Grade 6 | Module 3B

TEACHER GUIDE AND RESOURCE BOOK

Paths to College and Career
English Language Arts

Understanding Perspectives

JOSSEY-BASS
A Wiley Brand

Cover design by Wiley

Copyright © 2020 by Public Consulting Group, Inc. All rights reserved.

Published by Jossey-Bass
A Wiley Brand
111 River St., Hoboken NJ 07030—www.josseybass.com

No part of this publication may be reproduced, stored in a retrieval system, or transmitted in any form or by any means, electronic, mechanical, photocopying, recording, scanning, or otherwise, except as permitted under Section 107 or 108 of the 1976 United States Copyright Act, without either the prior written permission of the publisher, or authorization through payment of the appropriate per-copy fee to the Copyright Clearance Center, Inc., 222 Rosewood Drive, Danvers, MA 01923, 978-750-8400, fax 978-646-8600, or on the Web at www.copyright.com. Requests to the publisher for permission should be addressed to the Permissions Department, John Wiley & Sons, Inc., 111 River Street, Hoboken, NJ 07030, 201-748-6011, fax 201-748-6008, or online at www.wiley.com/go/permissions.

Limit of Liability/Disclaimer of Warranty: While the publisher and author have used their best efforts in preparing this book, they make no representations or warranties with respect to the accuracy or completeness of the contents of this book and specifically disclaim any implied warranties of merchantability or fitness for a particular purpose. No warranty may be created or extended by sales representatives or written sales materials. The advice and strategies contained herein may not be suitable for your situation. You should consult with a professional where appropriate. Neither the publisher nor author shall be liable for any loss of profit or any other commercial damages, including but not limited to special, incidental, consequential, or other damages. Readers should be aware that Internet Web sites offered as citations and/or sources for further information may have changed or disappeared between the time this was written and when it is read.

Jossey-Bass books and products are available through most bookstores. To contact Jossey-Bass directly call our Customer Care Department within the U.S. at 800-956-7739, outside the U.S. at 317-572-3986, or fax 317-572-4002.

Wiley publishes in a variety of print and electronic formats and by print-on-demand. Some material included with standard print versions of this book may not be included in e-books or in print-on-demand. If this book refers to media such as a CD or DVD that is not included in the version you purchased, you may download this material at http://booksupport.wiley.com. For more information about Wiley products, visit www.wiley.com.

ISBN: 978-1-119-73590-8

PB Printing   10 9 8 7 6 5 4 3 2 1

CONTENTS

About Public Consulting Group	xiii
What Is *Paths to College and Career*?	xv
Curriculum Maps	xxxiv
Grade 6 Curriculum Map	xxxvi
Grade 6 Unit-Level Assessments	xxxviii
ELA Curriculum: Grades 6–8 Curriculum Plan	xlvi
Module Overview	1

Unit 1 — 20

Unit Overview   Reading Closely and Writing to Learn: Point of View and Perspective — 20
Author's Point of View and Idea Development in *World Without Fish*

Lesson 1   Introducing *World Without Fish* — 34

  World Without Fish Word-Catcher — 40

  Text-Dependent Questions: Pages x–xii — 41

  Close Reading Guide: Pages x–xii (Teacher Reference) — 42

  Structured Notes: Pages x–xii — 46

Lesson 2   Introduction — 47
The Ideas of Charles Darwin

  Tracing the Development of an Idea Anchor Chart — 54

  Tracing the Development of an Idea Anchor Chart (Teacher Reference) — 55

  Text Dependent Questions: Pages xii–xvii — 56

Close Reading Guide: Pages xii–xvii (Teacher Reference) ... 58

Structured Notes: xii–xvii ... 61

Lesson 3   Introducing the Struggle for Survival in the Introduction of *World Without Fish* ... 62

Tracing the Development of an Idea Anchor Chart (Teacher Reference) ... 69

Text-Dependent Questions: Pages xx–xxiii ... 70

Text-Dependent Questions: Pages xx–xxiii (Teacher Reference) ... 72

Structured Notes: "The Story of Kram and Ailat: Part 1" ... 73

Lesson 4   Tracing the Idea of Fish Depletion ... 74
Chapter 1

Graphic Novel: Tracing the Development of an Idea Anchor Chart ... 81

Graphic Novel: Tracing the Development of an Idea Anchor Chart (Teacher Reference) ... 82

Text-Dependent Questions: Pages 1–8 ... 83

Close Reading Guide: Pages 1–8 (Teacher Reference) ... 85

Ocean Food Web ... 88

Tracing the Development of an Idea Anchor Chart (Teacher Reference) ... 89

Structured Notes: "The Story of Kram and Ailat: Part 2" ... 90

Lesson 5   Tracing the Idea of Fish Depletion ... 91
Chapter 2

Graphic Novel: Tracing the Development of an Idea Anchor Chart (Teacher Reference) ... 97

Text-Dependent Questions: Pages 28–33 ... 98

Text-Dependent Questions: Pages 28–33 (Teacher Reference) ... 100

Exit Ticket: Tracing the Development of an Idea, Chapter 2 ... 102

Exit Ticket: Tracing the Development of an Idea, Chapter 2 (Teacher Reference) ... 103

Structured Notes: "The Story of Kram and Ailat: Part 3" ... 104

Lesson 6   Mid-Unit 1 Assessment ... 105
Analyzing Idea Development in Chapter 3 of *World Without Fish*

Graphic Novel: Tracing the Development of an Idea Anchor Chart (Teacher Reference) ... 109

Mid-Unit 1 Assessment	110
Grade 6 2-Point Rubric—Short Response (Teacher Reference)	113
Mid-Unit 1 Assessment (Teacher Reference)	114
Structured Notes: "The Story of Kram and Ailat: Part 4"	116

Lesson 7   Reading for Gist and Answering Text-Dependent Questions — 117
Chapter 4 of *World Without Fish*

Graphic Novel: Tracing the Development of an Idea Anchor Chart (Teacher Reference)	124
Text-Dependent Questions: Pages 51–61	125
Text-Dependent Questions: Pages 51–61 (Teacher Reference)	127
Tracing the Development of an Idea Anchor Chart (Teacher Reference)	129
Structured Notes: Pages 51–61	130

Lesson 8   Analyzing Author's Point of View — 131
Chapter 4 of *World Without Fish*

Author's Point of View Graphic Organizer: Pages 51–61	137
Author's Point of View Graphic Organizer: Pages 51–61 (Teacher Reference)	139
Structured Notes: "The Story of Kram and Ailat: Part 5"	141

Lesson 9   Reading for Gist and Answering Text-Dependent Questions — 142
Chapter 5 of *World Without Fish*

Graphic Novel: Tracing the Development of an Idea Anchor Chart (Teacher Reference)	149
Text-Dependent Questions: Pages 63–69	150
Text-Dependent Questions: Pages 63–69 (Teacher Reference)	152
Tracing the Development of an Idea Anchor Chart (Teacher Reference)	154
Structured Notes: Pages 63–69	155

Lesson 10   Analyzing Author's Point of View — 156
Chapter 5 of *World Without Fish*

Author's Point of View Graphic Organizer: Pages 63–69	160
Author's Point of View Graphic Organizer: Pages 63–69 (Teacher Reference)	162
Structured Notes: "The Story of Kram and Ailat: Part 6"	164

Lesson 11 End-of-Unit 1 Assessment — 165
Analyzing Author's Point of View and How It Is Conveyed

   Graphic Novel: Tracing the Development of an Idea Anchor Chart (Teacher Reference) — 169

   End-of-Unit 1 Assessment — 170

   End-of-Unit 1 Assessment (Teacher Reference) — 173

   Grade 6 2-Point Rubric—Short Response (Teacher Reference) — 176

   Tracing the Development of an Idea Anchor Chart (Teacher Reference) — 177

Supplementary Assessment Items — 178

Supplementary Assessment Items Answer Key — 181

Unit 2 — 184

Unit Overview Reading Closely and Writing to Learn: Point of View and Perspective — 184
Narrator's Point of View and Evidence of Author's Perspective in *Flush*

Lesson 1 Learning from the Narrator's Point of View — 202
Introducing *Flush*

   Questions to Introduce *Flush* — 210

   Questions to Introduce *Flush* (Teacher Reference) — 211

   Flush Word-Catcher — 212

   Point of View Anchor Chart — 213

   Point of View Anchor Chart (Teacher Reference) — 214

   Thought, Word, Action Symbols — 215

   Structured Notes: Chapter 1 — 216

Lesson 2 Analyzing Point of View and Figurative Language — 217
Noah's Point of View of the *Coral Queen* and Dusty Muleman

   Noah's Point of View Graphic Organizer: Pages 7–9 — 228

   Noah's Point of View Graphic Organizer: Pages 7–9 (Teacher Reference) — 229

   Flush Plot Development Anchor Chart — 230

   Structured Notes: Chapters 2 and 3 — 231

Lesson 3   Analyzing Point of View and Figurative Language — 232
Noah's Point of View of Lice Peeking

- Noah's Point of View Graphic Organizer: Pages 17–19 — 241
- Noah's Point of View Graphic Organizer: Pages 17–19 (Teacher Reference) — 243
- Plot Development: The Rising Action in *Flush* Anchor Chart — 244
- Plot Development: The Rising Action in *Flush* Anchor Chart (Teacher Reference) — 245
- Structured Notes: Chapters 4 and 5 — 246

Lesson 4   Analyzing Point of View and Figurative Language — 247
Noah's Point of View of Florida

- Noah's Point of View Graphic Organizer: Pages 27–29 — 255
- Noah's Point of View Graphic Organizer: Pages 27–29 (Teacher Reference) — 257
- Exit Ticket: Chapters 4 and 5 Plot Development — 258
- Exit Ticket: Chapters 4 and 5 Plot Development (Teacher Reference) — 259
- Structured Notes: Chapters 6 and 7 — 260

Lesson 5   Mid-Unit 2 Assessment — 261
Analyzing Point of View and Plot Development in *Flush*

- Plot Development: The Rising Action in *Flush* Anchor Chart (Teacher Reference) — 266
- Mid-Unit 2 Assessment — 267
- Mid-Unit 2 Assessment (Teacher Reference) — 271
- Grade 6 2-Point Rubric—Short Response (Teacher Reference) — 274
- Structured Notes: Chapter 8 — 275

Lesson 6   Carl Hiaasen's Perspective of Florida: Part 1 — 276

- Five Creative Tips from Carl Hiaasen, Florida's Cleverest Chronicler — 283
- Gathering Evidence of Hiaasen's Perspective: Part 1 Graphic Organizer — 284
- Gathering Evidence of Hiaasen's Perspective: Part 1 Graphic Organizer (Teacher Reference) — 285
- Structured Notes: Chapters 9 and 10 — 286

Lesson 7   Carl Hiaasen's Perspective of Florida: Part 2 — 287

- "Florida 'A Paradise of Scandals'" Excerpt 1 — 293

Gathering Evidence of Hiaasen's Perspective: Part 2 Graphic Organizer	294
"Florida 'A Paradise of Scandals'" Excerpt 1 Close Reading Guide (Teacher Reference)	296
Gathering Evidence of Hiaasen's Perspective: Part 2 Graphic Organizer (Teacher Reference)	300
Structured Notes: Chapters 11 and 12	302

Lesson 8   Carl Hiaasen's Perspective of Florida: Part 3 — 303

"Florida 'A Paradise of Scandals'" Excerpt 2	309
Gathering Evidence of Hiaasen's Perspective: Part 3 Graphic Organizer	310
Gathering Evidence of Hiaasen's Perspective: Part 3 Graphic Organizer (Teacher Reference)	311
Structured Notes: Chapters 13 and 14	312

Lesson 9   Finding Evidence of Carl Hiaasen's Perspective in *Flush* — 313

Finding Evidence of Carl Hiaasen's Perspective in *Flush* Graphic Organizer	318
Finding Evidence of Carl Hiaasen's Perspective in *Flush* Graphic Organizer (Teacher Reference)	320
Structured Notes: Chapters 15 and 16	323

Lesson 10   Illustrating Carl Hiaasen's Perspective of Florida in *Flush* — 324

Illustrating a Scene Showing Perspective	330
Structured Notes: Chapter 17	331

Lesson 11   End-of-Unit 2 Assessment — 332
Finding Evidence of Carl Hiaasen's Perspective in *Flush* and Illustrating Perspective

End-of-Unit 2 Assessment	337
End-of-Unit 2 Assessment (Teacher Reference)	340
Grade 6 2-Point Rubric—Short Response (Teacher Reference)	342
Illustrating Perspective Rubric (Teacher Reference)	343
Structured Notes: End of *Flush*	344

Lesson 12   Analyzing Plot Development across *Flush* — 345

Reader's Review: *Flush*	349

Supplementary Assessment Items	351
Supplementary Assessment Items Answer Key	355

Unit 3 — 359

Unit Overview   Reading Closely and Writing to Learn: Point of View and Perspective — 359
Researching and Interpreting Information: What You Need to Know When Buying Fish

Lesson 1   Analyzing a Model Informative Consumer Guide — 379

- Performance Task Prompt — 386
- Grades 6–8 Expository Writing Evaluation Rubric — 387
- Model Informative Consumer Guide — 391
- Structured Notes: Chapter 7, Pages 87–97 — 392
- *World Without Fish* Word-Catcher — 393

Lesson 2   Researching Information about Overfishing — 394

- Researching Graphic Organizer: Lesson 2 — 401
- "Ending Overfishing" Video Transcript (Teacher Reference) — 403
- Threat 1: Overfishing — 404
- Destructive Fishing — 408
- Protecting Ocean Habitat from Bottom Trawling — 410
- Structured Notes: Chapter 7, Pages 98–106 — 413

Lesson 3   Researching Case Studies of Depleted Fish Species — 414

- Researching Graphic Organizer: Lesson 3 — 419
- A Rapidly Disappearing Fish — 421
- Case Study: Atlantic Bluefin Tuna — 422
- Structured Notes: Chapter 8 — 424

Lesson 4   Researching Information about Sustainable Fishing — 425

- Researching Graphic Organizer: Lesson 4 — 431

Sustainable Fishing Methods	433
Sustainable Fishing	436
Sustainable Seafood	438
Structured Notes: Chapter 11 through Page 153	440

Lesson 5   Mid-Unit 3 Assessment, Part 1 — 441
Researching Information about Buying Fish Caught Using Sustainable Methods

Mid-Unit 3 Assessment, Part 1	447
Choosing Sustainable	449
What We Eat Makes a Difference	452
Structured Notes: Chapter 9 through Page 127	453
Grade 6 2-Point Rubric—Short Response (Teacher Reference)	454

Lesson 6   Mid-Unit 3 Assessment, Part 2 — 455
Explaining How New Information Connects to the Topic

| Mid-Unit 3 Assessment, Part 2 | 459 |
| Structured Notes: Chapter 9, Pages 128–134 | 460 |

Lesson 7   Evaluating Research — 461

| Structured Notes: Chapter 10 | 467 |

Lesson 8   Planning Content of Informative Consumer Guide — 468
The Issue of Overfishing and Fish Depletion

| Model Quote Sandwich Graphic Organizer | 474 |
| Quote Sandwich Graphic Organizer | 475 |

Lesson 9   Planning Content of Informative Consumer Guide — 476
Sustainable Fishing Methods

| Quote Sandwich Graphic Organizer | 482 |

Lesson 10   End-of-Unit 3 Assessment — 483
Drafting the Informative Consumer Guide

| End-of-Unit 3 Assessment | 490 |
| Formal Style Examples | 491 |

| Lesson 11 | Analyzing the Features of an Informative Consumer Guide | 492 |

| Lesson 12 | Revising the Informative Consumer Guide | 498 |

Sentence Structure, Transitions, and Works Cited

| | Sentence Structure and Transitions | 503 |
| | Row 3 of the Grades 6–8 Expository Writing Evaluation Rubric: Self-Assessment | 504 |

| Lesson 13 | Performance Task | 507 |

Final Informative Consumer Guide

| | Peer Critique Guidelines | 513 |
| | Stars and Steps Recording Form | 514 |

Supplementary Assessment Items — 515

Supplementary Assessment Items Answer Key — 518

Vocabulary Included in This Module — 522

ABOUT PUBLIC CONSULTING GROUP

Public Consulting Group, Inc. (PCG) provides instructional and management services and technologies to schools, school districts, and state education agencies across the United States and internationally. We apply more than 30 years of management consulting expertise and extensive real-world experience as teachers and leaders to strengthen clients' instructional practice and organizational leadership, enabling student success.

As educators engage with rigorous standards for college and career readiness, PCG partners with practitioners at all stages of implementation. We work with clients to build programs, practices, and processes that align with the standards. Our team of experts develops and delivers standards-based instructional resources, professional development, and technical assistance that meet the needs of all learners.

In response to a wide range of needs, PCG's solutions leverage one or more areas of expertise, including College and Career Readiness, MTSS/RTI, Special Programs and Diverse Learners, School and District Improvement, and Strategic Planning. PCG's technologies expedite this work by giving educators the means to gather, manage, and analyze data, including student performance information, and by facilitating blended learning approaches to professional development.

To learn more about PCG, visit us at www.publicconsultinggroup.com.

WHAT IS *PATHS TO COLLEGE AND CAREER*?

Paths to College and Career is a comprehensive English Language Arts (ELA) curriculum that meets the rigorous requirements and instructional shifts of the Common Core State Standards (CCSS). *Paths to College and Career* (for grades 6–8) deeply engages middle-level students in authentic experiences while building their literacy skills and expanding their knowledge of the world around them as they grow toward college and career readiness. *Paths to College and Career* supports teachers' understanding of CCSS-aligned instruction that challenges and engages all students as they read, discuss, and write about complex texts.

Materials and Resources

- **Curriculum maps** that provide a bird's-eye view of standards, learning targets, core texts, and assessments across the year, both within each grade and across grades 6–8
- **Detailed plans** for curriculum modules, units, and lessons, with teacher instructional notes and student supports
- **Authentic literary and informational texts** at appropriate grade-level complexity working together to build students' knowledge
- **Supplementary resources** including protocols and practices, graphic organizers, and supports for students with a variety of learning needs
- **Flexibility,** encouraging teacher adaptation and student choice

Intentional Learning Progressions

- Engaging topics, and sequencing within topics, that draw students deeply into rigorous reading, writing, and thinking
- Deliberate **year-long instructional processes** that develop students' ability to read closely, analyze texts, and synthesize information across multiple texts
- Scaffolded **assignments** that help all students develop skill in evidence-based writing, including argument, explanation, and narrative
- **Regular, consistent writing** for many purposes, both informal and more formal, incorporating the writing process
- **Classroom protocols** that foster rich evidence-based discussions, research, and writing based on evidence from text

- **Academic vocabulary** development that builds students' ability to understand sophisticated words and complex language structures
- **Active learning** that encourages students' confidence in their ability to achieve at high levels

Assessment That Informs Instruction

- Daily and ongoing formative assessment opportunities
- Student self-assessment and feedback
- Mid-unit and end-of-unit assessments
- Curriculum-embedded performance tasks for each module in which students synthesize their work to demonstrate their deep learning of skills and content
- CCSS-based rubrics and models of expected student performance

Paths to College and Career provides a complete middle-level ELA curriculum, fully aligned with the Common Core State Standards and instructional shifts and designed to meet the needs of all students.

The Standards in Action: The Instructional Shifts and *Paths to College and Career*

The Common Core State Standards for ELA & Literacy set clear, high expectations for what students in each grade need to know as they grow toward college and career readiness. These rigorous expectations require shifts in the content and nature of instruction so that students will achieve the standards. *Paths to College and Career* embodies these instructional shifts.

Shift 1: Building Knowledge through Content-Rich Nonfiction

In college and career, most required reading is nonfiction and informational text. Students need to understand the structure of text and be able to learn independently through text.

- Expanding beyond fiction, students read a true **balance of literary and informational texts**.
- Through carefully selected text sets, students **build knowledge** about the world (domains/content areas) through interactions with **text** rather than through teacher talk or activities.

How does *Paths to College and Career* help teachers and students meet Shift 1?

All modules in *Paths to College and Career* pair literature with rich informational text (including primary source documents and literary nonfiction). Authentic reading materials include full-length books, excerpts, articles, and other texts. In addition, each unit includes a set of sequenced, coherent progressions of learning experiences that build knowledge and understanding of major concepts related to real-world issues and concerns. Students engage in significant topics as they read high-quality literature and fiction. They build expertise on topics and share that expertise with others.

Shift 2: Reading, Writing, and Speaking Grounded in Evidence from Text

The ability to locate and use evidence is a strong indicator of success in college and career. Too often, questions and tasks ask students to answer from their own experience, rather than requiring them to respond with evidence from text. The CCSS expects that most questions and tasks require students to read the text—and to identify what is directly stated and what is inferred. In the classroom, reading, writing, and speaking all emphasize the use of evidence.

- Students engage in **rich and rigorous evidence-based conversation** about text.
- Writing **uses evidence from sources** to inform or make an argument.

How does *Paths to College and Career* help teachers and students meet Shift 2?

Each module of the *Paths to College and Career* curriculum focuses on reading, writing, listening, and speaking in response to high-quality texts. *Paths to College and Career* supports teachers with careful and deliberate sequences of text-dependent questions and tasks which ensure that students return to the text for answers. Students use evidence, becoming skilled at asking and answering important text-dependent questions as they read. The curriculum also emphasizes writing from sources and research, matching the emphasis placed on these activities in the CCSS for a variety of purposes. Over the course of the academic year, students regularly write evidence-based informative/explanatory texts as they engage in text analysis. Writing instruction in *Paths to College and Career* frames writing as a recursive and iterative process of planning, drafting, revising, editing, and rewriting. Building the research skills outlined in the CCSS, students learn how to conduct effective, inquiry-based research. Through reading and analysis, students identify topics of interest, formulate questions for searches, assess sources, craft inquiry-based research questions, engage in research and writing, and, finally, analyze and synthesize their research in formal writing pieces.

Paths to College and Career regularly incorporates student discussion in order for students to process orally what they have read and what they will write or have already written in response to a text. Discussions take various forms, some more formal or structured than others. Discussions are student driven and share a common focus on evidence-based claims. Students engage with one another, rather than with the teacher, as they pose questions, build shared knowledge, and support each other. To facilitate classwide engagement, students work in pairs or small groups prior to whole-class discussion. These pair or small-group discussions allow students the space and time to collaboratively build evidence-based understandings of text(s) and share their ideas and understandings.

Students engage in peer-supported and independent research projects of varying lengths and on a range of topics. Using the text as the basis for forming claims and making inferences, students write in multiple contexts. End-of-module performance tasks require students to use textual evidence in authentic contexts.

Shift 3: Complex Text and Its Academic Vocabulary

There has existed a huge gap between the complexity of texts students read and the complexity of texts they need to be able to read to meet college and career expectations. The new standards have raised the overall level of text complexity, with clear expectations for independence at each grade level. One of the greatest factors in text complexity is the academic vocabulary that is more often found in text than in everyday speech. Because of this, teachers need to pay careful attention to building students' vocabulary and helping them learn how to build their own vocabulary in a variety of ways.

- Students **read appropriately complex texts for their grade level**. Instruction and learning center on those texts. Adequate time allows students to read closely and understand the text fully.
- Students **build the academic vocabulary** they need to access complex texts.

How does *Paths to College and Career* help teachers and students meet Shift 3?

The informational text and literature in each module meet the expected range of quantitative complexity. Students read and review texts for specific purposes. With a gradual release of support, students deconstruct, seek meaning, conduct analysis, define words in context, use and develop background knowledge, and work to understand the text at hand. The *Paths to College and Career* curriculum paces the learning so that students carefully read and reread complex text as they explore ideas, structures, and layers of meaning.

Paths to College and Career emphasizes depth of student understanding rather than the breadth of texts "covered." The process of achieving this depth of understanding includes annotating text. The curriculum frequently asks students to note specific parts of a text that contain important ideas and spark connections to other texts or require additional attention and discussion.

Paths to College and Career builds students' academic vocabulary, the words and language structures more likely to appear in complex literary and informational texts. Through guided practice, students gain familiarity with the words in context or, when appropriate, learn their meaning at point of use as they encounter the word in a text.

Other Features of *Paths to College and Career* That Support All the Instructional Shifts

In addition to directly addressing the instructional shifts, *Paths to College and Career* emphasizes instructional practices that promote achievement of high academic expectations.

Paired and Group Reading/Collaborative Work

Collaboration plays a major role in college and career readiness. The CCSS weave together the four strands of reading, writing, speaking and listening, and language to provide an integrated approach to learning. The lessons and units in *Paths to College and Career* provide students multiple opportunities to collaborate while reading, writing, speaking, and listening. This learning and sharing of insights also benefits students who require additional support in developing these skills.

Scaffolding to Independence

Paths to College and Career scaffolds student learning to promote independence in reading, writing, and speaking about complex texts. Each unit builds on the skills and knowledge students develop in the preceding units, just as each module in a year extends and refines students' work in earlier modules. Over the course of the year and across grade levels, teachers will notice students' increased capacity for independent work. As texts increase in complexity, tasks become more challenging.

Assessment in *Paths to College and Career*

Paths to College and Career provides a full complement of assessments, including ongoing formative assessment practices and protocols in each lesson, unit-level assessments, and a culminating performance task at the conclusion of each module.

- Formative assessment practices and opportunities are embedded in and across lessons. Students self-assess against daily learning targets and receive frequent feedback from the teacher and peers.
- Each unit includes two formal assessments. Mid-unit assessments typically are reading assessments requiring text-based answers. End-of-unit assessments often require using multiple sources in a written essay.
- The final assessment for each module is a performance task. In these culminating projects, students synthesize and apply their learning from the module in an engaging and authentic way. Performance tasks incorporate the writing process, scaffolds for students, and peer critique and revision.
- Assessments offer curriculum-embedded and supplemental opportunities to practice the types of skills needed on high-stakes assessments and include multiple items formats:
  - Selected response (multiple-choice questions)
  - Short constructed response
  - Extended response, either on demand or supported
  - Speaking and listening (discussion or oral presentation)
  - Formal argumentative, explanatory, and narrative essays (involving planning, drafting, and revision)

Paths to College and Career Organization and Structure

This curriculum is composed of seven grade levels (6–12). Each grade level includes four primary modules. Each module consists of up to three units, and each unit consists of a set of lesson plans.

Modules are arranged in units comprising one or more texts. The texts in each module share common elements in relation to genre, authors' craft, text structure, or central ideas. Each unit in a module builds on the skills and knowledge students develop in the preceding unit(s). The number of lessons in a unit varies based on the length of the text(s). Each lesson is designed to span one class period, but may extend beyond that time frame depending on student needs.

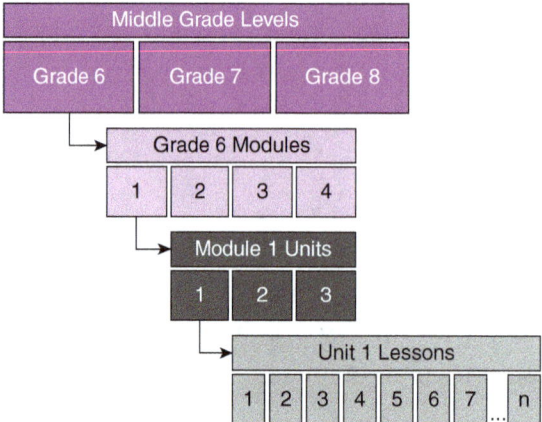

The standards assessed and addressed in each module specifically support the study of the module text(s), and include standards in all four domains: reading, writing, speaking and listening, and language. The modules include daily lesson assessments, mid- and end-of-unit assessments, and a culminating performance task in which students are asked to synthesize their learning across the module. The performance task also provides an option for teachers to engage students in writing or discussion of salient excerpts or ideas from the module texts in relation to outside texts, current events, the world writ large, or the human condition.

The *Paths to College and Career* curriculum provides a full year of modules and units, including

- Year-long scope and sequence
- Module framing and overview
- Unit-at-a-glance and week-at-a-glance guidance for the teacher
- Performance tasks and other summative and formative assessments
- Lesson plans
- Supporting materials (class work, homework, rubrics, and so on)

Structure of a Year of Instruction

There are four modules per grade level that focus on reading, writing, speaking and listening, and language in response to high-quality texts. Each module lasts one quarter of a school year.

Structure of a Module

Each module provides eight weeks of instruction constituting three units. Each unit includes a set of sequenced, coherent progressions of learning experiences that build knowledge and understanding of major concepts. The modules sequence and scaffold content aligned to CCSS for ELA & Literacy.

Module 1	Module 2	Module 3	Module 4
Close Reading and Writing to Learn	**Working with Evidence**	**Understanding Perspectives**	**Research, Decision Making, and Forming Positions**
Unit 1 Building Background Knowledge	Unit 1 Building Background Knowledge	Unit 1 Building Background Knowledge	Unit 1 Building Background Knowledge
Unit 2 Extended Reading and Research	Unit 2 Extended Reading and Research	Unit 2 Extended Reading and Research	Unit 2 Extended Reading and Research
Unit 3 Extended Writing	Unit 3 Extended Writing	Unit 3 Extended Writing	Unit 3 Extended Writing

Module 1 at each grade level establishes the foundation of instructional routines used throughout the year. Individual modules culminate in an end-of-module performance task, similar to those that students will encounter on high-stakes assessments. This assessment provides information to educators on whether students in their classrooms are achieving the standards.

Modules include daily lesson plans, guiding questions, recommended texts, scaffolding strategies, and other classroom resources. Instructional resources address the needs of all learners. Ancillary resources, including graphic organizers and collaborative protocols and formative assessment practices, apply to all modules.

Serving All Students

Paths to College and Career is planned and developed according to the principles of Universal Design for Learning (UDL) to support

- English language learners (ELL students)
- Students with disabilities
- Accelerated learners
- Students achieving below grade level

Each module is designed to be adapted to a group's specific instructional needs. Lessons are not scripts, but are intended to illustrate how instruction might be sequenced. Lessons are adaptable and allow for teacher preference and flexibility both to meet students' needs and to meet the requirements of the shifts and the standards. At the same time, Meeting Students' Needs boxes are embedded into each lesson to provide teachers with extra guidance around how to meet the needs of a variety of learners. The sections that follow describe how to use *Paths* to support the learning of all students.

Supporting English Language Learners

English language learners are a heterogeneous group of students who enter school with a variety of experiences and skills. The diversity among these students means that teachers need a flexible collection of strategies they can draw from to make sure students are mastering language and grade-level subject matter. *Paths* provides a focused and replicable collection of scaffolds teachers can use to help English language learners access the rigorous curriculum. This section describes some of the ways *Paths* embeds scaffolds for English language learners.

PCG's 10 Language and Literacy Practices to Support English Language Learners

Scaffolding instruction is key to the success of English language learners, regardless of their level of English proficiency. To support students throughout the curriculum, *Paths* scaffolds are based on PCG's 10 Language and Literacy Practices (LLPs) to support English language learners. These 10 practices are strategic approaches teachers can take to supporting students in any content area. This section describes each of the LLPs and how this practice is embedded in scaffolding throughout *Paths to College and Career.*

PCG's 10 Language and Literacy Practices	How *Paths* Supports This Practice
Practice 1: Develop oral language Oral language is the foundation of literacy, a predictor of reading and writing, and a main tool for learning and interacting in both academic and social settings. Regularly supporting the development of oral language also supports vocabulary development, text comprehension, and writing. Students benefit from daily meaningful opportunities to engage in teacher-planned structured academic talk and from sentence frames for conversation that support that talk.	• Additional scaffolds guide teachers to create sentence frames for academic discussions. Example: "One expectation I have for our group is _____, and this will help our group because _____." (Grade 6 Module 1 Unit 1 Lesson 2) • Activities include instructions to make discussion moves and expectations explicit for all students. Example: "Ask a student to read the learning targets for today and focus the class on SL.7.1. Inform students that today they will participate in an activity in which they build ideas through conversations with their classmates. Ask students to think of something they might say when they are building on someone else's ideas and to raise their hands when they have something. When most students have their hands raised, call on several to share." (Grade 7 Module 2 Unit 1 Lesson 1)

Practice 2: Teach targeted skills and meaning-making strategies Teaching foundational and reading comprehension skills gives English language learners access to reading strategies that will help them meet increasingly complex literacy demands. Building these meaning-making strategies provides students with a toolbox to approach future learning challenges. To become autonomous learners, students need to learn skills in context through authentic text and by learning meaning-making strategies modeled by the teacher.	• Instructions guide teachers to model meaning-making strategies for students. Example: "Display one of the photographs using the document camera. Model for students how to make an inference or take clues from the text and use your background knowledge to express something you think is true based on these facts." (Grade 8 Module 3 Unit 1 Lesson 1) • Graphic organizers provide support for students to make meaning independently. Example: "Distribute the Tracing an Argument Graphic Organizer to each student. Inform students that this graphic organizer provides a way to capture the argument, claims, and supporting evidence in an organized way." (Grade 6 Module 4 Unit 1 Lesson 3)
Practice 3: Build academic language Systematic and deliberate development of academic language both improves text comprehension and increases the chances that students will be able to integrate new words effectively into their language use and literacy experiences. Providing students with a variety of texts, vocabulary strategies, and opportunities to engage with other students in multiple ways helps them learn new vocabulary independently.	• Lessons regularly include targeted word work to build language. Example: "Invite students to sort the words by copying them down on the Word Connotation T-Chart, placing each word under either the 'positive' or 'negative' column. Explain that *connotation* means a feeling or association one has with a word." (Grade 8 Module 3 Unit 2 Lesson 2) • Lessons offer additional guidance for teachers to increase their support for academic language development where necessary. Example: "Even though the definitions are in the glossary, you will need to go over them and give students examples so that they understand how these words are used in the rubric to refer to writing." (Grade 7 Module 2 Unit 1 Overview)
Practice 4: Build and activate prior knowledge Building and activating prior knowledge helps improve student comprehension by allowing the brain to draw on previous experiences and understandings to learn new content. When a lack of historical or cultural context creates a significant barrier to comprehension, English language learners benefit from additional	• Lessons include guidance about how and when to provide additional suggestions for English language learners. Example: "Give basic background information without giving too much away. Mention that the video gives more information on the insecticide DDT and its use. John Stossel, an investigative journalist and reporter, and Richard Tren, author of *Excellent Powder*, detail how the DDT ban was a great victory for environmentalism. However, the ban has led to a multitude of deaths throughout the world." (Grade 6 Module 4 Unit 1 Lesson 3)

texts, videos, discussions, and targeted vocabulary instruction they can use to build a bridge to new learning.	• The first unit of each module focuses on knowledge building. Example: "Tell students that now they will read a short informational text to build background knowledge about Sudan's civil war. Tell them that having this background knowledge will help them better understand the novel, its characters, and their points of view." (Grade 7 Module 1 Unit 1 Lesson 6)
Practice 5: Develop language through writing Writing is a developmental process for English language learners, and writing itself is a powerful way to help students build language. By combining writing to learn with reading and analysis, English language learners can process their learning and can practice constructing ideas and expressions in English prior to discussion. Both help students master language and content. Students need daily writing opportunities to develop effective written language skills.	• The curriculum uses protocols to help students write to learn. Example: "Project or distribute the Entry Task, including the two images of modern garment factories. Invite students to look closely at each image and then write down what they notice and what they wonder." (Grade 7 Module 2 Unit 3 Lesson 2) • The first module for each grade level focuses on writing to learn.
Practice 6: Develop and support home language Developing and supporting students' home language helps them use those critical home language skills to learn English more effectively. English language learners benefit from support from teachers to leverage their home language as a tool to help them learn English.	• Lessons encourage teachers to be flexible and strategic when grouping students and provide guidance around when home-language groupings may make sense. Example: "Consider partnering an ELL student with a student who speaks the same home language when discussion of complex content is required. This can allow students to have more meaningful discussions and clarify points in their native language." (Grade 7 Module 1 Unit 1 Lesson 5) • The curriculum provides guidance around when to leverage a student's home language to improve learning, including reminding teachers to provide home-language definitions of key vocabulary. Example: "To further support ELL students, consider providing definitions of challenging vocabulary in students' home languages. Resources such as Google Translate and bilingual translation dictionaries can assist with one-word translation." (Grade 8 Module 3 Unit 2 Lesson 3)

Practice 7: Use ongoing classroom-based assessment Classroom-based assessment of English language learners requires measuring student progress in learning English and academic content. Ongoing assessment tasks should consider the students' level of English language proficiency. English language learners benefit when assessment results are regularly used for planning instruction.	• Lessons guide teachers to monitor comprehension during classroom activities to ensure that students comprehend the text and the task. "Example: As you monitor the groups, listen for main ideas of paragraphs . . ." (Grade 6 Module 1 Unit 2 Lesson 1) • Instructions continually remind teachers to look carefully at formative assessment data and to use that data to inform instruction, including providing specific guidance around strategies for reteaching. Example: "Review students' Exit Tickets as useful formative assessment data. Use them to evaluate how well students are able to use details to infer theme. You can then use this information to differentiate subsequent instruction through reteaching and differentiated mini lessons with small groups of students." (Grade 6 Module 1 Unit 2 Lesson 1)
Practice 8: Establish rituals and routines English language learners benefit from learning in a predictable environment that increases focused learning time. Rituals and routines such as lesson flows and protocols for completing common tasks help teachers and students use time efficiently by establishing processes and procedures for in-class time.	• The curriculum is built on replicable lesson flows so that students know what to expect each day. Lessons include several discussion protocols throughout the curriculum to provide support for students around a variety of activities. Examples: World Café protocol; Fishbowl; Socratic Seminar; Think-Pair-Share (throughout the curriculum). • Routines such as Quick Writes are used both as formative assessment tools and to provide students with a structure for writing to learn and reflect on learning. Example: "Use specific evidence from the text to write a paragraph in which you discuss one of Ha's personality traits. A complete paragraph includes a focus statement, several pieces of textual evidence, explanations about what each piece of evidence shows us about Ha, and a concluding sentence. Use the notes you collected in your journal to help you write this paragraph." (Grade 8 Module 1 Unit 1 Lesson 3)

Practice 9: Create classrooms with environmental supports	• Lessons regularly follow up instruction with guidance to post frames, anchor charts, and other supports for students. Example: "After the final text-dependent question, display the new Taking a Stand Anchor Chart. Tell students that throughout their reading of this novel, they will continue to think about this theme of when and why characters 'take a stand.'" (Grade 8 Module 2 Unit 1 Lesson 11)
Environmental supports can increase the effectiveness of instruction for English language learners and promote independent learning. Students benefit from posted vocabulary, word walls, protocols, co-constructed anchor charts, sentence frames, higher level prompts, and exemplary work. English language learners need many ways to access language and content relevant to what they are learning.	• Lessons guide teachers to provide nonlinguistic representations of key vocabulary and to post these for use throughout the year. Example: "Consider providing nonlinguistic symbols (for example, two people talking for *discuss,* a pen for *record,* a magnifying glass for *details,* a lightbulb for *main idea*) to assist ELL students in making connections with vocabulary." (Grade 7 Module 1 Unit 1 Lesson 1)
Practice 10: Maximize student grouping opportunities	• The curriculum provides opportunities for students to work in groups to maximize the benefits of those conversations through the development of shared expectations. Example: "Arrange students so that they are sitting in their triads. Give each group a half-sheet of chart paper and marker. Ask: 'When working in a group, what are important expectations you should have for one another?'" (Grade 6 Module 1 Unit 1 Lesson 2)
Grouping students in different configurations helps English language learners enter and participate in the classroom community and gain opportunities to practice language in a low-risk environment. Homogeneous and heterogeneous groupings include organizing students in different ways based on language proficiency in English, content knowledge, skills, or other characteristics. English language learners benefit from fluid and flexible student grouping that is determined by the task.	• Additional supports throughout *Paths* include explicit guidance for grouping students effectively. Example: "Heterogeneous pairing of students for regular discussion and close reading exercises will provide a collaborative and supportive structure for reading complex texts and close reading of the text. This also provides more talk-time per student when the processing and thinking requires more support and collaboration. Consider pairing students within existing small groups for ease in flexing students from pairs to small groups, and vice versa." (Grade 7 Module 2 Unit 3 Lesson 3)

Supporting Students with Disabilities

It is important to recognize that to enhance achievement for students with disabilities in meeting state and district standards and to support meeting their standards-based IEP goals, meaningful and regular consultation, planning, support, and coordination with special education teachers and related service providers are imperative. In addition to their participation in inclusive general education ELA classrooms and a tiered support system such as Response to Intervention (RtI) or Multi-Tiered System of Supports (MTSS), students with disabilities may be provided additional time, support, and robust scaffolding in resource classrooms, in before- and after-school programs, or through peer tutoring.

Because *Paths* was designed to support a wide range of learners, the curriculum already has a considerable amount of scaffolding built in. In general education classrooms, most of the planning is likely to involve determining what scaffolds are not necessary for a given lesson. To facilitate this work, in the next sections we describe potential challenges for students with disabilities around the four key CCSS areas: reading, speaking and listening, language, and writing. The tables describe existing *Paths* scaffolds and list additional scaffolds and supports to consider in daily planning and instructional implementation.

Reading

Students with disabilities who struggle with reading require additional scaffolds and supports designed to address their specific challenges. The following table provides a list of possible supports that could be used as a means to scaffold instruction in the general education setting. These supports may also require additional time and support from special education teachers. It is important to note that ongoing, frequent collaboration among all service providers is critical in enhancing the achievement of students with disabilities.

Potential Challenge	*Paths* Existing Scaffolds and Supplementary Supports
Fluency	Existing scaffolds: • Provide a masterful reading prior to analysis. Students should follow along as the text is read aloud (e.g., text-to-speech or digital text). This should be a preview, not a replacement for the reading assignment. • Provide multiple opportunities for students to read the text with assistance. Supplementary supports: • Pair students with a peer for reading. Students can take turns and provide feedback to each other, depending on each student's reading level.

Language comprehension	Existing scaffolds:
	• Chunk reading passages into small sections so that students do not feel overwhelmed by the amount of text.
	• Include masterful readings of text (see the previous row).
	• Teach and use annotation.
	Supplementary supports:
	• Provide students colored pens or markers and sticky notes to interact with and make sense of text as they read.
	• Teach students to generate questions as they read and/or assist with question generation to improve comprehension of key ideas.
	• Build in time for students to process or "consolidate" what they read.

Speaking and Listening

Difficulties related to speaking and listening may lead students with specific learning or other disabilities to struggle. Potential challenges in these areas include language processing and verbal expression. Possible adaptations for scaffolding instruction are listed in the following table. As with other areas, adaptations should be planned with careful consideration of the individual learner's needs and in consultation with special services providers.

Potential Challenge	*Paths* Existing Scaffolds and Supplementary Supports
Language processing	Existing scaffolds:
	• Segment class time into brief periods of language-intensive instruction followed by shorter and less language-intensive periods of work.
	Supplementary supports:
	• Provide additional think time to process questions.
	• Reword statements or questions, adding more details or using easier-to-understand terms.
	• Use additional visuals throughout the lesson. Create visual displays (e.g., bookmarks and posters) of routines and practices that students learn.
	• Give students a visual representation of important information that is provided orally.

Verbal expression	Existing scaffolds: • Provide ample opportunities for students to consolidate information before speaking. Supplementary supports: • Provide sufficient think time for students to formulate a response. • Provide written or alternate formats when appropriate. For example, if students are asked to respond orally to the entire class, scaffolding may include an option for a quick written response or use of technology to respond and display for class.

Writing

Writing can present particular difficulties for students with disabilities using the *Paths* curriculum. Students may have better comprehension than their written expression skills demonstrate. Additional scaffolds may help to build their ability to transfer that comprehension to the page. Adaptations for written expression are listed in the following table.

Potential Challenge	*Paths* Existing Scaffolds and Supplementary Supports
Written expression and mechanics of writing	Existing scaffolds: • Allow students to use *Paths* graphic organizers to either organize their thoughts or to provide their responses. • Before performance tasks, ask students to verbalize what they will need to express in writing. Assist as needed by demonstrating ways to organize thoughts using graphic organizers and/or technology. • Use sentence-starter frames for students who may need them to initiate their written responses. Supplementary supports: • Encourage use of technology to aid in formatting, spelling, grammar, and so on. • Schedule peer and/or teacher conferences regularly to review work and provide meaningful feedback.

Language

Language skills impact all the areas addressed in the previous sections: reading, speaking and listening, and writing. A deficit in general language skills is common among students with disabilities. Many of the supports listed in the previous tables provide examples of how teachers might scaffold specific instruction, activities, and assessments.

Potential Challenge	*Paths* Existing Scaffolds and Supplementary Supports
Conventions of Standard English grammar and usage when writing or speaking	Existing scaffolds: • Provide direct instruction and formative feedback for students in grammar, punctuation, and other conventions of Standard English. • Use peer editing for written and oral assignments. • Use anchor charts. Supplementary supports: • Provide additional teacher- or student-created reference guides. • Allow students to practice oral presentations and provide feedback prior to assessment.
Vocabulary acquisition and use	Existing scaffolds: • Provide multiple exposures to important vocabulary. • Use nonlinguistic representations of concepts or vocabulary. • Have students discuss vocabulary through cooperative learning activities. • Have students maintain vocabulary journals. Supplementary supports: • Provide written reference documents that students can refer to as needed. • Use challenging and engaging vocabulary games to practice and remember vocabulary. • Reteach vocabulary words germane to understanding concept or theme. • Teach students tools they can use when they are unable to decode or comprehend new or challenging words and content.

Application of language knowledge	Existing scaffolds: • Provide examples of how texts relate to one another to demonstrate language connections across contexts. • Use guided questions to support students in drawing conclusions regarding the use of language in particular texts. Supplementary supports: • Encourage students to formulate and ask questions of their peers. Then have students revise their questions to be more robust and challenging.

Supporting Struggling and Accelerated Learners

Because *Paths* was built using UDL principles, it includes more scaffolding in daily lessons than teachers will find in many other curricula. This allows for considerable flexibility when deciding which scaffolds to include for different types of learners. Teachers will find scaffolds embedded throughout the curriculum, both in the structure of the lesson itself and in additional Differentiation Considerations in every lesson. This means that teachers rarely need to create additional scaffolds in *Paths*. Instead, they are more likely to need to remove scaffolds when students don't need them. We refer to this process as subtractive planning. Accelerated learners may not need many of the existing scaffolds in the *Paths* curriculum, and they may benefit from additional enrichment activities. The following table lists several existing scaffolds in the *Paths* curriculum along with guidance for how to adapt or remove those scaffolds for accelerated learners.

Existing *Paths* Scaffold for Struggling Learners	Suggested Adaptations for Accelerated Learners
Masterful reading	This scaffold is designed to support fluency and comprehension for many students. Struggling students will benefit considerably. Consider eliminating for accelerated learners.
Text excerpts	Some complex texts are read in excerpted form and are carefully chunked. This scaffold supports struggling students by making sure they are grappling with grade-level complex text with the support of a teacher. Accelerated learners may be able to handle additional reading by consuming more of the text outside of class or by eliminating the chunking of texts.
Graphic organizers	The student journal contains graphic organizers designed to support student thinking with complex evidence gathering, analysis, and research tasks. Accelerated learners may not need these supports.

Pacing	*Paths* is paced slowly to ensure that all students have the time and space they need to engage in deep analysis of complex texts. Accelerated learners may benefit from a quicker pace, combining multiple lessons worth of reading and analysis into a single class period.
Vocabulary	*Paths* provides the definitions of many challenging vocabulary words, as well as those critical to accessing a text's central ideas. Accelerated learners may not need certain definitions to be provided, particularly those that are arcane, abstract, or unlikely to be encountered again.

Using *Paths to College and Career*

Paths to College and Career provides strong and engaging instruction and learning experiences in each lesson, throughout each unit and module, and across all grade levels. Students develop expertise in the standards as they practice them with a variety of topics and tasks. The routines and protocols are consistent throughout the lessons, units, and modules, and across grade levels. This predictable structure provides scaffolds for students as they grow toward independence and accountability for their own learning.

Launching a Module

Paths to College and Career provides multiple supports in each module to facilitate instructional planning.

The **Module Overview** provides a road map of the entire module, and includes the module's guiding questions and big ideas, a description of the final performance task, key features of the central texts, the standards addressed and assessed in the module, and long-term "I can" statements that translate the standards into student-centered targets.

The **Week-at-a-Glance Calendar** adds detail to the description provided in the Module Overview, including the instructional focus and a brief description of assessments.

A detailed description in the **Module Assessments** section, including the performance task, further clarifies the trajectory of instruction and the specific skills in context that students will understand by the end of the module.

The **Recommended Texts** chart explains the Lexile (quantitative complexity) measure and text type of each literary and nonfiction work in the module.

These overview documents provide a panoramic view of the module and include the information educators need to make decisions about adapting, enhancing, or changing learning activities.

Teaching a Unit

The **Unit Overview** includes the learning targets and standards addressed in this unit, the texts used in this unit, and a lesson-by-lesson overview. Especially helpful at this level of detail are the lesson-level (supporting) learning targets derived from the long-term targets for the module. "Anchor Charts and Protocols" identifies the introduced and reinforced routines in each lesson.

Inside the Lesson

Each lesson, regardless of the topic or timing within the unit, module, or year, has a dependable structure.

The lesson Opening engages students in the work of the lesson and reviews learning targets for the day. The lesson opening builds on the work of the prior lesson.

Work Time comprises the bulk of the lesson and may include close reading, note taking, journaling, teacher modeling, vocabulary development, and partner or group work. As students prepare for a mid-unit or end-of-unit assessment, Work Time may give them an opportunity to plan, draft, revise, and peer- or self-assess. Work Time varies from day to day according to the learning targets, texts, and tasks.

Closing and Assessment includes a debrief of the lesson and homework instructions. In lessons that do not include a specific assessment, there is a brief formative assessment, such as an Exit Ticket.

Support for the Teacher

In addition to information provided in the module and unit overviews, support is provided throughout the lesson in sections labeled Teaching Notes and Meeting Students' Needs, as well as in the supporting materials.

Teaching Notes describe protocols used in the lesson, and ongoing practices, such as journaling. They also suggest how to prepare for the lesson. The Teaching Notes also include background information that explains how a concept or routine introduced in this lesson will connect to or build toward other lessons.

Meeting Students' Needs discusses the purpose of particular protocols in the lesson and suggestions for visuals, tools, practices, models, or adaptations for students who may need extra support to achieve lesson goals.

Supporting Materials comprise those materials that might be required for the lesson. These materials may include specific reproducible maps, articles, and graphic organizers.

Paths to College and Career is truly a complete and integrated English Language Arts curriculum that ensures teaching and learning to the letter and in the spirit of the new standards and the related instructional shifts.

CURRICULUM MAPS

The grades 6–8 curriculum modules are designed to address CCSS outcomes during a 45-minute English Language Arts block. The overarching focus for all modules is on building students' literacy skills as they develop knowledge about the world.

Taken as a whole, these modules are designed to give teachers concrete strategies to address the "instructional shifts" required by the CCSS.

Structure of a Module

Each module provides eight weeks of instruction, broken into three shorter units. Each module includes a complete suite of assessments:

- Unit-level assessments that generally require students to complete on-demand, independent work on a reading, writing, speaking, or listening task
- A final performance task that is a more supported project, often involving research

Structure of a Year of Instruction

There are four modules per grade level. Teachers should begin the year with Module 1, which lays the foundation for both teachers and students regarding instructional routines.

How to Read the Curriculum Maps

The purpose of the curriculum map is to provide a high-level summary of each module and name the standards formally assessed in each module.

Module Focus: Read this first. The "focus" is the same across the grades 6–8 band and signals the progression of literacy skills across the year as well as alignment to the CCSS instructional shifts.

Module Title: This signals the topic students will be learning about (often connected to social studies or science) and aligns with Instructional Shift #1, building knowledge through content-rich nonfiction.

Description: These three or four sentences tell the basic "story" of the eight-week arc of instruction: the literacy skills, content knowledge, and central text(s).

Texts: This lists texts that all students read. The texts in bold are the extended texts for a given module: the texts with which students spend the most time. Remember that texts can be complex based on both qualitative and quantitative measures. Texts are listed in order from most quantitatively complex (based on Lexile measure) to least quantitatively complex. Texts near the bottom of the list are often complex in ways other than Lexile. Within a given module, the list shows the wide variety of texts students read as they build knowledge about a topic. This aligns with Instructional Shift #1, building knowledge through content-rich nonfiction.

Final Performance Task: This is a culminating project, which takes place during Unit 3 of every module. Performance tasks are designed to help students synthesize and apply their learning from the module in an engaging and authentic way. Performance tasks are developed using the writing process, are scaffolded, and almost always include peer critique and revision. Performance tasks are not "on-demand" assessments. (Note: The End-of-Unit 3 Assessment often addresses key components of the performance task.)

Unit-Level Assessments:

- Each unit includes two assessments, most of which are "on-demand" (that is, show what you know/can do on your own).
- Mid-Unit Assessments typically, though not always, are reading assessments: text-based answers.
- End-of-Unit Assessments typically, though not always, are writing assessments: writing from sources.
- Most assessments have a heavy emphasis on academic vocabulary, particularly on determining words in context.
- Assessments are designed to be curriculum-embedded opportunities to practice the types of skills needed on state assessments.
- The curriculum map that follows lists the title of each assessment, the standards assessed, and the assessment format, of which there are five types.
    - Selected response (multiple-choice questions)
    - Short constructed response (short-answer questions of the type that is scored using a 2-point rubric)
    - Extended response (longer writing or essays of the type that is scored using a 4-point rubric) (either on-demand or supported)
    - Speaking and listening (discussion or oral presentation)
    - Scaffolded essay (involving planning, drafting, and revision)

Standards: In each module, the standards formally assessed are indicated with a check mark.

Grade 6 Curriculum Map

	6.2B	6.3B
Focus	Working with Evidence	Understanding Perspectives
Module Title	Voices of Adversity	Sustaining the Oceans
Description	In this module, students explore the idea of adversity, historical and modern, as they study different writing genres. In Unit 1, students conduct research on the Middle Ages by analyzing informational articles about medieval life. They then write an informational essay based on their findings. In Unit 2, students read *Good Masters! Sweet Ladies! Voices from a Medieval Village*, identifying the various adversities the characters face and examining the author's figurative language, word choice, and tone. In Unit 3, they study modern voices of adversity by analyzing concrete poems in small-group discussions. Finally, students choose a writing format they studied in the module and write and perform their own piece about adversities faced by sixth-graders.	In this module, students consider authorial point of view and build academic vocabulary as they learn about the impact of human activities on ocean life. In Unit 1, students read an excerpt from Mark Kurlansky's informational text *World Without Fish*. They analyze how Kurlansky conveys his perspective and track the idea of fish depletion in both the main text and the graphic novel at the end of each chapter. In Unit 2, students read Carl Hiaasen's *Flush* and excerpts of an interview with Hiaasen to explore how authorial perspective informs a text. In Unit 3, students return to *World Without Fish* and pursue further research about overfishing to write a consumer guide to buying fish.

	6.2B	6.3B
Texts (central texts in bold)*	Simon Newman, "Serfs in the Middle Ages" (1150L) *Middle Ages Britannica Student Encyclopedia* (1060L) Kenneth S. Cooper, *Middle Ages* (980L) "Daily Life of a Noble Lord in the Middle Ages," Mr. Donn's Social Studies Site (930L) Sharon Fabian, "Lords and Ladies" (880L) "The Middle Ages for Kids: What Is a Fief?" Mr. Donn's Social Studies Site (790L) "The Middle Ages for Kids: The Manorial System & Common People," Mr. Donn's Social Studies Site (770L) "The Middle Ages for Kids: Life of the Nobility: Kings, Lords, Ladies, Knights," Mr. Donn's Social Studies Site (700L) **Laura Amy Schlitz, *Good Masters! Sweet Ladies! Voices from a Medieval Village*, illustrated by Robert Byrd (NP)** **John Grandits, *Blue Lipstick: Concrete Poems* (NP)** **John Grandits, *Technically, It's Not My Fault: Concrete Poems* (NP)**	**Mark Kurlansky, *World Without Fish* (1160L)** **Carl Hiaasen, *Flush* (770L)** Marine Conservation Institute, "Destructive Fishing." National Resources Defense Council, "Protecting Ocean Habitat from Bottom Trawling." "Threat 1: Overfishing." Overfishing. *PBS Newshour Extra*, "A Rapidly Disappearing Fish." Save Our Seas, "Case Study: Atlantic Blue Fin Tuna." Overfishing. *Sunset*, "Sustainable Fishing Methods." National Geographic's "Sustainable Fishing." Vancouver Aquarium, "Sustainable Seafood."
Performance Task	Giving Voice to Adversity (W.6.3, SL.6.4, SL.6.6, L.6.1, L.6.3, L.6.6)	Informative Consumer Guide: What You Need to Know When Buying Fish (W.6.2, W.6.4, L.6.2, L.6.3)
Lexile	Common Core band level text difficulty ranges for grades 6–8**: 925–1185L	

*Texts listed in order of informational text first, then literature; both categories shown from most to least quantitatively complex (based on Lexile®).
**Supplemental Information for Appendix A of the Common Core State Standards for English Language Arts and Literacy: New Research on Text Complexity http://www.corestandards.org/assets/E0813_Appendix_A_New_Research_on_Text_Complexity.pdf.

Grade 6 Unit-Level Assessments

	6.2B	6.3B
Mid-Unit 1	Research Reading: Medieval Times (CCSS RI.6.1, RI.6.2, RI.6.4, RI.6.5)	Analyzing Idea Development in Chapter 3 of *World Without Fish* (RI.6.3, RI.6.4)
End-of-Unit 1	Writing about Medieval Times (CCSS W.6.2, W.6.4, W.6.7, W.6.9)	Analyzing Author's Point of View and How It Is Conveyed in Chapter 5 of *World Without Fish* (RI.6.6)
Mid-Unit 2	Finding Theme and Interpreting Figurative Language: Monologues from a Medieval Village (CCSS RL.6.2, RL.6.4, L.6.5, L.6.5.a, b, c)	Analyzing Point of View and Plot Development in *Flush* (RL.6.4, RL.6.5, RL.6.6, L.6.4.a)
End-of-Unit 2	Argument Essay: Do We Face the Same Adversities as the Voices of *Good Masters! Sweet Ladies!*? (CCSS W.6.1, W.6.9)	Evidence of Author's Perspective in *Flush* (RL.6.6)
Mid-Unit 3	Small-Group Discussion: How Do Modern Poems Portray Modern Adversities? (CCSS RL.6.7, RL.6.9, SL.6.1, SL.6.4, SL.6.6)	Researching Information about How to Buy Fish Caught Using Sustainable Methods (W.6.7, SL.6.2)
End-of-Unit 3	Drafting a Modern Narrative of Adversity (CCSS W.6.3, L.6.1, L.6.3)	Draft Informative Consumer Guide: What You Need to Know When Buying Fish (RI.6.7, W.6.2.a–f, W.6.4, W.6.9)

Common Core ELA Standards Formally Assessed, by Module

In the following tables, any specific CCSS with a check mark indicates that the standard is formally assessed.

- Some standards are formally assessed in multiple modules.
- Because of the integrated nature of the standards, even standards that are not formally assessed are often embedded in instruction throughout every module (for example, RI/RL.6.1).
- Some standards are not applicable in an on-demand assessment context (for example, R.6.10 or W.6.10). In the following tables, these standards are noted as "integrated throughout."
- Some standards (for example, W.6.2) have a main or "parent" standard and then subcomponents (for example, W.6.2.a). Often, students' mastery of the entirety of this standard is scaffolded across multiple modules. Therefore, in the following tables, the "parent" standard is checked only if *all* components of that standard are formally assessed within that particular module. Otherwise, just the specific components are checked.

Reading Standards for Literature

	Module 6.2B	Module 6.3B
RL.6.1. Cite textual evidence to support analysis of what the text says explicitly as well as inferences drawn from the text.	✓	
RL.6.2. Determine a theme or central idea of a text and how it is conveyed through particular details; provide a summary of the text distinct from personal opinions or judgments.	✓	
RL.6.3. Describe how a particular story's or drama's plot unfolds in a series of episodes as well as how the characters respond or change as the plot moves toward a resolution.		
RL.6.4. Determine the meaning of words and phrases as they are used in a text, including figurative and connotative meanings; analyze the impact of a specific word choice on meaning and tone.	✓	✓
RL.6.5. Analyze how a particular sentence, chapter, scene, or stanza fits into the overall structure of a text and contributes to the development of the theme, setting, or plot.	✓	✓
RL.6.6. Explain how an author develops the point of view of the narrator or speaker in a text.		✓

	Module 6.2B	Module 6.3B
RL.6.7. Compare and contrast the experience of reading a story, drama, or poem to listening to or viewing an audio, video, or live version of the text, including contrasting what they "see" and "hear" when reading the text to what they perceive when they listen or watch.	✓	
RL.6.9. Compare and contrast texts in different forms or genres (e.g., stories and poems; historical novels and fantasy stories) in terms of their approaches to similar themes and topics.	✓	✓
RL.6.10. By the end of the year, read and comprehend literature, including stories, dramas, and poems, in the grades 6–8 text complexity band proficiently, with scaffolding as needed at the high end of the range.	Integrated throughout.	

Reading Standards for Informational Text

	Module 6.2B	Module 6.3B
RI.6.1. Cite textual evidence to support analysis of what the text says explicitly as well as inferences drawn from the text.	✓	
RI.6.2. Determine a central idea of a text and how it is conveyed through particular details; provide a summary of the text distinct from personal opinions or judgments.	✓	✓
RI.6.3. Analyze in detail how a key individual, event, or idea is introduced, illustrated, and elaborated in a text (e.g., through examples or anecdotes).		✓
RI.6.4. Determine the meaning of words and phrases as they are used in a text, including figurative, connotative, and technical meanings.	✓	✓
RI.6.5. Analyze how a particular sentence, paragraph, chapter, or section fits into the overall structure of a text and contributes to the development of the ideas.	✓	
RI.6.6. Determine an author's point of view or purpose in a text and explain how it is conveyed in the text.		✓
RI.6.7. Integrate information presented in different media or formats (e.g., visually, quantitatively) as well as in words to develop a coherent understanding of a topic or issue.		✓

	Module 6.2B	Module 6.3B
RI.6.8. Trace and evaluate the argument and specific claims in a text, distinguishing claims that are supported by reasons and evidence from claims that are not.		
RI.6.9. Compare and contrast one author's presentation of events with that of another (e.g., a memoir written by and a biography on the same person).		
RI.6.10. By the end of the year, read and comprehend literary nonfiction in the grades 6–8 text complexity band proficiently, with scaffolding as needed at the high end of the range.	Integrated throughout.	

Writing Standards

	Module 6.2B	Module 6.3B
W.6.1. Write arguments to support claims with clear reasons and relevant evidence. a. Introduce claim(s) and organize the reasons and evidence clearly. b. Support claim(s) with clear reasons and relevant evidence, using credible sources and demonstrating an understanding of the topic or text. c. Use words, phrases, and clauses to clarify the relationships among claim(s) and reasons. d. Establish and maintain a formal style. e. Provide a concluding statement or section that follows from the argument presented.	✓	
W.6.2. Write informative/explanatory texts to examine a topic and convey ideas, concepts, and information through the selection, organization, and analysis of relevant content. a. Introduce a topic; organize ideas, concepts, and information, using strategies such as definition, classification, comparison/contrast, and cause/effect; include formatting (e.g., headings), graphics (e.g., charts, tables), and multimedia when useful to aiding comprehension.	✓	✓ ✓

	Module 6.2B	Module 6.3B
b. Develop the topic with relevant facts, definitions, concrete details, quotations, or other information and examples.		✓
c. Use appropriate transitions to clarify the relationships among ideas and concepts.		✓
d. Use precise language and domain-specific vocabulary to inform about or explain the topic.		✓
e. Establish and maintain a formal style.		✓
f. Provide a concluding statement or section that follows from the information or explanation presented.		✓
W.6.3. Write narratives to develop real or imagined experiences or events using effective technique, relevant descriptive details, and well-structured event sequences.	✓	
a. Engage and orient the reader by establishing a context and introducing a narrator and/or characters; organize an event sequence that unfolds naturally and logically.	✓	✓
b. Use narrative techniques, such as dialogue, pacing, and description, to develop experiences, events, and/or characters.	✓	✓
c. Use a variety of transition words, phrases, and clauses to convey sequence and signal shifts from one time frame or setting to another.	✓	
d. Use precise words and phrases, relevant descriptive details, and sensory language to convey experiences and events.	✓	
e. Provide a conclusion that follows from the narrated experiences or events.	✓	
W.6.4. Produce clear and coherent writing in which the development, organization, and style are appropriate to task, purpose, and audience.	✓	✓
W.6.5. With some guidance and support from peers and adults, develop and strengthen writing as needed by planning, revising, editing, rewriting, or trying a new approach.	Integrated throughout.	
W.6.6. Use technology, including the Internet, to produce and publish writing as well as to interact and collaborate with others; demonstrate sufficient command of keyboarding skills to type a minimum of three pages in a single sitting.	Integrated throughout.	

	Module 6.2B	Module 6.3B
W.6.7. Conduct short research projects to answer a question, drawing on several sources and refocusing the inquiry when appropriate.	✓	✓
W.6.8. Gather relevant information from multiple print and digital sources; assess the credibility of each source; and quote or paraphrase the data and conclusions of others while avoiding plagiarism and providing basic bibliographic information for sources.		
W.6.9. Draw evidence from literary or informational texts to support analysis, reflection, and research.	✓	✓
a. Apply *grade 6 Reading standards* to literature (e.g., "Compare and contrast texts in different forms or genres [e.g., stories and poems; historical novels and fantasy stories] in terms of their approaches to similar themes and topics").		✓
b. Apply *grade 6 Reading standards* to literary nonfiction (e.g., "Trace and evaluate the argument and specific claims in a text, distinguishing claims that are supported by reasons and evidence from claims that are not").		
W.6.10. Write routinely over extended time frames (time for research, reflection, and revision) and shorter time frames (a single sitting or a day or two) for a range of discipline-specific tasks, purposes, and audiences.	Integrated throughout.	

Speaking & Listening Standards

	Module 6.2B	Module 6.3B
SL.6.1. Engage effectively in a range of collaborative discussions (one-on-one, in groups, and teacher-led) with diverse partners on *grade 6 topics, texts, and issues*, building on others' ideas and expressing their own clearly.	✓	
a. Come to discussions prepared, having read or studied required material; explicitly draw on that preparation by referring to evidence on the topic, text, or issue to probe and reflect on ideas under discussion.	✓	
b. Follow rules for collegial discussions, set specific goals and deadlines, and define individual roles as needed.	✓	
c. Pose and respond to specific questions with elaboration and detail by making comments that contribute to the topic, text, or issue under discussion.	✓	

	Module 6.2B	Module 6.3B
d. Review the key ideas expressed and demonstrate understanding of multiple perspectives through reflection and paraphrasing.	✓	
SL.6.2. Interpret information presented in diverse media and formats (e.g., visually, quantitatively, orally) and explain how it contributes to a topic, text, or issue under study.		✓
SL.6.3. Delineate a speaker's argument and specific claims, distinguishing claims that are supported by reasons and evidence from claims that are not.		
SL.6.4. Present claims and findings, sequencing ideas logically and using pertinent descriptions, facts, and details to accentuate main ideas or themes; use appropriate eye contact, adequate volume, and clear pronunciation.	✓	
SL.6.5. Include multimedia components (e.g., graphics, images, music, sound) and visual displays in presentations to clarify information.		
SL.6.6. Adapt speech to a variety of contexts and tasks, demonstrating command of formal English when indicated or appropriate.	✓	

Language Standards

	Module 6.2B	Module 6.3B
L.6.1. Demonstrate command of the conventions of standard English grammar and usage when writing or speaking. a. Ensure that pronouns are in the proper case (subjective, objective, possessive). b. Use intensive pronouns (e.g., *myself, ourselves*). c. Recognize and correct inappropriate shifts in pronoun number and person. d. Recognize and correct vague pronouns (i.e., ones with unclear or ambiguous antecedents). e. Recognize variations from standard English in their own and others' writing and speaking, and identify and use strategies to improve expression in conventional language.	✓	

	Module 6.2B	Module 6.3B
L.6.2. Demonstrate command of the conventions of standard English capitalization, punctuation, and spelling when writing. a. Vary sentence patterns for meaning, reader/listener interest, and style. b. Maintain consistency in style and tone.	✓	
L.6.3. Use knowledge of language and its conventions when writing, speaking, reading, or listening. a. Vary sentence patterns for meaning, reader/listener interest, and style. b. Maintain consistency in style and tone.	✓	✓ ✓
L.6.4. Determine or clarify the meaning of unknown and multiple-meaning words and phrases based on *grade 6 reading and content*, choosing flexibly from a range of strategies. a. Use context (e.g., the overall meaning of a sentence or paragraph; a word's position or function in a sentence) as a clue to the meaning of a word or phrase. b. Use common, grade-appropriate Greek or Latin affixes and roots as clues to the meaning of a word (e.g., *audience, auditory, audible*). c. Consult reference materials (e.g., dictionaries, glossaries, thesauruses), both print and digital, to find the pronunciation of a word or determine or clarify its precise meaning or its part of speech. d. Verify the preliminary determination of the meaning of a word or phrase (e.g., by checking the inferred meaning in context or in a dictionary).	✓	✓
L.6.5. Demonstrate understanding of figurative language, word relationships, and nuances in word meanings. a. Interpret figures of speech (e.g., personification) in context. b. Use the relationship between particular words (e.g., cause/effect, part/whole, item/ category) to better understand each of the words. c. Distinguish among the connotations (associations) of words with similar denotations (definitions) (e.g., *stingy, scrimping, economical, unwasteful, thrifty*).	✓ ✓ ✓ ✓	
L.6.6. Acquire and use accurately grade- appropriate general academic and domain-specific words and phrases; gather vocabulary knowledge when considering a word or phrase important to comprehension or expression.	Integrated throughout.	

ELA Curriculum: Grades 6–8 Curriculum Plan

GRADE 6

Topic	Module 6.2B **Voices of Adversity**	Module 6.3B **Sustaining the Oceans**
Central Texts*	Laura Amy Schlitz, *Good Masters! Sweet Ladies! Voices from a Medieval Village*, illustrated by Robert Byrd (NP) John Grandits, *Blue Lipstick: Concrete Poems* (NP) John Grandits, *Technically, It's Not My Fault: Concrete Poems* (NP)	Mark Kurlansky, *World Without Fish* (1160L) Carl Hiaasen, *Flush* (770L)
Writing Tasks**	• Writing about Medieval Times (W.6.2, W.6.4, W.6.7, W.6.9) • Argument Essay: "Do we still face the same adversities as the people of *Good Masters! Sweet Ladies!*?" (W.6.1, W.6.9)	• Researching Information about Buying Fish Caught Using Sustainable Methods (W.6.7) • Informative Consumer Guide: What You Need to Know When Buying Fish (W.6.2, W.6.4)

		7.2B	7.4B
GRADE 7	Topic	Identity and Transformation: Then and Now	Water Is Life
	Central Texts*	George Bernard Shaw, *Pygmalion*	Charles Fishman, *The Big Thirst: The Secret Life and Turbulent Future of Water*
	Writing Tasks**	• Argument Essay: Liza's Changes (W.7.1, W.7.9, W.7.5) • Writing a Research Synthesis (W.7.7, W 7.8) • Advertisement Analysis and Counter Ad (W.7.2 .a, b, d, f, W.7.4, W.7.6, W.7.7, W.7.8)	• Simulated Research Task: Water Management Strategies (W.7.7, W.7.8) • First Draft of Position Paper (W.7.1.a, b, e, W.7.4) • Final Draft of Position Paper and Reflection on the Writing Process (W.7.1.c, d, W.7.4, W.7.5)

		8.2B	8.3B
GRADE 8	Topic	*A Midsummer Night's Dream* and the Comedy of Control	The Civil Rights Movement and the Little Rock Nine
	Central Texts*	William Shakespeare, *A Midsummer Night's Dream* (590L)	Carlotta Walls LaNier, *A Mighty Long Way: My Journey to Justice at Little Rock Central High School* (1040L) Shelley Tougas, *Little Rock Girl 1957: How a Photograph Changed the Fight for Integration* (1010L)
	Writing Tasks**	• Argument Essay: Controlling Others in *A Midsummer Night's Dream* (W.8.1, W.8.1.b, c, d, e, W.8.a) • Confessional Narrative Character and Scene Selection: Justification (W.8.9.a) • Character Confessional Narrative (W.8.3, W.8.4, W.8.9.a)	• Informational Essay: The Role of the Media in the Story of the Little Rock Nine (W.8.2, W.8.9) • On-Demand Writing—Photograph and Song Choices for a Film (W.8.1, W.8.2)

*This plan shows most full-length books all students read and a few key articles. See separate document "Trade Books and Other Resources" for a complete list of resources needed in order to implement the modules.

**This plan shows the two main writing tasks per module and the standards most central to each task. See the curriculum map for the full list of standards assessed (including the writing process and language standards).

GRADE 6   Module 3B

MODULE OVERVIEW

Understanding Perspectives
Sustaining the Oceans

In this module, students study how an author develops point of view and how an author's perspective, based on his or her geographic location, is evident in his or her writing. Students consider point of view as they learn about ocean conservation and the impact of human activities on life in the oceans. Through close reading, students will learn multiple strategies for acquiring and using academic vocabulary. In Unit 1, students read the first five chapters of Mark Kurlansky's *World Without Fish*, a literary nonfiction text about fish depletion in the world's oceans. They analyze how point of view and perspective is conveyed in excerpts of the text and trace the idea of fish depletion in both the main text and the graphic novel at the end of each chapter to describe how the idea is introduced, illustrated, and elaborated on in the text. In Unit 2, students read Carl Hiaasen's *Flush*, a high-interest novel about a casino boat that is polluting the ocean and the effort of a family to stop it. As they read the novel, students also will read excerpts of an interview with Carl Hiaasen to determine how his geographic location in Florida shaped his perspective and how his perspective is evident in his novel *Flush*. At the end of Unit 2, having read the novel, students will write a short, on-demand response explaining how living in Florida affected Carl Hiaasen's perspective of the ocean and ocean conservation, supported by details from *Flush* that show evidence of Hiaasen's perspective. In Unit 3, students return to *World Without Fish* and pursue further research about overfishing to write an informative consumer guide about buying fish to be put in a grocery store. **This task addresses ELA CCSS W.6.2, W.6.6 (optional), W.6.7, L.6.2, L.6.2.a, L.6.2.b, L.6.3, L.6.3.a, and L.6.3.b**.

Guiding Questions and Big Ideas

- How does an author develop the narrator's point of view and perspective?
- How does an author's geographic location affect his perspective, and how is that perspective communicated through his writing?
- How does an author's purpose affect the narrator's point of view?
- How do human activities affect the balance of our ecosystem?
- *Understanding diverse points of view helps us to live in an increasingly diverse society.*

- *An author's culture, background, and purpose can affect the narrator's point of view.*
- *Organisms and their environment have an interconnected relationship. Human choices affect this relationship.*

Performance Task

Informative Consumer Guide: What Do People Need to Know about Overfishing and Fish Depletion When Buying Fish?

This task addresses ELA CCSS W.6.2, W.6.4, W.6.6 (optional), W.6.7, L.6.2, L.6.2.a, L.6.2.b, L.6.3, L.6.3.a, and L.6.3.b. In this performance task, students have an opportunity to apply what they have learned about fish depletion and the issue of overfishing to create an informative consumer guide to be handed out in grocery stores about buying sustainably caught fish. They research overfishing, sustainable fishing methods, specific case studies of fish having their numbers depleted, and suggestions for ways to buy fish caught using sustainable fishing methods. They then compile all this information in an eye-catching guide that consumers will want to pick up when they are at the fish counter in a grocery store.

Content Connections

This module is designed to address English Language Arts standards as students read literary and informational text about ocean conservation issues. However, the module intentionally incorporates social studies themes and practices to support potential interdisciplinary connections to this compelling content. These intentional connections are described below.

Social Studies Themes

Time, Continuity, and Change

- Analyzing causes and consequences of events and developments

Geography, Humans, and the Environment

- Relationship between human populations and the physical world (people, places, and environments)
- Impact of human activities on the environment

Creation, Expansion, and Interaction of Economic Systems

- Scarcity of resources and the challenges of meeting wants and needs
- Supply/demand and the coordination of individual choices

Science, Technology, and Innovation

- Relationship between human populations and the physical world
- Interactions between regions, locations, places, people, and environments

Social Studies Practices

Gathering, Interpreting, and Using Evidence

- Identify, effectively select, and analyze different forms of evidence used to make meaning in social studies.
- Identify evidence and explain content, authorship, point of view, purpose, and format; identify bias; explain the role of bias and potential audience.

English Language Arts Outcomes

CCS Standards: Reading—Literature	Long-Term Learning Targets
RL.6.4. Determine the meaning of words and phrases as they are used in a text, including figurative and connotative meanings; analyze the impact of a specific word choice on meaning and tone.	• I can determine the meaning of literal and figurative language (metaphors and similes) in a literary text. • I can analyze how an author's word choice affects tone and meaning in a literary text.
RL.6.5. Analyze how a particular sentence, chapter, scene, or stanza fits into the overall structure of a text and contributes to the development of the theme, setting, or plot.	• I can analyze how a particular sentence, stanza, scene, or chapter fits in and contributes to the development of a literary text.
RL.6.6. Explain how an author develops the point of view of the narrator or speaker in a text.	• I can analyze how an author develops a narrator or speaker's point of view.
RL.6.9. Compare and contrast texts in different forms or genres (e.g., stories and poems; historical novels and fantasy stories) in terms of their approaches to similar themes and topics.	• I can compare and contrast texts in different forms or genres (e.g., stories and poems; historical novels and fantasy stories) in terms of their approaches to similar themes and topics.
CCS Standards: Reading—Informational Texts	**Long-Term Learning Targets**
RI.6.3. Analyze in detail how a key individual, event, or idea is introduced, illustrated, and elaborated on in a text (e.g., through examples or anecdotes).	• I can analyze how key individuals, events, or ideas are developed throughout a text.
RI.6.4. Determine the meaning of words and phrases as they are used in a text, including figurative, connotative, and technical meanings.	• I can use a variety of strategies to determine word meaning in informational texts.

RI.6.6. Determine an author's point of view or purpose in a text and explain how it is conveyed in the text.	• I can determine an author's point of view or purpose in an informational text. • I can explain how an author's point of view is conveyed in an informational text.
RI.6.7. Integrate information presented in different media or formats (e.g., visually, quantitatively) as well as in words to develop a coherent understanding of a topic or issue.	• I can integrate information presented in different media or formats (e.g., visually, quantitatively) as well as in words to develop a coherent understanding of a topic or issue.
CCS Standards: Writing	**Long-Term Learning Targets**
W.6.2. Write informative/explanatory texts to examine a topic and convey ideas, concepts, and information through the selection, organization, and analysis of relevant content. a. Introduce a topic; organize ideas, concepts, and information using strategies such as definition, classification, comparison/contrast, and cause/effect; include formatting (e.g., headings), graphics (e.g., charts, tables), and multimedia when useful to aiding comprehension. b. Develop the topic with relevant facts, definitions, concrete details, quotations, or other information and examples. c. Use appropriate transitions to clarify the relationships among ideas and concepts. d. Use precise language and domain-specific vocabulary to inform about or explain the topic. e. Establish and maintain a formal style. f. Provide a concluding statement or section that follows from the information or explanation presented.	• I can write informative/explanatory texts that convey ideas and concepts using relevant information that is carefully selected and organized. a. I can introduce the topic of my text. a. I can organize my information using various strategies (e.g., definition/classification, comparison/contrast, cause/effect). a. I can include headings, graphics, and multimedia to help readers understand my ideas. b. I can develop the topic with relevant facts, definitions, concrete details, and quotations. c. I can use transitions to clarify relationships among my ideas. d. I can use contextually specific language/vocabulary to inform or explain about a topic. e. I can establish and maintain a formal style in my writing. f. I can construct a concluding statement or section of an informative/explanatory text.
W.6.4. Produce clear and coherent writing in which the development, organization, and style are appropriate to task, purpose, and audience.	• I can produce clear and coherent writing that is appropriate to task, purpose, and audience.

CCS Standards: Writing (cont.)	Long-Term Learning Targets
W.6.6. (optional) Use technology, including the Internet, to produce and publish writing as well as to interact and collaborate with others; demonstrate sufficient command of keyboarding skills to type a minimum of three pages in a single sitting.	• I can use technology to publish a piece of writing. • I can use technology to collaborate with others to produce a piece of writing. • I can type at least three pages of writing in a single sitting.
W.6.7. Conduct short research projects to answer a question, drawing on several sources, and refocusing the inquiry when appropriate.	• I can conduct short research projects to answer a question. • I can use several sources in my research. • I can refocus or refine my question when appropriate.

CCS Standards: Writing	Long-Term Learning Targets
W.6.9. Draw evidence from literary or informational texts to support analysis, reflection, and research. a. Apply sixth-grade reading standards to literature (e.g., "Compare and contrast texts in different forms or genres [e.g., stories and poems; historical novels and fantasy stories] in terms of their approaches to similar themes and topics"). b. Apply sixth-grade reading standards to literary nonfiction (e.g., "Trace and evaluate the argument and specific claims in a text, distinguishing claims that are supported by reasons and evidence from claims that are not").	• I can draw evidence from literary or informational texts to support analysis, reflection, and research. • I can apply sixth-grade reading standards to literary nonfiction (e.g., "Trace and evaluate the argument and specific claims in a text, distinguishing claims that are supported by reasons and evidence from claims that are not").

CCS Standards: Speaking and Listening	Long-Term Learning Targets
SL.6.2. Interpret information presented in diverse media and formats (e.g., visually, quantitatively, orally) and explain how it contributes to a topic, text, or issue under study.	• I can interpret information presented in different media and formats. • I can explain how new information connects to a topic, text, or issue I am studying.

CCS Standards: Language	Long-Term Learning Targets

L.6.2. Demonstrate command of the conventions of standard English capitalization, punctuation, and spelling when writing.
   a. Use punctuation (commas, parentheses, dashes) to set off nonrestrictive/parenthetical elements.
   b. Spell correctly.
	• I can use correct capitalization, punctuation, and spelling to send a clear message to my reader.
	   a. I can use punctuation (commas, parentheses, dashes) to set off nonrestrictive/parenthetical elements.
	   b. I can spell correctly.

L.6.3. Use knowledge of language and its conventions when writing, speaking, reading, or listening.
   a. Vary sentence patterns for meaning, reader/listener interest, and style.
   b. Maintain consistency in style and tone.
	• I can use knowledge of language and its conventions when writing, speaking, reading, or listening.
	   a. I can use a variety of sentence structures to make my writing and speaking more interesting.
	   b. I can maintain consistency in style and tone when writing and speaking.

L.6.4.a. Use context (e.g., the overall meaning of a sentence or paragraph; a word's position or function in a sentence) as a clue to the meaning of a word or phrase.	• I can use context (e.g., the overall meaning of a sentence or paragraph; a word's position or function in a sentence) to determine the meaning of a word or phrase.

Central Texts

1. Mark Kurlansky, *World Without Fish* (New York: Workman Publishing, 2011), ISBN: 978-0-7611-8500-0. (1160L)
2. Carl Hiaasen, *Flush* (New York: Random House, 1991), ISBN: 978-0-375-86125-3. (770L)
3. Marine Conservation Institute, "Destructive Fishing," October 23, 2015. (1280L)
4. National Resources Defense Council, "Protecting Ocean Habitat from Bottom Trawling," October 23, 2013. (1420L)
5. "Threat 1: Overfishing." Overfishing. Save Our Seas, Feb. 19, 2014. (1350L)
6. PBS Newshour Extra, "A Rapidly Disappearing Fish." (1160L)
7. "Case Study: Atlantic Bluefin Tuna," Overfishing, Feb. 19, 2014. (1280L)
8. Sunset. "Sustainable Fishing Methods," available at http://www.sunset.com/food-wine/flavors-of-the-west/sustainable-fishing-methods-00400000053176/. (1160L)
9. National Geographic, "Sustainable Fishing." (1130L)
10. Vancouver Aquarium. "Sustainable Seafood." (1310L)

Week-at-a-Glance Calendar

Week	Instructional Focus	Long-Term Targets	Assessments
Unit 1: Author's Point of View and Idea Development in *World Without Fish*			
Weeks 1–3	• Analyze excerpts of *World Without Fish* for figurative language, connotative language, word and phrase choice and meaning, and plot development. • Analyze excerpts of *World Without Fish* for evidence of Mark Kurlansky's point of view and how it is conveyed.	• I can analyze how key individuals, events, or ideas are developed throughout a text. (RI.6.3) • I can use a variety of strategies to determine word meaning in informational texts. (RI.6.4) • I can determine an author's point of view or purpose in an informational text. (RI.6.6) • I can explain how an author's point of view is conveyed in an informational text. (RI.6.6)	• **Mid-Unit 1 Assessment:** Analyzing Idea Development in Chapter 3 of *World Without Fish* (RI.6.2, RI.6.3 and RI.6.4) • **End-of-Unit 1 Assessment:** Analyzing Author's Point of View and How It Is Conveyed in Chapter 5 of *World Without Fish* (RI.6.6)
Unit 2: Narrator's Point of View and Evidence of Author's Perspective in *Flush*			
Weeks 3–5	• Closely read excerpts of *Flush* to analyze the narrator's point of view and how it is conveyed. • Analyze how Carl Hiaasen develops the plot in each chapter.	• I can determine the meaning of literal, and figurative language (metaphors and similes) in a literary text. (RL.6.4) • I can analyze how an author's word choice affects tone and meaning in a literary text. (RL.6.4) • I can analyze how a particular sentence, stanza, scene, or chapter fits in and contributes to the development of a literary text. (RL.6.5) • I can analyze how an author develops a narrator or speaker's point of view. (RL.6.6)	• **Mid-Unit 2 Assessment:** Analyzing Point of View and Plot Development in *Flush* (RL.6.4, RL.6.5, RL.6.6, and L.6.4.a)

Week	Instructional Focus	Long-Term Targets	Assessments
		• I can use context (e.g., the overall meaning of a sentence or paragraph; a word's position or function in a sentence) to determine the meaning of a word or phrase. (L.6.4.a)	
	• Closely read excerpts of interviews with Carl Hiaasen to analyze how his geographic location in Florida has affected his perspective. • Closely read excerpts of *Flush* looking for evidence of Carl Hiaasen's perspective.	• I can explain how the author develops the point of view of the narrator or speaker in a text. (RL.6.6)	• End-of-**Unit 2 Assessment**: Finding Evidence of Carl Hiaasen's Perspective in *Flush* and Illustrating Perspective (RL.6.6)
Unit 3: Researching and Interpreting Information: What You Need to Know When Buying Fish			
Weeks 6–8	• Researching information about overfishing, sustainable fishing methods, case studies of depleted fish species, and suggestions for buying fish caught using sustainable methods.	• I can conduct short research projects to answer a question. (W.6.7) • I can use several sources in my research. (W.6.7) • I can refocus or refine my question when appropriate. (W.6.7) • I can interpret information presented in different media and formats. (SL.6.2) • I can explain how new information connects to a topic, text, or issue I am studying. (SL.6.2)	• Mid-**Unit 3 Assessment (Parts 1 and 2)**: Researching Information about How to Buy Fish Caught Using Sustainable Methods (W.6.7 and SL.6.2)
	• Evaluate research to choose that which is most relevant and compelling.	• I can integrate information presented in different media or formats (e.g., visually, quantitatively) as well as in words to develop a coherent understanding of a topic or issue. (RI.6.7)	• End-of-**Unit 3 Assessment**: Draft Informative Consumer Guide: What You Need to Know When Buying Fish (RI.6.7, W.6.2.a–f, W.6.4, and W.6.9)

Week	Instructional Focus	Long-Term Targets	Assessments
	• Analyze authentic informative consumer guides to generate criteria for an effective informative consumer guide. • Compile the most relevant and compelling research into an informative consumer guide.	• I can write informative/explanatory texts that convey ideas and concepts using relevant information that is carefully selected and organized. (W.6.2) • I can introduce the topic of my text. (W.6.2.a) • I can organize my information using various strategies (e.g. definition/classification, comparison/contrast, cause/effect). (W.6.2.a) • I can include headings, graphics, and multimedia to help readers understand my ideas. (W.6.2.a) • I can develop the topic with relevant facts, definitions, concrete details, and quotations. (W.6.2.b) • I can use transitions to clarify relationships among my ideas. (W.6.2.c) • I can use contextually specific language/vocabulary to inform or explain about a topic. (W.6.2.d) • I can establish and maintain a formal style in my writing. (W.6.2.e) • I can construct a concluding statement or section of an informative/explanatory text. (W.6.2.f) • I can use correct capitalization, punctuation, and spelling to send a clear message to my reader. (L.6.2)	• **Final Performance Task:** Informative Consumer Guide: What You Need to Know When Buying Fish (W.6.2, W.6.4, L.6.2, and L.6.3)

Week	Instructional Focus	Long-Term Targets	Assessments
		• I can use punctuation (commas, parentheses, dashes) to set off nonrestrictive/parenthetical elements. (L.6.2.a) • I can spell correctly. (L.6.2.b) • I can use knowledge of language and its conventions when writing, speaking, reading, or listening. (L.6.3) • I can use a variety of sentence structures to make my writing and speaking more interesting. (L.6.3.a) • I can maintain consistency in style and tone when writing and speaking. (L.6.3.b)	

Preparation and Materials

This module is content-rich; consider previewing the full module with a science and social studies colleague and finding ways to collaborate to give an even richer experience. Students may benefit from spending more time with specific primary source documents with the support of the social studies teacher. That teacher also may identify natural connections or extensions with the compelling content of this module that she or he can address during science or social studies class.

This module continues an independent reading structure that was formally introduced in Module 2. See **Launching Independent Reading in Grades 6–8: Sample Plan** which provides practical guidance for a robust independent reading program. Students are expected to continue reading texts, completing the reading log, and selecting new independent reading texts throughout Module 3B. The independent reading routine takes about a half-class period per week, with an additional day near the end of a unit or module for students to review and share their books. There is an option to assess independent reading during Lesson 6 of Unit 3 of this module. Students can write a book review based on one of the independent books they have read this school year, and may also be given an opportunity to share their books through a book talk given to peers.

ASSESSMENT OVERVIEW

Performance Task

Informative Consumer Guide: What Do People Need to Know about Overfishing and Fish Depletion When Buying Fish?

This task addresses ELA CCSS W.6.2, W.6.4, W.6.6 (optional), W.6.7, L.6.2, L.6.2.a, L.6.2.b, L.6.3, L.6.3.a, and L.6.3.b. In this performance task, students have an opportunity to apply what they have learned about fish depletion and the issue of overfishing to create an informative consumer guide to be handed out in grocery stores about buying sustainably caught fish. They research overfishing, sustainable fishing methods, specific case studies of fish having their numbers depleted, and suggestions for ways to buy fish caught using sustainable fishing methods. They then compile all this information in an eye-catching guide that consumers will want to pick up when they are at the fish counter in a grocery store.

Mid-Unit 1 Assessment

Analyzing Idea Development in Chapter 3 of *World Without Fish*

This assessment addresses ELA CCSS RI.6.2, RI.6.3, and RI.6.4. For this assessment, students read a new excerpt of *World Without Fish* and use a graphic organizer to analyze how the author continues to illustrate and elaborate on the idea of fish depletion in the excerpt. They also answer selected-response questions about word and phrase meaning.

End-of-Unit 1 Assessment

Analyzing Author's Point of View and How It Is Conveyed in Chapter 5 of *World Without Fish*

This assessment addresses ELA CCSS RI.6.6. Students read a new excerpt from *World Without Fish* and complete a graphic organizer requiring them to make a claim about Mark Kurlansky's point of view of the codfish situation in the Grand Banks, use evidence from the text to support their claim, and analyze how the author conveys his point of view.

Mid-Unit 2 Assessment

Analyzing Point of View and Plot Development in *Flush*

This assessment addresses ELA CCSS RL.6.4, RL.6.5, RL.6.6, and L.6.4.a. For this assessment, students read a new excerpt of *Flush* and use a graphic organizer to analyze how the author develops the narrator's point of view. They also answer selected-response questions about word and phrase meaning, and how a sentence/paragraph fits into the overall structure of the text in the excerpt.

End-of-Unit 2 Assessment

Finding Evidence of Carl Hiaasen's Perspective in *Flush* and Illustrating Plot

This assessment addresses ELA CCSS RL.6.6. Students read an excerpt from *Flush* and fill out a graphic organizer to analyze the evidence of Carl Hiaasen's perspective of Florida in the excerpt, and then use their thinking to write an on-demand response to the questions: "How has being born and raised in Florida affected Carl Hiaasen's perspective of the place and where is the evidence of this perspective in the excerpt you have read today of the novel *Flush*? How does the evidence you have selected show evidence of his perspective?" Students also sketch and label or write about a scene from *Flush*, explaining how it shows evidence of Carl Hiaasen's perspective.

Mid-Unit 3 Assessment

Part 1: Researching Information about How to Buy Fish Caught Using Sustainable Methods

This assessment addresses ELA CCSS W.6.7. There are two parts to this assessment. In Part 1, students interpret the information presented in diverse media and formats to answer the question: How can we buy fish caught using sustainable methods? They record the information they find on a graphic organizer.

Part 2: Explaining How New Information Connects to the Topic

This assessment addresses ELA CCSS SL.6.2.

In Part 2, students explain orally how the resources they have looked at contribute to the topic of overfishing and fish depletion.

End-of-Unit 3 Assessment

Draft of Written Content of Informative Consumer Guide: What You Need to Know When Buying Fish

This assessment addresses ELA CCSS RI.6.7, W.6.2a–f, W.6.4, and W.6.9. Students write a first draft of their informative consumer guide to answer the question: What does a consumer need to know when buying fish? They select factual information from research that is most compelling and include all of the features of an informative guide that they have identified from authentic consumer guides.

PERFORMANCE TASK

Informative Consumer Guide: What Do People Need to Know about Overfishing and Fish Depletion When Buying Fish?

Summary of Task

This task addresses ELA CCSS W.6.2, W.6.4, W.6.6 (optional), W.6.7, L.6.2, L.6.2.a, L.6.2.b, L.6.3, L.6.3.a, and L.6.3.b. In this performance task, students have an opportunity to apply what they have learned about fish depletion and the issue of overfishing to create an informative consumer guide to be handed out in grocery stores about buying sustainably caught fish. They research overfishing, sustainable fishing methods, specific case studies of fish having their numbers depleted, and suggestions for ways to buy fish caught using sustainable fishing methods. They then compile all this information in an eye-catching guide that consumers will want to pick up when they are at the fish counter in a grocery store.

Format

- An informative consumer guide to be put in grocery stores near the fish counter to answer the question: What do you need to know when buying fish?
- The format of the guide will be based on a study of a model consumer guide and real-world consumer guides.
- The rough draft of the consumer guide will be assessed and then edited for revision.

Standards Assessed through This Task

- W.6.2. Write informative/explanatory texts to examine a topic and convey ideas, concepts, and information through the selection, organization, and analysis of relevant content.
- W.6.6. Use technology, including the Internet, to produce and publish writing as well as to interact and collaborate with others; demonstrate sufficient command of keyboarding skills to type a minimum of three pages in a single sitting.
- W.6.7. Conduct short research projects to answer a question, drawing on several sources and refocusing the inquiry when appropriate.

- L.6.2. Demonstrate command of the conventions of standard English capitalization, punctuation, and spelling when writing.
    a. Use punctuation (commas, parentheses, dashes) to set off nonrestrictive/parenthetical elements.
    b. Spell correctly.
- L.6.3. Use knowledge of language and its conventions when writing, speaking, reading, or listening.
    a. Vary sentence patterns for meaning, reader/listener interest, and style.
    b. Maintain consistency in style and tone.

Student-Friendly Writing Invitation/Task Description

For this performance task, you will create an informative consumer guide to answer the question: "What do people need to know about overfishing and fish depletion when buying fish?" Your guide can be placed in a grocery store, near the fish counter, to inform people about the issue of fish depletion due to overfishing and to guide them in how to buy fish caught using sustainable fishing methods. Your guide should fit onto one piece of paper so consumers don't have to carry a lot of paper around in the store with them. It should explain the problem, provide a case study to highlight the impact of the problem, and provide suggestions for how to buy fish caught using sustainable fishing methods. It should be eye-catching to encourage consumers to pick it up when they are standing at the fish counter deciding which fish to buy and compelling to encourage them to read to the end.

Key Criteria for Success (Aligned with ELA CCSS)

Below are key criteria students need to address when completing this task. Specific lessons during the module build in opportunities for students to understand the criteria, offer additional criteria, and review a rubric on which their work will be critiqued and formally assessed.

Your informative consumer guide needs to include relevant and compelling factual information and quotes about:

- The issue: overfishing and how it causes fish depletion.
- A case study of a fish species that has been severely depleted and the impact that it has had.
- A solution: sustainable methods for catching fish.
- Suggestions: buying fish that have been caught using sustainable methods.

Your informative consumer guide also needs to:

- Fit onto one piece of letter-sized paper.
- Include the features of a consumer guide: headline and subheadings.
- Include visuals like pictures and charts or graphs to make it eye-catching and to improve consumer understanding of the issue.
- Include a Works Cited list.

Options for Students

- Students might have a partner to assist as they work on planning their consumer guides, but the guide itself will be an individual's product.
- Student consumer guides could be various lengths, shorter for those for whom written English is a barrier.

Options for Teachers

- Student consumer guides could be displayed in a local grocery store or supermarket near the fish counter, with appropriate permission.
- Student consumer guides could be displayed in the classroom or somewhere else in the school.
- Consider working with a technology teacher if students are completing their work on computers.
- Consider working with an art teacher to help students improve the visual presentation of their work.

Resources and Links

- Save Our Seas Foundation: https://saveourseas.com/overfishing/
- Marine Conservation Institute: https://marine-conservation.org/what-we-do/program-areas/how-we-fish/destructive-fishing/
- NOAA FishWatch: https://www.fishwatch.gov/
- Monterey Bay Aquarium: https://www.seafoodwatch.org/seafood-recommendations/consumer-guides

RECOMMENDED TEXTS

The list below includes informational texts and fiction with a range of Lexile text measures about sustaining the world's oceans. This provides appropriate independent reading for each student to help build content knowledge about the topic. Note that districts and schools should consider their own community standards when reviewing this list. Some texts in particular units or modules address emotionally difficult content.

It is imperative that students read a high volume of texts at their reading level in order to continue to build the academic vocabulary and fluency demanded by the CCSS.

Where possible, texts in languages other than English are also provided. Texts are categorized into three Lexile measures that correspond to Common Core Bands: below grade band, within band, and above band. Note, however, that Lexile measures are just one indicator of text complexity, and teachers must use their professional judgment and consider qualitative factors as well. For more information, see Appendix A of the Common Core State Standards.

Common Core Band Level Text Difficulty Ranges

- Grades 2–3: 420–820L
- Grades 4–5: 740–1010L
- Grades 6–8: 925–1185L

Title	Author and Illustrator	Text Type	Lexile Measure
Lexile text measures in Grades 2–3 band level (below 740L)			
Oceans	Kate Riggs (author); Zack McLaughlin (illustrator)	Literature	330L
What Eats What in an Ocean Food Chain	Suzanne Slade (author)	Informational	560L

Title	Author and Illustrator	Text Type	Lexile Measure
Lexile text measures in Grades 4–5 band level (740–925L)			
Hoot	Carl Hiaasen (author)	Literature	760L
Fishing	Gary Newman (author)	Informational	IG770L
Make a Splash! A Kid's Guide to Protecting Our Oceans, Lakes, Rivers, and Wetlands	Cathryn Berger Kaye and Phillipe Cousteau (authors)	Informational	780L
What if There Were No Sea Otters? A Book about the Ocean Ecosystem	Suzanne Slade (author); Carol Schwartz (illustrator)	Informational	820L
Green Boy	Susan Cooper (author)	Literature	930L
Olivia's Birds: Saving the Gulf	Olivia Bouler (author)	Informational	880L
Lexile text measures within Grades 6–8 band level (925–1185L)			
Going Blue: A Teen Guide to Saving Our Oceans, Lakes, Rivers, and Wetlands	Cathryn Berger Kaye and Phillipe Cousteau (authors)	Informational	1170L
Overfishing (Habitat Havoc)	Therese Shea (author)	Informational	No LXL

Title	Author and Illustrator	Text Type	Lexile Measure
Lexile text measures above band level (over 1185L)			
Tracking Trash: Flotsam, Jetsam, and the Science of Motion	Loree Griffin Burns (author)	Informational	1200L
The River Cottage Fish Book: The Definitive Guide to Sourcing and Cooking Sustainable Fish and Shellfish	Hugh Fearnley-Whittingstall and Nick Fisher (authors)	Informational	No LXL

*Lexile based on a conversion from Accelerated Reading level.

GRADE 6   Module 3B: Unit 1

UNIT OVERVIEW

Reading Closely and Writing to Learn: Point of View and Perspective

Author's Point of View and Idea Development in *World Without Fish*

In this unit, students are involved in a study of how an author introduces, illustrates, and elaborates on an idea and how an author conveys his or her point of view. Students will begin reading Mark Kurlansky's *World Without Fish*, a literary nonfiction text about the causes of and solutions to the problem of fish depletion. The focus of Unit 1 is the first half of the book, in which Mark Kurlansky describes the problem. Students will return to the final chapters of the book and his suggested solutions in Unit 3. In the first half of the unit, the focus is on tracing the idea of fish depletion across the first five chapters of the book: how the idea is introduced at the beginning and how it is illustrated and elaborated on throughout the first half of the book. Through close reading of this text, students will learn multiple strategies for acquiring and using academic vocabulary. In the second half of the unit, students analyze Mark Kurlansky's point of view in excerpts of the text and how he conveys that point of view. At the end of Unit 1, students are assessed on their analysis of the point of view and how it is conveyed in a new excerpt of the text.

Guiding Questions and Big Ideas

- How does an author convey his or her point of view?
- How does an author introduce, illustrate, and elaborate on an idea?
- What is the impact of fish depletion?
- *All life on earth is interconnected, and altered circumstances will change the order of life at sea—which will also change life on land.*

Mid-Unit 1 Assessment

Analyzing Idea Development in Chapter 3 of *World Without Fish*

This assessment addresses ELA CCSS RI.6.2, RI.6.3, and RI.6.4. For this assessment, students read a new excerpt of *World Without Fish* and use a graphic organizer to analyze how the author continues to

illustrate and elaborate on the idea of fish depletion in the excerpt. They also answer selected-response questions about word and phrase meaning.

End-of-Unit 1 Assessment

Analyzing Author's Point of View and How It Is Conveyed in Chapter 5 of *World Without Fish*

This assessment addresses ELA CCSS RI.6.6. Students read a new excerpt from *World Without Fish* and complete a graphic organizer requiring them to make a claim about Mark Kurlansky's point of view of the codfish situation in the Grand Banks, use evidence from the text to support their claim, and analyze how the author conveys his point of view.

Supplementary Assessment Items

This unit also includes a small set of optional selected-response items. These are supplementary items that provide additional information about student mastery of a subset of the standards for this unit.

- Supplementary assessment items and teacher-facing answer keys are available at the end of each unit.
- To provide teachers with flexibility around how and when to use these materials, supplementary assessment items are located in this Teacher Guide and Resource Book only.

Content Connections

This module is designed to address English Language Arts standards as students read a literary nonfiction text about the causes of and solutions to the issue of fish depletion in the oceans. However, the module intentionally incorporates social studies themes and practices to support potential interdisciplinary connections to this compelling content. Descriptions of these intentional connections follow.

Social Studies Themes

- Time, Continuity, and Change
  - Analyzing causes and consequences of events and developments
- Geography, Humans, and the Environment
  - Relationship between human populations and the physical world (people, places, and environment)
  - Impact of human activities on the environment
- Creation, Expansion, and Interaction of Economic Systems
  - Scarcity of resources and the challenges of meeting wants and needs
  - Supply/demand and the coordination of individual choices

- Science, Technology, and Innovation
  - Relationship between human populations and the physical world
  - Interactions between regions, locations, places, people, and environments

Social Studies Practices

- Gathering, Interpreting, and Using Evidence
  - Identify, effectively select, and analyze different forms of evidence used to make meaning in social studies
  - Identify evidence and explain content, authorship, point of view, purpose, and format; identify bias; explain the role of bias and potential audience.

Central Text

1. Mark Kurlansky, *World Without Fish* (New York: Workman Publishing Company Inc., 2011), ISBN: 978-0-7611-8500-0. (1160L)

Unit-at-a-Glance Calendar

This unit is approximately 2 weeks or 11 sessions of instruction.

Lesson	Lesson Title	Long-Term Targets	Supporting Targets	Ongoing Assessment	Anchor Charts and Protocols
1	Introducing *World Without Fish*	• I can determine the main idea of an informational text based on details in the text. (RI.6.2) • I can analyze how key individuals, events, or ideas are developed throughout a text. (RI.6.3)	• I can find the gist of an excerpt of the Introduction of *World Without Fish*. • I can use evidence from the text to answer text-dependent questions.	• Sticky notes for gist • Text-Dependent Questions: Pages x–xii	

Lesson	Lesson Title	Long-Term Targets	Supporting Targets	Ongoing Assessment	Anchor Charts and Protocols
		• I can use a variety of strategies to determine word meaning in informational texts. (RI.6.4)			
2	Introduction: The Ideas of Charles Darwin	• I can determine the main idea of an informational text based on details in the text. (RI.6.2) • I can analyze how key individuals, events, or ideas are developed throughout a text. (RI.6.3) • I can use a variety of strategies to determine word meaning in informational texts. (RI.6.4)	• I can find the gist of an excerpt of the Introduction of *World Without Fish*. • I can use strategies to determine the meaning of words and phrases in this excerpt of the Introduction of *World Without Fish*. • I can use evidence from the text to answer text-dependent questions. • I can analyze how Mark Kurlansky introduces the problem of fish depletion in *World Without Fish*.	• Structured Notes: Pages x–xii (from homework) • Text-Dependent Questions: Pages xii–xvii	• Back-to-Back and Face-to-Face protocol

Lesson	Lesson Title	Long-Term Targets	Supporting Targets	Ongoing Assessment	Anchor Charts and Protocols
3	Introducing the Struggle for Survival in the Introduction of *World Without Fish*	• I can determine the main idea of an informational text based on details in the text. (RI.6.2) • I can analyze how key individuals, events, or ideas are developed throughout a text. (RI.6.3) • I can use a variety of strategies to determine word meaning in informational texts. (RI.6.4)	• I can find the gist of an excerpt of the Introduction of *World Without Fish*. • I can use strategies to determine the meaning of words and phrases in this excerpt of the Introduction of *World Without Fish*. • I can use evidence from the text to answer text-dependent questions. • I can analyze how Mark Kurlansky introduces the problem of fish depletion in *World Without Fish*.	• Structured Notes: Pages xii–xvii (from homework) • Text-Dependent Questions: Pages xx–xxiii	• Tracing the Development of an Idea Anchor Chart • Concentric Circles protocol

Lesson	Lesson Title	Long-Term Targets	Supporting Targets	Ongoing Assessment	Anchor Charts and Protocols
4	Tracing the Idea of Fish Depletion: Chapter 1	• I can determine the main idea of an informational text based on details in the text. (RI.6.2) • I can analyze how key individuals, events, or ideas are developed throughout a text. (RI.6.3) • I can use a variety of strategies to determine word meaning in informational texts. (RI.6.4)	• I can find the gist of pages 1-8 of *World Without Fish*. • I can use strategies to determine the meaning of words and phrases in this excerpt of Chapter 1 of *World Without Fish*. • I can use evidence from the text to answer text-dependent questions. • I can analyze how Mark Kurlansky illustrates/elaborates on the problem of fish depletion in an excerpt of Chapter 1 of *World Without Fish*.	• Structured notes for "The Story of Kram and Ailat: Part 1" (from homework) • Text-Dependent Questions: Pages 1–8	• Graphic Novel: Tracing the Development of an Idea Anchor Chart • Tracing the Development of an Idea Anchor Chart • Back-to-Back and Face-to-Face protocol

Lesson	Lesson Title	Long-Term Targets	Supporting Targets	Ongoing Assessment	Anchor Charts and Protocols
5	Tracing the Idea of Fish Depletion: Chapter 2	• I can determine the main idea of an informational text based on details in the text. (RI.6.2) • I can analyze how key individuals, events, or ideas are developed throughout a text. (RI.6.3) • I can use a variety of strategies to determine word meaning in informational texts. (RI.6.4)	• I can find the gist of pages 28–33 of *World Without Fish*. • I can use strategies to determine the meaning of words and phrases in this excerpt of Chapter 2 of *World Without Fish*. • I can use evidence from the text to answer text-dependent questions. • I can analyze how Mark Kurlansky illustrates/elaborates on the problem of fish depletion in an excerpt of Chapter 1 of *World Without Fish*.	• Structured notes for "The Story of Kram and Ailat: Part 2" (from homework) • Text-Dependent Questions: Pages 28–33	• Graphic Novel: Tracing the Development of an Idea Anchor Chart • Tracing the Development of an Idea Anchor Chart

Lesson	Lesson Title	Long-Term Targets	Supporting Targets	Ongoing Assessment	Anchor Charts and Protocols
6	**Mid-Unit 1 Assessment:** Analyzing Idea Development in Chapter 3 of *World Without Fish*	• I can determine the main idea of an informational text based on details in the text. (RI.6.2) • I can analyze how key individuals, events, or ideas are developed throughout a text. (RI.6.3) • I can use a variety of strategies to determine word meaning in informational texts. (RI.6.4)	• I can use strategies to determine the meaning of words and phrases in an excerpt of Chapter 3 of *World Without Fish*. • I can analyze how Mark Kurlansky illustrates/elaborates on the problem of fish depletion in an excerpt of Chapter 3 of *World Without Fish*.	• Structured notes for "The Story of Kram and Ailat: Part 3" (from homework) • Mid-Unit 1 Assessment: Analyzing Idea Development in Chapter 3 of *World Without Fish*	• Tracing the Development of an Idea Anchor Chart
7	Reading for Gist and Answering Text-Dependent Questions: Chapter 4 of *World Without Fish*	• I can determine an author's point of view or purpose in an informational text. (RI.6.6) • I can explain how an author's point of view is conveyed in an informational text. (RI.6.6)	• I can find the gist of an excerpt of Chapter 4 of *World Without Fish*. • I can determine the meaning of unfamiliar words and phrases in an excerpt of Chapter 4.	• Structured notes for "The Story of Kram and Ailat: Part 4" (from homework) • Text-Dependent Questions: Pages 51–61	• Graphic Novel: Tracing the Development of an Idea Anchor Chart • Tracing the Development of an Idea Anchor Chart

Lesson	Lesson Title	Long-Term Targets	Supporting Targets	Ongoing Assessment	Anchor Charts and Protocols
		• I can use a variety of strategies to determine word meaning in informational texts. (RI.6.4)	• I can use evidence from the text to answer text-dependent questions.		
8	Analyzing Author's Point of View: Chapter 4 of *World Without Fish*	• I can determine an author's point of view or purpose in an informational text. (RI.6.6) • I can explain how an author's point of view is conveyed in an informational text. (RI.6.6)	• I can analyze Mark Kurlansky's point of view in an excerpt of Chapter 4 of *World Without Fish*. • I can explain how he conveys his point of view.	• Structured notes for pages 51–61 (from homework) • Author's Point of View Graphic Organizer: pages 51–61 • Analyzing Author's Point of View Anchor Chart	• Analyzing Author's Point of View Anchor Chart
9	Reading for Gist and Answering Text-Dependent Questions: Chapter 5 of *World Without Fish*	• I can determine an author's point of view or purpose in an informational text. (RI.6.6) • I can explain how an author's point of view is conveyed in an informational text. (RI.6.6)	• I can find the gist of pages 63–69 of *World Without Fish*. • I can determine the meaning of unfamiliar words and phrases in pages 63–69 of *World Without Fish*.	• Structured notes for "The Story of Kram and Ailat: Part 5" (from homework) • Text-Dependent Questions: Pages 63–69	• Graphic Novel: Tracing the Development of an Idea Anchor Chart • Tracing the Development of an Idea Anchor Chart

Lesson	Lesson Title	Long-Term Targets	Supporting Targets	Ongoing Assessment	Anchor Charts and Protocols
		• I can use a variety of strategies to determine word meaning in informational texts. (RI.6.4)	• I can use evidence from the text to answer text-dependent questions.		
10	Analyzing Author's Point of View: Chapter 5 of *World Without Fish*	• I can determine an author's point of view or purpose in an informational text. (RI.6.6) • I can explain how an author's point of view is conveyed in an informational text. (RI.6.6)	• I can analyze Mark Kurlansky's point of view in an excerpt of Chapter 5. • I can explain how he conveys his point of view.	• Structured notes for pages 63–69 (from homework) • Author's Point of View Graphic Organizer: pages 63–69	
11	**End-of-Unit 1 Assessment:** Analyzing Author's Point of View and How It Is Conveyed	• I can determine an author's point of view or purpose in an informational text. (RI.6.6) • I can explain how an author's point of view is conveyed in an informational text. (RI.6.6)	• I can identify Mark Kurlansky's point of view. • I can explain how Mark Kurlansky conveys his point of view.	• Structured notes for "The Story of Kram and Ailat: Part 6" (from homework) • End-of-Unit 1 Assessment: Analyzing Author's Point of View and How It Is Conveyed in Chapter 5 of *World Without Fish*	• Graphic Novel: Tracing the Development of an Idea Anchor Chart • Tracing the Development of an Idea Anchor Chart

Optional: Experts, Fieldwork, and Service

Experts

Invite fishermen to speak to students about the methods they use for catching fish and the rules and regulations they have to follow. Invite a scientist to speak to students about biodiversity and fish depletion.

Fieldwork

Arrange for a visit to a local aquarium so students can learn more about biodiversity in the oceans. Arrange for a visit to a museum or exhibit about the Industrial Revolution. Arrange for a visit to a grocery store so students can see the fish available to buy.

Optional: Extensions

- An in-depth case study of depleted fish species and the impact of the depletion on humans and other species.
- A study of extinct species.
- A study of the depletion of a particular extinct species and the circumstances that led to its extinction, for example the Baiji white dolphin or the Javan tiger.

Preparation and Materials

This unit includes a number of routines. In Lessons 1–10, students frequently read the graphic novel at the end of each chapter or reread an excerpt of the book *World Without Fish* for homework. Once the routine is fully implemented (starting in Lesson 1), students will answer a focus question using evidence from the text each night.

Reading Calendar

- Students read excerpts of *World Without Fish* for homework in Lessons 1–10. Each night, they either read the graphic novel or reread the excerpt of text read in class that day.
- Consider providing a reading calendar to help students, teachers, and families understand what is due and when. See the Reading Calendar that follows.

Structured Notes

Structured notes record students' thinking about a focus question specific to what they have been asked to read. Structured notes are organized by chapter and require students to read the excerpt, answer the focus question for the excerpt, and record evidence from the excerpt to support their answers to the questions.

Reading Calendar *World Without Fish*

The calendar below shows what is due on each day. You may modify this document to include dates instead of lessons.

Due at Lesson	Reading	Focus Question
2	Introduction: pages x–xii	• How does Mark Kurlansky introduce his idea of fish depletion in the first few pages of *World Without Fish*? • Reread the excerpt of the Introduction you read today (pages x–xii), beginning with "Most stories about the destruction of the planet," and stopping after the bolded words, "and more responsibilities than any other generation in history." Use evidence flags to gather evidence as you read to answer the focus question on your structured notes. • **Key Vocabulary:** cormorants, unravel, Industrial Revolution, generation
3	Introduction: pages xii–xvii	• How does Mark Kurlansky continue to introduce his ideas about fish depletion in the Introduction of *World Without Fish*? • Reread the excerpt of the Introduction you read today (pages xii–xvii), beginning with "One of the great thinkers," and stopping at the end of page xvii. Use evidence flags to gather evidence as you read to answer the focus question on your structured notes. • **Key Vocabulary:** biologically, various, variations, evolved, evolution, interconnected, origin, dominate, idly, thus, elaborate, voraciously, revolting, adapt, conflict, eliminated, abundant, minuscule, tendency, unforeseen
4	Introduction: page xxiv	• What do we learn about fishing from the graphic novel? How does Mark Kurlansky introduce the idea of fish depletion in the graphic novel? • Read "The Story of Kram and Ailat: Part 1" (the graphic novel) at the end of the Introduction of *World Without Fish*. Answer the focus question on your structured notes.

Due at Lesson	Reading	Focus Question
5	Chapter 1: page 20	• What do we learn about fishing from the graphic novel? How does Mark Kurlansky illustrate and elaborate on the idea of fish depletion here? • Read "The Story of Kram and Ailat: Part 2" (the graphic novel) at the end of chapter 1. Answer the focus question on your structured notes.
6	Chapter 2: page 38	• What do we learn about fishing from the graphic novel? How does Mark Kurlansky illustrate and elaborate the idea of fish depletion here? • Read "The Story of Kram and Ailat: Part 3" (the graphic novel) at the end of chapter 2. Answer the focus question on your structured notes.
7	Chapter 3: page 50	• What do we learn about fishing from the graphic novel? How does Mark Kurlansky illustrate and elaborate the idea of fish depletion here? • Read "The Story of Kram and Ailat: Part 4" (the graphic novel) at the end of chapter 3. Answer the focus question on your structured notes.
8	Chapter 4: page 51–61	• What does Mark Kurlansky think about Thomas Henry Huxley's ideas and the things he did in the late nineteenth century? Does he agree with him? Does he disagree with him? How do you know? • Reread the excerpt of chapter 4 that you read in class. Use evidence flags to help you gather evidence to answer this focus question on your structured notes. • **Key Vocabulary:** myth, bounty, misconception, indestructible, Darwinism, posthumously, refuted, influential, promoting, anatomy, staunch, commissions, class, unobservant, avocations, contempt, preservation, interfering, objecting, Industrial Revolution, diminution, exhaustion, scarce

Due at Lesson	Reading	Focus Question
9	Chapter 4: page 62	• What do we learn about fishing from the graphic novel? How does Mark Kurlansky illustrate and elaborate on the idea of fish depletion here? • Read "The Story of Kram and Ailat: Part 5" (the graphic novel) at the end of chapter 4. Answer the focus question on your structured notes.
10	Chapter 5: pages 63–69	• What does Mark Kurlansky think about fishermen around the world? How do you know? • Reread the excerpt of chapter 5 that you read in class today (pages 63–69). Use evidence flags to help you gather evidence to answer this focus question on your structured notes. • **Key Vocabulary:** compensates, foreigners, rational, neglected, Viking, lava-encrusted, debate, intensified, economy, glaciers
11	Chapter 5: page 76	• What do we learn about fishing from the graphic novel? How does Mark Kurlansky illustrate and elaborate on the idea of fish depletion here? • Read "The Story of Kram and Ailat: Part 6" (the graphic novel) at the end of chapter 5. Answer the focus question on your structured notes.

LESSON 1

Introducing *World Without Fish*

Long-Term Targets Addressed (Based on ELA CCSS)

- I can determine the main idea of an informational text based on details in the text. (RI.6.2)
- I can analyze how key individuals, events, or ideas are developed throughout a text. (RI.6.3)
- I can use a variety of strategies to determine word meaning in informational texts. (RI.6.4)

Supporting Learning Targets

- I can find the gist of an excerpt of the Introduction of *World Without Fish*.
- I can use evidence from the text to answer text-dependent questions.

Ongoing Assessment

- Sticky notes for gist
- Text-Dependent Questions: Pages x–xii

Agenda

1. Opening
    A. Introducing the Text: *World Without Fish* (6 minutes)
    B. Unpacking Learning Targets (3 minutes)
2. Work Time
    A. Reading for Gist: Pages x–xii (15 minutes)
    B. Text-Dependent Questions: Pages x–xii (18 minutes)
3. Closing and Assessment
    A. Main Ideas (3 minutes)
4. Homework
    A. Reread the excerpt of the introduction you read today (pages x–xii). Use evidence flags to gather evidence as you read and answer the focus question on your structured notes.

Teaching Notes

- This lesson launches a new module. It starts with students becoming oriented to *World Without Fish*, one of the two central texts. Because of the complexity of the text, students will read only short excerpts of it at any given time. They will read excerpts first during the lesson—often with the assistance of a teacher-led close reading—to fully understand the content, and then they will reread at home, gathering evidence on evidence flags as they have in previous modules and answering a focus question that will challenge them to think more deeply.

- This lesson includes an opportunity for students to flip through *World Without Fish* to take note of its beautiful illustrations, images, and other striking text features. This will help build students' excitement for tackling this challenging text. Throughout the unit, students continue to focus on the text features during their initial "gist" reading of sections of text.

- Students will read excerpts of the Introduction over four lessons, reading for the gist in Lesson 1 and then digging deeper in Lessons 2–4.

- At the end of this lesson, students are given structured notes on which to record their homework. Establishing a routine will be important, as this homework structure will be repeated throughout the unit. The homework focus question is also on the reading calendar. The focus question is often quite similar from lesson to lesson, since students are tracing the author's argument.

- In advance:
  - Create triads who will work together to read, think, talk, and write about *World Without Fish*. Intentionally place students in groups that are different from previous triads.
  - Review pages x–xii of the Introduction of *World Without Fish*.

- Post: learning targets.

Lesson Vocabulary

gist, fish depletion; unravel, cormorants, Industrial Revolution, generation

Materials

- Equity sticks
- *World Without Fish* by Mark Kurlansky (book; one per student)
- *World Without Fish* Word-Catcher (one per student)
- Sticky notes (five per student)
- Dictionary (at least one per triad)
- Text-Dependent Questions: Pages x–xii (one per student)
- Close Reading Guide: Pages x–xii (Teacher Reference)
- Structured Notes: Pages x–xii (one to display or one per student; see Teaching Notes)

Opening

A. Introducing the Text: *World Without Fish* (6 minutes)

- Write the title of the text on the board. Ask students to discuss with an elbow partner:
  - "Imagine a *World Without Fish*. What would your life be like without fish? Would it be any different? How?"
- Select volunteers to share their responses. Ask for a show of hands:
  - "Who likes to eat fish?"
- Summarize what you see, for example: "Wow—most of you like fish!"
- Ask students to discuss with an elbow partner:
  - "What kinds of fish do you like to eat?"
- Consider using **equity sticks** to select students to share their responses.
  - Distribute *World Without Fish* by Mark Kurlansky to each student. Tell students that *World Without Fish* is an informational text.
- Invite students to spend a few minutes flipping through the book.
- Ask students to discuss with an elbow partner:
  - "What do you notice?"
  - "What do you wonder?"
  - "What excites you about this book?"
- Select students to share their responses with the whole group. Listen for students to notice the images, the large bold words, the graphic novel within the book, the illustrations, etc. Try to generate enthusiasm by pointing out the things that catch your eye when you look at the book, such as the colorful illustrations and the bold fonts.
- Post the list of new triads and invite students to get into their groups. Tell them that they will work with these same triads throughout the first half of this unit.

B. Unpacking Learning Targets (3 minutes)

- Invite students to read the learning targets along with you.
  - "I can find the gist of an excerpt of the Introduction of *World Without Fish*."
  - "I can use evidence from the text to answer text-dependent questions."
- Ask triads to discuss:
  - "What are the important words or phrases in the learning targets? Why do you think those are important?"
- Cold-call students to share their responses and circle the words and phrases they suggest. Make sure *gist* is circled.
- Focus students on the word *gist*. Ask triads to discuss:
  - "What is the gist, and how do we read for it?"

36 TEACHER GUIDE AND RESOURCE BOOK • Grade 6 • Module 3B • Unit 1 • Lesson 1

- Consider using equity sticks to select students to share their responses. Listen for them to explain that the gist is what the text is mostly about and that you summarize the main points as you do a first read.
- Remind students that they have been practicing reading for the gist in previous modules. Tell them that they will be using their reading skills to dive into the message from this author.

Meeting Students' Needs

Posting learning targets allows students to reference them throughout the lesson to check their understanding. Learning targets also provide a reminder to students and teachers about the intended learning behind a given lesson or activity.

Work Time

A. Reading for Gist: Pages x–xii (15 minutes)

- Invite a student to read aloud the learning target about reading for the gist.
  - "I can find the gist of an excerpt of the Introduction of *World Without Fish*.
- Explain to students that they are going to read in their heads as you read aloud from pages x to xii, beginning at "Most stories about the destruction of the planet" and stopping after the bolded words, "and more responsibilities than any other generation in history."
- When you have finished reading the excerpt aloud, ask students to discuss in triads:
  - "What do you now know about this book? What is it going to be about?"
- Consider using equity sticks to select students to share their ideas with the class. Listen for students to explain that from this excerpt, it seems like the book is going to be about how species of fish that we eat might die out in the next 50 years.
- Distribute **World Without Fish Word-Catchers** and five **sticky notes** to each student.
- Tell students that this a challenging text, but reassure them that you know they are going to be able to understand it by reading it in small pieces. Explain that now that students have read the excerpt once through, they are going to work with their triads to read it again for the gist, annotate the gist on sticky notes, and record unfamiliar words on their word-catchers. Remind students that they have been building reading stamina in previous modules and now they are ready to take on something more challenging.
- Model how to find the gist with page x. Reread it aloud and ask students to discuss in triads:
  - "What is this page mostly about?"
- Select volunteers to share their responses. Listen for students to explain that it is mostly about how *World Without Fish* is a story about how the earth could be destroyed. Record this on a sticky note and place it in your copy of the book, instructing students to do the same.
- Ask:
  - "Are there any unfamiliar words on this page?"

- Invite students to record any unfamiliar vocabulary on their word-catchers.
- Ask:
  - "What strategies do you already have for figuring out unfamiliar vocabulary?"
- Cold-call students to share their responses and listen for them to explain that they can look at the root word for clues, read around the word, use context clues, or use a dictionary to determine the meaning of the word. Pass out **dictionaries** to each triad. Remind students that if they can't work out the meaning of a word, they are to wait for those words to be shared and discussed with the whole group later.
- Ask students to find the gist for the remainder of pages x–xii. Remind students that the goal is for them to understand the basic idea of the excerpt one piece at a time. They will write the gist of each section on separate sticky notes as they read.
- Circulate and support students as they read. For those who need more support, ask them to practice telling you the gist of a section before they write it on their sticky note.
- As students finish up, refocus the whole group. Focus students on the word *unravel*, and ask them to discuss in triads:
  - "Read the sentence containing the word *unravel*. Using context clues from the rest of the sentence, what do you think it might mean? What words would you replace it with?"
- Cold-call students to share their responses. Listen for and guide students to understand that unravel means "to undo," so here the author means there could be serious negative consequences for life on earth.
- Invite students to share any unfamiliar vocabulary words they found, along with the definition if they found it. If they were unable to work out the definition from the context or find it in a dictionary, encourage other students to assist them with the definition. To keep things moving, if no one else knows what the word means, define it for the class. Be sure that the following words are discussed: *cormorants*, *Industrial Revolution*, and *generation*.
- Remind students to record new words on their word-catchers.

Meeting Students' Needs

- Hearing a complex text read slowly, fluently, and without interruption or explanation promotes fluency for students. They are hearing a strong reader read the text aloud with accuracy and expression and are simultaneously looking at and thinking about the words on the printed page. Be sure to set clear expectations that students read along silently in their heads as you read the text aloud.
- Allow students to grapple with a complex text before explicit teaching of vocabulary. After students have read for the gist, they can identify challenging vocabulary for themselves.
- Asking students to identify challenging vocabulary helps them monitor their understanding of a complex text. When students annotate the text by circling these words, it can also provide a formative assessment for the teacher.

B. Text-Dependent Questions: Pages x–xii (18 minutes)

- Distribute **Text-Dependent Questions: Pages x–xii** and guide students through it using the **Close Reading Guide: Pages x–xii (Teacher Reference)**.

Meeting Students' Needs

- Asking students to discuss challenging questions before recording them helps to ensure that all students have an idea about what to write and can give students confidence in their responses.
- Some students may benefit from having access to "hint cards": small slips of paper or index cards that they turn over for hints about how/where to find the answers to text-dependent questions. For example, a hint card might say, "Look in the third paragraph."
- Some students may benefit from having key sections pre-highlighted in their texts. This will help them focus on small sections rather than scanning the whole text for answers.

Closing and Assessment

A. Main Ideas (3 minutes)

- Ask students to discuss in triads:
    - "What main ideas are you are taking away after reading this excerpt?"
- Select volunteers to share their responses. Listen for students to explain that Mark Kurlansky thinks the planet is in danger because people are not looking after it as they should.
- Tell students that the way we can describe fish species dying out is *fish depletion*, because depletion means the numbers are going down.
- Distribute the **Structured Notes: Pages x–xii** for homework.

Homework

- Reread the excerpt of the Introduction you read in class today (pages x–xii), beginning at, "Most stories about the destruction of the planet," and stopping after the bolded words, "and more responsibilities than any other generation in history." Use evidence flags to gather evidence as you read to answer this focus question on your structured notes in your journal:
    - "How does Mark Kurlansky introduce his idea of fish depletion in the first few pages of *World Without Fish*?"

World Without Fish Word-Catcher

Name: _____

Date: _____

Mark literary words with an * (for example: *text feature).

A	B	C	D	E
F	G	H	I	J
K	L	M	N	O
P	Q	R	S	T
U	V	W	X	Y
Z	Use this space for notes.			

Text-Dependent Questions: Pages x–xii

Name: _____

Date: _____

Learning target:

- "I can use evidence from the text to answer text-dependent questions."

Questions	Answers (supported with evidence from the text)
1. On page x, according to Mark Kurlansky, who is causing the problem?	
2. According to Mark Kurlansky, how long could it take for most of the fish we commonly eat to be gone?	
3. What species of fish does that include?	
4. According to Mark Kurlansky, how did the Industrial Revolution change things?	
5. According to Mark Kurlansky, what does the survival of the planet depend on?	

Close Reading Guide: Pages x–xii
(Teacher Reference)

Time: 18 minutes

Questions	Teaching Notes

1. On page x, according to Mark Kurlansky, who is causing the problem?	**(3 minutes)**
	• Invite students to reread the first page beginning with "Most stories about the destruction . . ."
	• Ask students to discuss in triads
	  • "How does this page grab our attention immediately?"
	  • Select volunteers to share their responses. Listen for students to explain that the bold font captures our attention, but also the dramatic language, for example "the destruction of the planet," or "how the earth could be destroyed."
	• Ask students to discuss in triads:
	  • "What does 'well-meaning people' mean?"
	  • Cold-call students to share their responses. Listen for them to explain that well-meaning people are people who don't mean to do bad things—they are doing bad things unintentionally.
	  • Invite triads to discuss Question 1 and then record their answers in the Answer column of their worksheet. Remind students to use evidence from the text in their answers.
	  • Select volunteers to share their answers. Listen for students to explain that "well-meaning people" are causing the problem.

2. According to Mark Kurlansky, how long could it take for most of the fish we commonly eat to be gone?	**(3 minutes)** • Invite students to reread the words in bold font at the top of page xi. • Invite triads to discuss Question 2 and then record their answers in the Answer column of their worksheet. • Select volunteers to share their answers. Listen for students to explain that the fish could be gone in 50 years.

Questions	Teaching Notes

3. What species of fish does that include?	**(2 minutes)**
	• Invite triads to discuss Question 3 and then record their answers in the Answer column of their worksheet.
	• Select volunteers to share their answers. Listen for them to explain that salmon, tuna, cod, swordfish, and anchovies could be gone.
	• Invite students to discuss in triads:
	  • "Why will some seabirds and mammals be in trouble?"
	  • Cold-call students to share their responses. Listen for students to explain that they will be in trouble because they eat fish and if fish are gone, they will be too.

4. According to Mark Kurlansky, how did the Industrial Revolution change things?	**(5 minutes)**
	• Invite students to reread this sentence: "The Industrial Revolution, beginning in the mid-eighteenth century and continuing for the next 120 years shifted production from handcrafts to machine-made factory goods and in doing so completely changed the relationship of people to nature, the relationship of people to each other, politics, art, and architecture—the look and thought of the world."
	• Focus students on, "shifted production from handcrafts to machine-made factory goods" and ask students to discuss in triads:
	  • "What does the author mean by shifted production from handcrafts?"
	  • Cold-call students to share their ideas. Listen for and guide students to understand that it means people no longer made a lot of the things they needed by hand, as they had before.
	• Invite triads to discuss:
	  • "So how did it change? How did things begin to be made differently?"
	  • Select volunteers to share their responses and listen for students to explain that things began to be made by machines instead.
	• Invite triads to discuss Question 4 and then record their answers in the Answer column of their worksheet.
	• Select volunteers to share their answers. Listen for and guide students to understand that the Industrial Revolution was when things changed from being made by hand to being made by machines.

Questions	Teaching Notes
	• Focus students on "changed the relationship of people to nature." Ask students to discuss in triads: 　• "How do you think making things by machine rather than by hand would change the relationship people have with nature?" 　• Cold-call students to share their ideas. Students may struggle with this, so guide them to understand that when people made things by hand, they used things directly from nature. For example, if they needed milk, they would go outside and milk the cow to drink the cow's milk; however, once factories and machines started to make things, they no longer had that direct contact with nature. • Ask students to discuss in triads: 　• "How do you think losing a relationship with nature might make people less considerate of it?" 　• Select students to share their responses. Again students may struggle with this, so guide them to understand that if people don't have a relationship with nature, they don't understand how the things they do have an impact on it.
5. According to Mark Kurlansky, what does the survival of the planet depend on?	**(5 minutes)** • Focus students on, "In the next fifty years, much of your working life, there will be as much change in less than half the time." • Ask students to discuss in triads: 　• "Why do you think he says there will there be as much change in less than half the time? What does he mean?" 　• Cold-call students to share their ideas. They may struggle with this, so guide them to understand that things change more quickly now. We have improved technology to make things change more quickly than they did during the Industrial Revolution. • Invite triads to discuss Question 5 and then record their answers in the Answer column of their worksheet. • Select volunteers to share their answers. Listen for them to explain that it depends on how well we handle the changes that will happen. • Focus students on, "so you have more opportunities and responsibilities than any other generation in history."

Questions	Teaching Notes
	- Ask students to discuss in triads: - "What opportunities and responsibilities do you think he is referring to?" - Cold-call students to share their responses. Students may struggle with this, so guide them to understand that the author means they have the opportunity and responsibility to make sure that those changes are handled in a way that is good (rather than bad) for the environment and can make things better.

Structured Notes: Pages x–xii

Name: _____

Date: _____

Chapter	Homework Focus Question	Answer with Evidence from the Text (include page number)
_____	How does Mark Kurlansky introduce his idea of fish depletion in the first few pages of *World Without Fish*?	

LESSON 2

Introduction

The Ideas of Charles Darwin

Long-Term Targets Addressed (Based on ELA CCSS)

- I can determine the main idea of an informational text based on details in the text. (RI.6.2)
- I can analyze how key individuals, events, or ideas are developed throughout a text. (RI.6.3)
- I can use a variety of strategies to determine word meaning in informational texts. (RI.6.4)

Supporting Learning Targets

- I can find the gist of an excerpt of the Introduction of *World Without Fish*.
- I can use strategies to determine the meaning of words and phrases in this excerpt of the Introduction of *World Without Fish*.
- I can use evidence from the text to answer text-dependent questions.
- I can analyze how Mark Kurlansky introduces the problem of fish depletion in *World Without Fish*.

Ongoing Assessment

- Structured Notes: Pages x–xii (from homework)
- Text-Dependent Questions: Pages xii–xvii

Agenda

1. Opening
   A. Engaging the Reader: Excerpt 1 (6 minutes)
   B. Unpacking Learning Targets (2 minutes)
2. Work Time
   A. Reading for Gist: Pages xii–xvii (14 minutes)
   B. Text-Dependent Questions: Pages xii–xvii (20 minutes)

3. Closing and Assessment

    A. Link to Text Features (3 minutes)

4. Homework

    A. Reread the excerpt of the Introduction you read today (pages xii–xvii). Use evidence flags to gather evidence as you read to answer this focus question on your structured notes.

Teaching Notes

- In this lesson, students continue to discuss and analyze the Introduction of *World Without Fish*. The priority of this lesson is that students become familiar with the routine of reading for the gist, answering text-dependent questions, and analyzing the text to better understand Kurlansky's message about fish depletion. Students will follow this routine for chapters 1–3, including the mid-unit assessment.
- This section of the book discusses Darwin's theory of evolution. Emphasize that these are the ideas of one man, Charles Darwin, that have been widely accepted by the scientific community. There are other people who disagree with his ideas about evolution. Help students understand that Darwin's theory is one point of view and that there are other opposing points of view.
- Because of the introduction of the theories of Charles Darwin, there is a lot of science content in this excerpt of the text. Consider working with a science teacher to pair this with science lessons that can provide more detail on the theories—such as the classification of living things—that are mentioned in this excerpt.
- Students follow the same system for homework begun in Lesson 1, completing a structured notes worksheet.
- In advance:
    - Review pages xii–xvii of the Introduction of *World Without Fish* and Close Reading Guide: Pages xii–xvii (Teacher Reference).
    - Review Back-to-Back and Face-to-Face protocol (see Appendix).
    - Use Tracing the Development of an Idea Anchor Chart (Teacher Reference) to create the Tracing the Development of an Idea Anchor Chart.
- Post: learning targets.

Lesson Vocabulary

fish depletion, biologically, various , variations , evolved, evolution, interconnected; origin, dominate, idly, thus, elaborate, voraciously, revolting, adapt, conflict, eliminated, abundant, minuscule, tendency, unforeseen

Materials

- Structured Notes: x–xii (completed for homework)
- Tracing the Development of an Idea Anchor Chart (new; teacher-created; see Teaching Notes)
- Tracing the Development of an Idea Anchor Chart (Teacher Reference)
- *World Without Fish* (book; distributed in Lesson 1; one per student)
- Sticky notes (eight per student)
- Dictionaries (at least one per triad)
- *World Without Fish* Word-Catcher (students' own; begun in Lesson 1)
- Text-Dependent Questions: Pages xii–xvii (one per student, one for display)
- Close Reading Guide: Pages xii–xvii (Teacher Reference)
- Structured Notes: xii–xvii (one per student)

Opening

A. Engaging the Reader: Excerpt 1 (6 minutes)

- Remind students that the Introduction is where an author helps the reader understand what this whole book is going to be about and gives the reader a reason to keep reading. Consider explaining that the Introduction is like an outline of the author's message and the key concepts he will use to argue his message.
- Remind students of the homework focus question, "How does Mark Kurlansky introduce his ideas about fish depletion in the first few pages of *World Without Fish*?"
- Back-to-Back and Face-to-Face protocol:
  - Invite students to retrieve their **Structured Notes: x–xii** from their homework and pair up with someone to sit back-to-back.
  - Ask students the homework focus question: "How does Mark Kurlansky introduce his ideas about fish depletion in the first few pages of *World Without Fish*?"
  - Give students time to refer to their structured notes.
  - Invite students to turn face-to-face with their partner to share their ideas.
- Display the **Tracing the Development of an Idea Anchor Chart**. Remind students that the idea they are focusing on is *fish depletion*, which means fish dying out. Record this idea in the space provided at the top of the anchor chart.
- Ask students to discuss in triads:
  - "How does the author introduce the idea of fish depletion in the first part of the Introduction?"
- Cold-call students to share their responses. Listen for and guide students to understand that this idea is introduced through the use of very dramatic and almost scary sentences and words like, "But this is the story of how the Earth could be destroyed" and "life on planet Earth could completely unravel" to get our attention.

- Record this on the Tracing the Development of an Idea Anchor Chart. See **Tracing the Development of an Idea Anchor Chart (Teacher Reference)** for a model.

Meeting Students' Needs

Reviewing homework holds all students accountable for reading the text and completing their homework.

B. Unpacking Learning Targets (2 minutes)

- Invite students to follow along as you read the learning targets aloud.
    - "I can find the gist of an excerpt of the Introduction of *World Without Fish*."
    - "I can use strategies to determine the meaning of words and phrases in this excerpt of the Introduction of *World Without Fish*."
    - "I can use evidence from the text to answer text-dependent questions."
    - "I can analyze how Mark Kurlansky introduces the problem of fish depletion in *World Without Fish*."
- Remind students that they were introduced to two of these learning targets in the previous lesson and that this lesson will be much like the previous one in that they will read an excerpt of the text for the gist and then answer text-dependent questions in order to dig deeper into the text.

Meeting Students' Needs

- Posting learning targets allows students to reference them throughout the lesson to check their understanding. Learning targets also provide a reminder to students and teachers about the intended learning behind a given lesson or activity.
- Discussing and clarifying the language of learning targets helps build academic vocabulary.

Work Time

A. Reading for Gist: Pages xii–xvii (14 minutes)

- Invite students to turn to page xii of the Introduction of **World Without Fish**. Invite students to silently read along as you read aloud pages xii–xvii from "One of the great thinkers…" to "…that are extremely difficult to change back."
- As this section of the book discusses Darwin's theory of evolution, it is important to emphasize that these are the ideas of one man, Charles Darwin, and that there are other people who disagree with his ideas about evolution. Help students understand that these theories are one point of view and that there are other opposing points of view.
- Read aloud the learning target:
    - "I can find the gist of an excerpt of the Introduction of *World Without Fish*."

- Distribute eight **sticky notes** to each student. Remind students that the goal is for them to understand what the text is mostly about and that this is a challenging text, so they need to be prepared to use their reading stamina and to persevere, breaking the text into pieces (e.g., paragraphs) and working out the gist one piece at a time. Remind students to discuss the gist in triads before recording anything on their sticky notes.
- Remind students of the strategies they have practiced for determining the meaning of unknown vocabulary: reading around the word, replacing the word with one that fits, identifying the root word, using the dictionary, etc. Distribute **dictionaries** to each triad. Explain that if students still aren't sure what the word means after using the strategies, they should leave the definition to be discussed with the whole group later. Remind them to record unfamiliar vocabulary on their **World Without Fish Word-Catchers**.
- Ask students to begin at "One of the great thinkers . . ." on page xii and to finish at ". . . that are extremely difficult to change back" at the end of page xvii.
- Circulate and support students as they read. For those who need more support, ask them to practice telling you the gist of a section before they write it on their sticky note.
- As students finish up, refocus the whole group. Focus students on the word *biologically* on page xv. Tell students that the prefix *bio* means life and biology is the study of life.
- Focus students on the word *biological* within the word *biologically*. Explain that the suffix *ical* means "related to or about," so biological means "related to or about biology."
- Ask students to discuss in triads:
    - "So what do you think *biologically* might mean in this context? When the author describes 'organisms that are biologically close to us,' what do you think he means?"
- Select volunteers to share their responses. Listen for and guide students to understand that it means organisms that are related to/like us.
- Focus students on the words *various* (page xiii) and *variations* (page xv). Point out that the root of both of these words is *vari*. Ask students to discuss in triads:
    - "From what you already know about words with this root, what do you think this root means?"
- Cold-call students to share their responses. Listen for students to explain that it means different.
- Ask students to discuss in triads:
    - "So what do you think *various* and *variations* mean? What does he mean by 'nature puts out variations'?"
- Select volunteers to share their responses. Listen for students to explain that various and variations both mean different kinds of something and the author means that nature creates lots of different kinds.
- Focus students on the words *evolved* (page xiv) and *evolution* (page xvi). Explain to students that the root of these words is *evolve*. Ask students if they know what it means.
- If none of the students knows what it means, explain that evolve means to change and develop over time. Ask students to discuss in triads:
    - "So what do you think *evolved* means? What does adding *d* do to the word?"

- Select volunteers to share their responses with the whole group. Listen for students to explain that adding the *d* makes the word past tense, so evolved means it developed over time.
- Refocus students on the word *evolution*. Explain that the suffix *-tion* at the end of the word means the action of or the process of. Ask students to discuss in triads:
  - "Put those two parts of the word together. What do you think *evolution* means?"
- Select students to share their responses. Listen for students to explain that it means the process of developing and changing over time.
- Focus students on the word *interconnected* on page xvii. Point to the prefix *inter*. Tell students that this means between or among. Ask students to discuss in triads:
  - "What do you think *interconnected* might mean?"
- Cold-call students to share their responses. Listen for and guide students to understand that it means the way things are connected to each other.
- Ask students to suggest other words with the prefix *inter*. Listen for students to suggest words like: *interest*, *international*, and *interact*.
- Invite students to share any other unfamiliar vocabulary words they found, along with the definitions. If they were unable to work out the definition from the context or find it in a dictionary, encourage other students to assist them with the definition. To keep things moving, if no one else knows what the word means, define the word for the class.
- Students may struggle with these words, so be sure to address them here: *origin*, *dominate*, *idly*, *thus*, *elaborate*, *voraciously*, *revolting*, *adapt*, *conflict*, *eliminated*, *abundant*, *minuscule*, *tendency*, and *unforeseen*.
- If students are unable to work out the definition from the context or find it in a dictionary, encourage other students to assist them with the definition. To keep things moving, if no one else knows what the word means, define the word for the class.
- Ensure students record all new words on their word-catchers.

Meeting Students' Needs

- Hearing a complex text read slowly, fluently, and without interruption or explanation promotes fluency for students. They are hearing a strong reader read the text aloud with accuracy and expression and are simultaneously looking at and thinking about the words on the printed page. Be sure to set clear expectations that students read along silently in their heads as you read the text aloud.
- Allow students to grapple with a complex text before explicit teaching of vocabulary. After students have read for the gist, they can identify challenging vocabulary for themselves.
- Asking students to identify challenging vocabulary helps them monitor their understanding of a complex text. When students annotate the text by circling these words, it can also provide a formative assessment for the teacher.

B. Text-Dependent Questions: Pages xii–xvii (20 minutes)

- Distribute **Text-Dependent Questions: Pages xii–xvii** and guide students using the **Close Reading Guide: Pages xii–xvii (Teacher Reference)**.

Meeting Students' Needs

- Asking students to discuss challenging questions before recording them helps to ensure that all students have an idea about what to write and can give students confidence in their responses.
- Some students may benefit from having access to "hint cards": small slips of paper or index cards that they turn over for hints about how/where to find the answers to text-dependent questions. For example, a hint card might say, "Look in the third paragraph."
- Some students may benefit from having key sections pre-highlighted in their texts. This will help them focus on small sections rather than scanning the whole text for answers.

Closing and Assessment

A. Link to Text Features (3 minutes)

- Invite students to return to the page that opens the Introduction, the page that says, "Being a Brief Outline of the Problem."
- Ask students to discuss in triads:
  - "After reading about the ideas of Charles Darwin today, what do you notice about this page?"
- Cold-call students to share their responses. Listen for students to explain that there is a quote from Charles Darwin's book *On the Origin of Species* at the bottom of the page.
- Invite students to flip through the text and look at the introductory page of each chapter. Point out that that there is a quote from Darwin's book on each of the introductory pages and that this is a common text feature.

Homework

- Reread the excerpt of the Introduction you read in class today (pages xii–xvii), beginning with "One of the great thinkers," and stopping at the end of page xvii. Use evidence flags to gather evidence as you read to answer this focus question on your **Structured Notes: xii–xvii** worksheet:
  - "How does Mark Kurlansky continue to introduce his ideas about fish depletion in the Introduction of *World Without Fish*?"

Tracing the Development of an Idea Anchor Chart

Idea: _____

Chapter	How is the idea introduced, illustrated, or elaborated on in this chapter?

Tracing the Development of an Idea Anchor Chart
(Teacher Reference)

Idea: Fish depletion

Chapter	How is the idea introduced, illustrated, or elaborated on in this chapter?
Introduction	*The idea is introduced with the use of very dramatic and almost scary sentences and words like, "But this is the story of how the Earth could be destroyed" and "life on planet Earth could completely unravel" to get our attention.*

Text Dependent Questions: Pages xii–xvii

Name: _____

Date: _____

Learning target:

- "I can use evidence from the text to answer text-dependent questions."

Questions	Answers (supported with evidence from the text)
1. What is the full name of the famous book by Charles Darwin?	
2. In your own words and in no more than a couple of sentences, describe what Darwin explained in his book.	
3. What are the seven major levels or categories that plants and animals are organized into?	
4. What class and order are humans in? 5. What are some other mammals in that order? 6. What family, genus, and species are we in?	

Questions	Answers (supported with evidence from the text)
7. According to Mark Kurlansky, what was Charles Darwin's greatest contribution? Write your answer in your own words in no more than two sentences.	
8. Describe the process known as evolution in your own words.	
9. Why were Charles Darwin's ideas seen as controversial, and why do they still cause conflict now? Write your answer in your own words in no more than two sentences.	
10. According to page xvii, how is life interconnected?	

Close Reading Guide: Pages xii–xvii
(Teacher Reference)

Time: 20 minutes

Questions	Teaching Notes
1. What is the full name of the famous book by Charles Darwin?	• Invite students to reread the first paragraph beginning with "One of the great thinkers …" and ending with "… by its shortened title: *On the Origin of Species*." • Invite triads to discuss Question 1 and then record their answers in the Answer column of their worksheet. • Select volunteers to share their answers. Listen for them to explain that the book is titled *On the Origin of Species by Means of Natural Selection, or the Preservation of Favoured Races in the Struggle for Life*.

2. In your own words in no more than a couple of sentences, describe what Darwin explained in his book.	• Invite students to reread the next paragraph beginning with "In his book …" and ending with "… and are thus constantly destroying life."
	• Ask students to discuss in triads:
	  • "How would you paraphrase that paragraph? How would you put it into your own words in no more than a couple of sentences?"
	  • Select students to share their paraphrasing with the whole group. Listen for them to explain that Darwin saw nature as cruel because each species is constantly destroying life in what they eat.
	• Invite students to record their paraphrasing on their worksheet.

3. What are the seven major levels or categories that plants and animals are organized into?	• Invite students to read the next short paragraph, ending on the word "species." • Invite triads to discuss Question 3 and then record their answers in the Answer column of their worksheet. • Select volunteers to share their answers. Listen for them to explain that the seven levels are kingdom, phylum, class, order, family, genus (plural genera), and species.

Questions	Teaching Notes
4. What class and order are humans in? 5. What are some other mammals in that order? 6. What family, genus, and species are we in?	• Invite students to read the next paragraph beginning with "A codfish …" and ending with "… greatly favored by Homo sapiens," including the table underneath the paragraph. • Invite triads to discuss Questions 4–6 and then record their answers in the Answer column of their worksheets. • Select volunteers to share their answers. Listen for them to explain that humans are in the class known as mammals and the order known as primates. Other mammals in that order include monkeys and lemurs. We are in the family hominidae, the genus Homo, and the species Homo sapiens.
7. According to Mark Kurlansky, what was Charles Darwin's greatest contribution? Write your answer in your own words in no more than two sentences.	• Invite students to read from "Darwin's great contribution …" to "… genera became extinct." • Ask students to discuss in triads: 　• "How would you paraphrase that paragraph? How would you put it into your own words in no more than a couple of sentences?" • Select students to share their paraphrasing with the whole group. Listen for them to explain that Darwin understood that there are many variations in nature and those with successful adaptations survive whereas the others become extinct. • Invite students to record their paraphrasing on their worksheet.
8. Describe the process known as evolution in your own words.	• Invite students to reread page xvi up to "… developed into human beings." • Ask students to discuss in triads: 　• "According to Kurlansky, how were circumstances constantly changing?" • Cold-call students to share their responses. Listen for students to explain that species moved into and out of areas and there were changes in the weather. • Ask students to discuss in triads: 　• "According to Kurlansky, how did this change the order of nature?" • Select students to share their responses with the whole group. Listen for students to explain that changes in circumstances made some species die out and some thrive.

Questions	Teaching Notes

	• Ask students to discuss in triads:
	  • "Why do you think these changes in circumstances made some species die out and some thrive?"
	• Cold-call students to share their responses. Listen for and guide students to understand that when circumstances change—for example if the weather gets colder—some species with successful adaptations will survive, but some won't.
	• Ask students to discuss in triads:
	  • "How would you paraphrase that page? How would you describe evolution in your own words?"
	• Select students to share with the whole group. Listen for them to explain that evolution is the way some species fail and some succeed because of the adaptations they have that help them to survive in changing circumstances.
	• Invite students to record their paraphrasing on their worksheet.

9. Why were Charles Darwin's ideas seen as controversial, and why do they still cause conflict now? Write your answer in your own words in no more than two sentences.	• Invite students to reread the sidebar on the top left of page xvi. • Ask students to discuss in triads: • "How would you paraphrase that text? How would you put it into your own words in no more than a couple of sentences?" • Select students to share their paraphrasing with the whole group. Listen for them to explain that the ideas were seen as controversial because people didn't like the way Darwin said nature was cruel, and many also feel that it goes against what the Bible says about creation. • It is important to discuss this sensitively, making sure students understand that there are differing points of view on this issue—there are some who believe Darwin is correct and some who don't. Make it clear that students are not to take any of this as fact. They are to remember that this is a point of view and there are other points of view on this subject. • Invite students to record their paraphrasing on their worksheet.
10. According to page xvii, how is life interconnected?	• Invite students to reread from "In understanding what is happening…" at the bottom of page xvi to the end of page xvii. • Invite triads to discuss Question 10 and then record their answers in the Answer column of their worksheet. Remind students to use evidence from the text in their answers. • Select volunteers to share their answers. Listen for students to explain that what happens in the ocean affects life on earth and vice versa, and what plants and animals do alters human life and vice versa.

Structured Notes: xii–xvii

Name: _____

Date: _____

Chapter	Homework Focus Question	Answer with Evidence from the Text (include page number)
_____	How does Mark Kurlansky continue to introduce his ideas about fish depletion in the Introduction of *World Without Fish*?	

LESSON 3

Introducing the Struggle for Survival in the Introduction of *World Without Fish*

Long-Term Targets Addressed (Based on ELA CCSS)

- I can determine the main idea of an informational text based on details in the text. (RI.6.2)
- I can analyze how key individuals, events, or ideas are developed throughout a text. (RI.6.3)
- I can use a variety of strategies to determine word meaning in informational texts. (RI.6.4)

Supporting Learning Targets

- I can find the gist of an excerpt of the Introduction of *World Without Fish*.
- I can use strategies to determine the meaning of words and phrases in this excerpt of the Introduction of *World Without Fish*.
- I can use evidence from the text to answer text-dependent questions.
- I can analyze how Mark Kurlansky introduces the problem of fish depletion in *World Without Fish*.

Ongoing Assessment

- Structured Notes: Pages xii–xvii (from homework)
- Text-Dependent Questions: Pages xx–xxiii

Agenda

1. Opening
    A. Engaging the Reader: Excerpt 2 of the Introduction (6 minutes)
    B. Unpacking Learning Targets (2 minutes)
2. Work Time
    A. Reading for Gist: Pages xx–xxiii (15 minutes)
    B. Text-Dependent Questions: Pages xx–xxiii (16 minutes)

3. Closing and Assessment
   A. Discussion: Analyzing the Introduction (6 minutes)
4. Homework
   A. Reread the excerpt of the Introduction that you read in class today.
   B. Read "The Story of Kram and Ailat: Part 1" (the graphic novel) at the end of the Introduction of *World without Fish*. Answer the focus question on your structured notes.

Teaching Notes

- In this lesson, students continue to discuss and analyze the Introduction of *World Without Fish*. The priority of this lesson continues to be that students become familiar with the routine of reading for the gist, answering text-dependent questions, and analyzing their reading to understand how Kurlansky develops his message about fish depletion throughout the text. Students will follow this routine for chapters 1–3, including the mid-unit assessment.

- Due to time restraints, students do not closely read all of the Introduction. Instead, the excerpts containing the most relevant information have been selected for students to read. In this lesson they skip ahead a couple of pages from the last excerpt they read. You may want to explain this to students and invite them to read those pages in their own time if they desire.

- The Tracing the Development of an Idea Anchor Chart will continue to be used to capture and structure students' thinking about their homework focus questions and class reading and discussion.

- A close reading guide is not used to guide students through this excerpt because it isn't necessary for students to be able to answer the text-dependent questions. This also creates variety so that each lesson isn't exactly the same.

- Students will follow the same system for homework begun in Lesson 1, completing a structured notes worksheet.

- In advance:
  - Review pages xx–xxiii of the Introduction of *World Without Fish* and the Text-Dependent Questions: Pages xx–xxiii (Teacher Reference).
  - Review Concentric Circles protocol (see Appendix).
- Post: learning targets; Tracing the Development of an Idea Anchor Chart.

Lesson Vocabulary

fish depletion, ecosystem, aquatic species, polyp, reproduce, colony, organism, culprit, extinct, trawler, coined, biodiversity, inhabit, unprecedented, decline

Materials

- Structured Notes: xii–xvii (completed for homework)
- Tracing the Development of an Idea Anchor Chart (begun in Lesson 2)
- Tracing the Development of an Idea Anchor Chart (Teacher Reference)
- *World Without Fish* (book; distributed in Lesson 1; one per student)
- Sticky notes (eight per student)
- Dictionaries (at least one per triad)
- *World without Fish* Word-Catchers (students' own; begun in Lesson 1)
- Text Dependent Questions: Pages xx–xxiii (one per student, one for display)
- Text Dependent Questions: Pages xv–xxiii (Teacher Reference)
- Structured Notes: "The Story of Kram and Ailat: Part 1" (one per student)

Opening

A. Engaging the Reader: Excerpt 2 of the Introduction (6 minutes)

- Concentric Circles protocol:
  - Divide the group in half and invite both halves to get into two circles, one inside the other with their **Structured Notes: xii–xvii**. The circle on the inside should be facing out and the circle on the outside should be facing in.
  - Remind students of the of the homework focus question: "How does Mark Kurlansky continue to introduce his ideas about *fish depletion* in the Introduction of *World without Fish*?"
  - Invite students to refer to their structured notes from their homework.
  - Invite students in the inside circle to share their responses with the person opposite them in the outside circle.
  - Invite students in the outside circle to do the same.
  - Invite students in the inside circle to move two people to the left.
  - Repeat steps.
- Circulate and listen for students to explain that Kurlansky introduces his ideas by telling us what is going to happen to the planet if things don't change.
- Refocus the whole class and refer to the posted **Tracing the Development of an Idea Anchor Chart**.
- Cold-call students to share their responses. Listen for and guide students to understand that Mark Kurlansky continues to introduce his ideas about fish depletion by introducing very famous scientific ideas—like evolution and diversity of species by Charles Darwin—that provide a background to build his ideas on.
- Record this on the Tracing the Development of an Idea Anchor Chart. See **Tracing the Development of an Idea Anchor Chart (Teacher Reference)** for a model.

Meeting Students' Needs

- Reviewing homework holds all students accountable for reading the text and completing their homework.
- Capturing students' ideas on an anchor chart can ensure easy reference later and can enable students to see at a glance how an idea has developed through a text.

B. Unpacking Learning Targets (2 minutes)

- Invite students to follow along as you read the learning targets aloud:
  - "I can find the gist of an excerpt of the Introduction of *World Without Fish*."
  - "I can use strategies to determine the meaning of words and phrases in this excerpt of the Introduction of *World Without Fish*."
  - "I can use evidence from the text to answer text-dependent questions."
  - "I can analyze how Mark Kurlansky introduces the problem of fish depletion in *World Without Fish*."
- Remind students that they were introduced to these learning targets in the previous lessons and that this lesson will be much like the previous two in that they will read a new excerpt of the Introduction for the gist and then answer text-dependent questions in order to dig deeper into the text.

Meeting Students' Needs

Posting learning targets allows students to reference them throughout the lesson to check their understanding. Learning targets also provide a reminder to students and teachers about the intended learning behind a given lesson or activity.

Work Time

A. Reading for Gist: Pages xx–xxiii (15 minutes)

- Invite students to turn to page xx of the Introduction of **World Without Fish**. Invite students to silently read along as you read aloud pages xx–xxiii.
- Read aloud the learning target:
  - "I can find the gist of an excerpt of the Introduction of *World Without Fish*."
- Distribute eight **sticky notes** to each student. Remind students that the goal is for them to understand what the text is mostly about and that this is a challenging text, so they need to be prepared to use their reading stamina and to persevere, breaking the text into pieces (e.g., paragraphs) and working out the gist one piece at a time. Remind students to discuss the gist in triads before recording anything on their sticky notes.

- Remind students of the strategies they have practiced for determining the meaning of unknown vocabulary: reading around the word, replacing the word with one that fits, identifying the root word, using the dictionary, etc. Distribute **dictionaries** to each triad. Explain that if students still aren't sure what the word means after using the strategies, they should leave the definition to be discussed with the whole group later. Remind students to record unfamiliar vocabulary on their *World Without Fish* **Word-Catchers**.
- Remind students to begin at the top of page xx and stop at the end of page xxiii.
- Circulate and support students as they read. For those who need more support, ask them to practice telling you the gist of a section before they write it on a sticky note.
- As students finish up, refocus the whole group. Focus students on the word *ecosystem* on page xx. Tell students that the prefix *eco* means "the relationship between living things." Ask students to discuss in triads:
  - "So what do you think an *ecosystem* might be?"
- Select volunteers to share their responses. Listen for and guide students to understand that an ecosystem is a group of living things that live in an area.
- Focus students on the words *aquatic species* on page xx. Ask:
  - "What does the root of this word, *aqua*, mean?"
- Cold-call students to share their responses. Listen for students to explain that it means water.
- Ask students to discuss in triads:
  - "What do you think *aquatic species* means?"
- Select volunteers to share their responses. Listen for students to explain that it means species that live in the water.
- Focus students on the word *culprit* on page xx. Ask:
  - "Read around the word *culprit*. What do you think it means? What words would you replace it with?"
- Cold-call students to share their responses. Listen for and guide students to understand that it means "those responsible."
- Focus students on the word *biodiversity* on page xxii. Remind students that *bio* means life.
- Ask students to discuss in triads:
  - "What does *diversity* mean?"
- Select students to share their responses. Listen for students to explain that *diversity* means variety.
- Ask students to discuss in triads:
  - "So what does *biodiversity* mean?"
- Cold-call students to share their responses. Listen for students to explain that it means variety in life.
- Invite students to share any other unfamiliar vocabulary words they found, along with the definition. If they were unable to work out the definition from the context or find it in a dictionary, encourage other students to assist them with the definition. To keep things moving, if no one else knows what the word means, define the word for the class.

- Students may struggle with these words, so be sure to address them here: *polyp, colony, reproduce, organism, extinct, trawler, coined, inhabit, unprecedented,* and *decline.*
- If students are unable to work out the definition from the context or find it in a dictionary, encourage other students to assist with the definition. To keep things moving, if no one else knows what the word means, define the word for the class.

Meeting Students' Needs

- Hearing a complex text read slowly, fluently, and without interruption or explanation promotes fluency for students. They are hearing a strong reader read the text aloud with accuracy and expression and are simultaneously looking at and thinking about the words on the printed page. Be sure to set clear expectations that students read along silently in their heads as you read the text aloud.
- Allow students to grapple with a complex text before explicit teaching of vocabulary. After students have read for the gist, they can identify challenging vocabulary for themselves.

B. Text-Dependent Questions: Pages xx–xxiii (16 minutes)

- Display and distribute the **Text-Dependent Questions: Pages xx–xxiii**. Remind students that the purpose of this is to dig deeper into the text to understand what Mark Kurlansky is saying.
- Invite students to follow along silently as you read aloud the learning target at the top of the handout and the questions in the first column.
- Invite triads to work together to reread the text-dependent questions in column 1, then review pages xx–xxiii and discuss possible answers before recording their answers to the questions in column 2 using evidence from the text.
- Circulate and observe triads working. Support students as needed by asking them to use only evidence from the text to answer the questions. For answers, refer to the **Text-Dependent Questions: Pages xx–xxiii (Teacher Reference)**.
- As students finish up, refocus the whole class. Cold-call students you missed while circulating to check the understanding of the whole class. Guide students through each question, again using Text-Dependent Questions: Pages xx–xxiii (Teacher Reference).
- Invite students to make revisions to their responses as necessary.

Meeting Students' Needs

- Asking students to discuss challenging questions before recording them helps to ensure that all students have an idea about what to write and can give students confidence in their responses.
- Some students may benefit from having access to "hint cards": small slips of paper or index cards that they turn over for hints about how/where to find the answers to text-dependent questions. For example, a hint card might say, "Look in the third paragraph."
- Some students may benefit from having key sections pre-highlighted in their texts. This will help them focus on small sections rather than scanning the whole text for answers.

Closing and Assessment

A. Discussion: Analyzing the Introduction (6 minutes)

- Remind students that the Introduction is where an author helps the reader understand what this whole book is going to be about and gives the reader a reason to keep reading. Consider explaining that the Introduction is like an outline of the author's message and the key concepts he will use to argue his message.
- Display the Tracing the Development of an Idea Anchor Chart and create a new row to record new thinking based on the reading done in class. Ask students to discuss in triads:
  - "How does Mark Kurlansky continue to introduce his idea of fish depletion in the Introduction?"
- Cold-call students to share their responses. Listen for and guide students to understand that he sets up the rest of the book by introducing three main reasons (overfishing, pollution, and global warming) for the problem and presenting some research to support his claims.
- Record this on the Tracing the Development of an Idea Anchor Chart. See Tracing the Development of an Idea Anchor Chart (Teacher Reference) for a model.

Meeting Students' Needs

Capturing students' ideas on an anchor chart can ensure easy reference later and can enable students to see at a glance how an idea has developed through a text.

Homework

- Reread the excerpt of the Introduction that you read in class today.
- Read "The Story of Kram and Ailat: Part 1" (the graphic novel) at the end of the Introduction of *World Without Fish*. Answer this focus question on your **Structured Notes: "The Story of Kram and Ailat: Part 1"** worksheet:
  - "What do we learn about fishing from the graphic novel? How does Mark Kurlansky introduce the idea of fish depletion in the graphic novel?"

Tracing the Development of an Idea Anchor Chart
(Teacher Reference)

Idea: Fish depletion

Chapter	How is the idea introduced, illustrated, or elaborated on in this chapter?
Introduction	• *Kurlansky introduces very famous scientific ideas, like evolution and diversity of species by Charles Darwin, which provide a background to build his ideas on.*
Introduction	• *He sets up the book by introducing three main reasons for the problem (overfishing, pollution, and global warming), which it seems like the rest of the book will discuss in more detail. He also presents some research to support his claims.*

Text-Dependent Questions: Pages xx–xxiii

Name: _____

Date: _____

Learning target:

- "I can use evidence from the text to answer text-dependent questions."

Questions	Answers (supported with evidence from the text, include page numbers)
1. How does Mark Kurlansky describe coral reefs?	
2. What are coral reefs made up of?	
3. According to Mark Kurlansky, what three things are responsible for causing the reefs to die?	
4. According to Mark Kurlansky, about how many species of fish are known?	
5. According to Mark Kurlansky, how often is the list of fish species revised?	

Questions	Answers (supported with evidence from the text, include page numbers)
6. According to Mark Kurlansky, why are we losing species in the rainforest?	
7. According to scientists, how many animals face extinction?	
8. What are commercial fish species?	
9. According to the study by the United States government in 2002, how many of the most eaten types of fish are threatened?	
10. What are the most eaten types of fish threatened by?	

Text-Dependent Questions: Pages xx–xxiii (Teacher Reference)

Questions	Answers (supported with evidence from the text, include page numbers)
1. How does Mark Kurlansky describe coral reefs?	As "complex ecosystems that house a wide variety of plants and animals." (page xx)
2. What are coral reefs made up of?	"Coral reefs are made up of coral polyps, tiny, soft-bodied translucent animals related to sea anemones and jellyfish." (page xx)
3. According to Mark Kurlansky, what three things are responsible for causing the reefs to die?	"Overfishing, pollution and climate change." (page xx)
4. According to Mark Kurlansky, about how many species of fish are known?	"There are about 20,000 known species of fish." (page xxii)
5. According to Mark Kurlansky, how often is the list of fish species revised?	It is constantly being revised because "fish disappear and new ones are discovered." (page xxii)
6. According to Mark Kurlansky, why are we losing species in the rainforest?	Because they are "being cleared for people to live and chopped down for lumber at unprecedented rates." (page xxiii)
7. According to scientists, how many animals face extinction?	"One-fourth of all mammals, a third of amphibians, and 42 percent of all turtles and tortoise species also face extinction." (page xxiii)
8. What are commercial fish species?	"The fish caught for food." (page xxiii)
9. According to the study by the United States government in 2002, how many of the most eaten types of fish are threatened?	"One-third of the 274 most eaten types of fish are threatened by too much fishing." (page xxiii)
10. What are the most eaten types of fish threatened by?	They are "threatened by too much fishing." (page xxiii)

Structured Notes: "The Story of Kram and Ailat: Part 1"

Name: _____

Date: _____

Chapter	Homework Focus Question	Answer with Evidence from the Text (include page number)
_____	What do we learn about fishing from the graphic novel? How does Mark Kurlansky introduce the idea of fish depletion in the graphic novel?	

TEACHER GUIDE AND RESOURCE BOOK • Grade 6 • Module 3B • Unit 1 • Lesson 3 Supporting Materials

LESSON 4

Tracing the Idea of Fish Depletion
Chapter 1

Long-Term Targets Addressed (Based on ELA CCSS)

- I can determine the main idea of an informational text based on details in the text. (RI.6.2)
- I can analyze how key individuals, events, or ideas are developed throughout a text. (RI.6.3)
- I can use a variety of strategies to determine word meaning in informational texts. (RI.6.4)

Supporting Learning Targets

- I can find the gist of pages 1–8 of *World Without Fish*.
- I can use strategies to determine the meaning of words and phrases in an excerpt of chapter 1 of *World Without Fish*.
- I can use evidence from the text to answer text-dependent questions.
- I can analyze how Mark Kurlansky illustrates/elaborates on the problem of fish depletion in an excerpt of chapter 1 of *World Without Fish*.

Ongoing Assessment

- Structured Notes: "The Story of Kram and Ailat: Part 1" (from homework)
- Text-Dependent Questions: Pages 1–8

Agenda

1. Opening
   A. Engaging the Reader: Graphic Novel Part 1 (5 minutes)
   B. Unpacking Learning Targets (2 minutes)
2. Work Time
   A. Reading for Gist: Pages 1–8 (12 minutes)
   B. Text-Dependent Questions: Pages 1–8 (15 minutes)

3. Closing and Assessment
   A. Analyzing a Chart Showing Biodiversity and Tracing the Development of an Idea (12 minutes)
4. Homework
   A. Reread the excerpt of chapter 1 that you read in class today.
   B. Read "The Story of Kram and Ailat: Part 2" (the graphic novel) at the end of chapter 1. Answer the focus question on your structured notes.

Teaching Notes

- This lesson is similar in structure to Lessons 1–3. Students read a new excerpt of *World Without Fish* for the gist and then answer text-dependent questions to dig deeper into the text and analyze how Mark Kurlansky illustrates and elaborates on the idea of fish depletion in chapter 1.

- The content of chapter 1 is a worst-case scenario, so emphasize to students that this is a "could" situation rather than something that will happen, and that these are just ideas presented by one person.

- At the beginning of the lesson, students discuss the graphic novel. From this lesson onward, they will begin to trace how the idea of fish depletion is developed in the graphic novel as well as in the informational text. A new anchor chart is introduced in this lesson to trace the idea throughout the graphic novel. To distinguish this anchor chart from the title the anchor chart used to trace the idea through the main text in the chapters, ensure it has Graphic Novel at the beginning of the title.

- This lesson introduces a new Graphic Novel: Tracing the Development of an Idea Anchor Chart, which is similar to the Tracing the Development of an Idea Anchor Chart begun in Lesson 2, but focused specifically on the "novel within the text." Preview Closing, Part A for details.

- In advance:
  - Review *World Without Fish*, chapter 1, pages 1–8.
  - Read the Close Reading Guide: Pages 1–8 (see supporting materials).
  - Review the Back-to-Back and Face-to-Face protocol (see Appendix).

- Post: learning targets; Graphic Novel: Tracing the Development of an Idea Anchor Chart; Tracing the Development of an Idea Anchor Chart.

Lesson Vocabulary

illustrate, elaborate, exposition, cataclysm, genetic, deposit, grave, cooperation, vertebrates, evolved, invertebrates, krill

Materials

- Structured Notes: "The Story of Kram and Ailat: Part 1" (completed for homework)
- Graphic Novel: Tracing the Development of an Idea Anchor Chart (new; teacher-created; see supporting materials)

TEACHER GUIDE AND RESOURCE BOOK • Grade 6 • Module 3B • Unit 1 • Lesson 4

- Graphic Novel: Tracing the Development of an Idea Anchor Chart (Teacher Reference)
- *World Without Fish* Word-Catcher (students' own; begun in Lesson 1)
- *World Without Fish* (book; distributed in Lesson 1; one per student)
- Sticky notes (eight per student)
- Dictionaries (at least one per triad)
- Text-Dependent Questions: Pages 1–8 (one per student and one for display)
- Close Reading Guide: Pages 1–8 (Teacher Reference)
- Ocean Food Web (one for display)
- Tracing the Development of an Idea Anchor Chart (begun in Lesson 2)
- Tracing the Development of an Idea Anchor Chart (Teacher Reference)
- Structured Notes: "The Story of Kram and Ailat: Part 2" (one per student)

Opening

A. Engaging the Reader: Graphic Novel Part 1 (5 minutes)

- Back-to-Back and Face-to-Face:
    - Invite students to pair up and to sit back-to-back.
    - Remind students of the homework focus question: "What do we learn about fishing from the graphic novel? How does Mark Kurlansky introduce the idea of fish depletion here?"
    - Invite students to refer to the **Structured Notes: "The Story of Kram and Ailat: Part 1"** they completed for homework.
    - Invite students to turn face-to-face to share their answers with their partner.
- Select volunteers to share out with the whole group. Listen for students to explain that we learn that big fish drive small fish to the surface, and sea birds are an indicator that there are fish close to the surface. Also listen for students to explain that the author introduces the idea of fish depletion by having Kram explain to Ailat that they have to throw the one fish they have caught back because there aren't enough left.
- Record students' ideas on the posted **Graphic Novel: Tracing the Development of an Idea Anchor Chart**. See **Graphic Novel: Tracing the Development of an Idea Anchor Chart (Teacher Reference)** as a guide.

Meeting Students' Needs

- Reviewing homework holds all students accountable for reading the text and completing their homework.
- Capturing students' ideas on an anchor chart can ensure easy reference later and can enable students to see at a glance how an idea has developed through a text.

B. Unpacking Learning Targets (2 minutes)

- Ask a volunteer to read the learning targets aloud.
  - "I can find the gist of pages 1–8 of *World Without Fish*."
  - "I can use strategies to determine the meaning of words and phrases in an excerpt of chapter 1 of *World Without Fish*."
  - "I can use evidence from the text to answer text-dependent questions."
  - "I can analyze how Mark Kurlansky illustrates/elaborates on the problem of fish depletion in an excerpt of chapter 1 of *World Without Fish*."
- Underline *illustrates* and *elaborates*. Tell students that "illustrate," in this case, is how an author explains something with increasing detail, and not about drawing a picture, and that "elaborate" in this context is another way of saying developed. So students are going to be looking at how Mark Kurlansky continues to add detail and develop the idea of fish depletion in an excerpt of chapter 1.
- Direct students to record the new words on their **World Without Fish Word-Catchers**.

Meeting Students' Needs

- Posting learning targets allows students to reference them throughout the lesson to check their understanding. Learning targets also provide a reminder to students and teachers about the intended learning behind a given lesson or activity.
- Discussing and clarifying the language of learning targets helps build academic vocabulary.

Work Time

A. Reading for Gist: Pages 1–8 (12 minutes)

- Invite students to take out **World Without Fish** and turn to page 1, which is the first page of chapter 1. Ask students to read along in their heads as you read the page aloud. Instruct them to discuss in triads:
  - "What is this chapter going to be about? How do you know?"
- Select volunteers to share their ideas with the whole group. Listen for them to explain that it is going to be about what could happen and how it would happen. (It's fine if that is all students understand at this point).
- Focus students on the word *exposition*. Ask triads to discuss:
  - "What do you think this word might mean given the context?"
- Cold-call students to share their responses. Listen for and guide students to understand that it means a descriptive piece of writing.
- Focus students on the words *could* and *would*. Ask:
  - "Does this mean it definitely will happen?"

- Cold-call students to share their responses. Listen for and guide students to understand that this is something that Mark Kurlansky is saying is a possibility. It doesn't mean it definitely will happen, though. Also emphasize to students that these are just the ideas of one person, Mark Kurlansky.
- Ask students to turn to the next page and invite them to silently read along as you read aloud up to "seabirds would die out" on page 8. Ask students to discuss in triads:
  - "What is this excerpt mostly about?"
- Select volunteers to share their responses. Listen for students to explain that it is mostly about how losing some species of fish could have a huge impact on biodiversity—losing one species of fish could result in losing lots of species including mammals and birds.
- Invite a student to reread the learning target about reading for the gist aloud.
  - "I can find the gist of pages 1–8 of *World Without Fish*."
- Distribute eight **sticky notes** to each student. Remind students of the importance of summarizing smaller chunks of text as they read for the gist, and ask them to annotate the gist on the sticky notes. Remind students to ask questions as they read to help them monitor comprehension. Explain that the goal is for them to understand what this excerpt is mostly about. Direct students to include the text accompanying the images and any additional text at the side of the main excerpt of text as they read for the gist.
- Remind students that where possible, you would like them to use their word strategies to figure out the meaning of unfamiliar words: reading around unfamiliar words, looking for root words, replacing the word with other words that would make sense, and looking for context clues to figure out what they mean. Distribute **dictionaries** to each triad and tell students that if they can't figure out the meaning from the context, they can look the word up. If they aren't sure what the word means after looking for context clues and looking in the dictionary, they should leave the definition to be discussed with the whole group later.
- Invite students to work together as a triad to read for the gist, annotate sticky notes, and record unfamiliar words on their word-catchers.
- Circulate and support students as they read. For those who need more support, ask them to practice telling you the gist of a section before they write it on a sticky note.
- As students finish up, refocus the whole group. Focus students on the word *grave* on page 4. Ask them to discuss in triads:
  - "What does this word mean? Does it have more than one meaning?"
- Select volunteers to share their ideas. Listen for them to explain that *grave* means serious, but it can also mean a place where someone is buried.
- Invite students to share any unfamiliar vocabulary words they found, along with the definition. If they were unable to work out the definition from the context or find it in a dictionary, encourage other students to assist them with the definition. To keep things moving, if no one else knows what the word means, define the word for the class.
- Students may struggle with these words, so be sure to address them here: *cataclysm*, *genetic*, *deposit*, *cooperation*, *vertebrates*, *evolved*, *invertebrates*, and *krill*.

- If students are unable to work out the definition from the context or find it in a dictionary, encourage other students to assist them with the definition. To keep things moving, if no one else knows what the word means, define the word for the class.
- Remind students to record new words on their word-catchers.

Meeting Students' Needs

- Hearing a complex text read slowly, fluently, and without interruption or explanation promotes fluency for students. They are hearing a strong reader read the text aloud with accuracy and expression and are simultaneously looking at and thinking about the words on the printed page. Be sure to set clear expectations that students read along silently in their heads as you read the text aloud.
- Allow students to grapple with a complex text before explicit teaching of vocabulary. After students have read for the gist, they can identify challenging vocabulary for themselves.
- Asking students to identify challenging vocabulary helps them monitor their understanding of a complex text. When students annotate the text by circling these words, it can also provide a formative assessment for the teacher.

B. Text-Dependent Questions: Pages 1–8 (15 minutes)

- Display and distribute **Text-Dependent Questions: Pages 1–8**. Remind students that text-dependent questions help them to dig deeper into the text to have a better understanding of it.
- Guide students through the text-dependent questions using the **Close Reading Guide: Pages 1–8 (Teacher Reference)**.
- Finish by inviting students to read pages 17–19 as you read them aloud. Explain that you are jumping forward in the chapter because you want to make sure students are exposed to the most important information that Mark Kurlansky discusses.
- Emphasize to students that what Mark Kurlansky is presenting is an idea—it could happen, but it doesn't mean it definitely will.

Meeting Students' Needs

Asking students to discuss challenging questions before recording them helps to ensure that all students have an idea about what to write and can give students confidence in their responses.

Closing and Assessment

A. Analyzing a Chart Showing Biodiversity and Tracing the Development of an Idea (12 minutes)

- Display the **Ocean Food Web**. Invite students to notice the bottom, middle, and surface levels of the ocean, read aloud the species names, and explain how the arrows show the flow of energy (note the arrows show energy from the prey going to the predator).

- Remind students of what biodiversity means. Ask them to discuss in triads:
  - "How does this food web connect to what you have been reading today?"
- Cold-call students to share their responses. Listen for students to explain that this food web shows biodiversity in the ocean and the way one species depends on another, which is what they read about today.
- Cover up one of the species on the web and ask students to discuss in triads:
  - "What happens if this species disappears?"
- Select students to share their responses. Listen for them to explain that the other species that depend on it may also disappear.
- Repeat by covering different species.
- Focus students' attention on the posted **Tracing the Development of an Idea Anchor Chart**. Ask students to discuss in triads:
  - "So how does the author illustrate or elaborate on this idea in the excerpt you have read from chapter 1?"
- Remind students that *illustrate* and *elaborate* mean to add detail and develop the idea.
- Cold-call students to share their responses. Listen for and guide students to understand that the author illustrates and elaborates on the idea by explaining what could happen specifically to fish and then how that would affect other species.
- Record this on the Tracing the Development of an Idea Anchor Chart. See **Tracing the Development of an Idea Anchor Chart (Teacher Reference)** for a model.

Meeting Students' Needs

Capturing students' ideas on an anchor chart can ensure easy reference later and can enable students to see at a glance how an idea has developed through a text.

Homework

- Reread the excerpt of chapter 1 that you read in class today, pages 1–8 as well as 17–19.
- Read "The Story of Kram and Ailat: Part 2" (the graphic novel) at the end of Chapter 1. Answer this focus question on your Structured Notes: "The Story of Kram and Ailat: Part 2" worksheet:
  - "What do we learn about fishing from the graphic novel? How does Mark Kurlansky illustrate and elaborate on the idea of fish depletion here?"

Graphic Novel: Tracing the Development of an Idea Anchor Chart

What happens?	How is the idea of fish depletion introduced, illustrated, or elaborated on in the graphic novel?

Graphic Novel: Tracing the Development of an Idea Anchor Chart
(Teacher Reference)

What happens?	How is the idea of fish depletion introduced, illustrated, or elaborated on in the graphic novel?
Part 1: Kram and Ailat are fishing. They catch a small fish, which Ailat wants to take home to show her mom, but Kram explains that she can't because there aren't enough left.	The idea of fish depletion is introduced here by having Kram throw the fish that Ailat is so excited about back. We feel sorry for Ailat.

Text-Dependent Questions: Pages 1–8

Name: _____

Date: _____

Learning target:

- "I can use evidence from the text to answer text-dependent questions."

Questions	Answers (supported with evidence from the text)
1. What does Kurlansky say is key to the success of all life on earth? 2. According to Kurlansky, which are the most evolved animals in the sea?	
3. What is Kurlansky saying might happen if commercial fish were to disappear?	
4. What does Kurlansky mean by, "Their disappearance would mark the beginning of a process in which evolution goes in reverse"?	

Questions	Answers (supported with evidence from the text)
5. How old does Kurlansky say today's small fish species are?	
6. According to Kurlansky, why would the dolphin die off very quickly once the larger, more evolved fish were gone? 7. Why does Mark Kurlansky suggest seabirds would die out?	

Close Reading Guide: Pages 1–8
(Teacher Reference)

Time: 13 minutes

Questions	Teaching Notes
1. What does Kurlansky say is key to the success of all life on earth? 2. According to Kurlansky, which are the most evolved animals in the sea?	• Tell students they will work through Questions 1 and 2 together. • Invite students to reread pages 1–4 up to "... more difficult for the remaining animals to survive." • Invite students to work in triads to answer Questions 1 and 2 using evidence from the text. • Invite triads to pair up with another triad to share their answers to Questions 1 and 2. • Listen for the following answer to Question 1: "Biodiversity is key to success for all life on earth." • Listen for the following answer to Question 2: "Mammals are the most evolved animals in the sea: whales, porpoises, and seals."
3. What is Kurlansky saying might happen if commercial fish were to disappear?	• Invite students to reread, "If the top forty species of commercial fish were to disappear, or even have their populations decline in very small numbers, this would be a grave threat to all of biodiversity. Other species would begin disappearing, too, either because their lives depended on cooperation with these species or because they used to eat those fish—or even because those vanished species used to hunt predators that were now free to roam and prosper." • Ask students to discuss in triads: • "What does 'a grave threat to all of biodiversity' mean?" • Select volunteers to share their responses. Listen for and guide students to understand that it means a serious threat to the variety of life. • Invite students to work in triads to answer Question 3 using evidence from the text. • Refocus the whole group and invite triads to share their ideas. Listen for students to explain that it would be a threat to biodiversity because other species would begin to disappear too because they used to eat those fish. • Focus students on "... or even because those vanished species used to hunt predators that were now free to roam and prosper."

Questions	Teaching Notes

	• Ask students to discuss in triads:
	  • "What does this mean?"
	• Select volunteers to share their responses. Listen for and guide students to understand that it means that if species that used to hunt predators disappeared, there would be more of those predators than there were before.
	• Ask students to discuss in triads:
	  • "How would you synthesize what he is saying in this short section?"
	• Cold-call volunteers to share their ideas. Listen for and guide students to understand that the author is saying that the disappearance of the top forty fish species would be a threat to biodiversity—it would upset the balance of life because some species would die out and others would thrive as a result.

4. What does Mark Kurlansky mean by, "Their disappearance would mark the beginning of a process in which evolution goes in reverse?"	• Tell students they will work through Questions 4 and 5 together. • Invite students to reread "Their disappearance would mark the beginning of a process in which evolution goes in reverse . . . are only 100 million years old." • Remind students that *evolution* means "the process of developing and changing." • Ask students to work in triads to answer Question 4 using evidence from the text.
5. How old does Mark Kurlansky say today's small fish species are?	• Refocus the whole group and invite triads to share their ideas. Listen for students to explain that he means that the ocean would go back to how it was millions of years ago when there were no fish at all. • Invite students to work in triads to answer Question 5 using evidence from the text. • Refocus the whole group and invite triads to share their ideas. Listen for students to explain that he says they are only 100 million years old.

Questions	Teaching Notes
6. According to Mark Kurlansky, why would the dolphin die off very quickly once the larger, more evolved fish were gone? 7. Why does Mark Kurlansky suggest seabirds would die out?	• Tell students they will work through Questions 6 and 7 together. • Invite students to work in triads to answer Questions 6 and 7 using evidence from the text. • Invite triads to pair up with another triad to share their answers to Questions 6 and 7. • Listen for the following answer to Question 6: "Dolphins would die off quickly because the Bluefin tuna would be gone." • Listen for the following answer to Question 7: "Seabirds would die out because there wouldn't be large fish to drive the small fish to the surface."

Ocean Food Web

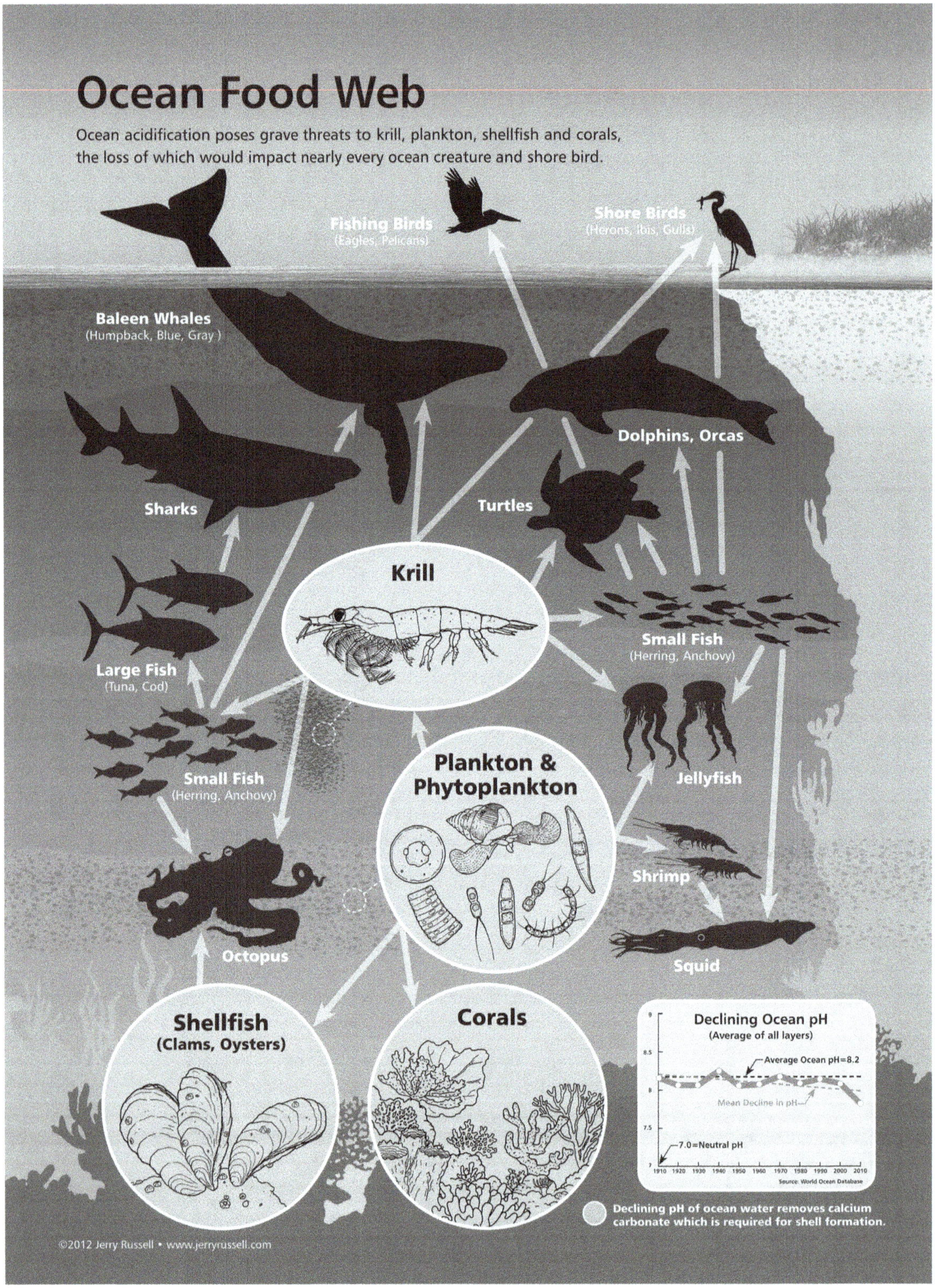

Ocean Food Web

Source: Jerry Russell. "Ocean Food Web," *The Environment Magazine*, May 1, 2012, http://www.emagazine.com/magazine/ocean-food-web.

Tracing the Development of an Idea Anchor Chart
(Teacher Reference)

Idea: Fish depletion

Chapter	How is the idea introduced, illustrated, or elaborated on in this chapter?
1	*Kurlansky illustrates and elaborates on the idea by explaining what could happen specifically to fish and then how that would affect other species.*

Structured Notes: "The Story of Kram and Ailat: Part 2"

Name: _____

Date: _____

Chapter	Homework Focus Question	Answer with Evidence from the Text (include page number)
_____	What do we learn about fishing from the graphic novel? How does Mark Kurlansky illustrate and elaborate on the idea of fish depletion here?	

LESSON 5

Tracing the Idea of Fish Depletion
Chapter 2

Long-Term Targets Addressed (Based on ELA CCSS)

- I can determine the main idea of an informational text based on details in the text. (RI.6.2)
- I can analyze how key individuals, events, or ideas are developed throughout a text. (RI.6.3)
- I can use a variety of strategies to determine word meaning in informational texts. (RI.6.4)

Supporting Learning Targets

- I can find the gist of pages 28–33 of *World Without Fish*.
- I can use strategies to determine the meaning of words and phrases in an excerpt of chapter 2 of *World Without Fish*.
- I can use evidence from the text to answer text-dependent questions.
- I can analyze how Mark Kurlansky illustrates/elaborates on the problem of fish depletion in an excerpt of chapter 2 of *World Without Fish*.

Ongoing Assessment

- Structured Notes: "The Story of Kram and Ailat: Part 2" (from homework)
- Text-Dependent Questions: Pages 28–33

Agenda

1. Opening
   A. Engaging the Reader: Graphic Novel Part 2 (6 minutes)
   B. Unpacking Learning Targets (2 minutes)

2. Work Time
   A. Reading for Gist: Pages 28–33 (16 minutes)
   B. Text-Dependent Questions: Pages 28–33 (15 minutes)
3. Closing and Assessment
   A. Tracing the Development of an Idea (6 minutes)
4. Homework
   A. Reread the excerpt of chapter 2 that you read in class today.
   B. Read "The Story of Kram and Ailat: Part 3" (the graphic novel) at the end of chapter 2. Answer the focus question on your structured notes.

Teaching Notes

- This lesson is similar in structure to Lessons 1–4. Students read a new excerpt of *World Without Fish* for the gist and then answer text-dependent questions to dig deeper into the text and analyze how Mark Kurlansky illustrates and elaborates on the idea of fish depletion in chapter 2.
- In advance:
  - Read *World Without Fish*, chapter 2, pages 28–33.
  - Review Text-Dependent Questions: Pages 28–33 (see supporting materials).
  - Review the Mix and Mingle protocol activity in Opening A and have music ready to use.
- Post: learning targets; Graphic Novel: Tracing the Development of an Idea Anchor Chart; Tracing the Development of an Idea Anchor Chart.

Lesson Vocabulary

industry, productive, sail power, innovations, fishing territories, beam trawler, efficient, advantages, well boats, technological, boon, teeming, lucrative

Materials

- Structured Notes: "The Story of Kram and Ailat: Part 2" (completed for homework)
- Graphic Novel: Tracing the Development of an Idea Anchor Chart (begun in Lesson 4)
- Graphic Novel: Tracing the Development of an Idea Anchor Chart (Teacher Reference)
- *World Without Fish* (book; distributed in Lesson 1; one per student)
- Sticky notes (eight per student)
- Dictionaries (at least one per triad)
- *World Without Fish* Word-Catchers (students' own; begun in Lesson 1)
- Text-Dependent Questions: Pages 28–33 (one per student, one for display)
- Text-Dependent Questions: Pages 28–33 (Teacher Reference)

- Exit Ticket: Tracing the Development of an Idea, Chapter 2 (one per student)
- Exit Ticket: Tracing the Development of an Idea, Chapter 2 (Teacher Reference)
- Structured Notes: "The Story of Kram and Ailat: Part 3" (one per student)

Opening

A. Engaging the Reader: Graphic Novel Part 2 (6 minutes)

- Remind students of the homework focus question: "What do we learn about fishing from the graphic novel? How does Mark Kurlansky illustrate and elaborate on the idea of fish depletion here?"
- Tell students they are going to start with the Mix and Mingle protocol:
    1. Play music. Invite students to move around the room with their **Structured Notes: "The Story of Kram and Ailat: Part 2"** homework.
    2. After 15 seconds, stop the music.
    3. Ask students to share their answer to the focus question with the person standing closest to them.
    4. Repeat until students have spoken to at least two people.
- Select volunteers to share their responses with the whole group. Listen for students to explain that we learn that fishing with nets catches a lot of fish and that the fishermen throw back the dead fish when they catch more than they are legally allowed to. Listen for students to also explain that the author illustrates and elaborates on the idea of fish depletion by introducing a way of fishing that is causing fish depletion and a loophole related to regulating how much fish fishermen can catch.
- Record students' ideas on the posted **Graphic Novel: Tracing the Development of an Idea Anchor Chart**. See the **Graphic Novel: Tracing the Development of an Idea Anchor Chart (Teacher Reference)** for a guide.

Meeting Students' Needs

- Reviewing homework holds all students accountable for reading the text and completing their homework.
- Capturing students' ideas on an anchor chart can ensure easy reference later and can enable students to see how an idea has developed through a text at a glance.

B. Unpacking Learning Targets (2 minutes)

- Ask for a volunteer to read the learning targets aloud.
    - "I can find the gist of pages 28–33 of *World Without Fish*."
    - "I can use strategies to determine the meaning of words and phrases in an excerpt of chapter 2 of *World Without Fish*."

- "I can use evidence from the text to answer text-dependent questions."
- "I can analyze how Mark Kurlansky illustrates/elaborates on the problem of fish depletion in an excerpt of chapter 2 of *World Without Fish*."

• Point out to students that these are the same learning targets they have encountered in previous lessons.

Meeting Students' Needs

Posting learning targets allows students to reference them throughout the lesson to check their understanding. Learning targets also provide a reminder to students and teachers about the intended learning behind a given lesson or activity.

Work Time

A. Reading for Gist: Pages 28–33 (16 minutes)

• Invite students to take out **World Without Fish** and turn to page 21, which is the first page of chapter 2. Invite students to read along in their heads as you read the page aloud. Ask students to discuss in triads:
  - "What is this chapter going to be about? How do you know?"

• Select volunteers to share their ideas with the whole group. Listen for students to explain that it is going to be about how humans began to fish and how fishing became an industry.

• Ask students to discuss in triads:
  - "What does it mean by 'fishing became an *industry*'? Think back to what you found out about the Industrial Revolution earlier in the unit."

• Select volunteers to share their responses. Listen for and guide students to understand that it means how fishing went from being a man on a small boat with a fishing rod to being huge boats with lots of motorized equipment to catch fish.

• Tell students to turn to page 28 of chapter 2.

• Invite students to silently read along as you read aloud from "Because the most productive fishing grounds . . ." on page 28 up to ". . . they simply moved on to new ones" on page 33. Ask students to discuss in triads:
  - "What is this excerpt mostly about?"

• Select volunteers to share their responses. Listen for students to explain that it is mostly about how the fishing industry began to change because technology was developed, such as steam-powered boats and rails to deliver fresh fish in the late 19th century.

• Invite a student to reread the learning target about reading for the gist aloud.
  - "I can find the gist of pages 28–33 of *World Without Fish*."

• Distribute eight **sticky notes** to each student. Remind students of the importance of summarizing smaller chunks of text as they read for the gist, and ask them to annotate the gist on the sticky

notes. Remind students to ask questions as they read to help them monitor comprehension. Explain that the goal is for them to understand what this excerpt is mostly about. Remind students that where possible, you would like them to use their word strategies to figure out the meaning of unfamiliar words: reading around unfamiliar words, looking for root words, replacing the word with other words that would make sense, and looking for context clues to figure out what they mean. Distribute **dictionaries** to each triad. If students can't figure out the meaning from the context, encourage them to look the word up. If they aren't sure what the word means after looking for context clues and looking in the dictionary, students should leave the definition to be discussed with the whole group later.

- Invite students to work together as a triad to read for the gist, annotate sticky notes, and record unfamiliar words on their *World Without Fish* **Word-Catchers**.

- Circulate and support students as they read. For those who need more support, ask them to practice telling you the gist of a section before they write it on a sticky note.

- As students finish up, refocus the whole group. Invite students to share any unfamiliar vocabulary words they found, along with the definition. If they were unable to work out the definition from the context or find it in a dictionary, encourage other students to assist them with the definition. To keep things moving, if no one else knows what the word means, define the word for the class.

- Students may struggle with these words, so be sure to address them here: *productive*, *sail power*, *innovations*, *fishing territories*, *beam trawler*, *efficient*, *advantages*, *well boats*, *technological*, *boon*, *teeming*, and *lucrative*.

- If students are unable to work out the definition from the context or find it in a dictionary, encourage other students to assist them with the definition. To keep things moving, if no one else knows what the word means, define the word for the class.

- Remind students to record new words on their word-catchers.

Meeting Students' Needs

Allow students to grapple with a complex text before explicit teaching of vocabulary. After students have read for the gist, they can identify challenging vocabulary for themselves.

B. Text-Dependent Questions: Pages 28–33 (15 minutes)

- Display and distribute **Text-Dependent Questions: Pages 28–33**. Remind students that the purpose of this is to dig deeper into the text to understand what Mark Kurlansky is saying.

- Invite students to read along with you as you read aloud the learning target at the top of the handout and the questions in the first column.

- Invite triads to work together to reread the text-dependent questions in column 1, review the excerpt of text, and discuss possible answers before recording their answers to the questions in column 2, using evidence from the text.

- Circulate and observe triads working. Support students as needed by asking them to use only evidence from the excerpt to answer the questions. Refer to the **Text-Dependent Questions: Pages 28–33 (Teacher Reference)** as needed.

Meeting Students' Needs

Asking students to discuss challenging questions before recording them helps to ensure that all students have an idea about what to write and can give students confidence in their responses.

Closing and Assessment

A. Tracing the Development of an Idea (6 minutes)

- Distribute the **Exit Ticket: Tracing the Development of an Idea, Chapter 2**. Explain to students that in previous lessons they have answered this question as a whole group on the **Tracing the Development of an Idea Anchor Chart**.
- Ask students to independently record on their exit tickets the answer to this question:
  - "How does the author illustrate and elaborate on this idea in the excerpt you have read from chapter 2?"
- Remind students that illustrate and elaborate mean to add detail and develop the idea.
- Collect in the exit tickets to check that all students are on the right track with filling out this chart independently.

Meeting Students' Needs

Capturing students' ideas on an anchor chart can ensure easy reference later and can enable students to see at a glance how an idea has developed through a text.

Homework

- Reread the excerpt of chapter 2 that you read in class today.
- Read "The Story of Kram and Ailat: Part 3" (the graphic novel) at the end of chapter 2. Answer this focus question on your Structured Notes: "The Story of Kram and Ailat: Part 3" worksheet:
  - "What do we learn about fishing from the graphic novel? How does Mark Kurlansky illustrate and elaborate on the idea of fish depletion here?"

Graphic Novel: Tracing the Development of an Idea Anchor Chart

(Teacher Reference)

What happens?	How is the idea of fish depletion introduced, illustrated, or elaborated on in this chapter?
Part 2: Kram is out on a boat with his friend Serrafino who is using nets to catch fish. Kram sees Serrafino catch too many fish, then throw dead fish back into the ocean because he had caught more than he was legally allowed to.	He illustrates and elaborates on the idea of fish depletion by introducing a way of fishing that is causing fish depletion and a loophole related to regulating how much fish fishermen can catch.

Text-Dependent Questions: Pages 28–33

Name: _____

Date: _____

Learning target:

- "I can use evidence from the text to answer text-dependent questions."

Questions	Answers (supported with evidence from the text, include page numbers)
1. When did innovations in fishing begin?	
2. Where is the North Sea?	
3. Who first started using the beam trawler and when?	
4. From the diagram on page 29, how would you describe a beam trawler?	

Questions	Answers (supported with evidence from the text, include page numbers)
5. What were the advantages of beam trawlers?	
6. What were well boats?	
7. What was different about the *Zodiac*?	
8. What four things started to happen between the 1870s and 1880s?	
9. What did fishermen do when fish declined in one place?	

Text-Dependent Questions: Pages 28–33
(Teacher Reference)

Questions	Answers (supported with evidence from the text, include page numbers)
1. When did innovations in fishing begin?	"It was in the North Sea in the late nineteenth century that innovations in fishing began to take place." (page 28)
2. Where is the North Sea?	"The North Sea is a body of water rich in fish, which is surrounded by the great European fishing nations, such as Scotland, England, France, Belgium, the Netherlands, Denmark, Germany, Sweden and Norway." (page 28)
3. Who first started using the beam trawler and when?	"It was the British that first started using a beam trawler in the fourteenth century." (page 29)
4. From the diagram on page 29, how would you describe a beam trawler?	It was a boat that pulled a net that dragged along the ocean floor.
5. What were the advantages of beam trawlers?	"The potential of dragging a net through the water and hauling up everything in its path had obvious advantages over setting lines with bait hooks. In addition to requiring no bait, a beam trawler seemed certain to haul in a much higher percentage of the fish it passed." (page 30)
6. What were well boats?	"These were ships that contained a tank of seawater into which the caught fish would be dumped, enabling fish to stay fresh longer than previously." (page 30)
7. What was different about the *Zodiac*?	It was "the first vessel built for dragging fishing nets under steam power." (page 31)

Questions	Answers (supported with evidence from the text, include page numbers)
8. What four things started to happen between the 1870s and 1880s?	**Steam engines got more powerful and could drag deeper.** **More powerful steam engines meant more places could be dragged.** **Britain became the greatest fishing nation because of the amount of fish they caught.** **The fish in the North Sea started showing signs of depletion. (page 32)**
9. What did fishermen do when fish declined in one place?	**"They simply moved on to new ones." (page 33)**

Exit Ticket: Tracing the Development of an Idea, Chapter 2

Name: _____

Date: _____

Learning target:

- "I can analyze how Mark Kurlansky illustrates/elaborates on the problem of fish depletion in an excerpt of chapter 2 of *World Without Fish*."

Idea: Fish depletion

Chapter	How is the idea introduced, illustrated, or elaborated on in this chapter?

Exit Ticket: Tracing the Development of an Idea, Chapter 2

(Teacher Reference)

Learning target:

- "I can analyze how Mark Kurlansky illustrates/elaborates on the problem of fish depletion in an excerpt of chapter 2 of *World Without Fish*."

Idea: Fish depletion

Chapter	How is the idea introduced, illustrated, or elaborated on in this chapter?
2	- **He illustrates and elaborates on the idea by going back and outlining the history of fishing technology, which illustrates how fish depletion started.**

Structured Notes: "The Story of Kram and Ailat: Part 3"

Name: _____

Date: _____

Chapter	Homework Focus Question	Answer with Evidence from the Text (include page number)
_____	What do we learn about fishing from the graphic novel? How does Mark Kurlansky illustrate and elaborate on the idea of fish depletion here?	

LESSON 6

Mid-Unit 1 Assessment

Analyzing Idea Development in Chapter 3 of *World Without Fish*

Long-Term Targets Addressed (Based on ELA CCSS)

- I can determine the main idea of an informational text based on details in the text. (RI.6.2)
- I can analyze how key individuals, events, or ideas are developed throughout a text. (RI.6.3)
- I can use a variety of strategies to determine word meaning in informational texts. (RI.6.4)

Supporting Learning Targets

- I can use strategies to determine the meaning of words and phrases in an excerpt of chapter 3 of *World Without Fish*.
- I can analyze how Mark Kurlansky illustrates/elaborates on the problem of fish depletion in an excerpt of chapter 3 of *World Without Fish*.

Ongoing Assessment

- Structured Notes: "The Story of Kram and Ailat: Part 3" (from homework)
- Mid-Unit 1 Assessment: Analyzing Idea Development in Chapter 3 of *World Without Fish*

Agenda

1. Opening
   A. Engaging the Reader: Graphic Novel Part 3 (6 minutes)
   B. Unpacking Learning Targets (3 minutes)
2. Work Time
   A. Mid-Unit 1 Assessment (33 minutes)
3. Closing and Assessment
   A. Debrief (3 minutes)

4. Homework

   A. Reread the excerpt of chapter 3 that you read in class today.

   B. Read "The Story of Kram and Ailat: Part 4" (the graphic novel) at the end of Chapter 3. Answer the focus question on your structured notes.

Teaching Notes

- In this Mid-Unit 1 Assessment, students analyze how Kurlansky develops the idea of an ocean food web in chapter 3 of *World Without Fish* and how this develops his message about fish depletion. Students are asked a series of questions to determine the main idea of the chapter and the meaning of unknown words to support their analysis, followed by a series of short constructed-response questions about analyzing idea development.
- Assess student responses using the Grade 6 2-Point Rubric—Short Response.
- In advance:
  - Review Fist-to-Five Checking for Understanding technique (see Appendix).
- Post: learning targets; Graphic Novel: Tracing the Development of an Idea Anchor Chart.

Lesson Vocabulary

Do not preview vocabulary.

Materials

- Structured Notes: "The Story of Kram and Ailat: Part 3" (completed for homework)
- Graphic Novel: Tracing the Development of an Idea Anchor Chart (begun in Lesson 4)
- Graphic Novel: Tracing the Development of an Idea Anchor Chart (Teacher Reference)
- Mid-Unit 1 Assessment: Analyzing Idea Development in Chapter 3 of *World Without Fish* (one per student)
- *World Without Fish* (book; distributed in Lesson 1; one per student)
- Sticky notes (eight per student)
- Grade 6 2-Point Rubric—Short Response (Teacher Reference)
- Mid-Unit 1 Assessment: Analyzing Idea Development in Chapter 3 of *World Without Fish* (Teacher Reference)
- Structured Notes: "The Story of Kram and Ailat: Part 4" (one per student)

Opening

A. Engaging the Reader: Graphic Novel Part 3 (6 minutes)

- Remind students of the homework focus question: "What do we learn about fishing from the graphic novel? How does Mark Kurlansky illustrate and elaborate on the idea of fish depletion here?"

- Invite students to refer to their **Structured Notes: "The Story of Kram and Ailat: Part 3"** homework to discuss the answers with their triads.
- Select volunteers to share their responses with the whole group. Listen for students to explain that he introduces a new idea—the idea of what happens when fishermen start catching different fish because the other fish are running out.
- Record students' ideas on the posted **Graphic Novel: Tracing the Development of an Idea Anchor Chart**. Refer to the **Graphic Novel: Tracing the Development of an Idea Anchor Chart (Teacher Reference)** as needed.

Meeting Students' Needs

- Reviewing homework holds all students accountable for reading the text and completing their homework.
- Capturing students' ideas on an anchor chart can ensure easy reference later and can enable students to see at a glance how an idea has developed through a text.

B. Unpacking Learning Targets (3 minutes)

- Invite students to read the learning targets aloud with you:
    - "I can use strategies to determine the meaning of words and phrases in an excerpt of chapter 3 of *World Without Fish*."
    - "I can analyze how Mark Kurlansky illustrates/elaborates on the problem of fish depletion in an excerpt of chapter 3 of *World Without Fish*."
- Remind students that these are similar to the learning targets they have been working with for the past five lessons. Tell them that today they will show how well they can demonstrate these targets independently in an assessment.

Meeting Students' Needs

Posting learning targets allows students to reference them throughout the lesson to check their understanding. Learning targets also provide a reminder to students and teachers about the intended learning behind a given lesson or activity.

Work Time

A. Mid-Unit 1 Assessment (33 minutes)

- Distribute **Mid-Unit 1 Assessment: Analyzing Idea Development in Chapter 3 of *World Without Fish*** to each student. They will also need their text ***World Without Fish*** and eight **sticky notes** each.
- Invite students to read through the learning targets and the questions with you.

- Remind the class that because this is an assessment, it is to be completed independently. However, if students need assistance, they should raise a hand to speak with a teacher.
- Explain to students that they should independently read the excerpt for the gist. They have the option of using the sticky notes as a tool to support their comprehension.
- Circulate and support students as they work. During an assessment, your prompting should be minimal.
- At the end of the time allotted, collect the Mid-Unit 1 Assessment, which you will assess using the **Grade 6 2-Point Rubric—Short Response** and the **Mid-Unit 1 Assessment: Analyzing Idea Development in Chapter 3 of** *World Without Fish* **(Teacher Reference)**.
- Congratulate students on their hard work during the assessment.

Meeting Students' Needs

If students receive accommodations for assessment, communicate with the cooperating service providers regarding the practices of instruction in use during this study, as well as the goals of the assessment.

Closing and Assessment

A. Debrief (3 minutes)

- Invite students to show how well they think they have achieved the learning targets with a Fist-to-Five.
- Tell students that they are going to continue reading *World Without Fish* in the second half of the unit, with a particular focus on how Mark Kurlansky is informing his audience of his point of view.

Homework

- Reread the excerpt of chapter 3 that you read in class today.
- Read "The Story of Kram and Ailat: Part 4" (the graphic novel) at the end of chapter 3. Answer this focus question on your Structured Notes: "The Story of Kram and Ailat: Part 4" worksheet:
  - "What do we learn about fishing from the graphic novel? How does Mark Kurlansky illustrate and elaborate the idea of fish depletion here?"

Note: Be prepared to return the Mid-Unit 1 Assessment with teacher feedback to students in Lesson 8.

Graphic Novel: Tracing the Development of an Idea Anchor Chart
(Teacher Reference)

What happens?	How is the idea of fish depletion introduced, illustrated, or elaborated on in the graphic novel?
Part 3: Kram and Ailat go to the Caribbean and go snorkeling. Then they go and look at what a fisherman has caught and see parrotfish. Kram tells the fisherman that parrotfish are important because they eat algae and without them the beach would be covered in it.	He introduces a new idea—the idea of what happens when fishermen start catching different fish because the other fish are running out.

Mid-Unit 1 Assessment

Analyzing Idea Development in Chapter 3 of *World Without Fish*

Name: _____

Date: _____

Long-Term Learning Targets Assessed:

- "I can use strategies to determine the meaning of words and phrases in an excerpt of chapter 3 of *World Without Fish*." (RI.6.4)
- "I can analyze how Mark Kurlansky illustrates/elaborates on the problem of fish depletion in an excerpt of chapter 3 of *World Without Fish*." (RI.6.3)

In this informational text, Kurlansky introduces us to and develops the idea of fish depletion. One way of understanding his message is to examine and analyze how Kurlansky develops his ideas in support of his message. In this assessment, you will have the opportunity to show what you have learned about examining the main ideas in this chapter. Then you will be able to show your analysis of how Kurlansky developed the main idea in the chapter and how that chapter develops his overall message about fish depletion.

Directions

- Read pages 39–49 of *World Without Fish* for the gist. It is optional for you to use the sticky notes to record the gist of each section as you read.
- Answer the selected-response questions.

Part 1: Selected Response

Circle the best answer for each question below.

1. What are phytoplankton?
   A. Creatures of the sea that eat zooplankton
   B. Land-based plants that pollute the oceans
   C. Microscopic plants that are the beginning of the ocean food chain

2. How are zooplankton, one of the smallest forms of sea life, essential to a healthy ocean ecosystem?
   A. Zooplankton eat masses of phytoplankton.
   B. Zooplankton are food for several ocean species such as the herring and the humpback whale.
   C. Zooplankton become larva that turn into coral.
   D. Zooplankton do all of the above.

Part 2: Short Response

Answer the following questions using evidence from chapter 3 of the text.

A healthy ecosystem is based on the destruction of life and the struggles for survival among species, and it is in such systems that men in the form of fishermen are drawn to take part in the killing. Ninety percent of the fishing they do is within 200 miles of land. Farther out to sea, there is life and there are fish. But many of them live at great depths that have not been explored because until recently we didn't have the ability to reach that far below the surface.

3. How do fishermen take part in the "destruction of life" in the ocean? How do you know?

   _____
   _____
   _____

4. More recently, how are fishermen exploring life at sea?

   _____
   _____
   _____

5. How is the orange roughy different from other commercial fish such as haddock or cod?

   _____

   _____

   _____

6. The title of the chapter is, "Being the Sad, Cautionary Tale of the Orange Roughy." What is a "cautionary tale"? How is the story of the orange roughy a cautionary tale?

   _____

   _____

   _____

7. How does chapter 3 illustrate and elaborate on Kurlansky's message about fish depletion?

   _____

   _____

   _____

   _____

   _____

Grade 6 2-Point Rubric—Short Response
(Teacher Reference)

Use the rubric below for determining scores on short answers in this assessment.

The features of a **2-point response** are:

- Valid inferences and/or claims from the text where required by the prompt
- Evidence of analysis of the text where required by the prompt
- Relevant facts, definitions, concrete details, and/or other information from the text to develop response according to the requirements of the prompt
- Sufficient number of facts, definitions, concrete details, and/or other information from the text as required by the prompt
- Complete sentences where errors do not impact readability

The features of a **1-point response** are:

- A mostly literal recounting of events or details from the text as required by the prompt
- Some relevant facts, definitions, concrete details, and/or other information from the text to develop response according to the requirements of the prompt
- Incomplete sentences or bullets

The features of a **0-point response** are:

- A response that does not address any of the requirements of the prompt or is totally inaccurate
- No response (blank answer)
- A response that is not written in English
- A response that is unintelligible or indecipherable

If the prompt requires two texts and the student references only one text, the response can be scored no higher than a 1.

Mid-Unit 1 Assessment

Analyzing Idea Development in Chapter 3 of *World Without Fish*
(Teacher Reference)

Part 1: Selected Response

Circle the best answer for each question below.

1. What are phytoplankton?
   A. Creatures of the sea that eat zooplankton
   B. Land-based plants that pollute the oceans
   C. **Microscopic plants that are the beginning of the ocean food chain**

2. How are zooplankton, one of the smallest forms of sea life, essential to a healthy ocean ecosystem?
   A. Zooplankton eat masses of phytoplankton.
   B. Zooplankton are food for several ocean species such as the herring and the humpback whale.
   C. Zooplankton become larva that turn into coral.
   D. **Zooplankton do all of the above**.

Part 2: Short Response

Answer the following questions using evidence from chapter 3 of the text.

A healthy ecosystem is based on the destruction of life and the struggles for survival among species, and it is in such systems that men in the form of fishermen are drawn to take part in the killing. Ninety percent of the fishing they do is within 200 miles of land. Farther out to sea, there is life and there are fish. But many of them live at great depths that have not been explored because until recently we didn't have the ability to reach that far below the surface.

3. How do fishermen take part in the "destruction of life" in the ocean? How do you know?
   Fishermen take part in the destruction of life by killing fish. I know this because it talks about them making money from bottom fish like haddock and middle fish like herring.

4. More recently, how are fishermen exploring life at sea?
   They are beginning to fish in deeper water and farther out, more than 200 miles from land.

5. How is the orange roughy different from other commercial fish such as haddock or cod?
   The orange roughy lives for about 150 years, which is longer than other fish. It grows very slowly and doesn't reproduce until it is much older than other fish.

6. The title of the chapter is, "Being the Sad, Cautionary Tale of the Orange Roughy." What is a "cautionary tale"? How is the story of the orange roughy a cautionary tale?

   A cautionary tale is a story that is warns the reader to be careful. And the story of how the orange roughy has almost been depleted is a warning about doing this to other fish species.

7. How does chapter 3 illustrate and elaborate on Kurlansky's message about fish depletion?

   Chapter 3 explains how fishermen are able to go farther and deeper out to sea to catch fish. It explains how this is very bad for orange roughy because fishermen didn't understand the fish's life cycle and almost fished it to extinction or depletion. So the chapter cautions fishermen to understand the deep ocean animals better before fishing them so they don't deplete those fish.

Structured Notes: "The Story of Kram and Ailat: Part 4"

Name: _____

Date: _____

Chapter	Homework Focus Question	Answer with Evidence from the Text (include page number)
_____	What do we learn about fishing from the graphic novel? How does Mark Kurlansky illustrate and elaborate the idea of fish depletion here?	

LESSON 7

Reading for Gist and Answering Text-Dependent Questions

Chapter 4 of *World Without Fish*

Long-Term Targets Addressed (Based on ELA CCSS)

- I can determine an author's point of view or purpose in an informational text. (RI.6.6)
- I can explain how an author's point of view is conveyed in an informational text. (RI.6.6)
- I can use a variety of strategies to determine word meaning in informational texts. (RI.6.4)

Supporting Learning Targets

- I can find the gist of an excerpt of chapter 4 of *World Without Fish*.
- I can determine the meaning of unfamiliar words and phrases in an excerpt of chapter 4.
- I can use evidence from the text to answer text-dependent questions.

Ongoing Assessment

- Structured Notes: "The Story of Kram and Ailat: Part 4" (from homework)
- Text-Dependent Questions: Pages 51–61

Agenda

1. Opening
   A. Engaging the Reader: Graphic Novel Part 4 (6 minutes)
   B. Unpacking Learning Targets (2 minutes)
2. Work Time
   A. Finding the Gist: Pages 51–61 (17 minutes)
   B. Text-Dependent Questions: Pages 51–61 (15 minutes)

3. Closing and Assessment
   A. Tracing the Development of an Idea (5 minutes)
4. Homework
   A. Reread the excerpt of chapter 4 that you read in class today. Use evidence flags to help you gather evidence to answer the focus question on your structured notes

Teaching Notes

- This lesson begins a two-lesson cycle during which students analyze Kurlansky's point of view (RI.6.6). The structure is similar to the lessons in the first part of this unit. The focus of this lesson is to help students dig deep into chapter 4 by reading for the gist and answering text-dependent questions to gain a deeper understanding of the text and prepare to analyze point of view in the next lesson.
- Be prepared to return the Mid-Unit 1 Assessment with teacher feedback to students in Lesson 8.
- Review:
  - Chapter 4 of *World Without Fish*.
  - Text-Dependent Questions: Pages 51–61 (Teacher Reference; see supporting materials).
  - Mix and Mingle protocol in Opening A.
- Post: learning targets; Graphic Novel: Tracing the Development of an Idea Anchor Chart; Tracing the Development of an Idea Anchor Chart.

Lesson Vocabulary

point of view, myth, bounty, misconception, indestructible, Darwinism, posthumously, refuted, influential, promoting, anatomy, staunch, commissions, class, unobservant, avocations, contempt, preservation, interfering, objecting, Industrial Revolution, diminution, exhaustion, scarce

Materials

- Structured Notes: "The Story of Kram and Ailat: Part 4" (from homework)
- Graphic Novel: Tracing the Development of an Idea Anchor Chart (begun in Lesson 4)
- Graphic Novel: Tracing the Development of an Idea Anchor Chart (Teacher Reference)
- *World Without Fish* (book; distributed in Lesson 1; one per student)
- Sticky notes (eight per student)
- Dictionaries (at least one per triad)
- *World Without Fish* Word-Catchers (begun in Lesson 1)
- Text-Dependent Questions: Pages 51–61 (one per student, one for display)
- Text-Dependent Questions: Pages 51–61 (Teacher Reference)

- Tracing the Development of an Idea Anchor Chart (begun in Lesson 2)
- Tracing the Development of an Idea Anchor Chart (Teacher Reference)
- Structured Notes: Pages 51–61 (one per student)

Opening

A. Engaging the Reader: Graphic Novel Part 4 (6 minutes)

- Remind students of the homework focus question: "What do we learn about fishing from the graphic novel? How does Mark Kurlansky illustrate and elaborate on the idea of fish depletion here?"
- Mix and Mingle:
  - Play music.
  - Invite students to move around the room with their **Structured Notes: "The Story of Kram and Ailat: Part 4"** homework.
  - Stop the music after 15 seconds.
  - Invite students to share their responses with the person standing closest to them.
  - Repeat two more time.
- Select volunteers to share their responses with the whole group. Listen for students to explain that he illustrates and elaborates on the idea by addressing it directly. Kram is interviewed about fish depletion on a talk show and while the presenter listens to some of what he says, he doesn't take it seriously. Instead he is mocked for a prediction he made previously.
- Record students' ideas on the posted **Graphic Novel: Tracing the Development of an Idea Anchor Chart**. See the **Graphic Novel: Tracing the Development of an Idea Anchor Chart (Teacher Reference)** as a guide.

Meeting Students' Needs

Opening the lesson by asking students to share their homework makes them accountable for completing it. It also gives you the opportunity to monitor which students are not doing their homework.

B. Unpacking Learning Targets (2 minutes)

- Invite students to read the learning targets aloud with you:
  - "I can find the gist of an excerpt of chapter 4 of *World Without Fish*."
  - "I can determine the meaning of unfamiliar words and phrases in an excerpt of chapter 4."
  - "I can use evidence from the text to answer text-dependent questions."

- Ask triads to briefly turn and talk:
  - "What are we going to be doing today? Why?"
- Cold-call on a student and listen for: "We are reading a new excerpt of *World Without Fish* for the gist and answering text-dependent questions in order to gain a deeper understanding of the text."

Meeting Students' Needs

- Learning targets are a research-based strategy that help all students, especially challenged learners.
- Posting learning targets allows students to reference them throughout the lesson to check their understanding. Learning targets also provide a reminder to students and teachers about the intended learning behind a given lesson or activity.
- Discussing and clarifying the language of learning targets helps build academic vocabulary.

Work Time

A. Finding the Gist: Pages 51–61 (17 minutes)

- Invite students to take out **World Without Fish** and turn to page 51, which is the first page of chapter 4. Invite students to read along silently as you read the page aloud. Ask students to discuss in triads:
  - "What is a myth?"
- Select volunteers to share their answers. Remind students of the work they did on myths in Module 1. Emphasize here that myth has two meanings. It can be a traditional story explaining something, or it can be a false belief or idea.
- Ask students to discuss in triads:
  - "What is a bounty?"
- Cold-call students to share their responses. Listen for them to explain that a bounty is a good thing that is given in large amounts.
- Ask students to discuss in triads:
  - "So what do you think the text means by 'the myth of nature's bounty'?"
- Cold-call students to share their responses. Listen for and guide students to understand that it means the false idea that nature is going to keep giving in large amounts.
- Ask students to discuss in triads:
  - "What is this chapter going to be about? How do you know?"
- Select volunteers to share their ideas with the whole group. Listen for students to explain that it is going to be about how people, including scientists, have falsely believed for a long time that nature is going to keep giving and giving.

- Remind students that good readers read complex texts multiple times to make sure they understand what is being written. Invite students to listen for the flow of the book and to follow along closely as you read the chapter aloud to the end of page 61.
- Ask students to discuss in triads:
  - "What is this chapter mostly about?"
- Cold-call students to share their responses. Listen for them to explain that it is mostly about how a scientist, Huxley, said that you can't overfish species. Many governments believed him and didn't control their fishing practices. Eventually, Huxley realized he was wrong.
- Invite a student to reread the first two learning targets aloud.
  - "I can find the gist of an excerpt of chapter 4 of *World Without Fish*."
  - "I can determine the meaning of unfamiliar words and phrases in an excerpt of chapter 4."
- Distribute eight **sticky notes** to each student. Remind students of the importance of summarizing smaller chunks of text as they read for the gist, and ask them to annotate the gist on sticky notes. Remind students to ask questions as they read to help them monitor comprehension. Explain that the goal is for them to understand the basic idea of this excerpt.
- Distribute **dictionaries** to each triad. Remind students that where possible, you would like them to read around unfamiliar words, looking for context clues to figure out what they mean; however, if they can't figure out the meaning from the context, encourage them to look the word up. If they aren't sure what the word means after looking for context clues and looking in the dictionary, they should leave the definition blank to be discussed with the whole group later.
- Invite students to work together as a triad to read for the gist, annotate sticky notes, and record unfamiliar words on their ***World Without Fish* Word-Catchers** as they reread pages 51–61 of chapter 4.
- Circulate and support students as they read. For those who need more support, ask them to practice telling you the gist of a section before they write it on a sticky note.
- As students finish up, refocus the whole group. Focus students on the word *indestructible* on page 53. Ask them to discuss in triads:
  - "If something is destructible, what does that mean?"
- Cold-call students to share their responses. Listen for them to explain that it means it can be destroyed.
- Ask students to discuss in triads:
  - "So what does the *in* prefix do to the word? How does it change the meaning?"
- Select volunteers to share their responses. Listen for them to explain that it makes the word have the opposite meaning. So instead of something that can be destroyed, *indestructible* means something that cannot be destroyed.
- Focus students on the word *Darwinism* on page 53. Remind students that they read about the ideas of Charles Darwin in Lesson 2 and that Darwinism means the ideas of Charles Darwin.

- Invite students to share any unfamiliar vocabulary words they found, along with the definition. If they were unable to work out the definition from the context or find it in a dictionary, encourage other students to assist them with the definition. To keep things moving, if no one else knows what the word means, define the word for the class.

- Students may struggle with these words, so be sure to address them here: *posthumously, refuted, influential, promoting, anatomy, staunch, commissions, class, unobservant, avocations, contempt, preservation, interfering, objecting, Industrial Revolution, diminution, exhaustion,* and *scarce*.

- If students are unable to work out the definition from the context or find it in a dictionary, encourage other students to assist them with the definition. To keep things moving, if no one else knows what the word means, define the word for the class.

- Remind students to record new words on their word-catchers.

B. Text-Dependent Questions: Pages 51–61 (15 minutes)

- Display and distribute **Text-Dependent Questions: Pages 51–61**. Remind students that the purpose of this is to dig deeper into the text to understand what Mark Kurlansky is saying.

- Invite students to read along with you as you read the learning target at the top of the handout and the questions in the first column aloud.

- Invite triads to work together to reread the text-dependent questions in column 1, review the excerpt of text, and discuss possible answers before recording their answers in column 2 using evidence from the text.

- Circulate and observe triads. Support students as needed by asking them to use only evidence from the excerpt to answer the questions. Refer to **Text-Dependent Questions: Pages 51–61 (Teacher Reference)** as needed.

Closing and Assessment

A. Tracing the Development of an Idea (5 minutes)

- Focus students' attention on the posted **Tracing the Development of an Idea Anchor Chart**. Ask students to discuss in triads:
  - "How does Kurlansky illustrate and elaborate on the idea of fish depletion in the excerpt you have read today?"

- Select volunteers to share their responses. Listen for them to explain that the author illustrates and elaborates on the idea by going back in history to explain why and how overfishing began, even though there were some warning signs.

- Record this on the **Tracing the Development of an Idea Anchor Chart. See Tracing the Development of an Idea Anchor Chart (Teacher Reference)** for guidance.

Meeting Students' Needs

Capturing student ideas on an anchor chart can ensure easy reference later and can enable students to see at a glance how an idea has developed through a text.

Homework

- Reread the excerpt of chapter 4 that you read in class today. Use evidence flags to help you gather evidence to answer this focus question on your **Structured Notes: Pages 51–61** worksheet:
  - "What does Mark Kurlansky think about Thomas Henry Huxley's ideas and the things he did in the late 19th century? Does he agree with him? Does he disagree with him? How do you know?"

Graphic Novel: Tracing the Development of an Idea Anchor Chart
(Teacher Reference)

What happens?	How is the idea of fish depletion introduced, illustrated, or elaborated on in the graphic novel?
Part 4: Kram is interviewed on a TV show, along with a man from government fishery management. They don't believe what he says about how bad fish depletion could be.	He illustrates and elaborates on the idea by addressing it directly. In the graphic novel, the character Kram talks directly about the implications of fish depletion.

Text-Dependent Questions: Pages 51–61

Name: _____

Date: _____

Learning target:

- "I can use evidence from the text to answer text-dependent questions."

Questions	Answers (supported with evidence from the text, include page numbers)
1. In the 1800s, who was afraid the fish populations could be destroyed—fishermen or scientists?	
2. What is "nature's bounty"?	
3. Why did scientists in the late 19th century think it was "impossible to destroy fish populations"?	
4. Why was this idea refuted by Darwin?	

Questions	Answers (supported with evidence from the text, include page numbers)
5. How did Huxley misunderstand Darwin?	
6. Why did the commissions to examine the fears of fish depletion reject what the fishermen were telling them?	
7. At the 1883 International Fisheries Exhibition, how did Huxley suggest we would know if fish were being depleted?	
8. What had many government officials and scientists failed to notice?	
9. Why did Huxley change his mind in the end?	

Text-Dependent Questions: Pages 51–61
(Teacher Reference)

Questions	Answers (supported with evidence from the text, include page numbers)
1. In the 1800s, who was afraid the fish populations could be destroyed—fishermen or scientists?	Fishermen. "In the 1800s, when the study of fish and oceans was a relatively new science, it was the fishermen who were afraid that fish populations could be destroyed by catching too many fish, especially small fish." (page 53)
2. What is "nature's bounty"?	Nature's bounty is "the belief that nature is such a powerful force that it is indestructible." (page 53)
3. Why did scientists in the late 19th century think it was "impossible to destroy fish populations"?	Because scientist Anton van Leeuwenhoek "counted 9,384,000 eggs in a single, average-sized fish," (page 54) people thought that if every fish had that many eggs and they all hatched, there would be plenty of fish regardless of how many were caught by fishermen.
4. Why was this idea refuted by Darwin?	Because "the reason nature provided fish with so many eggs is that few can survive in the sea . . . a fish will usually only have between one and six surviving babies, just like a mammal or a bird." (page 55)
5. How did Huxley misunderstand Darwin?	"He believed that Darwin's theory of survival proved that fish were indestructible." (page 56)
6. Why did the commissions to examine the fears of fish depletion reject what the fishermen were telling them?	They thought that the fishermen didn't have the scientific understanding to know what was going on. They also thought the fishermen were interfering in "the progress of technology." (page 58)

Questions	Answers (supported with evidence from the text, include page numbers)
7. At the 1883 International Fisheries Exhibition, how did Huxley suggest we would know if fish were being depleted?	". . . we would realize we were overfishing by the simple fact that we were hauling in fewer fish." (pages 58–59)
8. What had many government officials and scientists failed to notice?	"Many government officials and scientists had failed to notice that there was new technology being used with entirely new results." (page 60)
9. Why did Huxley change his mind in the end?	"Huxley himself, after studying the impact of engine-driven net draggers in the North Sea a few years later, completely reversed his beliefs. Overfishing, he acknowledged, was not only possible—it was happening." (pages 60–61)

Tracing the Development of an Idea Anchor Chart
(Teacher Reference)

Idea: Fish depletion

Chapter	How is the idea introduced, illustrated, or elaborated on in this chapter?
4	• He illustrates and elaborates on the idea by going back in history to explain why and how overfishing began, even though there were warning signs.

Structured Notes: Pages 51–61

Name: _____

Date: _____

Chapter	Homework Focus Question	Answer with Evidence from the Text (include page number)
_____	What does Mark Kurlansky think about Thomas Henry Huxley's ideas and the things he did in the late 19th century? Does he agree with him? Does he disagree with him? How do you know?	

LESSON 8

Analyzing Author's Point of View

Chapter 4 of *World Without Fish*

Long-Term Targets Addressed (Based on ELA CCSS)

- I can determine an author's point of view or purpose in an informational text. (RI.6.6)
- I can explain how an author's point of view is conveyed in an informational text. (RI.6.6)

Supporting Learning Targets

- I can analyze Mark Kurlansky's point of view in an excerpt of chapter 4 of *World Without Fish*.
- I can explain how he conveys his point of view.

Ongoing Assessment

- Structured Notes: Pages 51–61 (from homework)
- Author's Point of View Graphic Organizer: Pages 51–61
- Analyzing Author's Point of View Anchor Chart

Agenda

1. Opening
   A. Feedback from Mid-Unit 1 Assessment (4 minutes)
   B. Unpacking Learning Targets (4 minutes)
2. Work Time
   A. Think-Aloud: Analyzing Kurlansky's Point of View of Thomas Henry Huxley (10 minutes)
   B. Triad Work: Analyzing Kurlansky's Point of View of Thomas Henry Huxley (17 minutes)
3. Closing and Assessment
   A. Partner and Whole-Group Share (10 minutes)

4. Homework
   A. Read "The Story of Kram and Ailat: Part 5" (the graphic novel) at the end of chapter 4. Answer the focus question on your structured notes.

Teaching Notes

- This is the second lesson of the two-lesson cycle begun in Lesson 7. Students analyze the same excerpt they read for the gist in the previous lesson: pages 51–61 of *World Without Fish*. Now, students identify Kurlansky's point of view of Thomas Henry Huxley and how Kurlansky conveyed his point of view.
- There is a think-aloud and an opportunity for the class to work through an example together before triads work independently, but some students still may need further modeling and guidance. Modify the lesson as needed according to your students' needs.
- Working in triads to analyze Mark Kurlansky's point of view helps students gain confidence as they hear and discuss the ideas and thinking of others.
- In advance:
  - Ensure the Mid-Unit 1 Assessments are ready to return to students with feedback.
- Review:
  - Author's Point of View: Pages 51–61 (Teacher Reference; see supporting materials). Note that these are just suggestions. Students may have additional ideas.
- Post: learning targets.

Lesson Vocabulary

point of view, convey, infer

Materials

- Mid-Unit 1 Assessments with teacher feedback (completed in Lesson 6)
- Equity sticks
- *World Without Fish* Word-Catchers (begun in Lesson 1)
- Structured Notes: Pages 51–61 (from homework)
- Author's Point of View Graphic Organizer: Pages 51–61 (one per student, one for display)
- Highlighters (any color; one per student and one for the teacher)
- *World Without Fish* (book; distributed in Lesson 1; one per student)
- Author's Point of View Graphic Organizer: Pages 51–61 (Teacher Reference)
- Structured Notes: "The Story of Kram and Ailat: Part 5" (one per student)

Opening

A. Feedback from Mid-Unit 1 Assessment (4 minutes)

- Hand back the **Mid-Unit 1 Assessments with teacher feedback** and invite students to spend time reading your feedback.
- Invite students to write their name on the board if they have questions so you can follow up either immediately or later in the lesson.
- Name some patterns you noticed in students' work, particularly things the class did well.

B. Unpacking Learning Targets (4 minutes)

- Invite students to read the learning targets aloud with you:
  - "I can analyze Mark Kurlansky's point of view in an excerpt of chapter 4 of *World Without Fish*."
  - "I can explain how he conveys his point of view."
- Focus students on *point of view*. Ask triads to discuss:
  - "What does *point of view* mean?"
- Consider using **equity sticks** to select students to share their responses. Listen for them to explain that people have different ways of looking at things, and a person's point of view is his or her way of looking at things.
- Tell students that in literature, every story is told from a point of view. It can be a first-person point of view, where the narrator is the "I" or "me" telling the story; a third-person limited point of view, in which an author appears to know the thoughts and feelings of just one of the characters in a story; or a third-person omniscient point of view, in which an author captures the points of view of all the characters.
- Ask triads to discuss:
  - "What do you think *convey* means?"
- Select volunteers to share their responses. Listen for them to explain that *convey* means "communicates."
- Direct students to add *point of view* and *convey* to their **World Without Fish Word-Catchers**.

Meeting Students' Needs

- Posting learning targets allows students to reference them throughout the lesson to check their understanding. Learning targets also provide a reminder to students and teachers about the intended learning behind a given lesson or activity.
- Discussing and clarifying the language of learning targets helps build academic vocabulary.

Work Time

A. Think-Aloud: Analyzing Kurlansky's Point of View of Thomas Henry Huxley (10 minutes)

- Remind students that for homework they analyzed what Mark Kurlansky thinks of Thomas Henry Huxley's ideas and the things he did in the late nineteenth century. Invite students to share their thinking from their **Structured Notes: Pages 51–61** homework with their triads.

- Display and distribute the **Author's Point of View Graphic Organizer: Pages 51–61** and **highlighters** and ask students to take out their *World Without Fish* books. Invite students to read the column headings aloud with you. Ask:
  - "What do you notice?"
  - "What do you wonder?"

- Cold-call students to share their ideas with the whole group.

- Explain to students that you will model how to analyze this text for Kurlansky's point of view. First you will do a think-aloud, and then students will have time to practice as triads. Direct students to follow along and listen closely to your thought process, or how you analyze for point of view.

- The following is an example of a possible think-aloud with the first couple of paragraphs on page 56:
  - "My first step is to scan the excerpt of *World Without Fish* for where Kurlansky begins to talk about Huxley. I can see he starts talking about Huxley on page 56, so I'm going to read the first paragraph. Straight away from the first paragraph I know that Kurlansky thinks Huxley was influential and played an important role in helping people to accept Charles Darwin's ideas, so I'm going to record that in the first column of my graphic organizer."

- Record in the first column of the displayed organizer. **Refer to the Author's Point of View Graphic Organizer: Pages 51–61 (Teacher Reference)** for guidance. Continue the think-aloud:
  - "In the middle column I need to support my claim about his point of view with evidence from the text, or quotes."

- Record in the middle column of the displayed organizer. Refer to the Author's Point of View Graphic Organizer: Pages 51–61 (Teacher Reference) for guidance. Continue the think-aloud:
  - "The final column asks how Mark Kurlansky conveyed his point of view. The first direction asks me to highlight text clues. The words 'influential' and 'important role' are the parts of the paragraph that showed me his point of view. I'm going to use a highlighter to highlight those."

- Highlight those words on the displayed organizer. Refer to the Author's Point of View Graphic Organizer: Pages 51–61 (Teacher Reference) for guidance. Continue the think-aloud:
  - "The second instruction in the final column asks whether the words I have highlighted told me his point of view directly, or whether they led me to infer it. What does 'infer' mean?"

- Select students to share their responses. Listen for them to explain that infer means to use clues in evidence to make a claim.

- Point out that by using the words "influential" and "important role," Kurlansky tells us directly. Record this in the final column of the graphic organizer. Refer to the Author's Point of View Graphic Organizer: Pages 51–61 (Teacher Reference) for guidance. Continue the think-aloud:
  - "Now I'm going to move on to the next section of text, these words in bold, colored font."
- Reread the words in bold, colored font on page 56 aloud. Ask students to discuss in triads:
  - "What does this change in font tell you? What do the large, capital letters and the colors suggest?"
- Cold-call students to share their responses. Listen for them to explain that it suggests he wants to emphasize this information because it is particularly important in this chapter, that the capital letters suggest shock/disbelief, and that he is angry, as suggested by the use of the color red. Point out that often using all capital letters in a text is perceived as "shouting."
- Record a claim in the first column of the displayed graphic organizer. Refer to the Author's Point of View Graphic Organizer: Pages 51–61 (Teacher Reference) for guidance.
- Record the text evidence in the second column.
- Ask students to discuss in triads:
  - "In addition to the use of different sized and colored font, which words suggest the author's point of view?"
- Select volunteers to share their responses. Listen for them to suggest that the word "completely" in front of misunderstood really emphasizes the word, which makes him seem shocked or angry. Highlight those words in the middle column of the displayed organizer.
- Ask students to discuss in triads:
  - "Does he tell us directly that he is angry or shocked? Or do we use clues to infer it from the text? If so, how?"
- Cold-call students to share their responses. Listen for them to explain that we infer it from the large capital letters and the use of red font.

Meeting Students' Needs

- Providing models of expected work supports all learners, but especially supports challenged learners.
- When reviewing graphic organizers or recording forms, consider using a document camera to display the document for students who struggle with auditory processing.

B. Triad Work: Analyzing Kurlansky's Point of View of Thomas Henry Huxley (17 minutes)

- Invite students to engage with their triads in the same process you just modeled for the rest of the chapter. Remind students to take it paragraph by paragraph and explain that some paragraphs may not contain evidence of Mark Kurlansky's point of view, but they should discuss it as a triad before moving on to the next paragraph.

- Circulate to support triads as they work. Ask questions and refer to the Author's Point of View Graphic Organizer: Pages 51–61 (Teacher Reference) as needed to guide students. Ask:
  - "What words or text features led you to make that claim about his point of view?"

Meeting Students' Needs

Invite triads you think may struggle with this to focus on just pages 56 and 57.

Closing and Assessment

A. Partner and Whole-Group Share (10 minutes)

- Invite students to pair up with someone from another triad to share their answers and to make revisions/additions as they see fit (e.g., if their partner has a different idea that didn't come up in their own triad).
- Select volunteers to share their ideas with the whole group. Invite students to make revisions/additions based on the whole-group discussion as they see fit. Refer to the Author's Point of View Graphic Organizer: Pages 51–61 (Teacher Reference) for guidance.

Homework

- Read "The Story of Kram and Ailat: Part 5" (the graphic novel) at the end of chapter 4. Answer this focus question on your Structured Notes: "The Story of Kram and Ailat: Part 5" worksheet:
  - "What do we learn about fishing from the graphic novel? How does Mark Kurlansky illustrate and elaborate on the idea of fish depletion here?"

Author's Point of View Graphic Organizer: Pages 51–61

Name: _____

Date: _____

Learning targets:

- "I can analyze Mark Kurlansky's point of view in an excerpt of chapter 4 of *World Without Fish*."
- "I can explain how he conveys his point of view."

What is Mark Kurlansky's point of view of Thomas Henry Huxley's ideas and actions?	How do you know? (Quote specific words, phrases, and sentences.)	How does Mark Kurlansky convey his point of view? 1. Highlight the text clues in the middle column. 2. Note whether these text clues tell you directly or if they led you to infer Kurlansky's point of view.

What is Mark Kurlansky's point of view of Thomas Henry Huxley's ideas and actions?	How do you know? (Quote specific words, phrases, and sentences.)	How does Mark Kurlansky convey his point of view? 1. Highlight the text clues in the middle column. 2. Note whether these text clues tell you directly or if they led you to infer Kurlansky's point of view.

Author's Point of View Graphic Organizer: Pages 51–61

(Teacher Reference)

What is Mark Kurlansky's point of view of Thomas Henry Huxley's ideas and actions?	How do you know? (Quote specific words, phrases, and sentences.)	How does Mark Kurlansky convey his point of view? 1. Highlight the text clues in the middle column. 2. Note whether these text clues tell you directly or if they led you to infer Kurlansky's point of view.
1. He thought Huxley was an influential scientist who played an important role in helping people to accept the ideas of Charles Darwin.	"One of the most **influential** figures promoting the idea that it was impossible for fishermen to endanger fishing populations was Thomas Henry Huxley, a British scientist.... He was a staunch supporter of Darwin's theories and played an **important role** in the public acceptance of Darwin's theory of evolution." (page 56)	He says it directly.
2. He is shocked and angry that such an important scientist misunderstood Darwin's ideas in relation to fish.	"But on the subject of fish, Huxley **completely misunderstood** Darwin." (page 56)	Inferred from the use of powerful language and bold, large font in capital letters and two different colors in the middle of the page.

What is Mark Kurlansky's point of view of Thomas Henry Huxley's ideas and actions?	How do you know? (Quote specific words, phrases, and sentences.)	How does Mark Kurlansky convey his point of view? 1. Highlight the text clues in the middle column. 2. Note whether these text clues tell you directly or if they led you to infer Kurlansky's point of view.
3. He is dismayed at the way Huxley rejected what the fishermen were saying.	Huxley's reaction "established the **very harmful tradition** of showing **contempt** for the knowledge fishermen acquire through experience.... **The fact is that fishermen need to know almost everything about fish** in order to do a good job of catching them, and **no one has a deeper involvement** in or greater concern for the preservation of fish populations." (page 57)	Inferred from the use of language and the use of bold, large font in capital letters and two different colors in the middle of the page.
4. He is disappointed and angry that Huxley didn't understand Darwin's ideas.	"But Huxley had **overlooked an important part** of Darwin's findings, which was that the survival struggle of a species depended on maintaining a large population." (page 59)	Inferred from the use of language and the use of bold, large font in capital letters and two different colors in the middle of the page.
5. He is disappointed and angry that Huxley's ideas and actions had such an impact on fish depletion because governments and scientists listened to him for too long.	"Here was the **hidden trap**. Many government officials and scientists had **failed to notice** that there was new technology being used with entirely new results. They **held on** to the view Huxley and others ... shared **long after the reality of the situation indicated otherwise.**" (page 60)	Inferred from the use of language and the use of bold, large font in capital letters and two different colors.

Structured Notes: "The Story of Kram and Ailat: Part 5"

Name: _____

Date: _____

Chapter	Homework Focus Question	Answer with Evidence from the Text (include page number)
_____	What do we learn about fishing from the graphic novel? How does Mark Kurlansky illustrate and elaborate on the idea of fish depletion here?	

LESSON 9

Reading for Gist and Answering Text-Dependent Questions

Chapter 5 of *World Without Fish*

Long-Term Targets Addressed (Based on ELA CCSS)

- I can determine an author's point of view or purpose in an informational text. (RI.6.6)
- I can explain how an author's point of view is conveyed in an informational text. (RI.6.6)
- I can use a variety of strategies to determine word meaning in informational texts. (RI.6.4)

Supporting Learning Targets

- I can find the gist of pages 63–69 of *World Without Fish*.
- I can determine the meaning of unfamiliar words and phrases in pages 63–69 of *World Without Fish*.
- I can use evidence from the text to answer text-dependent questions.

Ongoing Assessment

- Structured Notes: "The Story of Kram and Ailat: Part 5" (from homework)
- Text-Dependent Questions: Pages 63–69

Agenda

1. Opening
   A. Engaging the Reader: Graphic Novel Part 5 (6 minutes)
   B. Unpacking Learning Targets (2 minutes)
2. Work Time
   A. Finding the Gist: Pages 63–69 (17 minutes)
   B. Text-Dependent Questions: Pages 63–69 (15 minutes)

3. Closing and Assessment
   A. Tracing the Development of an Idea (5 minutes)
4. Homework
   A. Reread the excerpt of chapter 5 that you read in class today (pages 63–69). Use evidence flags to help you gather evidence to answer the focus question on your structured notes.

Teaching Notes

- This lesson is the start of a new two-lesson cycle—very similar to the cycle in Lessons 7 and 8—in which students analyze Mark Kurlansky's point of view (RI.6.6). The focus of this lesson is to help students dig deep into pages 63–69 of the text by reading for the gist and answering text-dependent questions to gain a deeper understanding of the text and prepare to analyze point of view in the next lesson.
- As students are now more familiar with the structure of these lessons, in order to gradually release them in this lesson, they work independently to answer text-dependent questions.
- In Lesson 10 students will do a whole-group critique of a completed point of view graphic organizer. Begin to consider which students may be suitable candidates for this process and would be willing to do so.
- Review:
  - Text-Dependent Questions: Pages 63–69 (Teacher Reference; see supporting materials).
- Post: learning targets; Graphic Novel: Tracing the Development of an Idea Anchor Chart; Tracing the Development of an Idea Anchor Chart.

Lesson Vocabulary

politics, compensates, foreigners, rational, neglected, Viking, lava-encrusted, debate, intensified, economy, glaciers

Materials

- Structured Notes: "The Story of Kram and Ailat: Part 5" (from homework)
- Graphic Novel: Tracing the Development of an Idea Anchor Chart (begun in Lesson 4)
- Graphic Novel: Tracing the Development of an Idea Anchor Chart (Teacher Reference)
- *World Without Fish* (book; distributed in Lesson 1; one per student)
- Sticky notes (eight per student)
- Dictionaries (at least one per triad)
- *World Without Fish* Word-Catchers (students' own; from Lesson 1)
- Text-Dependent Questions: Pages 63–69 (one per student, one for display)

- Text-Dependent Questions: Pages 63–69 (Teacher Reference)
- Tracing the Development of an Idea Anchor Chart (begun in Lesson 2)
- Tracing the Development of an Idea Anchor Chart (Teacher Reference)
- Structured Notes: Pages 63–69 (one per student)

Opening

A. Engaging the Reader: Graphic Novel Part 5 (6 minutes)

- Remind students of the homework focus question: "What do we learn about fishing from the graphic novel? How does Mark Kurlansky illustrate and elaborate on the idea of fish depletion here?"
- Invite students to refer to their **Structured Notes: "The Story of Kram and Ailat: Part 5"** homework and discuss the answers with their triads.
- Select volunteers to share their responses with the whole group. Listen for students to explain that the author illustrates and elaborates on the idea by talking about the impact of fish depletion on other species like seabirds and crabs.
- Record students' ideas on the posted **Graphic Novel: Tracing the Development of an Idea Anchor Chart**. See the **Graphic Novel: Tracing the Development of an Idea Anchor Chart (Teacher Reference)** as a guide.

Meeting Students' Needs

Opening the lesson by asking students to share their homework makes them accountable for completing it. It also gives you the opportunity to monitor which students are not doing their homework.

B. Unpacking Learning Targets (2 minutes)

- Invite students to read the learning targets aloud with you:
  - "I can find the gist of pages 63–69 of *World Without Fish*."
  - "I can determine the meaning of unfamiliar words and phrases in pages 63–69 of *World Without Fish*."
  - "I can use evidence from the text to answer text-dependent questions."
- Ask triads to briefly turn and talk:
  - "What are we going to be doing today? Why?"
- Cold-call on a student and listen for: "We are reading a new excerpt of *World Without Fish* for the gist and answering text-dependent questions to gain a deeper understanding of the text."

Meeting Students' Needs

- Learning targets are a research-based strategy that helps all students, especially challenged learners.
- Posting learning targets allows students to reference them throughout the lesson to check their understanding. Learning targets also provide a reminder to students and teachers about the intended learning behind a given lesson or activity.
- Discussing and clarifying the language of learning targets helps build academic vocabulary.

Work Time

A. Finding the Gist: Pages 63–69 (17 minutes)

- Invite students to take out **World Without Fish** and turn to page 63, which is the first page of chapter 5. Invite students to follow along silently as you read the page aloud. Ask students to discuss in triads:
    - "What does *politics* mean?"
- Select volunteers to share their answers. Listen for and guide students to understand that it means activities related to the actions and policies of the government—the people who run a country.
- Ask students to discuss in triads:
    - "So what is this chapter going to be about? How do you know?"
- Select volunteers to share their ideas with the whole group. Listen for them to explain that it is going to be about the laws and rules about fish.
- Invite students to listen for the flow of the book and to follow along closely as you read the chapter aloud to the end of page 69.
- Ask students to discuss in triads:
    - "What is this excerpt mostly about?"
- Cold-call students to share their responses. Listen for students to explain that it is mostly about other countries overfishing and causing fish depletion in Iceland.
- Invite a student to reread the first two learning targets aloud.
    - "I can find the gist of pages 63–69 of *World Without Fish*."
    - "I can determine the meaning of unfamiliar words and phrases on pages 63–69 of *World Without Fish*."
- Distribute eight **sticky notes** to each student. Remind students of the importance of summarizing smaller chunks of text as they read for the gist, and ask them to annotate the gist on sticky notes. Remind students to ask questions as they read to help them monitor comprehension. Explain that the goal is for them to understand the basic idea of this excerpt.

- Distribute **dictionaries** to each triad. Remind students that where possible you would like them to read around unfamiliar words, looking for context clues to figure out what they mean; however, if they can't figure out the meaning from the context, encourage them to use a dictionary. If they aren't sure what the word means after looking for context clues and looking in the dictionary, they should leave the definition blank to be discussed with the whole group later.
- Invite students to work together as a triad to read for the gist, annotate sticky notes, and record unfamiliar words on their *World Without Fish* **Word-Catchers** as they reread pages 63–69 of chapter 5.
- Circulate and support students as they read. For those who need more support, ask them to practice telling you the gist of a section before they write it on a sticky note.
- As students finish up, refocus the whole group. Focus students on the word *intensified* on page 68. Invite students to discuss in triads:
  - "What does the word *intense* mean?"
- Select students to share their responses with the whole group. Listen for students to explain that it means of great force or strength.
- Focus students on the *ified* at the end of the word. Write the word *intensify* on the board and underline the *fy*. Tell students that this suffix means *to make* or *to cause to be*. So intensify means to make more intense or to cause to be more intense.
- Remind students that the *ed* makes the word past tense. Invite students to discuss in triads:
  - "What does the word *intensified* mean?"
- Cold-call students to share their responses with the whole group and listen for students to explain that intensified means made more intense.
- Invite students to share any unfamiliar vocabulary words they found, along with the definition. If they were unable to work out the definition from the context or find it in a dictionary, encourage other students to assist them with the definition. To keep things moving, if no one else knows, define the word for the class.
- Students may struggle with these words, so be sure to address them here: *compensates*, *foreigners*, *rational*, *neglected*, *Viking*, *lava-encrusted*, *debate*, *economy*, and *glaciers*.
- If students are unable to work out the definition from the context or find it in a dictionary, encourage other students to assist them with the definition. To keep things moving, if no one else knows, define the word for the class.
- Remind students to record new words on their word-catchers.

Meeting Students' Needs

- Hearing a complex text read slowly, fluently, and without interruption or explanation promotes fluency for students. They are hearing a strong reader read the text aloud with accuracy and expression and are simultaneously looking at and thinking about the words on the printed page. Be sure to set clear expectations that students read along silently in their heads as you read the text aloud.

- Allow students to grapple with a complex text before explicit teaching of vocabulary. After students have read for the gist, they can identify challenging vocabulary for themselves.
- Asking students to identify challenging vocabulary helps them monitor their understanding of a complex text. When students annotate the text by circling these words, it can also provide a formative assessment for the teacher.

B. Text-Dependent Questions: Pages 63–69 (15 minutes)

- Display and distribute **Text-Dependent Questions: Pages 63–69**. Remind students that the purpose of this is to dig deeper into the text to understand what Mark Kurlansky is saying.
- Invite students to follow along as you read aloud the learning target at the top of the handout and the questions in the first column.
- Invite students to work independently to reread the text-dependent questions in column 1 and review the excerpt of text before recording their answers to the questions in column 2, using evidence from the text.
- Circulate and observe triads working. Support students as needed by asking them to use only evidence from the excerpt to answer the questions. For answers, refer to the **Text-Dependent Questions: Pages 63–69 (Teacher Reference)**.

Meeting Students' Needs

Asking students to discuss challenging questions before recording them helps to ensure that all students have an idea about what to write and can give students confidence in their responses.

Closing and Assessment

A. Tracing the Development of an Idea (5 minutes)

- Focus students' attention to the posted **Tracing the Development of an Idea Anchor Chart**. Ask them to discuss in triads:
  - "How does Kurlansky illustrate and elaborate on the idea of fish depletion in the excerpt you have read today?"
- Select volunteers to share their responses. Listen for them to explain that he illustrates and elaborates on the idea by providing examples of politics in the fishing industry in different parts of the world.
- Record this on the Tracing the Development of an Idea Anchor Chart. See **Tracing the Development of an Idea Anchor Chart (Teacher Reference)** for guidance.

Homework

- Reread the excerpt of chapter 5 that you read in class today (pages 63–69). Use evidence flags to help you gather evidence to answer this focus question on your **Structured Notes: Pages 63–69** worksheet:

    - "What does Mark Kurlansky think about fishermen around the world? How do you know?"

Graphic Novel: Tracing the Development of an Idea Anchor Chart
(Teacher Reference)

What happens?	How is the idea of fish depletion introduced, illustrated, or elaborated on in the graphic novel?
Part 5: Kram and Ailat go out on another fishing trip with Serrafino, who is using a different net because there aren't any fish on the bottom to catch anymore. He points out that there aren't any seabirds, and when they get back to land Ailat goes looking for crabs but can't find any.	*He illustrates and elaborates on the idea by introducing the idea of the impact of fish depletion on other species like seabirds and crabs.*

Text-Dependent Questions: Pages 63–69

Name: _____

Date: _____

Learning target:

- "I can use evidence from the text to answer text-dependent questions."

Questions	Answers (supported with evidence from the text, include page numbers)
1. Why did the argument about overfishing end in the 1990s on the Grand Banks?	
2. Why were the fish getting smaller?	
3. Who was most concerned about the problem?	
4. Who do fishermen blame for the problem?	
5. Who did William Hooper blame first for overfishing?	

Questions	Answers (supported with evidence from the text, include page numbers)
6. Who did he blame next when he was told the first group couldn't be responsible?	
7. According to Mark Kurlansky, who were the first foreigners to start fishing in Iceland?	
8. What was the debate in Iceland?	
9. What did they decide?	
10. How did the British respond?	
11. What happened in Iceland and around the world as a result?	

Text-Dependent Questions: Pages 63–69
(Teacher Reference)

Questions	Answers (supported with evidence from the text, include page numbers)
1. Why did the argument about overfishing end in the 1990s on the Grand Banks?	Because fishermen started to see the effects of overfishing: "1. They had to travel greater distances to find the same amount of fish they used to find so close to shore. 2. The fish were getting smaller." (Page 65)
2. Why were the fish getting smaller?	"... since the big fish that produce the most eggs are also the easiest to catch they get taken first, leaving a population of small fish behind. Nature also compensates for a shortage of food by making fish grow more slowly." (Page 65)
3. Who was most concerned about the problem?	The fishermen. "Once again, it was the fishermen and not the scientists who were expressing the most concern about the size of the fish and the distances needed to travel in order to catch them." (Page 65)
4. Who do fishermen blame for the problem?	Other fishermen in other countries. "Most fishermen in the world, no matter where they live, will say that the worst fishing practices are those done by foreigners." (Page 65)
5. Who did William Hooper blame first for overfishing?	The Spanish. "The biggest problem we have is the Spanish." (Page 66)
6. Who did he blame next when he was told the first group couldn't be responsible?	The Scottish. "Yes, the Scots used to overfish." (Page 67)
7. According to Mark Kurlansky, who were the first foreigners to start fishing in Iceland?	The English. "In the 1890s, however, modern, steel-hulled, engine-powered fishing boats from England started dragging their enormous nets through Icelandic waters." (Page 67)

Questions	Answers (supported with evidence from the text, include page numbers)
8. What was the debate in Iceland?	Whether the English fishing boats should stay or if they should get some boats of their own: "there was a debate in Iceland between those who thought these boats should be kept out of their waters and those who thought Iceland should get a few of their own." (Page 68)
9. What did they decide?	They asked the English to leave. "And so they asked the foreign fishermen to leave." (Page 69)
10. How did the British respond?	They attacked the Icelandic Coast Guard. "The British Royal Navy attacked the Icelandic Coast Guard, which protected their water." (Page 69)
11. What happened in Iceland and around the world as a result?	Iceland established a 200-mile zone around their territories, and other countries did the same thing. "But once the Icelanders had their 200-mile limit, the other nations of the world wanted theirs. Countries began measuring 200 miles from every farthest rock they could claim." (Page 69)

Tracing the Development of an Idea Anchor Chart
(Teacher Reference)

Idea: Fish depletion

Chapter	How is the idea introduced, illustrated, or elaborated on in this chapter?
5	• **He illustrates and elaborates on the idea by providing examples of politics in the fishing industry in different parts of the world.**

Structured Notes: Pages 63–69

Name: _____

Date: _____

Chapter	Homework Focus Question	Answer with Evidence from the Text (include page number)
_____	What does Mark Kurlansky think about fishermen around the world? How do you know?	

LESSON 10

Analyzing Author's Point of View
Chapter 5 of World Without Fish

Long-Term Targets Addressed (Based on ELA CCSS)

- I can determine an author's point of view or purpose in an informational text. (RI.6.6)
- I can explain how an author's point of view is conveyed in an informational text. (RI.6.6)

Supporting Learning Targets

- I can analyze Mark Kurlansky's point of view in an excerpt of chapter 5.
- I can explain how he conveys his point of view.

Ongoing Assessment

- Structured Notes: Pages 63–69 (from homework)
- Author's Point of View Graphic Organizer: Pages 63–69

Agenda

1. Opening
   A. Unpacking Learning Targets (2 minutes)
2. Work Time
   A. Analyzing Kurlansky's Point of View of Fishermen (30 minutes)
   B. Triad and Whole-Group Critique (10 minutes)
3. Closing and Assessment
   A. Self-Assessment (3 minutes)
4. Homework
   A. Read "The Story of Kram and Ailat: Part 6" (the graphic novel) at the end of chapter 5. Answer the focus question on your structured notes.

Teaching Notes

- This is the second of the two-lesson cycle started in Lesson 9. Students analyze the same excerpt they read for the gist in the previous lesson: pages 63–69 of *World Without Fish*. In this lesson, students identify Kurlansky's point of view of fishermen and how he conveyed his point of view.

- In order to gradually prepare for the end-of-unit assessment in the next lesson, students work independently to complete their point of view graphic organizer in this lesson.

- Students also perform a whole-group critique of a completed graphic organizer to help them improve their work and their understanding of the process of analyzing point of view. Ensure this is done carefully and sensitively—invite a volunteer who would like to share his or her work and make it clear what the student is volunteering for. Ensure that the focus is on how to improve, rather than what is wrong with the work. The suggested questions in Work Time B help to make it a positive learning experience.

- Review:
  - Author's Point of View: Pages 63–69 (Teacher Reference; see supporting materials). Please note that these are just suggestions. Students may have additional ideas.
  - Review Fist-to-Five in Checking for Understanding techniques (see Appendix).
- Post: learning targets.

Lesson Vocabulary

point of view, convey, infer

Materials

- Structured Notes: Pages 63–69 (from homework)
- Author's Point of View Graphic Organizer: Pages 63–69 (one per student)
- *World Without Fish* (book; distributed in Lesson 1; one per student)
- Highlighters (any color; one per student)
- Author's Point of View Graphic Organizer: Pages 63–69 (Teacher Reference)
- Structured Notes: "The Story of Kram and Ailat: Part 6" (one per student)

Opening

A. Unpacking Learning Targets (2 minutes)

- Invite students to read the learning targets aloud with you:
  - "I can analyze Mark Kurlansky's point of view in an excerpt of chapter 5."
  - "I can explain how he conveys his point of view."
- Remind students of what *point of view*, *convey*, and *infer* mean.

Meeting Students' Needs

- Posting learning targets allows students to reference them throughout the lesson to check their understanding. Learning targets also provide a reminder to students and teachers about the intended learning behind a given lesson or activity.
- Discussing and clarifying the language of learning targets helps build academic vocabulary.

Work Time

A. Analyzing Kurlansky's Point of View of Fishermen (30 minutes)

- Remind students that for homework they analyzed Mark Kurlansky's point of view of fishermen. Invite students to share their thinking with their triads using their **Structured Notes: Pages 63–69** homework.
- Distribute the **Author's Point of View Graphic Organizer: Pages 63–69** and ask students to take out their *World Without Fish* texts. Remind students that they filled in the same organizer in Lesson 8 using an excerpt from chapter 4. Invite students to read the column headings with you.
- Point out that to get them started there are already two claims, which they need to complete with evidence from the text and by explaining how the author conveys his point of view.
- Tell students you want them to work independently this time, taking pages 63–69 one paragraph at a time and analyzing for point of view, recording their ideas on the graphic organizer. Remind students that some paragraphs may not contain evidence of Mark Kurlansky's point of view, so they can continue reading if that is the case.
- Distribute **highlighters** and circulate to support students as they work. Ask guiding questions and refer to the **Author's Point of View Graphic Organizer: Pages 63–69 (Teacher Reference)** to guide students:
    - "What words or text features led you to make that claim about his point of view?"

Meeting Students' Needs

- Providing models of expected work supports all learners, but especially supports challenged learners.
- When reviewing graphic organizers or recording forms, consider using a document camera to display the document for students who struggle with auditory processing.

B. Triad and Whole-Group Critique (10 minutes)

- Invite students to get into their triads to share their answers and to make revisions/additions as they think necessary.

- Invite a volunteer to share his or her work with the whole group for a critique. Take each part of the organizer one claim at a time and invite students to help you make suggestions to improve the work. Ask students:
  - "Does this quote support the claim?"
  - "Are there any other words you would highlight here?"
  - "Would you add anything to this explanation about how the author conveys his point of view?"
- Refer to the Author's Point of View Graphic Organizer: Pages 63–69 (Teacher Reference) to make suggestions to improve student work.

Closing and Assessment

A. Self-Assessment (3 minutes)

- Read each learning target. Invite students to show a Fist-to-Five for how confident they feel about each one. Make a note of those students who are still unsure and be sure to make time to address their concerns before the assessment in the next lesson.
- Preview homework and distribute the structured notes.

Homework

- Read "The Story of Kram and Ailat: Part 6" (the graphic novel) at the end of chapter 5. Answer this focus question on your **Structured Notes: "The Story of Kram and Ailat: Part 6"** worksheet:
  - "What do we learn about fishing from the graphic novel? How does Mark Kurlansky illustrate and elaborate on the idea of fish depletion here?"

Author's Point of View Graphic Organizer: Pages 63–69

Name: _____

Date: _____

Learning targets:

- "I can analyze Mark Kurlansky's point of view in an excerpt of chapter 5."
- "I can explain how the text evidence conveys his point of view."

What is Mark Kurlansky's point of view of fishermen?	How do you know? (Quote specific words, phrases, and sentences.)	How does the text evidence convey Kurlansky's point of view? 1. Highlight the text clues in the middle column. 2. Note whether these text clues tell you directly or if they led you to infer Kurlansky's point of view.
1. He is smug/proud that the fishermen were right.		
2. He is frustrated and disappointed that fishermen still blame others.		

What is Mark Kurlansky's point of view of fishermen?	How do you know? (Quote specific words, phrases, and sentences.)	How does the text evidence convey Kurlansky's point of view? 1. Highlight the text clues in the middle column. 2. Note whether these text clues tell you directly or if they led you to infer Kurlansky's point of view.

Author's Point of View Graphic Organizer: Pages 63–69
(Teacher Reference)

What is Mark Kurlansky's point of view of fishermen?	How do you know? (Quote specific words, phrases, and sentences.)	How does the text evidence convey Kurlansky's point of view? 1. Highlight the text clues in the middle column. 2. Note whether these text clues tell you directly or if they led you to infer Kurlansky's point of view.
1. He is smug/proud that the fishermen were right.	"**Once again**, it was the fishermen and not the scientists where were expressing concern." (page 65)	The use of the words "once again" shows a sense of smugness and pride.
2. He is frustrated and disappointed that fishermen still blame others.	"The **only problem** was that most fishermen thought of overfishing as something that was done by fishermen in other countries. **Even today**, most fishermen in the world, no matter where they live, will say the worst fishing practices are those done by foreigners." (page 65)	Inferred from the words "the only problem," which suggests a sense of frustration and disappointment.
3. He seems almost amused that fishermen blame each other.	"**His answer was clear:** 'The biggest problem we have is the Spanish.'… which meant they couldn't have been responsible for the overfishing in his water, he thought in silence for a moment and then said: 'Yes, the Scots used to overfish.'" (pages 66 and 67)	Inferred from the words "His answer was clear," which sounds almost mocking.

What is Mark Kurlansky's point of view of fishermen?	How do you know? (Quote specific words, phrases, and sentences.)	How does the text evidence convey Kurlansky's point of view? 1. Highlight the text clues in the middle column. 2. Note whether these text clues tell you directly or if they led you to infer Kurlansky's point of view.
4. He is angry with the English fishermen because he feels bad for the hardships faced by the Icelandic people and the Icelandic fishermen.	"But Iceland is an unusual place: an island of volcanoes and glaciers in a **harsh climate** where neither trees nor grains will grow, and **children took a small piece of cod to school for a snack because there was no bread for sandwiches**. One of their few natural resources was their sea full of fish, and they **could not risk losing their main food supply**." (page 68)	*Inferred because he highlights the hardships faced by the Icelandic people after explaining how the English moved in to fish in their waters. The large and colored font in capital letters emphasizes this at the end of the quote.*
5. He thought the British fishermen were unfair to the Icelandic people.	"The British, **although they were trying to do the same thing to other Europeans in their own waters**, claimed that having their fishing boats banned from Icelandic waters was an act of war." (page 69)	*Inferred by mentioning that the British were trying to do the same thing themselves.*

Structured Notes: "The Story of Kram and Ailat: Part 6"

Name: _____

Date: _____

Chapter	Homework Focus Question	Answer with Evidence from the Text (include page number)
_____	What do we learn about fishing from the graphic novel? How does Mark Kurlansky illustrate and elaborate on the idea of fish depletion here?	

LESSON 11

End-of-Unit 1 Assessment

Analyzing Author's Point of View and How It Is Conveyed

Long-Term Targets Addressed (Based on ELA CCSS)

- I can determine an author's point of view or purpose in an informational text. (RI.6.6)
- I can explain how an author's point of view is conveyed in an informational text. (RI.6.6)

Supporting Learning Targets

- I can identify Mark Kurlansky's point of view.
- I can explain how Mark Kurlansky conveys his point of view.

Ongoing Assessment

- Structured Notes: "The Story of Kram and Ailat: Part 6" (from homework)
- End-of-Unit 1 Assessment: Analyzing Author's Point of View and How It Is Conveyed in Chapter 5 of *World Without Fish*
- Optional Supplementary Assessment Items

Agenda

1. Opening
    A. Engaging the Reader: Graphic Novel Part 6 (6 minutes)
    B. Unpacking Learning Targets (2 minutes)
2. Work Time
    A. End-of-Unit 1 Assessment (32 minutes)
3. Closing and Assessment
    A. Tracing the Development of an Idea (5 minutes)
4. Homework
    A. None.

Teaching Notes

- This lesson is the End-of-Unit 1 Assessment. Students repeat what they have been practicing over the past few lessons in analyzing point of view with a new excerpt of text: pages 70–75 from chapter 5 of *World Without Fish*.
- Assess student responses using the Grade 6 2-Point Rubric—Short Response.
- Post: learning targets; Graphic Novel: Tracing the Development of an Idea Anchor Chart; Tracing the Development of an Idea Anchor Chart.

Lesson Vocabulary

Do not preview vocabulary.

Materials

- Structured Notes: "The Story of Kram and Ailat: Part 6" (from homework)
- Graphic Novel: Tracing the Development of an Idea Anchor Chart (begun in Lesson 4)
- Graphic Novel: Tracing the Development of an Idea Anchor Chart (Teacher Reference)
- End-of-Unit 1 Assessment: Analyzing Author's Point of View and How It Is Conveyed in Chapter 5 of *World Without Fish* (one per student; one for display)
- Sticky notes (eight per student)
- Highlighters (any color; one per student)
- *World Without Fish* (book; distributed in Lesson 1; one per student)
- End-of-Unit 1 Assessment: Analyzing Author's Point of View and How It Is Conveyed in Chapter 5 of *World Without Fish* (Teacher Reference)
- Grade 6 2-Point Rubric—Short Response (Teacher Reference)
- Tracing the Development of an Idea Anchor Chart (begun in Lesson 2)
- Tracing the Development of an Idea Anchor Chart (Teacher Reference)

Opening

A. Engaging the Reader: Graphic Novel Part 6 (6 minutes)

- Remind students of the homework focus question: "What do we learn about fishing from the graphic novel? How does Mark Kurlansky illustrate and elaborate on the idea of fish depletion here?"
- Invite students to refer to their **Structured Notes: "The Story of Kram and Ailat: Part 6"** homework and discuss their answers with their triads.

- Select volunteers to share their responses with the whole group. Listen for them to explain that the author illustrates and elaborates on the idea by returning to an idea discussed in an earlier part of the graphic novel and describing how overfishing had impacts in the ocean and on land.
- Record students' ideas on the posted **Graphic Novel: Tracing the Development of an Idea Anchor Chart**. See the **Graphic Novel: Tracing the Development of an Idea Anchor Chart (Teacher Reference)** as a guide.

Meeting Students' Needs

- Opening the lesson by asking students to share their homework makes them accountable for completing it. It also gives you the opportunity to monitor which students are not doing their homework.
- Capturing students' ideas on an anchor chart can ensure easy reference later and can enable students to see at a glance how an idea has developed through a text.

B. Unpacking Learning Targets (2 minutes)

- Invite students to read the learning targets aloud with you:
    - "I can identify Mark Kurlansky's point of view."
    - "I can explain how Mark Kurlansky conveys his point of view."
- Remind students that these are similar to the learning targets they have been working with for the past several lessons. Tell them that today they will show how well they can demonstrate these targets independently in an assessment.

Meeting Students' Needs

Posting learning targets allows students to reference them throughout the lesson to check their understanding. Learning targets also provide a reminder to students and teachers about the intended learning behind a given lesson or activity.

Work Time

A. End-of-Unit 1 Assessment (32 minutes)

- Distribute an **End-of-Unit 1 Assessment: Analyzing Author's Point of View and How It Is Conveyed** to each student, along with **sticky notes** and **highlighters**. Remind students they will also need their text *World Without Fish*.
- Invite students to read through the questions with you:
    - "Read pages 70–75 of *World Without Fish* for the gist from 'Some governments . . .' on page 70 to the end of page 75. It is optional for you to use the sticky notes to annotate the gist as you read."

- - "Analyze the excerpt for Mark Kurlansky's point of view of the Great Banks codfish situation, one paragraph at a time, and complete the point of view graphic organizer as you have in previous lessons. Provide at least three examples of his point of view of the Great Banks codfish situation."
- Remind students that the graphic organizer on the assessment handout is similar to the one they have been using to analyze point of view in previous lessons.
- Remind the class that because this is an assessment, it is to be completed independently. However, if students need assistance, they should raise a hand to speak with a teacher.
- Circulate and support students as they work. During an assessment, your prompting should be minimal.
- At the conclusion of the allotted time, collect the End-of-Unit 1 Assessment, which you will assess using the **End-of-Unit 1 Assessment: Analyzing Author's Point of View and How It Is Conveyed (Teacher Reference)** and the **Grade 6 2-Point Rubric—Short Response**.
- Congratulate students on their hard work during the assessment and throughout the unit.

Meeting Students' Needs

If students receive accommodations for assessment, communicate with the cooperating service providers regarding the practices of instruction in use during this study, as well as the goals of the assessment.

Closing and Assessment

A. Tracing the Development of an Idea (5 minutes)

- Focus students' attention on the posted **Tracing the Development of an Idea Anchor Chart**. Ask students to discuss in triads:
  - "How does Kurlansky illustrate and elaborate on the idea of fish depletion in the excerpt you have read today?"
- Select volunteers to share their responses. Listen for them to explain that he illustrates and elaborates on the idea by providing an example of fish depletion that could have been avoided.
- Record this on the Tracing the Development of an Idea Anchor Chart. See **Tracing the Development of an Idea Anchor Chart (Teacher Reference)** for a model.

Meeting Students' Needs

Capturing students' ideas on an anchor chart can ensure easy reference later and can enable students to see at a glance how an idea has developed through a text.

Homework

- None

Graphic Novel: Tracing the Development of an Idea Anchor Chart
(Teacher Reference)

What happens?	How is the idea of fish depletion introduced, illustrated, or elaborated on in the graphic novel?
Part 6: Kram and Ailat return to the Caribbean, where everything has changed because of overfishing. As Kram predicted, algae has overtaken the area because the fish that ate it have been depleted.	*He illustrates and elaborates on the idea by returning to an idea discussed in an earlier part of the graphic novel and describing how overfishing had impacts in the ocean and on land.*

End-of-Unit 1 Assessment

Analyzing Author's Point of View and How It Is Conveyed in Chapter 5 of *World Without Fish*

Name: _____

Date: _____

Long-Term Learning Targets Assessed

- "I can identify Mark Kurlansky's point of view."
- "I can explain how Mark Kurlansky conveys his point of view."

One of the features that makes Mark Kurlansky's book *World Without Fish* interesting is his expression of his point of view. Through his use of text features and descriptive language, we come to know his point of view on issues related to fish depletion.

Directions

1. Read pages 70–75 of *World Without Fish* for the gist from "Some governments . . ." on page 70 to the end of page 75. It is optional for you to use the sticky notes to annotate the gist as you read.

2. Analyze the excerpt for Mark Kurlansky's point of view of the Great Banks codfish situation, one paragraph at a time, and complete the point of view graphic organizer as you have in previous lessons. Provide at least three examples of his point of view of the Great Banks codfish situation.

What is Mark Kurlansky's point of view of the Great Banks codfish situation?	How do you know? (Quote specific words, phrases, and sentences.)	How does the text evidence convey Kurlansky's point of view? 1. Highlight the text clues in the middle column. 2. Note whether these text clues tell you directly or if they led you to infer Kurlansky's point of view.

What is Mark Kurlansky's point of view of the Great Banks codfish situation?	How do you know? (Quote specific words, phrases, and sentences.)	How does the text evidence convey Kurlansky's point of view? 1. Highlight the text clues in the middle column. 2. Note whether these text clues tell you directly or if they led you to infer Kurlansky's point of view.

End-of-Unit 1 Assessment

Analyzing Author's Point of View and How It Is Conveyed in Chapter 5 of *World Without Fish*

(Teacher Reference)

What is Mark Kurlansky's point of view of the Great Banks codfish situation?	How do you know? (Quote specific words, phrases, and sentences.)	How does the text evidence convey Kurlansky's point of view? 1. Highlight the text clues in the middle column. 2. Note whether these text clues tell you directly or if they led you to infer Kurlansky's point of view.
He respects the fishermen of Newfoundland.	"These were **tough and hearty** men.... It was dangerous work in icy waters full of **treacherous** icebergs that had broken off from the polar cap. The water was so cold that they would **freeze to death in minutes** if they fell in." (page 71)	Inferred through his description of the fishermen and the hardships they faced.
He thinks the fishermen of Newfoundland were observant and aware of the situation, more so than others.	"When their catches got smaller and smaller, **they thought it was because the big, new boats far out at sea were taking all the fish**. At that point, it was only their inshore fish that were vanishing, so the deepwater fishermen paid little attention." (page 71)	Inferred through his description of their awareness of the problem when no one else was concerned.

What is Mark Kurlansky's point of view of the Great Banks codfish situation?	How do you know? (Quote specific words, phrases, and sentences.)	How does the text evidence convey Kurlansky's point of view? 1. Highlight the text clues in the middle column. 2. Note whether these text clues tell you directly or if they led you to infer Kurlansky's point of view.
He is surprised and disappointed that people didn't learn from the past.	"**Even in the 1980s, a century after trawlers were found to be destroying the North Sea**, many still believed that the codfish population of the Grand Banks, known as the northern stock, was in no danger because it was one of the most plentiful populations in recorded history." (pages 72 and 73)	Inferred through his use of the word "even," which signifies disbelief.
He is angry with the government for denying there was a problem in order to continue catching fish, making money, and providing jobs.	"The skiff fishermen went to scientists, and many scientists agreed with them. But the government had their own scientists who reported that the northern **stock was not in danger. So many fish were being caught and so much money was being made** that the government didn't want to listen to a few old-fashioned skiff fishermen. They were providing jobs processing fish at sea **for many people who had not had any work** before the 200-mile limit." (page 73)	Inferred through the use of bold, colored font in capital letters. Also said directly.

What is Mark Kurlansky's point of view of the Great Banks codfish situation?	How do you know? (Quote specific words, phrases, and sentences.)	How does the text evidence convey Kurlansky's point of view? 1. Highlight the text clues in the middle column. 2. Note whether these text clues tell you directly or if they led you to infer Kurlansky's point of view.
He thinks the government was silly to not see the obvious.	"But they didn't consider the **other possibility**: that the catches were large because they were catching all of the fish." (page 74)	Inferred through the use of bold, colored font in capital letters.
He is angry with the fishermen that the problem was recognized too late, and he is sad for the loss of the fish.	"What happened on the Grand Banks is that modern fishing had become so powerful, so effective, the fishermen were able to **hunt down every last fish in a dying population** without realizing it was dying." (page 74)	Inferred through his use of language in describing what happened. "Hunt down" suggests mean, aggressive fishermen, and "dying population" suggests vulnerable fish.
He is sad for the people who lost their livelihoods as a result of the situation.	"Thirty thousand Newfoundland fishermen instantly lost their jobs. **The island province was plunged into poverty**." (page 75)	It is inferred through his use of language such as the word "plunged."

Grade 6 2-Point Rubric—Short Response
(Teacher Reference)

Use the rubric below for determining scores on short answers in this assessment.

The features of a **2-point response** are:

- Valid inferences and/or claims from the text where required by the prompt
- Evidence of analysis of the text where required by the prompt
- Relevant facts, definitions, concrete details, and/or other information from the text to develop response according to the requirements of the prompt
- Sufficient number of facts, definitions, concrete details, and/or other information from the text as required by the prompt
- Complete sentences where errors do not impact readability

The features of a **1-point response** are:

- A mostly literal recounting of events or details from the text as required by the prompt
- Some relevant facts, definitions, concrete details, and/or other information from the text to develop response according to the requirements of the prompt
- Incomplete sentences or bullets

The features of a **0-point response** are:

- A response that does not address any of the requirements of the prompt or is totally inaccurate
- No response (blank answer)
- A response that is not written in English
- A response that is unintelligible or indecipherable

If the prompt requires two texts and the student references only one text, the response can be scored no higher than a 1.

Tracing the Development of an Idea Anchor Chart
(Teacher Reference)

Idea: Fish depletion

Chapter	How is the idea introduced, illustrated, or elaborated on in this chapter?
5	• He illustrates and elaborates on the idea by providing an example of fish depletion that could have been avoided.

Supplementary Assessment Items

World Without Fish

Name: _____

Date: _____

Directions: Read the following passage. Answer the questions that follow.

Excerpt from *World Without Fish* by Mark Kurlansky (pp. 45–49)

[P1] Darwin was right. A healthy ecosystem is based on the destruction of life and the struggles for survival among species, and it is in such systems that men in the form of fishermen are drawn to take part in the killing. Ninety percent of the fishing they do is within 200 miles of land.

[P2] Farther out to sea, there is life and there are fish. But many of them live at great depths that have not been explored because until recently we didn't have the ability to reach that far below the surface.

[P3] Most attempts to commercialize fish hauled in from farther out at sea have proven disastrous in a very short time because of our lack of understanding of this deepwater life system. The orange roughy is an excellent example.

[P4] Fishermen were not capable of reaching the orange roughy until the 1970s, but once they did, eating orange roughy became fashionable in Australia, the United States, and many other places in the world well into the 1990s.

[P5] It was not understood that this species was not like other fish we had known. For one thing, many scientists think that an orange roughy lives for 150 years, which is at least five times as long as most of the fish we know. The age is disputed, with some saying it lives even longer, but the problem with this long-lived species is that it grows very slowly. The fish doesn't even become capable of producing offspring until it is twenty years old, which would be an older fish in most of the species we know. This means that many orange roughy that appear to be mature are actually quite young and haven't yet reproduced.

[P6] The large-scale killing of fish that haven't yet reproduced will in time destroy them, and that's exactly what happened to the orange roughy populations off the coast of New Zealand and Australia, where the fish was first discovered. After little more than ten years, the Australian orange roughy population was only 10 percent of what it had been in the 1990s. So fishermen went looking somewhere else for this popular new species, and found it in the Atlantic Ocean off southern Africa, as well as farther north from Morocco to Iceland. Just as it happened with the Australian orange roughy, these populations very quickly showed signs of vanishing.

Source: From *World Without Fish* by Mark Kurlansky (pp. 45–49), Chapter 3 "Being the Sad, Cautionary Tale of the Orange Roughy."

[P7] The sad story of how the orange roughy became one of the world's most threatened fish populations within decades of being discovered by us should serve as a caution to what could happen. Who knows what years of dragging nets through these deep unknown oceans is doing to deepwater ecosystems—we are probably damaging and destroying species we haven't even discovered yet and will never know about. It would follow the laws of Darwin if it turned out that rare fish in hard-to-reach places had fewer chances of survival than large populations of more familiar fish living in ideal environments closer to shore.

This question has two parts. First answer Part A. Then answer Part B.

Part A: Which is one way the author introduces the tale of the orange roughy in paragraphs 1–3?

   A. by using emotional language
   B. by paraphrasing an expert
   C. by making an accusation
   D. by asking a question

Part B: Which detail from the opening paragraph best supports the answer in Part A?

   A. "Ninety percent of the fishing they do is within 200 miles of land."
   B. "Until recently we didn't have the ability to reach that far . . ."
   C. "A healthy ecosystem is based on the destruction of life . . ."
   D. "The orange roughy is an excellent example."

This question has two parts. First answer Part A. Then answer Part B.

Part A: Which detail best explains how our lack of understanding of the orange roughy has proved disastrous for the species?

   A. The age of orange roughy is a well-disputed topic.
   B. Fish caught deeper at sea are less likely to survive.
   C. The fish lived up to 150 years with no natural enemies.
   D. Within 20 years, the orange roughy became nearly extinct.

Part B: Which **two** sentences from the passage best support your answer to **Part A?**

_____A. "It was not understood that this species was not like other fish we had known." (p. 5)

_____B. "… many scientists think that an orange roughy lives for 150 years, which is at least five times as long as most of the fish we know." (p. 5)

_____C. "… many orange roughy that appear to be mature are actually quite young …" (p. 5)

_____D. "After little more than ten years, the Australian orange roughy population was only 10 percent of what it had been in the 1990s." (p. 6)

_____E. "The large-scale killing of fish that haven't yet reproduced will in time destroy them …" (p. 6)

_____F. "Who knows what years of dragging nets through these deep unknown oceans is doing to deepwater ecosystems …" (p. 7)

_____G. "It would follow the laws of Darwin if it turned out that rare fish in hard-to-reach places had fewer chances of survival …" (p. 7)

Supplementary Assessment Items Answer Key

World Without Fish

Standards Assessed: RI.6.3

Note: Supplementary Assessment Items are located in the Teacher Guide And Resource Book only. Distribute a copy of the student version of this assessment to each student.

Directions: Read the following passage. Answer the questions that follow.

Excerpt from *World Without Fish* by Mark Kurlansky (pp. 45–49)

Source: From *World Without Fish* by Mark Kurlansky (p. 45-49), Chapter 3 "Being the Sad, Cautionary Tale of the Orange Roughy"

[P1] Darwin was right. A healthy ecosystem is based on the destruction of life and the struggles for survival among species, and it is in such systems that men in the form of fishermen are drawn to take part in the killing. Ninety percent of the fishing they do is within 200 miles of land.

[P2] Farther out to sea, there is life and there are fish. But many of them live at great depths that have not been explored because until recently we didn't have the ability to reach that far below the surface.

[P3] Most attempts to commercialize fish hauled in from farther out at sea have proven disastrous in a very short time because of our lack of understanding of this deepwater life system. The orange roughy is an excellent example.

[P4] Fishermen were not capable of reaching the orange roughy until the 1970s, but once they did, eating orange roughy became fashionable in Australia, the United States, and many other places in the world well into the 1990s.

[P5] It was not understood that this species was not like other fish we had known. For one thing, many scientists think that an orange roughy lives for 150 years, which is at least five times as long as most of the fish we know. The age is disputed, with some saying it lives even longer, but the problem with this long-lived species is that it grows very slowly. The fish doesn't even become capable of producing offspring until it is twenty years old, which would be an older fish in most of the species we know. This means that many orange roughy that appear to be mature are actually quite young and haven't yet reproduced.

[P6] The large-scale killing of fish that haven't yet reproduced will in time destroy them, and that's exactly what happened to the orange roughy populations off the coast of New Zealand and Australia, where the fish was first discovered. After little more than ten years, the Australian orange roughy population was only 10 percent of what it had been in the 1990s. So fishermen went looking somewhere else for this popular new species, and found it in the Atlantic Ocean off southern Africa, as well as farther north from Morocco to Iceland. Just as it happened with the Australian orange roughy, these populations very quickly showed signs of vanishing.

[P7] The sad story of how the orange roughy became one of the world's most threatened fish populations within decades of being discovered by us should serve as a caution to what could happen. Who knows what years of dragging nets through these deep unknown oceans is doing to deepwater ecosystems—we are probably damaging and destroying species we haven't even discovered yet and will never know about. It would follow the laws of Darwin if it turned out that rare fish in hard-to-reach places had fewer chances of survival than large populations of more familiar fish living in ideal environments closer to shore.

This question has two parts. First answer Part A. Then answer Part B.

Part A: Which is one way the author introduces the tale of the orange roughy in paragraphs 1–3?

   A. by using emotional language
   B. by paraphrasing an expert
   C. by making an accusation
   D. by asking a question

Part A: Choice B is correct. The author introduces the topic by paraphrasing Darwin. Choice A is partially correct. Overall, while the opening statement is an opinion, the language is largely not emotional. Choice C is not supported because the author is not making an accusation in this section of the text. Choice D is not supported by the text. There are no questions in this section.

Part B: Which detail from the opening paragraph best supports the answer in Part A

   A. "Ninety percent of the fishing they do is within 200 miles of land."
   B. "Until recently we didn't have the ability to reach that far . . ."
   C. "A healthy ecosystem is based on the destruction of life . . ."
   D. "The orange roughy is an excellent example."

Part B: Choice C is correct. This statement paraphrases Darwin's claim. Choice A is a statistic to support how humans have historically participated in fishing by staying closer to shore. Choice B is about the historical limits of technology. Choice D serves as a transition to the rest of the article.

This question has two parts. First answer Part A. Then answer Part B.

Part A: Which detail best explains how our lack of understanding of the orange roughy has proved disastrous for the species?

   A. The age of orange roughy is a well-disputed topic.
   B. Fish caught deeper at sea are less likely to survive.
   C. The fish lived up to 150 years with no natural enemies.
   D. Within 20 years, the orange roughy became nearly extinct.

Part A: Choice D is correct. The author's purpose is to show how the lack of understanding has almost decimated an entire species of fish to extinction and should serve as a caution to the impact man has on the ocean in the search for food. This supports the author's initial claim that fisherman have caused the destruction of one species in a fight for their own survival, which is the basic premise of Darwin. Choice A does not address the disaster to the species. Choice B does not address man's lack of understanding of species at this ocean depth or the disastrous effects man has had on this species. Choice C does not address the lack of understanding nor the disastrous effect of human impact.

Part B: Which **two** sentences from the passage best support your answer to **Part A?**

_____ A. "It was not understood that this species was not like other fish we had known." (p. 5)

_____ B. "… many scientists think that an orange roughy lives for 150 years, which is at least five times as long as most of the fish we know." (p. 5)

_____ C. "… many orange roughy that appear to be mature are actually quite young …" (p. 5)

_____ D. "After little more than ten years, the Australian orange roughy population was only 10 percent of what it had been in the 1990s." (p. 6)

_____ E. "The large-scale killing of fish that haven't yet reproduced will in time destroy them …" (p. 6)

_____ F. "Who knows what years of dragging nets through these deep unknown oceans is doing to deepwater ecosystems …" (p. 7)

_____ G. "It would follow the laws of Darwin if it turned out that rare fish in hard-to-reach places had fewer chances of survival …" (p. 7)

Part B: Choices D and E are correct. Choice D supports the idea that man's impact has been disastrous in a very short time. Choice E demonstrates that the lack of understanding of how the orange roughy reproduces may have played the largest contributing factor to the decimation of that species' population. Choices A, B, and C speak to man's lack of understanding, but do not address man's impact on the species' destruction. Choices F and G both address how a lack of understanding of a species has consequences, but the impact is on animals in general and not the orange roughy specifically.

GRADE 6   Module 3B: Unit 2

UNIT OVERVIEW

Reading Closely and Writing to Learn: Point of View and Perspective

Narrator's Point of View and Evidence of Author's Perspective in *Flush*

In this unit, students are involved in a study of how an author develops point of view and how an author's perspective, based on his or her geographic location, is evident in his or her writing. Students will begin reading Carl Hiaasen's *Flush*, a high-interest novel about a boy whose father has been arrested for sinking a casino boat that was polluting the ocean by pumping sewage into it. As they read the novel, students will also read excerpts of interviews with Carl Hiaasen in order to determine how his geographic location has shaped his perspective, and how his perspective is evident in *Flush*. Through the close reading of these texts, students will learn multiple strategies for acquiring and using academic vocabulary. At the end of the unit, having read most of the novel, students will analyze an excerpt of text for evidence of Carl Hiaasen's perspective.

Guiding Questions and Big Ideas

- How does an author develop the narrator's point of view?
- How does an author develop the plot of a novel?
- *The geographic location of an author affects his or her perspective and can be evident in the work he or she produces.*

Mid-Unit 2 Assessment

Analyzing Point of View and Plot Development in *Flush*

This assessment addresses ELA CCSS RL.6.4, RL.6.5, RL.6.6, and L.6.4.a. For this assessment, students read a new excerpt of *Flush* and use a graphic organizer to analyze how the author develops the narrator's point of view. They also answer selected-response questions about word and phrase meaning, and how a sentence/paragraph fits into the overall structure of the text in the excerpt.

End-of-Unit 2 Assessment

Finding Evidence of Carl Hiaasen's Perspective in *Flush* and Illustrating Plot

This assessment addresses ELA CCSS RL.6.6. Students read an excerpt from *Flush* and fill out a graphic organizer to analyze the evidence of Carl Hiaasen's perspective of Florida in the excerpt, and then use their thinking to write an on-demand response to the questions: "How has being born and raised in Florida affected Carl Hiaasen's perspective of the place? Where is the evidence of this perspective in the excerpt you have read today of the novel *Flush*? How does the evidence you have selected illustrate his perspective?"

Supplementary Assessment Items

This unit also includes a small set of optional selected-response items. These are supplementary items that provide additional information about student mastery of a subset of the standards for this unit.

- Supplementary assessment items and teacher-facing answer keys are available at the end of each unit.
- To provide teachers with flexibility around how and when to use these materials, supplementary assessment items are located in this Teacher Guide and Resource Book only.

Content Connections

This module is designed to address English Language Arts standards as students read a novel set in the present day about a man polluting the ocean with sewage from a casino boat in Florida and how local people try to stop him. However, the module intentionally incorporates social studies themes and practices to support potential interdisciplinary connections to this compelling content. These intentional connections are described next.

Social Studies Themes

- Time, Continuity, and Change
  - Analyzing causes and consequences of events and developments
- Geography, Humans, and the Environment
  - Relationship between human populations and the physical world (people, places, and environment)
  - Impact of human activities on the environment
- Creation, Expansion, and Interaction of Economic Systems
  - Scarcity of resources and the challenges of meeting wants and needs
  - Supply/demand and the coordination of individual choices
- Science, Technology, and Innovation
  - Relationship between human populations and the physical world
  - Interactions between regions, locations, places, people, and environments

Social Studies Practices

- Gathering, Interpreting, and Using Evidence
  - Identify, effectively select, and analyze different forms of evidence used to make meaning in social studies
  - Identify evidence and explain content, authorship, point of view, purpose, and format; identify bias; explain the role of bias and potential audience.

Central Text

1. Carl Hiaasen, *Flush* (New York: Yearling Publishing, 2010), ISBN: 978-0-375-86125-3. (770L)

Unit-at-a-Glance Calendar

This unit is approximately 2.5 weeks or 12 sessions of instruction.

Lesson	Lesson Title	Long-Term Targets	Supporting Targets	Ongoing Assessment	Anchor Charts and Protocols
1	Learning from the Narrator's Point of View: Introducing *Flush*	• I can analyze how an author develops a narrator or speaker's point of view. (RL.6.6) • I can compare and make connections between *World Without Fish* and *Flush* (RL.6.9)	• I can make connections between *World Without Fish* and *Flush*. • I can identify Noah's point of view of his father's situation using text evidence from the novel.	• Point of View Anchor Chart: Chapter 1	• Point of View Anchor Chart: Chapter 1 • Triad Talk Expectations Anchor Chart

Lesson	Lesson Title	Long-Term Targets	Supporting Targets	Ongoing Assessment	Anchor Charts and Protocols
			• I can explain how Carl Hiaasen develops the point of view of Noah. • I can follow Triad Talk expectations when I participate in a discussion.		
2	Analyzing Point of View and Figurative Language: Noah's Point of View of the *Coral Queen* and Dusty Muleman	• I can determine the meaning of literal, and figurative language (metaphors and similes) in a literary text. (RL.6.4) • I can analyze how an author's word choice affects tone and meaning in a literary text. (RL.6.4)	• I can find the gist of pages 7–9 of *Flush*. • I can analyze how Carl Hiaasen conveys Noah's point of view of the *Coral Queen* and Dusty Muleman. • I can determine connotative and figurative meanings of language and analyze how the author's choice of words affects tone and meaning.	• Structured Notes: Chapter 1 (from homework) • Gist annotated on sticky notes • Noah's Point of View Graphic Organizer: Pages 7–9	• Back-to-Back, Face-to-Face protocol • *Flush* Plot Development Anchor Chart

Lesson	Lesson Title	Long-Term Targets	Supporting Targets	Ongoing Assessment	Anchor Charts and Protocols
		• I can analyze how a particular sentence, stanza, scene, or chapter fits in and contributes to the development of a literary text. (RL.6.5) • I can analyze how an author develops a narrator or speaker's point of view. (RL.6.6) • I can use context (e.g., the overall meaning of a sentence or paragraph, a word's position or function in a sentence) to determine the meaning of a word or phrase. (L.6.4.a)	• I can explain how chapter 1 contributes to plot development.		

Lesson	Lesson Title	Long-Term Targets	Supporting Targets	Ongoing Assessment	Anchor Charts and Protocols
3	Analyzing Point of View and Figurative Language: Noah's Point of View of Lice Peeking	• I can determine the meaning of literal and figurative language (metaphors and similes) in a literary text. (RL.6.4) • I can analyze how an author's word choice affects tone and meaning in a literary text. (RL.6.4) • I can analyze how a particular sentence, stanza, scene, or chapter fits in and contributes to the development of a literary text. (RL.6.5) • I can analyze how an author develops a narrator or speaker's point of view. (RL.6.6)	• I can analyze how Carl Hiaasen develops Noah's point of view of Lice Peeking. • I can determine connotative and figurative meanings of language and analyze how the author's choice of words affects tone and meaning. • I can analyze how chapters 2 and 3 contribute to plot development.	• Structured Notes: Chapters 2 and 3 (from homework) • Noah's Point of View Graphic Organizer: Pages 17–19	• *Flush* Plot Development Anchor Chart • Plot Development: The Rising Action in *Flush* Anchor Chart

Lesson	Lesson Title	Long-Term Targets	Supporting Targets	Ongoing Assessment	Anchor Charts and Protocols
		• I can use context (e.g., the overall meaning of a sentence or paragraph, a word's position or function in a sentence) to determine the meaning of a word or phrase. (L.6.4.a)			
4	Analyzing Point of View and Figurative Language: Noah's Point of View of Florida	• I can determine the meaning of literal and figurative language (metaphors and similes) in a literary text. (RL.6.4) • I can analyze how an author's word choice affects tone and meaning in a literary text. (RL.6.4)	• I can determine connotative and figurative meanings of language and analyze how the author's choice of words affects tone and meaning. • I can analyze how Carl Hiaasen develops Noah's point of view of the area he lives in.	• Structured Notes: Chapters 4 and 5 (from homework) • Noah's Point of View Graphic Organizer: Pages 27–29 • Exit Ticket: Chapters 4 and 5 Plot Development	• Plot Development: The Rising Action in *Flush* Anchor Chart • *Flush* Plot Development Anchor Chart

Lesson	Lesson Title	Long-Term Targets	Supporting Targets	Ongoing Assessment	Anchor Charts and Protocols
		• I can analyze how a particular sentence, stanza, scene, or chapter fits in and contributes to the development of a literary text. (RL.6.5) • I can analyze how an author develops a narrator or speaker's point of view. (RL.6.6) • I can use context (e.g., the overall meaning of a sentence or paragraph, a word's position or function in a sentence) to determine the meaning of a word or phrase. (L.6.4.a)	• I can analyze how chapters 4 and 5 contribute to plot development.		

Lesson	Lesson Title	Long-Term Targets	Supporting Targets	Ongoing Assessment	Anchor Charts and Protocols
5	**Mid-Unit 2 Assessment:** Analyzing Point of View and Plot Development in *Flush*	• I can determine the meaning of literal and figurative language (metaphors and similes) in a literary text. (RL.6.4) • I can analyze how an author's word choice affects tone and meaning in a literary text. (RL.6.4) • I can analyze how a particular sentence, stanza, scene, or chapter fits in and contributes to the development of a literary text. (RL.6.5) • I can analyze how an author develops a narrator or speaker's point of view. (RL.6.6)	• I can determine the meaning of words and phrases in the text. • I can analyze how the word choice affects tone and meaning. • I can analyze how Hiaasen develops Noah's point of view. • I can explain how a chapter contributes to plot development.	• Structured Notes: Chapters 6 and 7 (from homework) • Mid-Unit 2 Assessment: Point of View, Figurative Language, and Plot Development in *Flush* • *Flush* Plot Development Anchor Chart	• Plot Development: The Rising Action in *Flush* Anchor Chart • *Flush* Plot Development Anchor Chart

Lesson	Lesson Title	Long-Term Targets	Supporting Targets	Ongoing Assessment	Anchor Charts and Protocols
		• I can use context (e.g., the overall meaning of a sentence or paragraph, a word's position or function in a sentence) to determine the meaning of a word or phrase. (L.6.4.a)			
6	Carl Hiaasen's Perspective of Florida: Part 1	• I can explain how the author develops the point of view of the narrator or speaker in a text. (RL.6.6)	• I can find the gist of an excerpt of "Five Creative Tips from Carl Hiaasen." • I can use evidence from the text to answer text-dependent questions. • I can infer Carl Hiaasen's perspective of Florida.	• Structured Notes: Chapter 8 (from homework) • Gathering Evidence of Hiaasen's Perspective: Part 1 Graphic Organizer	• *Flush* Plot Development Anchor Chart

Lesson	Lesson Title	Long-Term Targets	Supporting Targets	Ongoing Assessment	Anchor Charts and Protocols
7	Carl Hiaasen's Perspective of Florida: Part 2	• I can explain how the author develops the point of view of the narrator or speaker in a text. (RL.6.6)	• I can find the gist of "Florida 'A Paradise of Scandals'" Excerpt 1. • I can use evidence from the text to answer text-dependent questions. • I can identify evidence of Carl Hiaasen's perspective of his geographic location in *Flush*.	• Structured Notes: Chapters 9 and 10 (from homework) • Gathering Evidence of Hiaasen's Perspective: Part 2 Graphic Organizer	• Concentric Circles protocol
8	Carl Hiaasen's Perspective of Florida: Part 3	• I can explain how the author develops the point of view of the narrator or speaker in a text. (RL.6.6)	• I can find the gist of "Florida 'A Paradise of Scandals'" Excerpt 2. • I can use evidence from the text to answer text-dependent questions. • I can infer Carl Hiaasen's perspective of Florida.	• Structured Notes: Chapters 11 and 12 (from homework) • Gathering Evidence of Hiaasen's Perspective: Part 3 Graphic Organizer	• *Flush* Plot Development Anchor Chart

Lesson	Lesson Title	Long-Term Targets	Supporting Targets	Ongoing Assessment	Anchor Charts and Protocols
9	Finding Evidence of Carl Hiaasen's Perspective in *Flush*	• I can explain how the author develops the point of view of the narrator or speaker in a text. (RL.6.6)	• I can identify evidence of Carl Hiaasen's perspective in *Flush*.	• Structured notes: Chapters 13 and 14 (from homework) • Finding Evidence of Carl Hiaasen's Perspective in *Flush* Graphic Organizer	• *Flush* Plot Development Anchor Chart
10	Illustrating Carl Hiaasen's Perspective of Florida in *Flush*	• I can draw evidence from literary or informational texts to support analysis, reflection, and research. (W.6.9) • I can explain how the author develops the point of view of the narrator or speaker in a text. (RL.6.6) • I can draw evidence from literary or informational texts to support analysis, reflection, and research. (W.6.9)	• I can illustrate a scene from *Flush* that shows evidence of Carl Hiaasen's perspective of Florida.	• Structured Notes: Chapters 15 and 16 (from homework) • Illustrating a Scene Showing Perspective	• Concentric Circles protocol • *Flush* Plot Development Anchor Chart

TEACHER GUIDE AND RESOURCE BOOK • Grade 6 • Module 3B • Unit 2 • Unit Overview   195

Lesson	Lesson Title	Long-Term Targets	Supporting Targets	Ongoing Assessment	Anchor Charts and Protocols
11	**End-of-Unit 2 Assessment:** Finding Evidence of Carl Hiaasen's Perspective in *Flush* and Illustrating Perspective	• I can explain how the author develops the point of view of the narrator or speaker in a text. (RL.6.6) • I can draw evidence from literary or informational texts to support analysis, reflection, and research. (W.6.9)	• I can identify evidence of Carl Hiaasen's perspective in *Flush*. • I can illustrate a scene from *Flush* that shows evidence of Carl Hiaasen's perspective of Florida.	• Structured Notes: Chapter 17 (from homework) • End-of-Unit 2 Assessment	• *Flush* Plot Development Anchor Chart
12	Analyzing Plot Development Across *Flush*	• I can analyze how a particular sentence, stanza, scene, or chapter fits in and contributes to the development of a literary text. (RL.6.5)	• I can explain how chapters 18–21 contribute to plot development. • I can explain how Carl Hiaasen develops the plot across the novel. • I can write a Reader's Review of the novel *Flush*.	• Structured Notes: End of *Flush* (from homework) • Reader's Review of *Flush*	• *Flush* Plot Development Anchor Chart

Optional: Experts, Fieldwork, and Service

Experts

- Invite local authors to talk with students about how their geographic location has affected their perspective and how that is evident in their work.
- Invite a scientist to speak with students about the causes and effects of water pollution.

Optional: Extensions

- A study of local causes and effects of water pollution

Preparation and Materials

This unit includes a number of routines.

In Lessons 1–11, students read chapters of the book *Flush* for homework. Once the routine is fully implemented (starting in Lesson 1), students will answer a focus question using evidence from the text each night.

Independent Reading

This module introduces a more robust independent reading structure. However, it makes sense to wait until after students have completed *Flush* to launch this—specifically, after the End-of-Unit 2 Assessment. See **Launching Independent Reading in Grades 6–8: Sample Plan**, which provides practical guidance for a robust independent reading program. Once students have all learned how to select books and complete the reading log, it takes less class time. After the launch period, the independent reading routine takes about half of a class period per week, with an additional day near the end of a unit or module for students to review and share their books. You may wish to review the independent reading materials now to give yourself time to gather texts and to make a launch plan that meets your students' needs.

After launching independent reading, resume the second half of the module, where independent reading is used regularly in homework and during independent reading reviews in the openings of lessons.

Reading Calendar

- Students read chapters of the novel *Flush* for homework for Lessons 1–11. Each night, they answer a focus question about point of view (in the first half of the unit) or about plot development (in the second half of the unit).
- Consider providing a reading calendar to help students, teachers, and families understand what is due and when. See the following Reading Calendar.
- *Flush* is a high-interest novel about a boy whose father has been arrested for sinking a casino boat that was polluting the ocean by pumping sewage into. It has been chosen for this unit because there is clear evidence of the author's perspective as a result of his geographic location, and because it links to the module topic of human impact on life in the oceans. It is not a complex text, so students

are required to read two chapters of the novel each night for homework. Depending on your students, you may need to allow additional time in lessons for students to catch-up on reading the novel if they have been unable to do so at home. Students must finish the novel by the end of unit.

Structured Notes

Structured notes record students' thinking about a focus question specific to what they have been asked to read. Structured notes are organized by chapter and require students to read the excerpt, answer the focus question for the excerpt, and record evidence from the excerpt to support their answers to the questions.

Reading Calendar *Flush*

The calendar below shows what is due on each day.

You may modify this document to include dates instead of lessons.

Due at Lesson	Reading	Focus Question
2	Chapter 1	• Read chapter 1 of *Flush*. As you read, mark the text with at least three evidence flags to help you answer this focus question in your structured notes: • "What is Noah's point of view of his father's crime?" • Remember to record any new vocabulary on your word-catcher.
3	Chapters 2 and 3	• Read chapters 2 and 3 of *Flush*. As you read, mark the text with at least three evidence flags to help you answer this focus question in your structured notes: • "What is Noah's point of view of Jasper? How do you know?" • Remember to record any new vocabulary on your word-catcher.

Due at Lesson	Reading	Focus Question
4	Chapters 4 and 5	• Read chapters 4 and 5 of *Flush*. As you read, mark the text with at least three evidence flags to help you answer this focus question in your structured notes: • "What does Noah think about Miles Umlatt? How do you know?" • Remember to record any new vocabulary on your word catcher.
5	Chapters 6 and 7	• Read chapters 6 and 7. As you read, mark the text with at least three evidence flags to help you answer this focus question in your structured notes: • "What does Shelly think of Lice in chapter 6? How do you know?" • Remember to record any new vocabulary on your word-catcher.
6	Chapter 8	• Read the rest of chapter 8. As you read, mark the text with at least three evidence flags to help you answer this focus question in your structured notes: • "What happens in this chapter and how do those events contribute to the plot development?" • Remember to record new vocabulary words on your word-catcher.
7	Chapter 9 and 10	• Read chapters 9 and 10 of *Flush*. As you read, mark the text with at least three evidence flags to help you answer this focus question in your structured notes: • "What happens in these chapters and how do those events contribute to the plot development?" • Remember to record any new vocabulary on your word-catcher.

Due at Lesson	Reading	Focus Question
8	Chapters 11 and 12	• Read chapters 11 and 12 of *Flush*. As you read, mark the text with at least three evidence flags to help you answer this focus question in your structured notes: • "What happens in these chapters and how do those events contribute to the plot development?" • Remember to record any new vocabulary on your word-catcher.
9	Chapters 13 and 14	• Read chapters 13 and 14 of *Flush*. As you read, mark the text with at least three evidence flags to help you answer this focus question in your structured notes: • "What happens in these chapters and how do those events contribute to the plot development?" • Remember to record any new vocabulary on your word-catcher.
10	Chapters 15 and 16	• Read chapters 15 and 16 of *Flush*. As you read, mark the text with at least three evidence flags to help you answer this focus question in your structured notes: • "What happens in these chapters and how do those events contribute to the plot development?" • Remember to record any new vocabulary on your word-catcher.

Due at Lesson	Reading	Focus Question
11	Chapter 17	• Read chapter 17 of *Flush*. As you read, mark the text with at least three evidence flags to help you answer this focus question in your structured notes: • "What happens in this chapter and how do those events contribute to the plot development?" • Remember to record any new vocabulary on your word-catcher.
12	Chapters 18–21	• Read to the end of *Flush*. As you read, mark the text with at least three evidence flags to help you answer this focus question in your structured notes: • "What is the resolution?" • Remember to record any new vocabulary on your word-catcher.

LESSON 1

Learning from the Narrator's Point of View
Introducing *Flush*

Long-Term Targets Addressed (Based on ELA CCSS)

- I can analyze how an author develops a narrator or speaker's point of view. (RL.6.6)
- I can compare and make connections between *World Without Fish* and *Flush*. (RL6.9)

Supporting Learning Targets

- I can make an ethical connection between *World Without Fish* and *Flush*.
- I can identify Noah's point of view of his father's situation using text evidence from the novel.
- I can explain how Carl Hiaasen develops the point of view of Noah.
- I can follow Triad Talk expectations when I participate in a discussion.

Ongoing Assessment

- Point of View Anchor Chart: Chapter 1

Agenda

1. Opening
    A. Engaging the Reader: Introducing the Novel (10 minutes)
    B. Unpacking Learning Targets (3 minutes)
2. Work Time
    A. First Read: Chapter 1 (15 minutes)
    B. Identifying Noah's Point of View: Chapter 1 (10 minutes)
    C. Determining Author's Techniques for Developing Point of View (5 minutes)

3. Closing and Assessment

    A. Previewing Homework (2 minutes)

4. Homework

    A. Read chapter 1 of *Flush*. As you read, mark the text with evidence flags to help you answer the focus question in your structured notes.

Teaching Notes

- This lesson introduces students to the primary focus of this unit: point of view (RL.6.6). Students begin to identify the narrator Noah's point of view in *Flush* and analyze the techniques that Carl Hiaasen uses to develop it.

- At the beginning of the lesson, students work in triads to guess the title of the book from visual and sound clues. Prepare pictures of a flushing toilet and a flushed face (can be found via internet searches) to display for students.

- In this lesson, students are introduced to the novel by reading pages 1–3. They also revisit the concept of point of view, but this time the point of view of the narrator in a literary text, rather than the author of an informational text as in Unit 1. Together, the class completes an anchor chart as they analyze point of view in the first three pages of the novel. The anchor chart prepares students for the graphic organizer they will use in later lessons to independently analyze point of view. This lesson focuses on the character Noah and his point of view about his father's situation.

- Help students distinguish between the basic meaning of "point of view" (e.g., "perspective") and the literary terms used to describe the point of view of a character (e.g., "first-person," "third-person"). These literary terms are addressed in a fourth-grade standard (RL.4.6), but may need to be reviewed with students. The basic meaning of point of view will be more heavily emphasized throughout this unit.

- The homework routine in this unit is similar to that in Unit 1. At the end of the lesson, students are given a structured notes handout on which to record their homework. Post or display the homework focus question at the conclusion of the lesson and instruct students to copy it down. Establishing a routine will be important, as this homework structure will be repeated throughout the unit. The homework focus question is also on the reading calendar. Consider giving each student one baggie with evidence flags, rather than distributing new flags each day.

- In advance:

    - Group students into new triads who will work together to read, think, talk, and write about *Flush* and other texts. Be intentional in placing students in groups that are different from their previous triads.

    - Review pages 1–3 of *Flush*. Identify Noah's point of view of his father and the evidence from those pages that supports your claims.

    - Prepare the Point of View Anchor Chart (see supporting materials). Note that part of the chart will be co-created with students in this lesson and part of it will be co-created with students in Lesson 2.

- Search the internet to find an audio of the sound of toilet flushing.
- Locate the Triad Talk Expectations Anchor Chart created in Module 1.
- Post: learning targets.

Lesson Vocabulary

point of view, evidence, first person, third person, omniscient, technique, synopsis; flush, pitiful, smuggling, bail

Materials

- Triad Talk Expectations Anchor Chart (from Module 1, Unit 1, Lesson 2)
- Lined paper (one sheet per triad)
- Image of a flushing toilet (one for display; see Teaching Notes)
- Image of a flushed face (one for display; see Teaching Notes)
- Sound of a flushing toilet (audio; to play for the whole group)
- *Flush* by Carl Hiaasen (book; one per student)
- Questions to Introduce *Flush* (one for display)
- Questions to Introduce *Flush* (Teacher Reference)
- Equity sticks
- *Flush* Word-Catcher (one per student)
- Dictionary (at least one per triad)
- Point of View Anchor Chart (new; co-created with students during Work Time B; see supporting materials)
- Point of View Anchor Chart (Teacher Reference)
- Thought, Word, Action Symbols (one for display)
- Blue markers/pencils (one per student and one for teacher use)
- Structured Notes: Chapter 1 (one per student and one for display)
- Evidence flags (at least three per student)

Opening

A. Engaging the Reader: Introducing the Novel (10 minutes)

- Post the list of new triads and invite students to get into their groups. Tell them that they will work with these students for the duration of this unit.
- Review the **Triad Talk Expectations Anchor Chart** (from Module 1, Unit 1, Lesson 2).
- Tell students that you are going to give them three clues to the title of the novel they are going to read. Tell students that the novel has a one-word title and they are going to try to guess what it is

- based on the clues. Distribute a piece of lined paper to each triad so they can record the words they think are possible titles, based on the clues they are given.
- First show students the **image of a flushing toilet**. Ask students to discuss in triads:
  - "What do you see?"
- Give triads time to discuss what they see and record possible single-word titles.
- Next show the **image of a flushed face**. Ask students to discuss in triads:
  - "What do you see?"
- Give triads time to discuss what they see and record possible single-word titles.
- Next play the **sound of a flushing toilet**. Ask students to discuss in triads:
  - "What do you hear?"
- Give triads time to discuss what they hear and record possible single-word titles.
- Invite triads to discuss the images and the sound bite and choose a single word that they think might be the title of the novel. Cold-call triads to share their ideas with the whole group. Congratulate those who guessed correctly!
- Write the title of the novel *Flush* on the board and ask students to discuss in triads:
  - "You've just seen some images and heard some sounds that relate to the word flush. What does the word 'flush' mean?"
  - "Given this title and the work you did in Unit 1 about the ocean and fish depletion, what do you think this novel might be about?"
- Cold-call students to share their responses. Listen for students to explain that flush can mean to clean something, like flushing a toilet or flushing an illness out of your body, or it can also mean to go red, to have a flushed face. Student ideas about the novel have no right or wrong answer at this stage, as long as students can justify why they think the way they do based on the meaning of the word.
- Distribute the novel *Flush* by Carl Hiaasen to each student. Focus students on the cover of the book. Ask them to discuss in triads:
  - "Based on the cover, what do you think this book will be about now? Why?"
- Select volunteers to share their ideas with the whole group.
- Invite students to look at the synopsis of the book on the back cover. Explain that a synopsis gives the reader an overview of what the book is going to be about. Read the synopsis aloud and ask students to follow along silently in their heads.
- Display the **Questions to Introduce *Flush***. Ask triads to discuss each question using text evidence from the synopsis.
- Cold-call a few triads to share their answers with the whole group. Use the **Questions to Introduce *Flush* (Teacher Reference)** to guide student responses. Ask students to discuss in triads:
  - "What problems do you think might arise from flushing human waste into the ocean?"
- Select students to share their responses. Listen for students to suggest something like: "It's dangerous for humans to swim in and dangerous for sea life."

Meeting Students' Needs

Heterogeneous groups support students in discussing and answering questions about texts.

B. Unpacking Learning Targets (3 minutes)

- Invite students to read the learning targets aloud with you:
  - "I can make an ethical connection between *World Without Fish* and *Flush*."
  - "I can identify Noah's point of view of his father's situation using text evidence from the novel."
  - "I can explain how Carl Hiaasen develops the point of view of Noah."
  - "I can follow Triad Talk expectations when I participate in a discussion."
- Ask triads to discuss:
  - "What are the important words or phrases in the learning targets? Why do you think those are important?"
- Cold-call students to share their responses and circle the words and phrases they suggest. Make sure point of view and evidence are circled.
- Focus students on the term *point of view*. Ask triads to discuss:
  - "What does *point of view* mean?"
- Consider using **equity sticks** to select students to share their responses. Listen for them to explain that people have different ways of looking at things, and your point of view is your way of looking at things.
- Tell students that in literature, every story is told from a point of view. It can be a first-person point of view, where the narrator is in the story and is the "I" or "me" telling the story; a third-person limited point of view, in which an author appears to know the thoughts and feelings of only one of the characters in a story, or a third-person omniscient point of view, in which an author captures the points of view of all the characters.

Meeting Students' Needs

- Learning targets are a research-based strategy that helps all students, especially challenged learners.
- Posting learning targets allows students to reference them throughout the lesson to check their understanding. Learning targets also provide a reminder to students and teachers about the intended learning behind a given lesson or activity.

Work Time

A. First Read: Chapter 1 (15 minutes)

- Explain to students that Carl Hiaasen is a well-known author from Florida. He is known for writing adventurous stories that often make you laugh out loud. In *Flush*, he gets us thinking about pollution in the oceans with a clever tale of crime and mystery.

- Ask students to follow along silently as you read the first few paragraphs and opening dialogue on page 1 up to, "'Thanks, Noah,' he said."
- Ask triads to discuss:
  - "What do we know so far?"
  - "Who is the narrator of the story?"
  - "Is this first-person, third-person, or omniscient narration? How do you know?"
- Refocus the whole class and use equity sticks to call on a few students. Listen for students to explain that *Flush* is written in first-person because the narrator Noah speaks from the perspective of "I" as he tells the story.
- Invite students to follow along silently as you read aloud to the bottom of page 3, up to, "Dad smiled. 'I believe you are, Noah.'" Ask triads to discuss:
  - "What do we know now?"
- Select volunteers to share their responses with the whole group.
- Distribute a **Flush Word-Catcher** to each student. Students should be familiar with word-catchers, but they may need to be reminded how to fill it out. Invite students to add any unfamiliar words from the first few pages of the novel to the word-catcher.
- Refocus the whole group. Focus students on the word *pitiful*. Ask:
  - "What root word can you see and hear in the word *pitiful*?"
- Cold-call students to share their responses. Listen for students to say "pity." Ask:
  - "What does the word *pity* mean?"
- Consider using equity sticks to select students to share their responses. Listen for students to explain that when you pity someone or something, you feel sorry for them. Ask:
  - "So what do you think the word *pitiful* means?"
- Select volunteers to share their responses. Listen for students to explain that the word *pitiful* means in a sorry state. When someone is pitiful, it makes you feel sorry for him or her.
- Students may also struggle with the words *smuggling* and *bail*, as they may not be able to figure out what they mean from the context. Ensure that each triad has a **dictionary** and remind students that looking up words is another strategy for understanding the meaning of words you don't know when you are reading.

B. Identifying Noah's Point of View: Chapter 1 (10 minutes)

- Remind students of the learning target:
  - "I can identify Noah's point of view of his father's situation using text evidence from the novel."
- Explain that you want students to pay attention to Noah's point of view of his father's situation in what they have read so far. Ask students to discuss in triads:
  - "What is his father's situation?"
- Select volunteers to share their responses. Listen for students to explain that his father is in jail because he sunk someone's boat.

- Post this question and ask students to discuss in triads:
  - "What is Noah's point of view of his father's situation? How do you know? What does he do or say in the text to make you think that?"
- Refocus the whole group. Display the **Point of View Anchor Chart**. Focus students on the first two columns, Claim and Evidence. Explain that in their triads, students have already begun to make a claim about Noah's point of view of his father. They have also identified what he does or says in the text to make them think that, which is finding evidence.
- Invite each triad to briefly orally share their claims and evidence with the whole group.
- Record appropriate claims in the first column of the anchor chart and evidence cited in the middle column. Refer to **Point of View Anchor Chart (Teacher Reference)** for guidance.

Meeting Students' Needs

- Giving students the opportunity to discuss answers to questions in small groups before asking them to share with the whole group can ensure that all are able to contribute to the whole-group discussion.
- Anchor charts serve as note-catchers when the class is co-constructing ideas.

C. Determining Author's Techniques for Developing Point of View (5 minutes)

- Draw students' attention to the final column on the Point of View Anchor Chart, Technique. Explain that technique is about how the author, Carl Hiaasen, develops point of view. Tell students that now that they have identified Noah's point of view of his father's situation, they are going to consider how Hiaasen conveyed that point of view. Review the learning target:
  - "I can explain how Carl Hiaasen develops the point of view of Noah."
- Ask students to look at the first claim on the anchor chart and the evidence that goes along with it and then discuss with their triads:
  - "How did Carl Hiaasen develop this point of view? How is that point of view conveyed so that we understand it?"
  - "Is it through the narrator's words, thoughts, or actions? Is it through another character's words or actions?"
- Select volunteers to share their responses. Listen for students to explain that in this excerpt we mostly understand Noah's point of view through what he says to his dad.
- Display the **Thought, Word, Action Symbols** and explain that we can color and text-code the Point of View Anchor Chart so that we can quickly see how Carl Hiaasen developed that point of view.
- Explain that you are going to use blue when it is Noah, the narrator saying, thinking, or doing something. If it were someone else saying, thinking, or doing something, we would use a different color to make it easy to see at a glance how the author has developed point of view.

- In the Evidence column, underline the evidence in blue.
- In the Technique column, draw word bubbles in blue and explain that you are doing so because they are Noah's words—what he is saying. See Point of View Anchor Chart (Teacher Reference) for guidance.

Closing and Assessment

A. Previewing Homework (2 minutes)

- Preview homework and distribute **Structured Notes: Chapter 1** and **evidence flags**.
- Tell students that each night they will have a point of view focus question for homework, based on the chapter they are reading. They are to record the chapter number, the question, the answer to the question, and evidence to support their answer in the appropriate columns.
- Model for students how to fill in the focus question and chapter number for today's homework. (For example, write, "What is Noah's point of view of his father's crime?" in the Homework Focus Question column and write, "1" in the Chapter column).

Meeting Students' Needs

Writing the focus question at the top of the structured notes will support students to recall their purpose for reading.

Homework

- Read chapter 1 of *Flush*. As you read, mark the text with at least three evidence flags to help you answer this focus question in your structured notes:
    - "What is Noah's point of view of his father's crime?"
- Remember to record any new vocabulary on your word-catcher.

Questions to Introduce *Flush*

1. What is the book mainly going to be about?

2. What connections can you make to the cover of the book now?

3. What was the *Coral Queen* "dumping illegally"?

4. Is dumping this in the ocean waterways an ethical or unethical action—a right or wrong choice? Use evidence from the text to explain your answer.

Questions to Introduce *Flush*
(Teacher Reference)

1. What is the book mainly going to be about?

   This book is going to be about Noah trying to catch the "fiendish flusher," who is dumping raw sewage in the ocean.

2. What connections can you make to the cover of the book now?

   The fish is swimming through the toilet bowl ring because the dumping is turning the ocean into a toilet bowl.

3. What was the *Coral Queen* "dumping illegally"?

   It was dumping the raw sewage, the human waste from the boat.

4. Is dumping this in the ocean waterways an ethical or unethical decision—a right or wrong choice? Use evidence from the text to explain your answer.

   It is unethical because the dumping causes great damage to both human and animal life, and it's breaking the law.

Flush Word-Catcher

Name: _____

Date: _____

Mark literary words with an * (for example: *inference).

A	B	C	D	E
F	G	H	I	J
K	L	M	N	O
P	Q	R	S	T
U	V	W	X	Y
Z	Use this space for notes.			

Point of View Anchor Chart

Claim	Evidence	Technique
What is Noah's point of view of his father's situation?	How do you know? (Choose specific words, phrases, and sentences from the text that support your claim.)	How does he tell us about it? (Thoughts? Words? Actions? By whom?)

Point of View Anchor Chart
(Teacher Reference)

Claim	Evidence	Technique
What is Noah's point of view of his father's situation?	**How do you know?** (Choose specific words, phrases, and sentences from the text that support your claim.)	**How does he tell us about it?** (Thoughts? Words? Actions? By whom?)
• He doesn't want his dad to be in jail—he wants him to say he's sorry and offer to pay for what he did so that he can come out.	• Noah asks his father, "How come you won't let Mom bail you out?" (page 1) • Noah asks his father, "Dad, what if you just said you're sorry and offered to pay for what you did?" (page 2) • Noah says to his father, "If you just paid to get it fixed, maybe then—" (page 3)	Word Word Word

Thought, Word, Action Symbols

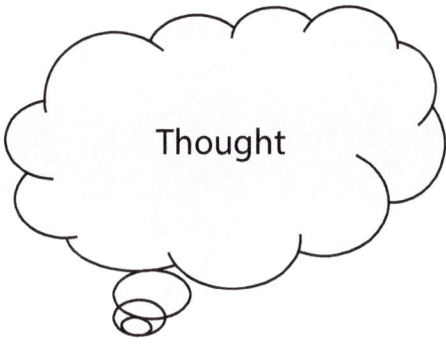

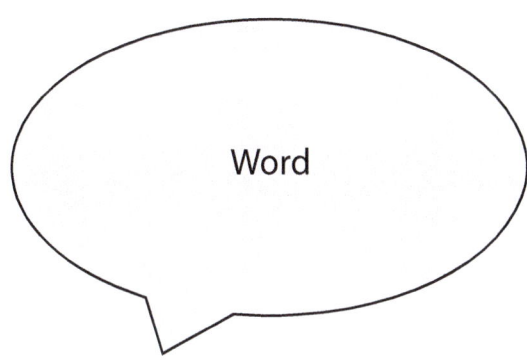

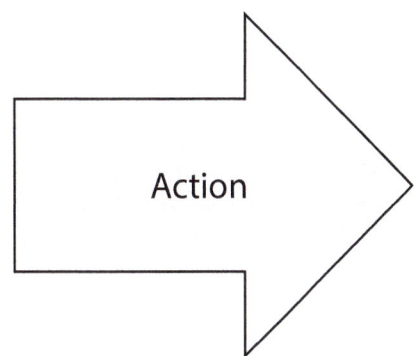

Structured Notes: Chapter 1

Name: _____

Date: _____

Chapter	Homework Focus Question	Answer to Homework Focus Question with Evidence from the Text (include page numbers)

LESSON 2

Analyzing Point of View and Figurative Language
Noah's Point of View of the *Coral Queen* and Dusty Muleman

Long-Term Targets Addressed (Based on ELA CCSS)

- I can determine the meaning of literal and figurative language (metaphors and similes) in a literary text. (RL.6.4)
- I can analyze how an author's word choice affects tone and meaning in a literary text. (RL.6.4)
- I can analyze how a particular sentence, stanza, scene, or chapter fits in and contributes to the development of a literary text. (RL.6.5)
- I can analyze how an author develops a narrator or speaker's point of view. (RL.6.6)
- I can use context (e.g., the overall meaning of a sentence or paragraph, a word's position or function in a sentence) to determine the meaning of a word or phrase. (L.6.4.a)

Supporting Learning Targets

- I can find the gist of pages 7–9 of *Flush*.
- I can analyze how Carl Hiaasen conveys Noah's point of view of the *Coral Queen* and Dusty Muleman.
- I can determine connotative and figurative meanings of language and analyze how the author's choice of words affects tone and meaning.
- I can explain how chapter 1 contributes to plot development.

Ongoing Assessment

- Structured Notes: Chapter 1 (from homework)
- Gist annotated on sticky notes
- Noah's Point of View Graphic Organizer: Pages 7–9

Agenda

1. Opening
   A. Engaging the Reader: Chapter 1 of *Flush* (5 minutes)
   B. Unpacking Learning Targets (5 minutes)
2. Work Time
   A. Rereading for Gist: Pages 7–9 (8 minutes)
   B. Analyzing Noah's Point of View: Connotative and Figurative Language (13 minutes)
   C. Analyzing Author's Craft: Point of View, Tone, and Meaning (8 minutes)
3. Closing and Assessment
   A. Analyzing Plot Development: Chapter 1 (6 minutes)
4. Homework
   A. Read chapters 2 and 3 of *Flush*. As you read, mark the text with evidence flags to help you answer the focus question in your structured notes.

Teaching Notes

- The primary focus of this unit is point of view, addressing standard RL.6.6. This unit also focuses on RL.6.4, analyzing the meaning and tone of figurative language. In this lesson, students build on their previous work on figurative language from Module 2.

- Students are introduced to a Point of View Graphic Organizer that will support both their analysis of the point of view of Noah and their analysis of the tone and meaning of words. This builds directly on the Point of View Anchor Chart begun in Lesson 1.

- In this lesson, students are reintroduced to the familiar routine of reading for gist and then analyzing the text. This routine will be repeated in Lessons 2–5.

- The closing of this lesson focuses students on RL.6.5, asking them to explain how chapter 1 contributes to the development of plot. Students are reminded of the plot work they did in Module 1 with the narrative story line of the Hero's Journey. Students are introduced to the *Flush* Plot Development Anchor Chart, which they will continue adding to in Lessons 3–10.

- From this lesson onward, students read two chapters of the novel for homework after each lesson. The volume of reading picks up here because by Module 3 students should have improved their reading stamina. This novel is fast-moving, high-interest, and of a level that sixth-grade students should be comfortable with. This volume of reading will also ensure that students encounter the content necessary to gather evidence to support their claims later on in the unit and will help them see how the author develops the plot from the beginning to the end of the book. Where possible, consider providing students with additional time to read or to catch up on reading the novel.

- In advance:
  - Read pages 7–9 of *Flush* as well as the answer key for the Point of View Graphic Organizer to familiarize yourself with what students will be doing and the answers you will need to guide them toward (see supporting materials).
  - Review the Back-to-Back and Face-to-Face protocol (see Appendix).
- Post: learning targets; Point of View Anchor Chart; Thought, Word, Action Symbols.

Lesson Vocabulary

literal language, figurative language, connotative language, tone, simile, metaphor, plot; gambling, marina, reservation

Materials

- Structured Notes: Chapter 1 (from homework)
- Equity sticks
- *Flush* Word-Catcher (begun in Lesson 1)
- *Flush* (book; distributed in Lesson 1; one per student)
- Sticky notes (five per student)
- Dictionaries (at least one per triad)
- Noah's Point of View Graphic Organizer: Pages 7–9 (one per student and one to display)
- Point of View Anchor Chart (begun in Lesson 1)
- Noah's Point of View Graphic Organizer: Pages 7–9 (Teacher Reference)
- Thought, Word, Action Symbols (one for display; from Lesson 1)
- Colored pencils or markers (blue and one other color; one of each color per student)
- *Flush* Plot Development Anchor Chart (new, co-created with students during Closing and Assessment A; see supporting materials)
- Structured Notes: Chapters 2 and 3 (one for display; one per student)
- Evidence flags (at least three per student)

Opening

A. Engaging the Reader: Chapter 1 of *Flush* (5 minutes)

- Direct students to retrieve their **Structured Notes: Chapter 1** homework.
- Tell students that they will engage in the Back-to-Back and Face-to-Face protocols:
  1. With their structured notes in hand, invite students to pair up with someone.
  2. Invite pairs to stand back-to-back.
  3. Ask students: "What are the main scenes or actions that happen in chapter 1?"

4. Give students a minute to think before asking them to turn face-to-face with their partner to share the answer.
5. Invite pairs to stand back-to-back again.
6. Ask students the homework focus question: "What is Noah's point of view of his father's crime?"
7. Give them a minute to think and refer to the answers and evidence they wrote in their structured notes before asking them to turn face-to-face with their partner to share the answer.

- Direct students to return to their seats. Use **equity sticks** to call on a student to share Noah's point of view of his father's crime and one piece of evidence that supports that claim. Listen for students to explain that he thought his dad had messed up by committing the crime because he says, "Even for him this was a major screw-up," and he also describes the sunken ship—the scene of the crime—as "bad."

Meeting Students' Needs

Opening the lesson by asking students to share their homework makes them accountable for completing it. It also gives you the opportunity to monitor which students are not doing their homework.

B. Unpacking Learning Targets (5 minutes)

- Invite students to get into triads and read the learning targets with you:
  - "I can find the gist of pages 7–9 of *Flush*."
  - "I can analyze how Carl Hiaasen conveys Noah's point of view of the *Coral Queen* and Dusty Muleman."
  - "I can determine connotative and figurative meanings of language and analyze how the author's choice of words affects tone and meaning."
  - "I can explain how chapter 1 contributes to plot development."
- Explain to students that the first two learning targets are linked because figurative language and the tone of words both contribute to the point of view we understand from a text.
- Remind students that they should be familiar with gist from their work in Modules 1 and 2, and with point of view from the previous lesson's learning target.
- Circle the italicized words below and ask triads to discuss each of these questions in turn:
  - "What is *literal language*?"
  - "What is *figurative language*?"
  - "What is *tone*?"
  - "What is *connotative meaning*?"
- Refocus the whole class and ask for volunteers to share their responses. Listen for and guide students to recall that *literal language* means exactly what it says, *figurative language* is describing something by comparing it to something else, and *tone* is the author's or narrator's attitude toward something in the novel.

- Explain that *connotative meaning* is the association connected to a word. For example, you could trudge through the snow or you could stroll through the snow. Both suggest a similar pace, but trudge brings a sense of a negative association like it is something you really don't want to do, whereas stroll sounds leisurely and fun.
- Direct students to add these terms to their **Flush** Word-Catcher, as they will be referring to them throughout the unit.

Meeting Students' Needs

- Learning targets are a research-based strategy that helps all students, especially challenged learners.
- Posting learning targets allows students to reference them throughout the lesson to check their understanding. Learning targets also provide a reminder to students and teachers about the intended learning behind a given lesson or activity.

Work Time

A. Rereading for Gist: Pages 7–9 (8 minutes)

- Ask students to keep their word-catchers out, and also take out **Flush**. Distribute about five **sticky notes** to each student. Tell them they are going to reread pages 7–9 of the novel for gist.
- Remind students that they read for gist a lot in *World Without Fish* in Unit 1. Remind them that the sticky notes are for them to annotate the text as they read. Also remind students to ask questions as they read.
- Ensure that each triad has a **dictionary**. Tell students that where possible, you would like them to read around unfamiliar words, looking for context clues to figure out what they mean; however, if they can't figure out the meaning from the context, encourage them to look the word up. If they aren't sure what the word means after looking for context clues and looking in the dictionary, they should leave the definition to be discussed with the whole group later on.
- Explain to students that they are going to reread from the section break on page 7, from "The *Coral Queen* had gone down stern-first" to the end of page 9. Tell them to work with their triads to read for gist, annotate sticky notes, and record unfamiliar words on their word-catchers. Note to students that in this narrative there is a lot of dialogue. As they chunk the text for gist, they might want to group the dialogue into one section. (For example on page 9 there is a discussion between Abbey and Noah which goes on for approximately 10 lines that could be grouped into one paragraph).
- Circulate and support students as they read. For those who need more support, ask them to practice telling you the gist of a section before they write it on a sticky note.
- Refocus the whole group and focus students on the word *marina*. Ask students to discuss in triads:
  - "What root word can you see in the word *marina*?"
  - "Think back to *World Without Fish*. What does the word *marine* mean?"

- Cold-call students to share their responses. Listen for students to explain that marine means relating to the ocean or sea. Ask students to discuss in triads:
  - "So what is a marina? You know it is something to do with the sea or ocean, so knowing that and looking at the sentence around the word, what does *marina* mean?"
- Select students to share their responses. Listen for students to explain that a marina is a dock with places to tie up boats.
- Focus students on the word *reservation*. Ask students to discuss in triads:
  - "What does *reservation* mean? Is there more than one meaning?"
- Cold-call students to share their responses. Listen for students to explain that there is more than one meaning. One meaning is to reserve something or to save a space, for example a table at a restaurant or a room in a hotel. Another meaning, as in this example, is a protected area of land managed by someone. For example, in *Flush* the reference is to an American Indian reservation—an area of land protected by a Native American tribe.
- Invite students to share any unfamiliar vocabulary words they found on pages 7–9. If students were unable to work out the definition from the context or find it in a dictionary, encourage other students to assist them with the definition. To keep things moving, if no one else knows what the word means, define it for the class.
- Consider probing students to make sure they understand that the law allows Native American tribes to operate casinos only on reservation land, and that the Miccosukees had bought a marina to be part of reservation land. This allowed Dusty to operate a casino there.
- Ensure that students understand what the word *gambling* means.
- Remind students to record new words on their word-catchers.

Meeting Students' Needs

- Asking students to identify challenging vocabulary helps them monitor their understanding of a complex text.
- ELL students may be unfamiliar with more vocabulary words than are mentioned in this lesson. Check for comprehension of general words that most students would know.

B. Analyzing Noah's Point of View: Connotative and Figurative Language (13 minutes)

- Refocus the whole class. Ask a volunteer to reread the point of view learning target to the class:
  - "I can analyze how Carl Hiaasen conveys Noah's point of view of the *Coral Queen* and Dusty Muleman.'"
- Display and distribute **Noah's Point of View Graphic Organizer: Pages 7–9**.
- Explain that for the next several lessons, students are going to work on analyzing Noah's point of view using this graphic organizer. Remind students that they began examining Noah's point of view

of his father's situation in the previous lesson and for homework. Direct students' attention to the posted **Point of View Anchor Chart** from Lesson 1. Ask students to discuss in triads:

- "How are the anchor chart and your new graphic organizer similar? How are they different?"

- Use equity sticks to call on students and listen for them to explain that they are similar because the first two columns ask for a claim and evidence to support the claim. The third columns are different since the anchor chart focused on author technique and the graphic organizer focuses on tone and meaning.

- Focus the class on the three paragraphs at the bottom of page 7 in *Flush*. Invite them to reread those paragraphs silently in their heads as you read them aloud.

- Explain that you are going to think aloud as you model how to analyze Noah's point of view of the boat the *Coral Queen* and Dusty Muleman on this graphic organizer. Direct students to pay attention to your thinking and analysis process.

- The think-aloud should sound something like this:
  - "As I look over the paragraphs, I think that Noah didn't like the *Coral Queen* very much and thought it was big and ugly."

- Record this in the first column of the displayed graphic organizer and invite students to do the same on their own copy. Continue with the think-aloud:
  - "Column 2 of the organizer asks me what words or phrases really support my claim about Noah's point of view. As I look back at page 7 in the book, I see evidence in paragraph 2 where it says, 'It was like a big ugly apartment building had fallen out of the sky and landed in the basin.'"

- Record this in the middle column of the displayed graphic organizer and invite students to do the same on their own copy.

- Invite students to work in triads to repeat this process for the rest of pages 7–9.

- Circulate to support students as they work. Refer to **Noah's Point of View Graphic Organizer: Pages 7–9 (Teacher Reference)**. As you circulate, refocus students as necessary by asking:
  - "What is Noah's point of view of the boat and Dusty Muleman?"
  - "How do you know? What does he say? What does he do to make you think that?"
  - "Where can you see that in the text?"

- Refocus the whole class.

- Tell students that *Flush* uses figurative language such as *similes* and *metaphors* to help us better understand how things look and what characters think and feel.

- Invite the class to reread the figurative language learning target with you:
  - "I can determine connotative and figurative meanings of language and analyze how the author's choice of words affects tone and meaning."

- Direct students to look back at the evidence they recorded in the middle column of their graphic organizers and ask triads to discuss:
  - "Can you identify any figurative language in the notes you have taken? Remember that figurative language is when you describe something by comparing it to something else."

- Use equity sticks to select students to share their responses. Listen for them to point out: "It was like a big ugly apartment building had fallen out of the sky and landed in the basin." Circle this example on your displayed model and invite students to do the same on their own copies.
- Ask triads to discuss:
  - "What kind of figurative language is this example? How do you know?"
- Use equity sticks to call on students for their responses. Listen for them to explain that it is a simile, because similes often use "like" or "as" to compare two things.
- Ask triads to discuss:
  - "What do these phrases literally mean? Does it mean that the boat is an apartment building?"
- Use equity sticks to select students to share their responses. Listen for them to explain that it means the boat looked huge and the part of the boat that looked like a boat was under water, with just the cabins showing above water. As a result, it looked like an apartment building.
- Ask triads to discuss:
  - "So why did Hiaasen use figurative language here?"
- Cold-call students to share their responses. Listen for students to explain that it paints a picture in the reader's mind of what the *Coral Queen* looked like submerged, as some people may never have seen a half-sunken boat to be able to picture what it looks like.
- Focus students on the phrase, "'He's lost his marbles,' Abbey muttered."
- Ask triads to discuss:
  - "So what does this literally mean? Did Noah's dad really lose his marbles?"
- Select volunteers to share their responses. Listen for students to explain that it means to go insane.
- Ask triads to discuss:
  - "So why did Hiaasen use figurative language here?"
- Cold-call students to share their responses. Listen for students to explain that this is a common saying that is an informal way of saying someone has gone insane, and it's something that a child like Abbey is more likely to say.
- Remind students that another focus of the learning target was connotative language. Focus students on the phrase, "I locked my bike to a buttonwood tree and walked down to the charter docks, Abbey trailing behind."
- Focus students particularly on the word *trailing* and ask them to discuss in triads:
  - "What connotation does the word *trailing* suggest?"
  - "What words could have been used instead with a different connotation?"'
- Consider using equity sticks to select students to share their responses. Listen for students to explain that trailing suggests Abbey didn't want to keep up and that she was purposely hanging back. *Following* could have been used to create a sense of her wanting to keep up willingly, but being just slightly behind.

Meeting Students' Needs

- Graphic organizers and recording forms engage students more actively and provide scaffolding that is especially critical for learners with lower levels of language proficiency and/or learning.

- When reviewing graphic organizers or recording forms, consider using a document camera to display the document for students who struggle with auditory processing.

- Providing models of expected work supports all learners, especially challenged learners.

C. Analyzing Author's Craft: Point of View, Tone, and Meaning (8 minutes)

- Refocus the whole class.
- Continue with the think-aloud using the example started on the displayed graphic organizer:
  - "This third column is new to us. As I read over the top of it, I ask myself, what tone and meaning can I infer from the evidence I have recorded? As I read back over this text evidence, the words 'big' and 'ugly' stand out to me. I don't think Noah likes the *Coral Queen*, so the tone I infer from this is dislike."
- Record "dislike" in the final column of the organizer.
- Invite students to work in triads to do the same for the evidence they have recorded in the second column of their organizers.
- Circulate to support students as they work. Refer to **Noah's Point of View Graphic Organizer: Pages 7–9 (Teacher Reference)** as needed. As you circulate, refocus students as necessary by asking:
  - "What tone can you infer from what he says or thinks here? Does he seem disappointed? Angry? Excited?"
- As students begin to finish, refocus the whole class.
- Refer to the posted **Thought, Word, Action Symbols** and remind students that an author can develop a point of view using the narrator's or another character's thoughts, words, or actions. Pick up a blue pen/marker and continue with the think-aloud:
  - "We still want to identify how Carl Hiaasen developed point of view. As I look back at column 2, I see that this is from Noah, not another character. Remember that we determined in Lesson 1 that we would use blue to represent Noah's point of view. So I will draw a blue line under the evidence in column 2. Next, I notice these are Noah's thoughts, not an action or a conversation. So I'm going to draw a thought bubble next to the evidence."
- Distribute **colored pencils or markers**. Direct students to copy the blue you just drew onto their Noah's Point of View Graphic Organizer: Pages 7–9 and to make sure they have row 1 completed as you modeled it.

- Invite students to work in triads to do the same with the rest of the evidence they have recorded in the second column of their organizer. Remind students to underline the rest of the evidence they have recorded as follows:
  - Noah's own thoughts, actions, and feelings—blue
  - The words and actions of others—another color
- Remind students to then code each piece of evidence as a thought, word, or action.
- Circulate to support students as they work. Refer to Noah's Point of View Graphic Organizer: Pages 7–9 (Teacher Reference) as needed. As you circulate, refocus students as necessary by asking:
  - "Is this something Noah is saying? Something he is thinking? Something he is doing? How do you know?"

Meeting Students' Needs

Asking students to color code and add symbols to their text provides a clear visual reference for analysis.

Closing and Assessment

A. Analyzing Plot Development: Chapter 1 (6 minutes)

- Read aloud the learning target about plot:
  - "I can explain how chapter 1 contributes to plot development."
- Display the **Flush** Plot Development Anchor Chart. Remind students that they worked on *plot* in Module 1 when they created their narrative story lines for the Hero's Journey. Remind students of what each of the words in the boxes means:
  - Exposition: introduces the theme, setting, and character
  - Rising Action: what happens in the story to lead toward the main event
  - Climax: the main event
  - Resolution: what happens after the main event
- Explain that you want students to determine how chapter 1 exposes the plot—the exposition. Post the following questions and invite students to discuss them with their triads:
  - "Whom did we meet and how are they connected to each other?"
  - "Where is the story taking place?"
  - "What plot does the beginning of the story set up?"
- Refocus the whole class and use equity sticks to call on a few triads. As students share their answers, write the gist of who, where, and what under "Exposition." Listen for students to share:
  - Who: Noah, his Dad, Abbey, his Mom, and Dusty Muleman. The first four are family. Dusty is the owner of the casino boat.

- - Where: The story is taking place in Key West, Florida, near the ocean.
  - What: The main conflict is that Dusty Muleman is dumping sewage into the waterway from his boat and the family wants to stop it.
- Ask students to synthesize the information they have just recorded on the *Flush* Plot Development Anchor Chart by discussing in triads:
  - "How did chapter 1 contribute to plot development in *Flush*?"
- Select volunteers to share their ideas with the whole group. Listen for students to explain that it introduces the characters and setting and sets up the plot.
- Preview homework and distribute **Structured Notes: Chapters 2 and 3** and **evidence flags**.

Meeting Students' Needs

Capturing ideas on an anchor chart can ensure quick reference later on and can also enable students to quickly see how the plot has developed throughout a novel.

Homework

- Read chapters 2 and 3 of *Flush*. As you read, mark the text with at least three evidence flags to help you answer this focus question in your structured notes:
  - "What is Noah's point of view of Jasper? How do you know?"
- Remember to record any new vocabulary on your word-catcher.

Noah's Point of View Graphic Organizer: Pages 7–9

Name: _____

Date: _____

Learning targets:

- "I can analyze how an author's word choice affects tone and meaning in a literary text." (RL.6.4)
- "I can analyze how an author develops a narrator or speaker's point of view." (RL.6.6)

Claim	Evidence	Word Choice
What is Noah's point of view of the *Coral Queen* and Dusty Muleman?	How do you know? How did Hiaasen develop Noah's point of view of the *Coral Queen* and Dusty Muleman? (Use specific words, phrases, and sentences from the text.)	Describe the tone of the text with one word (for example, angry or sad).

Noah's Point of View Graphic Organizer: Pages 7–9
(Teacher Reference)

Claim	Evidence	Word Choice
What is Noah's point of view of the *Coral Queen* and Dusty Muleman?	How do you know? How did Hiaasen develop Noah's point of view of the *Coral Queen* and Dusty Muleman? (Use specific words, phrases, and sentences from the text.)	Describe the tone of the text with one word (for example, angry or sad).
Noah sees the *Coral Queen* as a big, ugly boat.	*It was like a big ugly apartment building had fallen out of the sky and landed in the basin.* (page 7) THOUGHT	Dislike
Noah supports his father because he sees Dusty's actions as disgusting.	*"He's lost his marbles,"* Abbey muttered. *"Who—Dad? No way,"* I said. *"Then why did he do it?"* *"Because Dusty Muleman has been dumping his holding tank into the water,"* I said. Abbey grimaced. *"Yuck. From the toilets?"* *"Yep. In the middle of the night, when there's nobody around."* *"That's so gross."* (page 9) WORDS OF NOAH AND ABBEY	Sickened; revulsion
Noah's sees Dusty as a greedy criminal	*"And totally illegal,"* I said. *"He only does it to save money."* (page 9) WORDS	Upset; angry

Flush Plot Development Anchor Chart

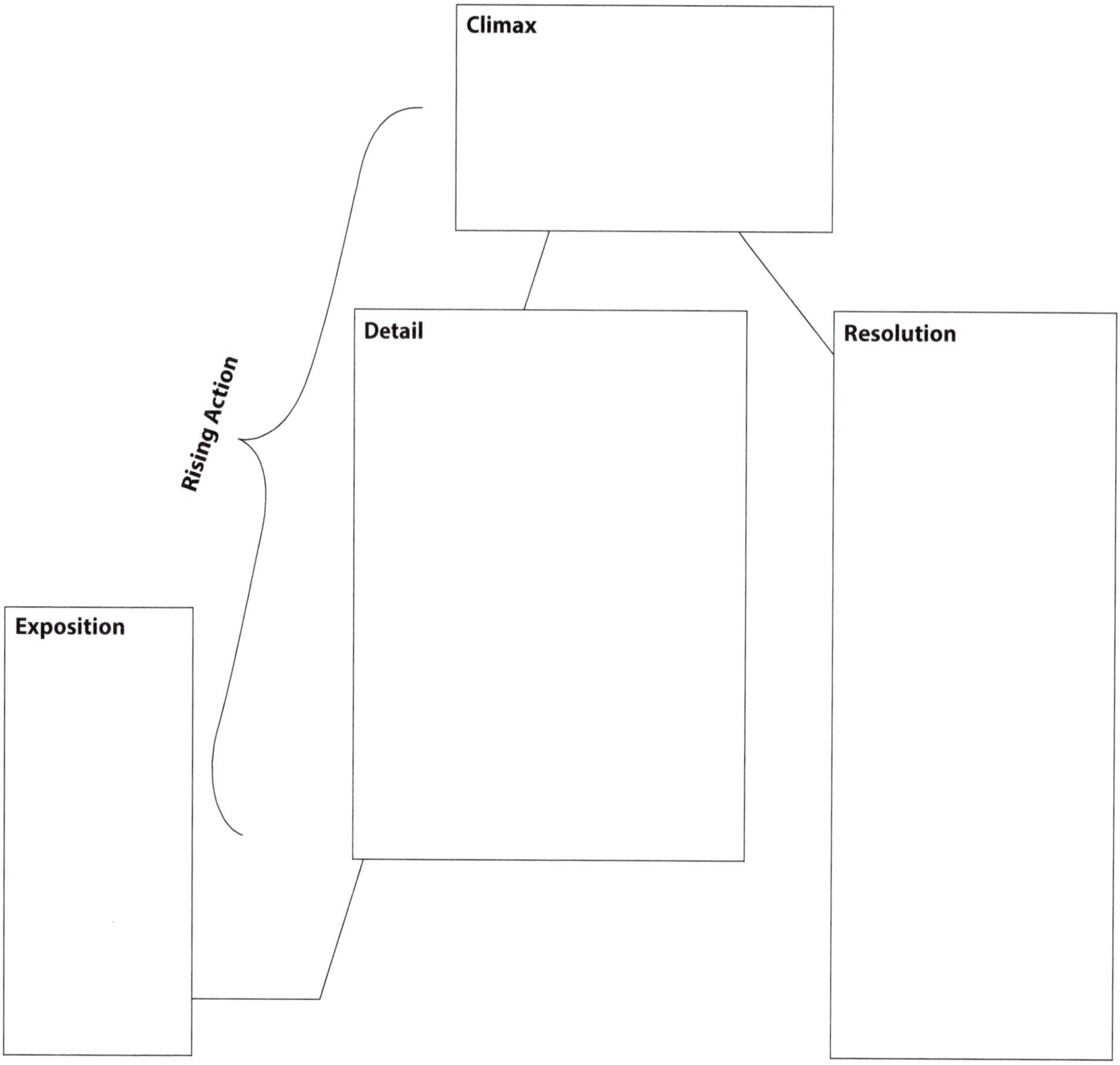

Climax

Detail

Resolution

Rising Action

Exposition

Structured Notes: Chapters 2 and 3

Name: _____

Date: _____

Chapter	Homework Focus Question	Answer to Homework Focus Question with Evidence from the Text (include page numbers)

LESSON 3

Analyzing Point of View and Figurative Language

Noah's Point of View of Lice Peeking

Long-Term Targets Addressed (Based on ELA CCSS)

- I can determine the meaning of literal and figurative language (metaphors and similes) in a literary text. (RL.6.4)
- I can analyze how an author's word choice affects tone and meaning in a literary text. (RL.6.4)
- I can analyze how a particular sentence, stanza, scene, or chapter fits in and contributes to the development of a literary text. (RL.6.5)
- I can analyze how an author develops a narrator or speaker's point of view. (RL.6.6)
- I can use context (e.g., the overall meaning of a sentence or paragraph, a word's position or function in a sentence) to determine the meaning of a word or phrase. (L.6.4.a)

Supporting Learning Targets

- I can analyze how Carl Hiaasen develops Noah's point of view of Lice Peeking.
- I can determine connotative and figurative meanings of language and analyze how the author's choice of words affects tone and meaning.
- I can analyze how chapters 2 and 3 contribute to plot development.

Ongoing Assessment

- Structured Notes: Chapters 2 and 3 (from homework)
- Noah's Point of View Graphic Organizer: Pages 17–19

Agenda

1. Opening
   A. Engaging the Reader: Chapters 2 and 3 of *Flush* (5 minutes)
   B. Unpacking Learning Targets (2 minutes)

2. Work Time
   A. Rereading Pages 17–19 for Unfamiliar Vocabulary (6 minutes)
   B. Analyzing Point of View, Figurative Language, and Tone: Pages 17–19 (15 minutes)
   C. Determining Author's Techniques: Point of View, Tone, and Meaning (8 minutes)
3. Closing and Assessment
   A. Analyzing Plot Development in Chapters 2 and 3 (9 minutes)
4. Homework
   A. Read chapters 4 and 5 of *Flush*. As you read, mark the text with evidence flags to help you answer the focus question in your structured notes.
   B. Record any new vocabulary words on your word-catcher.

Teaching Notes

- In preparation for the mid-unit assessment, this lesson begins to gradually release students to work more independently. They work in triads without any teacher modeling to analyze an excerpt of *Flush* for point of view, figurative language, tone, and meaning.
- At the end of Work Time C, collect Noah's Point of View Graphic Organizer: Pages 17–19 to check students' understanding of making a claim, selecting text evidence, and determining tone. Consider making a list of students who need extra support, noting what they are doing well and what concrete next steps will lead to improvement.
- In advance:
  - Read pages 17–19 of *Flush* and Noah's Point of View Graphic Organizer: Pages 17–19 (Teacher Reference) to familiarize yourself with what students will be doing and the answers you will need to guide them toward (see supporting materials).
  - Review Plot Development: The Rising Action in *Flush* Graphic Organizer to familiarize yourself with what students will be doing in the Closing and Assessment (see supporting materials).
  - Review the Mix and Mingle protocol activity in Opening A and have music ready to use for the opening of this lesson.
- Post: learning targets; Thought, Word, Action Symbols.

Lesson Vocabulary

rising action; snuffed, accustomed

Materials

- Structured Notes: Chapters 2 and 3 (from homework)
- Equity sticks
- *Flush* (book; distributed in Lesson 1; one per student)

- *Flush* Word-Catcher (begun in Lesson 1)
- Noah's Point of View Graphic Organizer: Pages 17–19 (one per student)
- Noah's Point of View Graphic Organizer: Pages 17–19 (Teacher Reference)
- Thought, Word, Action Symbols (from Lesson 1)
- Colored pencils or markers (blue and one other color; one of each color per student)
- *Flush* Plot Development Anchor Chart (from Lesson 2)
- Plot Development: The Rising Action in *Flush* Anchor Chart (new; co-created with students in Closing and Assessment)
- Plot Development: The Rising Action in *Flush* Anchor Chart (Teacher Reference)
- Structured Notes: Chapters 4 and 5 (one per student)
- Evidence flags (at least three per student)

Opening

A. Engaging the Reader: Chapters 2 and 3 of *Flush* (5 minutes)

- Ask students to retrieve their **Structured Notes: Chapters 2 and 3** homework and remind them of how Mix and Mingle works.
- Mix and Mingle:
    1. Play music. Invite students to move around the room with their structured notes homework.
    2. After 15 seconds, stop the music.
    3. Invite students to share their answer to the following question with the person standing closest to them: "What happens in chapter 2?"
    4. Repeat Steps 1 and 2.
    5. Invite students to share their answer to the following question with the person standing closest to them: "What happens in chapter 3?"
    6. Repeat Steps 1 and 2.
    7. Invite students to share their answer to the following question with the person standing closest to them: "What is Noah's point of view of Jasper and how do you know?"
- Refocus the whole class and direct students to sit in their triads as they return to their seats.

Meeting Students' Needs

Opening the lesson by asking students to share their homework makes students accountable for completing it. It also gives you the opportunity to monitor which students have not been completing their homework.

B. Unpacking Learning Targets (2 minutes)

- Invite students to read the learning targets aloud with you:
  - "I can analyze how Carl Hiaasen develops Noah's point of view of Lice Peeking."
  - "I can determine connotative and figurative meanings of language and analyze how the author's choice of words affects tone and meaning."
  - "I can analyze how chapters 2 and 3 contribute to plot development."
- Students should be familiar with these learning targets from previous lessons. Remind students of vocabulary they have explored in previous lessons: gist, connotative language, figurative language, tone, point of view, and plot.

Meeting Students' Needs

- Learning targets are a research-based strategy that helps all students, especially challenged learners.
- Posting learning targets allows students to reference them throughout the lesson to check their understanding. Learning targets also provide a reminder to students and teachers about the intended learning behind a given lesson or activity.

Work Time

A. Rereading Pages 17–19 For Unfamiliar Vocabulary (6 minutes)

- Ask students to take out their copies of **Flush**. Invite two students to read the parts of Noah and Lice, and invite the rest of the class to read along silently in their heads from "'Mr. Peeking?' I said. His real name was Charles," on page 17 to the end of page 19.
- Ask students to take out their **Flush Word-Catchers**. As students have already read this section of *Flush* for homework and should have already recorded unfamiliar vocabulary on their word-catchers, invite them to work in triads to share any unfamiliar vocabulary words they found on pages 17–19, along with the definition. If they were unable to work out the definition from the context or find it in a dictionary, encourage other students to assist them with the definition.
- Focus students on the word *snuffed* on page 18. Invite them to read the sentence around the word to see if they can work out what it means from the context. Ask:
  - "What word or words could you use in place of *snuffed* in this sentence?"
- Cold-call students to share their responses. Listen for students to explain that they could use the words "put out" or "extinguished" because that is what *snuff* means.
- Focus students on the word *accustomed* on page 18. Again invite them to read the sentence around the word to see if they can work out what it means from the context. Ask:
  - "What word or words could you use in place of *accustomed* in this sentence?"

- Consider using equity sticks to select students to share their responses. Listen for students to explain that they could use the words "used to" or "familiar with" because that is what *accustomed* means.
- Remind students to record new words on their word-catchers.

Meeting Students' Needs

- Asking students to identify challenging vocabulary helps them to monitor their understanding of a complex text.
- ELL students may be unfamiliar with more vocabulary words than are mentioned in this lesson. Check for comprehension of general words that most students would know.

B. Analyzing Point of View, Figurative Language, and Tone: Pages 17–19 (15 minutes)

- Distribute **Noah's Point of View Graphic Organizer: Pages 17–19** and remind students that they filled out a similar organizer in Lesson 2 to analyze Noah's point of view of the *Coral Queen* and Dusty Muleman.
- Invite students to read through the directions at the beginning of the organizer with you and encourage them to ask questions if they don't understand.
- Circulate to assist students with analyzing the text for point of view, language, and tone. Refer to **Noah's Point of View Graphic Organizer: Pages 17–19 (Teacher Reference)** to guide students. As you circulate, ask probing questions such as:
    - "What is Noah's point of view about Lice Peeking?"
    - "How do you know? Which specific words, phrases, and sentences from the text support your claim about Noah's point of view?"
- Refocus the whole class.
- Remind students that *Flush* uses figurative language such as similes and metaphors to help us better understand how things look and what characters think and feel.
- Invite the class to reread the figurative language learning target aloud with you:
    - "I can determine connotative and figurative meanings of language and analyze how the author's choice of words affects tone and meaning."
- Direct students to look back at the evidence they recorded in the middle column of their graphic organizers and ask them to discuss in triads:
    - "Can you identify any figurative language in the notes you have taken? Remember that figurative language is when you describe something by comparing it to something else."
- Invite students to circle figurative language on their graphic organizers.
- Use equity sticks to select students to share their responses. Listen for students to point out: "He looked like a sick iguana." If this isn't suggested, draw students' attention to it on page 19 and ask triads to discuss:
    - "So what kind of figurative language is this example? How do you know?"

- Use equity sticks to call on students for their responses. Listen for them to explain that it is a simile, because similes often use "like" or "as" to compare two things.
- Ask triads to discuss:
  - "Why does Hiaasen use figurative language here? What does it do for the reader?"
- Listen for students to explain that it helps the reader create a mental picture of what Lice Peeking looked like and his character.
- Focus students on the name "Lice." Ask students to discuss in triads:
  - "What connotation does that name have?"
- Select volunteers to share their responses. Listen for students to explain that it suggests something dirty that no one wants or likes because lice are generally associated with dirtiness and are never wanted.
- Focus students on the phrase, "Lice Peeking propped himself against the wall of the trailer."
- Ask students to discuss in triads:
  - "What connotation does the word 'propped' have? What does it make you think?"
  - "What words could have been used instead with a different connotation?"
- Cold-call students to share their responses. Listen for students to explain that the word *propped* has the connotation that he was unable to stand and that the wall stopped him from falling over. *Leaned* could have been used instead, but that would suggest that instead of stopping him from falling over, the wall was just helping to relieve the weight on his feet.

Meeting Students' Needs

- Graphic organizers and recording forms engage students more actively and provide the necessary scaffolding that is especially critical for learners with lower levels of language proficiency and/or learning.
- When reviewing graphic organizers or recording forms, consider using a document camera to display the document for students who struggle with auditory processing.

C. Determining Author's Techniques: Point of View, Tone, and Meaning (8 minutes)

- Refer to the posted **Thought, Word, Action Symbols** and remind students of the ways authors can develop point of view.
- Tell students that now they are going to continue to work in triads to analyze how the author has developed point of view by looking at the evidence from the text recorded in the middle column of their Noah's Point of View Graphic Organizer: Pages 17–19. Distribute **colored pencils or markers** and remind students to underline evidence as follows:
  - Noah's own thoughts, actions, and feelings—blue
  - The words and actions of others—another color
- Remind students to then code each piece of evidence as a thought, word, or action.

- Refocus the whole group. Ask students:
  - "So what techniques does Hiaasen use most often to develop Noah's point of view of Lice Peeking in this excerpt?"
- Cold-call students to share their responses with the whole group. Listen for students to explain that in this excerpt, most of Noah's point of view comes from his own thoughts.
- Invite students to focus on the Tone column of the graphic organizer. Ask triads to share the words they chose and to justify why they infer that tone.
- Remind students that the tone helps to determine the point of view because it gives us an idea of what the narrator thinks of or feels about the subject.
- Collect students' Noah's Point of View Graphic Organizers: Pages 17–19 to check for understanding.

Meeting Students' Needs

- Asking students to color code and add symbols to their text provides a clear visual reference for analysis.
- Collecting students' graphic organizers allows a quick check for understanding of the learning targets so that instruction can be adjusted or tailored to students' needs during the lesson or before the next lesson.

Closing and Assessment

A. Analyzing Plot Development in Chapters 2 and 3 (9 minutes)

- Ask a student to read aloud the learning target about plot:
  - "I can analyze how chapters 2 and 3 contribute to plot development."
- Display the *Flush* **Plot Development Anchor Chart** begun in Lesson 2.
- Focus students on the words *Rising Action* along the left side diagonal line. Explain that the bulk of a novel is the rising action. Ask triads to discuss:
  - "What is rising action?"
- Refocus the whole class and listen for students to share something like: "It is how the action, tension, or conflicts grow or increase throughout the book."
- Explain that something in each chapter is going to cause the action to rise or an increase in conflict or tension. It is like a drum solo building up to a really big and fast pattern. Tell students you want them to determine how chapter 2 contributes to the rising action of the plot.
- Display **Plot Development: The Rising Action in *Flush* Anchor Chart** and read aloud the headings in row 1. Emphasize that in order to analyze the rising action, students first need to determine the main events in the chapters, determine how each event impacted the conflict or tension, and then explain how they know this. Ask students to discuss in triads:
  - "What were the main events in chapter 2?"

- Select volunteers to share their answers with the whole group. Listen for and list each event in the second column. For suggested answers, see **Plot Development: The Rising Action in *Flush* Anchor Chart (Teacher Reference)**.
- Ask students to discuss in triads:
  - "What were the main events in chapter 3?"
- Select volunteers to share their answers with the whole group. Listen for and list each event in the second column. For suggested answers, see Plot Development: The Rising Action in *Flush* Anchor Chart (Teacher Reference).
- Explain that the events help to develop the plot by introducing new characters, information, conflicts, or tensions, or by adding one that has already been introduced. Ask students to discuss in their triads:
  - "How do the events in chapter 2 contribute to the plot development? Do they provide/build on conflict or tension?"
- Select volunteers to share their answers with the whole group. Listen for and list student responses in the final column. For suggested answers, see Plot Development: The Rising Action in *Flush* Anchor Chart (Teacher Reference).
- Ask students to discuss in their triads:
  - "How do the events in chapter 3 contribute to the plot development? Do they provide/build on conflict or tension?"
- Select volunteers to share their answers with the whole group. Listen for and list student responses in the final column. For suggested answers, see Plot Development: The Rising Action in *Flush* Anchor Chart (Teacher Reference).
- Ask students to synthesize information:
  - "So how did chapters 2 and 3 contribute to the rising action of the plot in *Flush*?"
- Refocus the whole class and use equity sticks to call on a few triads to share their answer. On the *Flush* Plot Development Anchor Chart, record next to the Rising Action line something similar to: "Chapters 2 and 3 introduce: Lice, who might help; conflicts with Jasper; and tension between Noah's mom and dad."
- Preview homework and distribute **Structured Notes: Chapters 4 and 5** and **evidence flags**.

Meeting Students' Needs

- Graphic organizers and recording forms engage students more actively and provide the necessary scaffolding that is especially critical for learners with lower levels of language proficiency and/or learning
- When reviewing graphic organizers or recording forms, consider using a document camera to display the document for students who struggle with auditory processing.

Homework

- Read chapters 4 and 5 of *Flush*. As you read, mark the text with at least three evidence flags to help you answer this focus question in your structured notes:
    - "What does Noah think about Miles Umlatt? How do you know?"
- Record any new vocabulary on your word-catcher.

Noah's Point of View Graphic Organizer: Pages 17–19

Name: _____

Date: _____

Learning targets:

- "I can analyze how an author's word choice affects tone and meaning in a literary text." (RL.6.4)
- "I can analyze how an author develops a narrator or speaker's point of view." (RL.6.6)

Directions

1. Reread pages 17–19 of *Flush* from "'Mr. Peeking?' I said. His real name was Charles," on page 17 to the end of page 19.
2. In triads, discuss the question: What is Noah's point of view of Lice Peeking? Use evidence from the text to support your answer.
3. Record your claims in the first column of the organizer.
4. Record evidence from the text to support those claims in the middle column. Remember to use quotation marks and to include the page number.
5. Choose one word to describe the tone of the evidence you have recorded and record it in the final column.

Claim	Evidence	Word Choice
What is Noah's point of view of Lice Peeking?	How do you know? How did Hiaasen develop Noah's point of view of Lice Peeking? (Use specific words, phrases, and sentences from the text.) Circle figurative language.	Describe the tone of the text with one word (for example, angry or sad).

Noah's Point of View Graphic Organizer: Pages 17–19
(Teacher Reference)

Claim	Evidence	Word Choice
What is Noah's point of view of Lice Peeking?	How do you know? How did Hiaasen develop Noah's point of view of Lice Peeking? (Use specific words, phrases, and sentences from the text.) Circle figurative language.	Describe the tone of the text with one word (for example, angry or sad).
Noah sees Lice as dirty and unkempt.	"… everyone called him Lice, for obvious reasons. … It didn't look like his bathing habits had improved much since then." (page 17) – THOUGHT	Disgusted; repelled
Noah sees Lice as mean.	"Lice Peeking started laughing so hard, I thought he might have an asthma attack and fall on the floor. Obviously the news about my father had brightened his day." (page 17) – THOUGHT	Sad; disappointed
Noah sees Lice as selfish and greedy.	"Dad had warned me that Lice Peeking wasn't accustomed to doing something because it was decent and right. He predicted that Lice Peeking might demand something in return." (page 18) – THOUGHT	Disgusted; disappointed
Noah sees Lice as weak and sickly.	"To keep from wobbling, Lice Peeking braced himself with both arms … His face was pasty in the sunlight, and his eyes were glassy and dim. He looked like a sick old iguana, … he was only twenty-nine. It was hard to believe." (page 19) – THOUGHT	Pitying

Plot Development: The Rising Action in *Flush* Anchor Chart

Learning target:

- "I can analyze how each chapter contributes to plot development."

Chapter	Main Events in Chapter	How do these events contribute to the plot development? (Do they introduce a new character? Provide/build on conflict or tension?)

Plot Development: The Rising Action in *Flush* Anchor Chart
(Teacher Reference)

Learning target:

- "I can analyze how each chapter contributes to plot development."

Chapter	Main Events in Chapter	How do these events contribute to the plot development? (Do they introduce a new character? Provide/build on conflict or tension?)
2	1. Noah goes to the marina and runs into Jasper. 2. Noah goes to Lice Peeking's trailer to ask for his help. 3. Noah goes home and talks with Mom.	1. Introduces a conflict with a new character, Jasper, because he is angry with Noah because of what Noah's dad did to Jasper's dad's boat. 2. Introduces a new character, Lice Peeking, who may possibly help Noah get his dad out of jail. 3. Develops more tension around Dad being in jail, because Mom is angry and it hints that their family might break apart.
3	1. Noah visits his father in jail. 2. Noah visits Thunder Beach with his friends. 3. Noah visits Lice but mostly talks to Shelly.	1. Develops more tension about Dad staying in jail because they talk about sacrificing the skiff and Paine being away from the family. 2. Illustrates how wildlife is being affected by the pollution from Dusty Muleman's casino boat. 3. Develops more tension about Noah trying to solve this crime for his dad, because he is trying to get Lice to help but Shelly makes him nervous.

Structured Notes: Chapters 4 and 5

Name: _____

Date: _____

Chapter	Homework Focus Question	Answer to Homework Focus Question with Evidence from the Text (include page numbers)

LESSON 4

Analyzing Point of View and Figurative Language

Noah's Point of View of Florida

Long-Term Targets Addressed (Based on ELA CCSS)

- I can determine the meaning of literal and figurative language (metaphors and similes) in a literary text. (RL.6.4)
- I can analyze how an author's word choice affects tone and meaning in a literary text. (RL.6.4)
- I can analyze how a particular sentence, stanza, scene, or chapter fits in and contributes to the development of a literary text. (RL.6.5)
- I can analyze how an author develops a narrator or speaker's point of view. (RL.6.6)
- I can use context (e.g., the overall meaning of a sentence or paragraph, a word's position or function in a sentence) to determine the meaning of a word or phrase. (L.6.4.a)

Supporting Learning Targets

- I can determine connotative and figurative meanings of language and analyze how the author's choice of words affects tone and meaning.
- I can analyze how Carl Hiaasen develops Noah's point of view of the area he lives in.
- I can analyze how chapters 4 and 5 contribute to plot development.

Ongoing Assessment

- Structured Notes: Chapters 4 and 5 (from homework)
- Noah's Point of View Graphic Organizer: Pages 27–29
- Exit Ticket: Chapters 4 and 5 Plot Development

Agenda

1. Opening
    A. Engaging the Reader: Chapters 4 and 5 of *Flush* (5 minutes)
    B. Unpacking Learning Targets (2 minutes)
2. Work Time
    A. Rereading Pages 27–29 for Unfamiliar Vocabulary (6 minutes)
    B. Analyzing Point of View, Figurative Language, and Tone: Pages 27–29 (14 minutes)
    C. Determining Author's Techniques: Point of View, Tone, and Meaning (10 minutes)
3. Closing and Assessment
    A. Exit Ticket: Chapters 4 and 5 Plot Development (8 minutes)
4. Homework
    A. Read chapters 6 and 7. As you read, mark the text with evidence flags to help you answer the focus question in your structured notes.

Teaching Notes

- This lesson is similar in structure to Lesson 3: students work in triads without any teacher modeling to analyze an excerpt of *Flush* for point of view, figurative language, tone, and meaning. This time, the focus of the analysis is Noah's point of view of the area he lives in. Students go back to chapter 3 in the book for this analysis. The reason for this is that Noah's point of view of the area he lives in is important in the second half of the unit, when students look for evidence of Carl Hiaasen's perspective of where he lives to address standard RI.6.6.

- Instead of filling out the anchor chart to track plot development in this lesson, students fill out an exit ticket that looks exactly like the anchor chart to practice for the upcoming mid-unit assessment.

- As students are reading two chapters of this novel per night, consider providing catch-up reading time to ensure that all students are at the same place in the text as they go into the mid-unit assessment in the next lesson.

- In advance:
    - Read pages 27–29 and Noah's Point of View Graphic Organizer (Teacher Reference) to familiarize yourself with what students will be doing and the answers you will need to guide them toward (see supporting materials).
    - Informally assess Noah's Point of View Graphic Organizer: Pages 17–19, collected in Lesson 3. Look for students' ability to make a claim, select text evidence, and appropriately determine tone. Consider making a list of students who need extra support and providing them with descriptive feedback (one thing they did well and one thing they can improve upon with concrete next steps). Pre-determine if you will reteach these students as a small group or circulate to them individually during Work Time B.

- Post: learning targets; Thought, Word, Action Symbols.

Lesson Vocabulary

Everglades, squall, hunkered, mangroves

Materials

- *Flush* (book; distributed in Lesson 1; one per student)
- Structured Notes: Chapters 4 and 5 (from homework)
- Equity sticks
- Dictionaries (at least one per triad)
- *Flush* Word-Catcher (begun in Lesson 1)
- Noah's Point of View Graphic Organizer: Pages 27–29 (one per student)
- Noah's Point of View Graphic Organizer: Pages 27–29 (Teacher Reference)
- Thought, Word, Action Symbols (from Lesson 1; one for display)
- Colored pencils or markers (blue and one other color; one of each color per student)
- Plot Development: The Rising Action in *Flush* Anchor Chart (from Lesson 3)
- Exit Ticket: Chapters 4 and 5 Plot Development (one per student)
- Exit Ticket: Chapters 4 and 5 Plot Development (Teacher Reference)
- *Flush* Plot Development Anchor Chart (from Lesson 2)
- Structured Notes: Chapters 6 and 7 (one per student)
- Evidence flags (at least three per student)

Opening

A. Engaging the Reader: Chapters 4 and 5 of *Flush* (5 minutes)

- Invite students to take out **Flush**. Ask students to discuss in triads:
  - "What happened in chapters 4 and 5?"
- Select volunteers to share their answers. Listen for students to explain that Noah helps to sink Jasper's boat, the reporter comes to talk to Noah, Noah goes to visit Lice Peeking again to ask for his help in exchange for his dad's skiff, and Noah and Abbey go to the marina at night to see what Dusty Muleman's people are doing to the *Coral Queen*.
- Invite students to refer to their **Structured Notes: Chapters 4 and 5** homework to discuss the answer to the focus question in triads: "What does Noah think of Miles Umlatt? How do you know?"
- Refocus the whole class. Select students to share their answers using **equity sticks**. Listen for students to share something like: "Noah doesn't like him because he makes him nervous." Listen for students to provide evidence like: "He was thin and blotchy, and his nose was scuffed up like an old shoe," (page 41), or "Miles Umlatt wrote that down on his pad, which made me a little nervous. So did the tiny green light blinking on his tape recorder" (page 44).

Meeting Students' Needs

Opening the lesson by asking students to share their homework makes students accountable for completing homework. It also gives you the opportunity to monitor which students have not been completing their homework.

B. Unpacking Learning Targets (2 minutes)

- Invite students to read the learning targets with you:
  - "I can determine connotative and figurative meanings of language and analyze how the author's choice of words affects tone and meaning."
  - "I can analyze how Carl Hiaasen develops Noah's point of view of the area he lives in."
  - "I can analyze how chapters 4 and 5 contribute to plot development."
- Students should be familiar with these learning targets from previous lessons. Remind students of vocabulary they have explored in previous lessons: gist, connotative language, figurative language, tone, point of view, and plot.

Meeting Students' Needs

- Learning targets are a research-based strategy that helps all students, especially challenged learners.
- Posting learning targets allows students to reference them throughout the lesson to check their understanding. Learning targets also provide a reminder to students and teachers about the intended learning behind a given lesson or activity.

Work Time

A. Rereading Pages 27–29 for Unfamiliar Vocabulary (6 minutes)

- Ask students to follow along silently as you read aloud from "In July days get long and stream together," on page 27 to "Rado took him home while I skated alone down the old road, back toward Lice Peeking's place," in the middle of page 29.
- Distribute **dictionaries** to each triad. Remind students that they have already read this chapter and recorded unfamiliar words on their **Flush** Word-Catchers for homework. Invite students to share any new vocabulary and definitions with their triad. If they were unable to work out the meaning of a word, encourage other students to assist them with the definition. You may need to explain to students that the *Everglades* is a large area of wetland in Florida and that *mangroves* are trees that grow in wetland areas.
- Focus students' attention on the word *squall*. Invite them to read the sentence containing the word *squall* and the two sentences after to try and figure out what the word means from the context. Ask students to discuss in triads:

- "What do you think a *squall* might be? Why do you think that? What in those sentences suggests that?"
- Cold-call students to share their responses. Listen for students to explain that a squall must be a storm because it says that they held their skateboards over their heads to keep the raindrops from their eyes and that it took half an hour for the storm to pass. Invite a volunteer to check the meaning of the word in a dictionary and explain to students that squalls are common in the area of Florida that Carl Hiaasen is writing about in *Flush*.
- Focus students' attention on the word *hunkered*. Invite a volunteer to look up the word in a dictionary and to share the meaning with the whole group, as this isn't an easy one to get from context.
- Remind students to record new words on their word-catchers.

Meeting Students' Needs

- Asking students to identify challenging vocabulary helps them monitor their understanding of a complex text.
- ELL students may be unfamiliar with more vocabulary words than are mentioned in this lesson. Check for comprehension of general words that most students would know.

B. Analyzing Point of View, Figurative Language, and Tone: Pages 27–29 (14 minutes)

- Distribute **Noah's Point of View Graphic Organizer: Pages 27–29**. Remind students that they filled out a similar organizer in Lessons 2 and 3.
- Explain that in this lesson, they use the graphic organizer to help them analyze pages 27–29 to identify Noah's point of view of the area he lives in.
- Remind students to read the directions at the beginning of the graphic organizer.
- Direct students to work independently to analyze the text. Explain that they will discuss their answers with their triads after they have tried to complete the organizer on their own.
- Circulate to assist students with analyzing the text for point of view, figurative language, and tone. Refer to **Noah's Point of View Graphic Organizer: Pages 27–29 (Teacher Reference)** to guide students. Consider doing some small-group instruction or circulating to certain individuals based on their work on the graphic organizers you collected in the previous lesson. Consider providing students who need it with clear descriptive feedback (for example, one thing they are doing well and one thing they can improve upon with concrete next steps). As you circulate, ask probing questions such as:
  - "What is Noah's point of view of the area he lives in?"
  - "How do you know? Which specific words, phrases, and sentences from the text support your claim about Noah's point of view?"
  - "Based on the images, words, and phrases you have selected, how would you describe the tone of the text with one word?"

- Invite students to get into triads to share their graphic organizers. Encourage them to add to and revise their graphic organizers based on what they learn from the other people in their triads.
- Refocus the whole group. Remind students that *Flush* uses figurative language such as similes and metaphors to help us better understand how things look and what characters think and feel.
- Invite the class to reread the figurative language learning target with you:
  - "I can determine connotative and figurative meanings of language and analyze how the author's choice of words affects tone and meaning."
- Direct students to look back at the evidence they recorded in the middle column and ask them to discuss in triads:
  - "Can you identify any figurative language in the notes you have taken? Remember that figurative language is when you describe something by comparing it to something else."
- Invite students to circle figurative language on their graphic organizers.
- Use equity sticks to select students to share their responses. Listen for students to say: "I've always enjoyed watching the sky drop down like a foamy purple curtain when a summer storm rumbles across Florida Bay" on pages 27–28.
- Ask triads to discuss:
  - "What kind of figurative language is this example? How do you know?"
- Use equity sticks to call on students for their responses. Listen for them to explain that it is a simile, because similes often use "like" or "as" to compare two things.
- Ask triads to discuss:
  - "Why does Hiaasen use figurative language here? What does it do for the reader?"
- Listen for students to explain that it helps the reader create a mental picture of what a storm looks like when it rolls into the Florida Bay.
- Focus students on the sentence, "Thom, Rado, and I hunkered in the mangroves . . ."
- Ask students to discuss in triads:
  - "What connotation does the word *hunkered* suggest? What words could the author have used instead with a different connotation?"
- Cold-call students to share their responses. Listen for students to explain that *hunkered* has the connotation of having to get down really low in a strong, solid position to avoid being blown over. The author could have used the words *squatted* or *crouched down*, but those don't have the same effect.
- Focus students on the sentence, "Only a certified moron would dive in when the beach was posted."
- Ask students to discuss in triads:
  - "What connotation does the word *moron* suggest? What words could the author have used instead with a different connotation?"
- Cold-call students to share their responses. Listen for students to explain that *moron* has the connotation of someone being dangerously foolish. The author could have used the word *fool*, but that doesn't make the person sound like such an unclear thinker for doing something that could endanger their life.

Meeting Students' Needs

- Graphic organizers and recording forms engage students more actively and provide the necessary scaffolding that is especially critical for learners with lower levels of language proficiency and/or learning

- When reviewing graphic organizers or recording forms, consider using a document camera to display the document for students who struggle with auditory processing.

- By using formative assessment, teachers can provide differentiated instruction to students during individual work time through small-group or individual instruction.

- Descriptive feedback is a research-based strategy that supports student achievement by providing feedback on what students are doing well to replicate their thinking and increase engagement. And by providing feedback on what students can do to improve with specific next steps, to build success and increases student engagement.

C. Determining Author's Techniques: Point of View, Tone, and Meaning (10 minutes)

- Direct students' attention to the posted **Thought, Words, Actions Symbols** and remind them of the ways authors can develop point of view.

- Tell students that now they are going to continue to work in triads to analyze how the author has developed point of view by looking at the evidence from the text recorded in the middle column of their graphic organizers. Distribute **colored pencils or markers** and remind students to underline evidence as follows:
    - Noah's own thoughts, actions, and feelings—blue
    - The words and actions of others—another color

- Remind students to then code each piece of evidence as a thought, word, or action.

- Refocus the whole group. Ask:
    - "So what techniques does Hiaasen use most often to develop Noah's point of view of where he lives in this excerpt?"

- Cold-call students to share their responses with the whole group. Listen for students to explain that in this excerpt, most of Noah's point of view comes from his own thoughts.

- Invite students to focus on the Tone column of the graphic organizer. Ask triads to share the words they chose and to justify why they infer that tone.

- Remind students that the tone helps them to determine the point of view because it gives us an idea of what the narrator thinks of or feels about the subject.

Meeting Students' Needs

Asking students to color code and add symbols to their text provides a clear visual reference for analysis.

Closing and Assessment

A. Exit Ticket: Chapters 4 and 5 Plot Development (8 minutes)

- Display the **Plot Development: The Rising Action in *Flush* Anchor Chart**. Invite students to reread what has been recorded so far. Read aloud the learning target:
  - "I can analyze how chapters 4 and 5 contribute to plot development."
- Distribute **Exit Ticket: Chapters 4 and 5 Plot Development** and explain to students that it is identical to the anchor chart they have been filling out over the past couple of lessons. Explain to students that in the next lesson they are going to be doing their mid-unit assessment, so this exit ticket is good practice for that. Ask:
  - "What were the main events in chapters 4 and 5?"
- Invite students to independently refer to their text and record the main things that happened on the exit ticket.
- Ask:
  - "How do these events contribute to the plot development? Do they introduce a new character? Do they provide/build on conflict or tension?"
- Invite students to independently refer to their text and record how the things they recorded in the middle column contributed to the plot development.
- Select volunteers to share their answers with the whole group. For suggested answers, see **Exit Ticket: Chapters 4 and 5 Plot Development (Teacher Reference)**.
- Display the ***Flush* Plot Development Anchor Chart**. Invite students to synthesize their thinking about plot development:
  - "How did chapters 4 and 5 contribute to the rising action and plot development in *Flush*?"
- Use equity sticks to call on a few students to share their statements with the class. Listen for students to share that in chapters 4 and 5 the conflict between Jasper and Noah continues, and there is tension as Abbey and Noah realize their dad might be in the wrong. Record this next to the Rising Action line on the *Flush* Plot Development Anchor Chart.
- Distribute **Structured Notes: Chapters 6 and 7** and **evidence flags** for homework.

Meeting Students' Needs

Exit tickets allow a check for understanding of the learning targets so that instruction can be adjusted or tailored to students' needs during the lesson or before the next lesson.

Homework

- Read chapters 6 and 7. As you read, mark the text with at least three evidence flags to help you answer this focus question in your structured notes:
  - "What does Shelly think of Lice in chapter 6? How do you know?"
- Remember to record any new vocabulary on your word-catcher.

Noah's Point of View Graphic Organizer: Pages 27–29

Name: _____

Date: _____

Learning targets:

- "I can analyze how an author's word choice affects tone and meaning in a literary text." (RL.6.4)
- "I can analyze how an author develops a narrator or speaker's point of view." (RL.6.6)

Directions

1. Reread pages 27–29 of *Flush* from "In July days get long and stream together," on page 27 to "Rado took him home while I skated alone down the old road, back toward Lice Peeking's place" in the middle of page 29.
2. In triads discuss the question: What is Noah's point of view of the area he lives in? Use evidence from the text to support your answer.
3. Record your claims in the first column of the organizer.
4. Record evidence from the text to support those claims in the middle column. Remember to use quotation marks and to include the page number.
5. Choose one word to describe the tone of the evidence you have recorded and write it in the final column.

Claim	Evidence	Word Choice
What is Noah's point of view of the area he lives in?	How do you know? How did Hiaasen develop Noah's point of view of the area he lives in? (Use specific words, phrases, and sentences from the text.)	Describe the tone of the text with one word (for example, angry or sad).

Noah's Point of View Graphic Organizer: Pages 27–29
(Teacher Reference)

Learning targets:

- "I can analyze how an author's word choice affects tone and meaning in a literary text." (RL.6.4)
- "I can analyze how an author develops a narrator or speaker's point of view." (RL.6.6)

Claim	Evidence	Word Choice
What is Noah's point of view of the area he lives in?	How do you know? How did Hiaasen develop Noah's point of view of the area he lives in? (Use specific words, phrases, and sentences from the text.)	Describe the tone of the text with one word (for example, angry or sad).
Noah likes the storms.	"I've always liked watching the sky drop like a foamy purple curtain when a summer storm rumbles across Florida Bay." (pages 27–28) – THOUGHT "Then the wind dropped out, and the only sound was a soft sleepy drizzle." (page 28) –THOUGHT	Comforted
Noah sees the beach as a special place to be kept clean.	"I was glad to see that the water was okay, especially when a big loggerhead turtle bobbed up the surface." (page 28) – THOUGHT	Relieved
Noah sees the turtles as something to watch and respect.	"The three of us stayed real quiet because we thought the turtle might be coming ashore to lay her eggs" (page 28) – ACTION	Anticipation
Noah sees it as his duty to help the turtles by leaving them alone	"The momma turtles down here don't have lots of options, so we leave them alone. It's the law, too." (page 29) – ACTION	Protective

Exit Ticket: Chapters 4 and 5 Plot Development

Name: _____

Date: _____

Learning target:

- "I can analyze how chapters 4 and 5 contribute to plot development."

Chapter	Main Events in Chapter	How do these events contribute to the plot development? (Do they introduce a new character? Provide/build on conflict or tension?)
4		
5		

Exit Ticket: Chapters 4 and 5 Plot Development
(Teacher Reference)

Learning target:

- "I can analyze how chapters 4 and 5 contribute to plot development."

Chapter	Main Events in Chapter	How do these events contribute to the plot development? (Do they introduce a new character? Provide/build on conflict or tension?)
4	1. Noah helps to sink Jasper's boat with Jasper and Bull in it. 2. Miles Umlatt interviews Noah and discusses his dad's history of breaking the law.	1. Develops conflict between Noah and Jasper because although Noah won this one, we know Jasper will be angry and will want revenge. 2. Develops tension about the punishment Noah's dad will receive because now we know he has been in trouble with the law many times before.
5	1. Noah and Abbey go to the marina at night to see what Dusty Muleman's people are doing to the Coral Queen. 2. At the end of the chapter, someone grabs Abbey.	1. Tension builds between Noah and his father because what Noah and Abbey find at the marina makes them question whether their father was right. 2. Builds tension because we don't know what happens next.

Structured Notes: Chapters 6 and 7

Name: _____

Date: _____

Chapter	Homework Focus Question	Answer to Homework Focus Question with Evidence from the Text (include page numbers)

LESSON 5

Mid-Unit 2 Assessment

Analyzing Point of View and Plot Development in *Flush*

Long-Term Targets Addressed (Based on ELA CCSS)

- I can determine the meaning of literal and figurative language (metaphors and similes) in a literary text. (RL.6.4)
- I can analyze how an author's word choice affects tone and meaning in a literary text. (RL.6.4)
- I can analyze how a particular sentence, stanza, scene, or chapter fits in and contributes to the development of a literary text. (RL.6.5)
- I can analyze how an author develops a narrator or speaker's point of view. (RL.6.6)
- I can use context (e.g., the overall meaning of a sentence or paragraph, a word's position or function in a sentence) to determine the meaning of a word or phrase. (L.6.4.a)

Supporting Learning Targets

- I can determine the meaning of words and phrases in the text.
- I can analyze how the word choice affects tone and meaning.
- I can analyze how Hiaasen develops Noah's point of view.
- I can explain how a chapter contributes to plot development.

Ongoing Assessment

- Structured Notes: Chapters 6 and 7 (from homework)
- Mid-Unit 2 Assessment: Point of View, Figurative Language, and Plot Development in *Flush*
- *Flush* Plot Development Anchor Chart

Agenda

1. Opening
    A. Engaging the Reader: Chapters 6 and 7 of Flush (7 minutes)
    B. Unpacking Learning Targets (2 minutes)
2. Work Time
    A. Mid-Unit 2 Assessment (33 minutes)
3. Closing and Assessment
    A. Debrief (3 minutes)
4. Homework
    A. Read the rest of chapter 8. As you read, mark the text with evidence flags to help you answer the focus question in your structured notes.
    B. Record new vocabulary words on your word-catcher.

Teaching Notes

- In this Mid-Unit 2 Assessment, students read a passage of *Flush* and are asked to identify and interpret the point of view and use of figurative language in the passage. They do this in a graphic organizer nearly identical to the one they have been using to track point of view throughout the novel so far. Students are then asked a series of short constructed-response questions about figurative language, word choice, and plot development.
- Assess student responses using the Grade 6 2-Point Rubric—Short Response. There are also suggested answers in the supporting materials, but be aware that student answers may differ from those suggested—they are to be used as a guideline for the kind of responses to look for.
- Consider allowing time for catch-up reading to ensure all students are at the same place in the book.
- In advance:
    - Review the Concentric Circles protocol (see Appendix).
- Post: learning targets; Plot Development: The Rising Action in *Flush* Anchor Chart; *Flush* Plot Development Anchor Chart.

Lesson Vocabulary

Do not preview vocabulary.

Materials

- Structured Notes: Chapters 6 and 7 (from homework)
- Plot Development: The Rising Action in *Flush* Anchor Chart (from Lesson 3)
- Plot Development: The Rising Action in *Flush* Anchor Chart (Teacher Reference)
- *Flush* Plot Development Anchor Chart (from Lesson 2)

- Mid-Unit 2 Assessment: Analyzing Point of View and Plot Development in *Flush* (one per student)
- *Flush* (book; distributed in Lesson 1; one per student)
- Sticky notes (five per student)
- Colored pencils or markers (blue and one other color; one of each color per student)
- Mid-Unit 2 Assessment: Analyzing Point of View and Plot Development in Flush (Teacher Reference)
- Grade 6 2-Point Rubric—Short Response (Teacher Reference)
- Structured Notes: Chapter 8 (one per student)
- Evidence flags (at least three per student)

Opening Meeting

A. Engaging the Reader: Chapters 6 and 7 of *Flush* (7 minutes)

- Concentric Circles protocol:
    1. Divide the group in half and invite both halves to get into two circles, one inside the other with their **Structured Notes: Chapters 6 and 7**. The circle on the inside should be facing out and the circle on the outside should be facing in.
    2. Ask: "What happened in chapter 6?"
    3. Invite students to share their answers with the person opposite them.
    4. Invite students on the inside circle to move two people to the right.
    5. Ask: "What happened in chapter 7?"
    6. Invite students to share their answers with the person opposite them.
    7. Invite students on the inside circle to move two people to the right.
    8. Ask: "What does Shelly think of Lice in chapter 6? How do you know?"
    9. Invite students to share their answers to with the person opposite them.
- Refocus the whole group. Invite volunteers to share their answers with the whole group. Listen and write student answers on the displayed **Plot Development: The Rising Action in *Flush* Anchor Chart**. For guidance, see **Plot Development: The Rising Action in *Flush* Anchor Chart (Teacher Reference)**.
- Direct students' attention to the posted ***Flush* Plot Development Anchor Chart** and add a summative statement for chapters 6 and 7. For example: "Tension builds with the possibility that Noah's dad could actually be wrong and there is disappointment that Lice, who Noah's dad has been pinning his hopes on, has gone. The tension about the sewage tank is relieved when we find out the sewage tank isn't used."

Meeting Students' Needs

Opening the lesson by asking students to share their homework makes them accountable for completing it. It also gives you the opportunity to monitor which students are not doing their homework.

B. Unpacking Learning Targets (2 minutes)

- Invite students to read the learning targets with you:
  - "I can determine the meaning of words and phrases in the text."
  - "I can analyze how the word choice affects tone and meaning."
  - "I can analyze how Hiaasen develops Noah's point of view."
  - "I can explain how a chapter contributes to plot development."
- Remind students that these are the same learning targets they have been working with for the past four lessons. Tell them that today they will show how well they can demonstrate these targets independently in an assessment.

Meeting Students' Needs

- Learning targets are a research-based strategy that helps all students, especially challenged learners.
- Posting learning targets allows students to reference them throughout the lesson to check their understanding. Learning targets also provide a reminder to students and teachers about the intended learning behind a given lesson or activity.

Work Time

A. Mid-Unit 2 Assessment (33 minutes)

- Distribute a **Mid-Unit 2 Assessment: Analyzing Point of View and Plot Development in** *Flush* to each student. They will also need their text *Flush*, **five sticky notes**, and **colored pencils or markers**.
- Invite students to read through the learning targets and the prompt with you. Remind them that the graphic organizer on the assessment handout is similar to the one they have been using to analyze point of view in previous lessons.
- Invite students to read through the questions that follow the graphic organizer with you. Explain that once they have analyzed the point of view and tone, they are to answer those questions.
- Remind the class that because this is an assessment, it is to be completed independently. However, if students need assistance, they should raise their hand to speak with a teacher.
- Explain to students they should independently read the excerpt for gist, and they have the option of using the sticky notes to write down the gist as a tool to support their comprehension.
- Circulate and support students as they work. During an assessment, your prompting should be minimal.
- At the conclusion of the allotted time, collect the Mid-Unit 2 Assessment.
- Congratulate students on their hard work during the assessment.

Meeting Students' Needs

If students receive accommodations for assessment, communicate with the cooperating service providers regarding the practices of instruction in use during this study, as well as the goals of the assessment.

Closing and Assessment

A. Debrief (3 minutes)

- Fist-to-Five: Invite students to reread each of the learning targets with you and to show on their fingers how well they achieved each target with 0 being "not at all" and 5 being "achieved it successfully."
- Take note of students who show low numbers on their fingers and be sure to address their concerns in the next lesson.
- Preview homework and distribute **Structured Notes: Chapter 8** and **evidence flags**.

Homework

- Read the rest of chapter 8. As you read, mark the text with at least three evidence flags to help you answer this focus question in your structured notes:
  - "What happens in this chapter and how do those events contribute to the plot development?"
- Record new vocabulary words on your word-catcher.

Plot Development: The Rising Action in *Flush* Anchor Chart

(Teacher Reference)

Learning target:

- "I can explain how each chapter contributes to plot development."

Chapter	Main Events in Chapter	How do these events contribute to the plot development? (Do they introduce a new character? Provide/build on conflict or tension?)
6	1. Noah and Abbey escape from the marina knowing that there is a sewage tank in the marina that it looks like the Coral Queen has been using. Noah goes to visit his dad in jail again and tells him about the sewage tank. 2. Noah goes to visit Lice only to find he has run away.	1. Tension builds with the possibility that Noah's dad could actually be wrong. 2. Tension builds when Noah finds out that Lice, who Noah's dad has been pinning his hopes on, has gone.
7	1. Noah's dad's interview is on TV, so Noah and Abbey try to stop their mom from seeing it. 2. Noah sneaks down to the marina again in the dark and finds that the sewage tank is rusty and useless, so cannot have been used by the Coral Queen.	1. Tension builds as Noah and Abbey do everything they can to stop their mom watching the interview. 2. Tension about the sewage tank is relieved when we find out the sewage tank isn't used.

Mid-Unit 2 Assessment

Analyzing Point of View and Plot Development in *Flush*

Name: _____

Date: _____

Long-Term Learning Targets Assessed

- "I can determine the meaning of literal and figurative language (metaphors and similes) in a literary text." (RL.6.4)
- "I can analyze how an author's word choice affects tone and meaning in a literary text." (RL.6.4)
- "I can analyze how a particular sentence, stanza, scene, or chapter fits in and contributes to the development of a literary text." (RL.6.5)
- "I can analyze how an author develops a narrator or speaker's point of view." (RL.6.6)
- "I can use context (e.g., the overall meaning of a sentence or paragraph, a word's position or function in a sentence) to determine the meaning of a word or phrase." (L.6.4.a)

Assessment Prompt

One of the characteristics that makes Carl Hiaasen's novel *Flush* a compelling story is his development of the narrator's point of view. Through his use of details and descriptive language that capture Noah's observations and thoughts, the reader comes to know Noah's point of view of his father, of Lice Peeking, and of where he lives in Florida. In this assessment, you will have the opportunity to show what you have learned about determining how Noah's point of view has been developed, how figurative language, connotative meanings, and word choice can affect the tone of a novel, and how each chapter contributes to the development of the plot in the novel.

Directions: In chapter 8 of *Flush*, read from the last paragraph on page 82, beginning with "The next afternoon Mom insisted," and ending with "In a matter of moments he had hustled to his car and sped away" on page 84. After you read, complete the organizer and answer the questions.

1. Complete the following organizer.

Claim	Evidence	Word Choice
What is Noah's point of view of his dad's interview?	How do you know? How did Hiaasen develop Noah's point of view of his dad's interview? Provide three examples of specific words, phrases, and sentences that support your claim.	Describe the tone of the text with one word (for example, angry or sad).
	1.	1.
	2.	2.
	3.	3.

2. On your completed organizer:
   A. Underline each piece of text evidence with a colored pencil or marker as follows:
      - Noah's own thoughts, actions, and feelings—blue
      - The words and actions of others—another color
   B. Code each piece of evidence as a thought, word, or action using the Thought, Word, Action Symbols.

3. "My father ended the interview by saying he intended to stay locked behind bars until the law dealt **squarely** with Dusty Muleman." (page 82)
   - What do you think the word **squarely** means?
   - What word(s) would you replace **squarely** with? Use that strategy to help you determine what this word might mean. Explain why you would replace it with that word(s).

   _____
   _____
   _____

4. "Mr. Shine sucked air through his teeth. 'Sorry. I'm **obliged** to tell your mother first.'" (page 83)
   - What do you think the word **obliged** means?
   - Use the context to determine the meaning and record it below. Explain how you know the meaning from the context clues in the text.

   _____
   _____
   _____

5. "Dad's TV interview was the **buzz** of the Keys . . ." (page 82)
   - What is the connotation of **buzz**?
   - What other words could have been used here with a similar meaning but a different connotation?
   - Why has the author used this connotation here?

   _____
   _____
   _____

TEACHER GUIDE AND RESOURCE BOOK • Grade 6 • Module 3B • Unit 2 • Lesson 5 Supporting Materials

6. "Next to show up on camera was a rodent-faced man who identified himself as Dusty's attorney." (page 82)

   - Circle the figurative language about Dusty Muleman's attorney in this sentence. What does it mean?
   - Why has the author used this figurative language here? In your explanation, include the specific words or phrase that helped you determine the meaning.

   _____
   _____
   _____

7. "Mr. Shine looked like he'd swallowed a bad clam. 'What?' he croaked. 'Where in the world did you get that idea?'" (page 84)

   - Circle the figurative language in this sentence. What does it mean?
   - Why has the author used this figurative language here?

   _____
   _____
   _____

8. How does the excerpt you read from pages 82–84 contribute to plot development? Describe the main events in this excerpt and how they contribute to the rising action of the plot.

   Main events in excerpt:

   _____
   _____
   _____

   How do these events contribute to the development of the plot's rising action? Do they introduce new characters? Do they build tension? Do they introduce/continue conflict?

   _____
   _____
   _____

Mid-Unit 2 Assessment

Analyzing Point of View and Plot Development in *Flush*
(Teacher Reference)

Long-Term Learning Targets Assessed

- "I can determine the meaning of literal and figurative language (metaphors and similes) in a literary text." (RL.6.4)
- "I can analyze how an author's word choice affects tone and meaning in a literary text." (RL.6.4)
- "I can analyze how a particular sentence, stanza, scene, or chapter fits in and contributes to the development of a literary text." (RL.6.5)
- "I can analyze how an author develops a narrator or speaker's point of view." (RL.6.6)
- "I can use context (e.g., the overall meaning of a sentence or paragraph, a word's position or function in a sentence) to determine the meaning of a word or phrase." (L.6.4.a)

1. Complete the following organizer.

Claim	Evidence	Word Choice
What is Noah's point of view of his dad's interview?	How do you know? How did Hiaasen develop Noah's point of view of his dad's interview? Provide three examples of specific words, phrases, and sentences that support your claim.	Describe the tone of the text with one word (for example, angry or sad).
He seems to be quite relieved and pleased with it. It seems that he thinks his dad didn't come across as badly as he had feared.	1. "My father was in rare form." (page 82) – NOAH'S THOUGHT	1. Relief
	2. "He came off more like a college professor than a boat vandal." (page 82) – NOAH'S THOUGHT	2. Relief

Claim	Evidence	Word Choice
What is Noah's point of view of his dad's interview?	How do you know? How did Hiaasen develop Noah's point of view of his dad's interview? Provide three examples of specific words, phrases, and sentences that support your claim.	Describe the tone of the text with one word (for example, angry or sad).
	3. "He had the good sense not to compare himself to Nelson Mandela (or if he did, the TV people were nice enough to cut that part out)." (page 82) – NOAH'S THOUGHT	3. Relief

2. On your completed organizer:
   A. Underline each piece of text evidence with a colored pencil or marker as follows:
      • Noah's own thoughts, actions, and feelings—blue
      • The words and actions of others—another color
   B. Code each piece of evidence as a thought, word, or action using the Thought, Word, Action symbols.

3. "My father ended the interview by saying he intended to stay locked behind bars until the law dealt **squarely** with Dusty Muleman." (page 82)
   • What do you think the word **squarely** means?
   • What word(s) would you replace **squarely** with? Use that strategy to help you determine what this word might mean. Explain why you would replace it with that word(s).

   I would replace "squarely" with "fairly." I would replace it with "fairly" because I know that Noah's dad thinks the law is being very unfair by arresting him rather than Dusty Muleman.

4. "Mr. Shine sucked air through his teeth. 'Sorry. I'm **obliged** to tell your mother first.'" (page 83)
   • What do you think the word **obliged** means?
   • Use the context to determine the meaning and record it below. Explain how you know the meaning from the context clues in the text.

   I think the word "obliged" means that he has to tell her first. I think this because Mr. Shine refuses to tell Noah before he has told his mother.

5. "Dad's TV interview was the **buzz** of the Keys . . ." (page 82)
   - What is the connotation of **buzz**?
   - What other words could have been used here with a similar meaning but a different connotation?
   - Why has the author used this connotation here?

   The word "buzz" has the connotation that it was alive and active. The word "talk" could have also been used here, but that sounds more passive. The author has used this word here to make the reader understand that everyone was talking about it.

6. "Next to show up on camera was a **rodent-faced** man who identified himself as Dusty's attorney." (page 82)
   - Circle the figurative language about Dusty Muleman's attorney in this sentence. What does it mean?
   - Why has the author used this figurative language here? In your explanation, include the specific words or phrase that helped you determine the meaning.

   It means his face looked like a rat or a mouse, and I think the author chose to use that figurative language because he wants us to know that Noah doesn't like Dusty Muleman's attorney.

7. "Mr. Shine **looked like he'd swallowed a bad clam**. 'What?' he croaked. 'Where in the world did you get that idea?'" (page 84)
   - Circle the figurative language in this sentence. What does it mean?
   - Why has the author used this figurative language here?

   It means he pulled a face like he tasted something bad that made him feel unwell. I think the author chose to use it because it makes us understand how uncomfortable Mr. Shine was about answering Noah's question.

8. How does the excerpt you read on pages 82–84 contribute to plot development? Describe the main events in this excerpt and how they contribute to the rising action of the plot.

   Main events in excerpt:

   Noah watches his dad's TV interview and Mr. Shine comes to deliver some news.

   How do these events contribute to the development of the plot's rising action? Do they introduce new characters? Do they build tension? Do they introduce/continue conflict?

   The tension about what Noah thought his father might say in the interview is taken away because it wasn't as bad as he thought. The visit from Mr. Shine builds tension again because we wonder what news he has.

Grade 6 2-Point Rubric—Short Response
(Teacher Reference)

Use the rubric below for determining scores on short answers in this assessment.

The features of a **2-point response** are:

- Valid inferences and/or claims from the text where required by the prompt
- Evidence of analysis of the text where required by the prompt
- Relevant facts, definitions, concrete details, and/or other information from the text to develop response according to the requirements of the prompt
- Sufficient number of facts, definitions, concrete details, and/or other information from the text as required by the prompt
- Complete sentences where errors do not impact readability

The features of a **1-point response** are:

- A mostly literal recounting of events or details from the text as required by the prompt
- Some relevant facts, definitions, concrete details, and/or other information from the text to develop response according to the requirements of the prompt
- Incomplete sentences or bullets

The features of a **0-point response** are:

- A response that does not address any of the requirements of the prompt or is totally inaccurate
- No response (blank answer)
- A response that is not written in English
- A response that is unintelligible or indecipherable

If the prompt requires two texts and the student references only one text, the response can be scored no higher than a 1.

Structured Notes: Chapter 8

Name: _____

Date: _____

Chapter	Homework Focus Question	Answer to Homework Focus Question with Evidence from the Text (include page numbers)

LESSON 6

Carl Hiaasen's Perspective of Florida: Part 1

Long-Term Target Addressed (Based on ELA CCSS)

- I can explain how an author develops the point of view of the narrator or speaker in a text. (RL.6.6)

Supporting Learning Targets

- I can find the gist of an excerpt of "Five Creative Tips from Carl Hiaasen."
- I can use evidence from the text to answer text-dependent questions.
- I can infer Carl Hiaasen's perspective of Florida.

Ongoing Assessment

- Structured Notes: Chapter 8 (from homework)
- Gathering Evidence of Hiaasen's Perspective: Part 1 Graphic Organizer

Agenda

1. Opening
   A. Engaging the Reader: Chapter 8 of *Flush* (8 minutes)
   B. Unpacking Learning Targets (5 minutes)
2. Work Time
   A. Reading an Excerpt of "Five Creative Tips from Carl Hiaasen" for Gist (12 minutes)
   B. Text-Dependent Questions: An Excerpt of "Five Creative Tips from Carl Hiaasen" (10 minutes)
3. Closing and Assessment
   A. Inferring Carl Hiaasen's Perspective of Florida (10 minutes)
4. Homework
   A. Read chapters 9 and 10 of *Flush*. As you read, mark the text with evidence flags to help you answer the focus question in your structured notes.
   B. Record any new vocabulary on your word-catcher.

Teaching Notes

- In this lesson, students are introduced to an excerpt from an interview titled "Five Creative Tips from Carl Hiaasen, Florida's Cleverest Chronicler." This introduces students to the two main perspectives of Hiaasen: that he loves Florida and that he is angry about the development of Florida.

- The graphic organizer introduced in this lesson is designed to support students in gathering evidence and inferring Hiaasen's perspective about Florida from an excerpt of an interview with him. Initially this is done with a lot of teacher guidance and modeling, but over the course of the unit, students are gradually released to use the graphic organizer more independently, scaffolding toward the End-of-Unit Assessment.

- In this unit, point of view and perspective are used synonymously. To address the same standard in the first half of the unit, "point of view" is discussed in relation to the narrator of *Flush*, Noah, and the way he sees objects, people, and events. To address standard RL.6.6.a in the second half of the unit, "perspective" is used in relation to how Carl Hiaasen views the world as a result of his geographic location and how we see that perspective come through in the novel *Flush*.

- Students will look for evidence of Carl Hiaasen's perspective in *Flush* in later lessons.

- In advance:
  - Read the excerpt from "Five Creative Tips," focusing on gist.
  - Review Gathering Evidence of Hiaasen's Perspective: Part 1 Graphic Organizer (Teacher Reference).

- Post: learning targets; *Flush* Plot Development Anchor Chart.

Lesson Vocabulary

infer, perspective, satire, emotional attachment, exploitation, development

Materials

- *Flush* (book; distributed in Lesson 1; one per student)
- Structured Notes: Chapter 8 (from homework)
- Equity sticks
- *Flush* Plot Development Anchor Chart (from Lesson 2)
- *Flush* Word-Catcher (begun in Lesson 1)
- "Five Creative Tips from Carl Hiaasen, Florida's Cleverest Chronicler" (one per student and one to display)
- Dictionaries (at least one per triad)
- Gathering Evidence of Hiaasen's Perspective: Part 1 Graphic Organizer (one per student and one to display)
- Gathering Evidence of Hiaasen's Perspective: Part 1 Graphic Organizer (Teacher Reference)

- Structured Notes: Chapters 9 and 10 (one per student)
- Evidence flags (at least three per student)

Opening

A. Engaging the Reader: Chapter 8 of *Flush* (8 minutes)

- Invite students to take out **Flush** and their **Structured Notes: Chapter 8** homework and discuss the following question with an elbow partner:
  - "What happens in this chapter and how do those events contribute to the plot development?"
- Consider using **equity sticks** to call on a few students to share with the whole class. Direct students' attention to the posted **Flush Plot Development Anchor Chart**. Add a summative statement to the Rising Action line based on student responses. Listen for and record a response like: "8—Noah watches the interview with his father, which relieves tension because it wasn't as bad as he thought," "Mr. Shine visits, which builds tension again because we want to know the news he has," and "tension builds when Shelly tells Noah she believes Lice may have been killed by Dusty Muleman."

Meeting Students' Needs

Opening the lesson by asking students to share their homework makes them accountable for completing it. It also gives you the opportunity to monitor which students are not doing their homework.

B. Unpacking Learning Targets (5 minutes)

- Invite students to silently follow along as you read the learning targets aloud:
  - "I can find the gist of an excerpt of 'Five Creative Tips from Carl Hiaasen.'"
  - "I can use evidence from the text to answer text-dependent questions."
  - "I can infer Carl Hiaasen's perspective of Florida."
- Remind students what the word *gist* means (understanding what the text is mostly about).
- Ask:
  - "What does it mean to *infer*?"
- Ask for volunteers and listen for students to share that to *infer* means to draw a conclusion using both text evidence and your own background knowledge.
- Ask:
  - "What does *perspective* mean?"
- Consider using equity sticks to select students to share their responses. Listen for: "It means how you see something, based on your background and your previous experiences." Make it clear to students that *point of view* and *perspective* mean something very similar, but when talking about

Noah in *Flush*, they have been using *point of view*; when talking about Carl Hiaasen, they are going to use the word *perspective*.

- Direct students to define *infer* and *perspective* on their **Flush Word-Catchers**.

Meeting Students' Needs

- Learning targets are a research-based strategy that helps all students, especially challenged learners.
- Posting learning targets allows students to reference them throughout the lesson to check their understanding. Learning targets also provide a reminder to students and teachers about the intended learning behind a given lesson or activity.
- Discussing and clarifying the language of learning targets helps build academic vocabulary.

Work Time

A. Reading an Excerpt of "Five Creative Tips from Carl Hiaasen" for Gist (12 minutes)

- Tell students that the cultural background and/or geographic location of an author can often affect his or her perspective and that we can often see evidence of that perspective in the author's writing. Explain to students that in this half of the unit they are going to find out more about Carl Hiaasen—where he is from and how that has affected his perspective. Tell them that they are then going to look for evidence of that perspective in *Flush*.
- Display and distribute **"Five Creative Tips from Carl Hiaasen."**
- Invite students to follow along silently in their heads as you read the excerpt aloud slowly, fluently, and without interruption. Tell the class to listen for details about his geographic location that have influenced Hiaasen's life and that may have shaped his beliefs, values, and ideas.
- Ask students to Think-Pair-Share:
  - "What did you learn about Hiaasen in this excerpt from 'Five Creative Tips from Carl Hiaasen'?"
- Select students to share their responses. Listen for students to explain that he loves Florida and this helps him write.
- Invite students to first pair up with a new person and work together to annotate the gist of the paragraph in the margin of the text and record unfamiliar words on their word-catchers. If students struggle with getting the gist of the whole paragraph, encourage them to separate the text into smaller chunks.
- Distribute **dictionaries**. Remind students that if they aren't sure what a word means after looking for context clues and looking in the dictionary, they should leave the definition to be discussed with the whole group later on.
- Circulate and support students as they read. For those who need more support, ask them to practice telling you the gist of a section before they write it down.

TEACHER GUIDE AND RESOURCE BOOK • Grade 6 • Module 3B • Unit 2 • Lesson 6

- Then, invite students to get into their regular triads to compare what they wrote for their gist statements and to help each other with any unfamiliar vocabulary they haven't been able to figure out.
- Refocus the whole class and invite students to share any unfamiliar vocabulary words they found, along with the definitions. If students were unable to work out the definition from the context or find it in a dictionary, encourage other students to assist them with the meaning.
- Focus students' attention on the word *satire* in the subheading and in the body of the text. Explain that this is quite an important word when talking about the writing of Carl Hiaasen, but as it isn't easy to figure out the meaning from the context or from the way the word is put together, you are going to need a volunteer to look up this word for the whole class in the dictionary. Make sure students understand that *satire* is humor about weaknesses or bad qualities and that Carl Hiaasen uses a lot of satire in his writing.
- Focus students' attention on the words *emotional attachment*. Ask:
  - "What do you think this means? What is an *emotional attachment*? So what is he saying in this sentence?"
- Cold-call students to share their responses. Listen for students to explain that emotional attachment is a sense of feeling close to something emotionally—it is special to you and you have a connection with it—and in this sentence it means that there are very few places in Florida that he doesn't feel a special connection to.
- Focus students' attention on the word *exploitation*. Point out that the root of the word is "exploit." As this word isn't easy to figure out from the context, invite a volunteer to look up this word for the whole class in the dictionary. Make sure students understand that when you exploit, you make full use of something or someone.
- Tell students that the suffix *tion* at the end of a word means the action of, or the process of, so *exploitation* is "the process of exploiting something."
- Invite students to consider other words ending in *tion* and discuss how the suffix is added to the root word to mean the action of, or the process of. Words students may suggest include: *motion*, *action*, *connection*, and *communication*.
- Focus students on the word *development* and explain that in this context Carl Hiaasen means the building of buildings, housing, roads, etc.

Meeting Students' Needs

- Hearing a complex text read slowly, fluently, and without interruption or explanation promotes fluency for students. They are hearing a strong reader read the text aloud with accuracy and expression and are simultaneously looking at and thinking about the words on the printed page. Be sure to set clear expectations that students read along silently in their heads as you read the text aloud.
- Allow students to grapple with a complex text before explicit teaching of vocabulary. After students have read for gist, they can identify challenging vocabulary for themselves.

- Asking students to identify challenging vocabulary helps them monitor their understanding of a complex text. When students annotate the text by circling these words, it can also provide a formative assessment for the teacher.

B. Text-Dependent Questions: An Excerpt of "Five Creative Tips from Carl Hiaasen" (10 minutes)

- Display and distribute the **Gathering Evidence of Hiaasen's Perspective: Part 1 Graphic Organizer**.
- Focus students' attention on the questions in the first column of the table. Explain that the responses to these questions can be found in the text. Invite students to read through the questions with you.
- Work through the first question as a class:
  1. Ask the question.
  2. Invite students to refer to the text to find the answer.
  3. Invite students to discuss the answer in their triads.
  4. Select students to share their responses.
  5. Model how to fill out the answer in the Answers column of the graphic organizer. Refer to **Gathering Evidence of Hiaasen's Perspective: Part 1 Graphic Organizer (Teacher Reference)** for guidance.
- Tell students that triads will work together to reread the rest of the text-dependent questions in column 1, review their excerpt, discuss possible answers, and then record their answers to the questions in column 2, using evidence from the text. Make it clear that for now, they should leave the column 3 blank. Clarify directions as needed.
- Circulate and observe triads working. While circulating, ask students:
  - "Where in the text did you find this answer?"
- Refocus the whole class after a few minutes. Invite students to share their answers with the whole group. Guide students through each question using the Gathering Evidence of Hiaasen's Perspective: Part 1 Graphic Organizer (Teacher Reference).
- Invite students to make revisions to their answers if necessary.

Meeting Students' Needs

- Asking students to discuss challenging questions before recording them helps to ensure that all students have an idea about what to write and can give students confidence in their responses.
- Some students may benefit from having access to "hint cards": small slips of paper or index cards that they turn over for hints about how/where to find the answers to text-dependent questions. For example, a hint card might say, "Look in the third line."
- Some students may benefit from having key sections pre-highlighted in their texts. This will help them focus on small sections rather than scanning the whole text for answers.

Closing and Assessment

A. Inferring Carl Hiaasen's Perspective of Florida (10 minutes)

- Focus students' attention on the third column of the organizer, "Perspective: Based on what you have read so far, how has being born and raised in Florida affected Carl Hiaasen's perspective of the place?" Ask students to discuss this question in triads.

- Select volunteers to share their answers with the whole group. Listen for students to explain something like: "As a result of being born and raised in Florida, Carl Hiaasen loves the place and sees it as special. He doesn't like the way it is being developed and exploited."

- Record this in the third column of the displayed graphic organizer as a model for students. Invite students to record their ideas in the third column of their own organizers.

- Distribute **Structured Notes: Chapters 9 and 10** and **evidence flags** for homework.

Meeting Students' Needs

Asking students to discuss challenging questions before recording their answer helps to ensure that all students have an idea about what to write and can give students confidence in their responses.

Homework

- Read chapters 9 and 10 of *Flush*. As you read, mark the text with at least three evidence flags to help you answer this focus question in your structured notes:
  - "What happens in these chapters and how do those events contribute to the plot development?"
- Record any new vocabulary on your word-catcher.

Five Creative Tips from Carl Hiaasen, Florida's Cleverest Chronicler

Jessica Grose

By any measure, Carl Hiaasen is a prolific writer—he's the author of more than a dozen books and continues to write a newspaper column. Here, he shares with us the secrets of getting it done (when you're surrounded by beautiful distractions)

Excerpt

From Fast Company, July 24 © 2013 Mansueto Ventures. All rights reserved. Used by permission and protected by the Copyright Laws of the United States. The printing, copying, redistribution, or retransmission of this Content without express written permission is prohibited.

TIP NUMBER 4

THE BEST SATIRE COMES FROM A PLACE OF AFFECTION.

I feel lucky to be born and raised in Florida, and have genuine family roots there. It affects the way I work—it affects the degree to which I care about the place. As much as I write about the crazy aspect and what's wrong with it, I have tremendous affection—all my grandkids are here; it's not a throwaway location for me. There are very few places in the state that don't have an emotional attachment for me. It helps the writing; it helps the satire. I have a lot of strong feelings, and it's a great sharp edge. When you grow up in Florida where it's completely flat, it's so vulnerable to development and exploitation. I've always said that in writers' groups, I couldn't write—or be as funny in my writing about Florida—if I didn't care about it so much.

Gathering Evidence of Hiaasen's Perspective: Part 1 Graphic Organizer

Name: _____

Date: _____

Learning targets:

- "I can use evidence from the text to answer text-dependent questions."
- "I can infer Carl Hiaasen's perspective of Florida."

Questions	Answers	Perspective
	Use evidence from the text to support your answers.	Based on what you have read so far, how has being born and raised in Florida affected Carl Hiaasen's perspective of the place?
"Five Creative Tips from Carl Hiaasen"		
1. What affects the way Carl Hiaasen cares about Florida?		
2. Why does Carl Hiaasen have "tremendous affection" for Florida?		
3. According to Hiaasen, why is Florida vulnerable?		

Gathering Evidence of Hiaasen's Perspective: Part 1 Graphic Organizer
(Teacher Reference)

Questions	Answers	Perspective
	Use evidence from the text to support your answers.	Based on what you have read so far, how has being born and raised in Florida affected Carl Hiaasen's perspective of the place?
"Five Creative Tips from Carl Hiaasen"		
1. What affects the way Carl Hiaasen cares about Florida?	*The fact that he was born and raised there and has family roots there. "I feel lucky to be born and raised in Florida, and have genuine family roots there."*	*As a result of being born and raised in Florida, Carl Hiaasen loves and cares about it and sees it as a special place. He doesn't like the way it is being developed and exploited.*
2. Why does Carl Hiaasen have "tremendous affection" for Florida?	*He was born and raised there, has family roots there, and has grandchildren there. "all my grandkids are here..."*	
3. According to Hiaasen, why is Florida vulnerable?	*It is vulnerable because it is flat. "When you grow up in Florida where it's completely flat, it's so vulnerable..."*	

Structured Notes: Chapters 9 and 10

Name: _____

Date: _____

Chapter	Homework Focus Question	Answer to Homework Focus Question with Evidence from the Text (include page numbers)

LESSON 7

Carl Hiaasen's Perspective of Florida: Part 2

Long-Term Target Addressed (Based on ELA CCSS)

- I can explain how an author develops the point of view of the narrator or speaker in a text. (RL.6.6)

Supporting Learning Targets

- I can find the gist of "Florida 'A Paradise of Scandals'" Excerpt 1.
- I can use evidence from the text to answer text-dependent questions.
- I can identify evidence of Carl Hiaasen's perspective of his geographic location in *Flush*.

Ongoing Assessment

- Structured Notes: Chapters 9 and 10 (from homework)
- Gathering Evidence of Hiaasen's Perspective: Part 2 Graphic Organizer

Agenda

1. Opening
   A. Engaging the Reader: Chapters 9 and 10 (8 minutes)
   B. Unpacking Learning Targets (2 minutes)
2. Work Time
   A. Reading for Gist: "Florida 'A Paradise of Scandals'" Excerpt 1 (8 minutes)
   B. Guided Close Reading and Answering Text-Dependent Questions: "Florida 'A Paradise of Scandals'" Excerpt 1 (20 minutes)
3. Closing and Assessment
   A. Inferring Carl Hiaasen's Perspective of Florida (7 minutes)

4. Homework

   A. Read chapters 11 and 12 of *Flush*. As you read, mark the text with evidence flags to help you answer the focus question in your structured notes.

   B. Record any new vocabulary on your word-catcher.

Teaching Notes

- In this lesson, students read the first of a two-part excerpt of the transcript of an interview with Carl Hiaasen that was aired on CBS's *60 Minutes* in 2005. In Lesson 8, students will read Excerpt 2 of the transcript.

- This lesson is similar in structure to Lesson 6 and uses the same graphic organizer, which is designed to support students in gathering evidence and inferring Hiaasen's perspective based on his geographical location; however, as this is a more complex text and contains more complex language and ideas that students may not understand independently, students are guided through the text with a Close Reading Guide (see supporting materials).

- In this lesson, students continue adding to the *Flush* Plot Development Anchor Chart. Continued tracking of plot development is an intentional scaffold to support students in Lessons 9 and 10, when they address standard W.6.9.

- As students are reading two chapters of this novel per night, consider providing catch-up reading time to ensure all students are at the same place in the text.

- In advance:
  - Read "Florida 'A Paradise of Scandals'" Excerpt 1, focusing on gist.
  - Review "Florida 'A Paradise of Scandals'" Excerpt 1 Close Reading Guide (Teacher Reference) and Gathering Evidence of Hiaasen's Perspective: Part 2 Graphic Organizer (Teacher Reference).
  - Review the Concentric Circles protocol (see Appendix).

- Be prepared to return the Mid-Unit 2 Assessment in Lesson 8.

- Post: learning targets; *Flush* Plot Development Anchor Chart.

Lesson Vocabulary

geographic location, urban sprawl, quaint, strip malls, appealing, appalling, manufacture, tourism, therapy, transformed, collision

Materials

- Structured Notes: Chapters 9 and 10 (from homework)
- *Flush* Plot Development Anchor Chart (from Lesson 2)
- Equity sticks
- "Florida 'A Paradise of Scandals'" Excerpt 1 (one per student and one to display)

- *Flush* Word-Catcher (begun in Lesson 1)
- Dictionaries (at least one per triad)
- Gathering Evidence of Hiaasen's Perspective: Part 2 Graphic Organizer (one per student and one to display)
- "Florida 'A Paradise of Scandals'" Excerpt 1 Close Reading Guide (Teacher Reference)
- Gathering Evidence of Hiaasen's Perspective: Part 2 Graphic Organizer (Teacher Reference)
- Structured Notes: Chapters 11 and 12 (one per student)
- Evidence flags (at least three per student)

Opening

A. Engaging the Reader: Chapters 9 and 10 of *Flush* (8 minutes)

- Concentric Circles protocol:
    1. Divide the group in half and invite both halves to get into two circles, one inside the other with their **Structured Notes: Chapters 9 and 10**. The circle on the inside should be facing out and the circle on the outside should be facing in.
    2. Ask: "What happened in chapter 9 of *Flush*?"
    3. Invite students to share their answers to this question with the person opposite them.
    4. Invite students on the inside circle to move two people to the right.
    5. Ask: "What happened in chapter 10 of *Flush*?"
    6. Invite students to share their answers to this question with the person opposite them.
    7. Invite students on the inside circle to move two people to the right.
    8. Ask: "How did those events contribute to the plot development?"
    9. Invite students to share their answers with the person opposite them.

- Direct students to return to their seats and direct students' attention to the posted **Flush Plot Development Anchor Chart**. Consider using **equity sticks** to call on a few students to summarize the plot development in chapters 9 and 10. Add to the anchor chart something like: "9 and 10—Tension builds and is relieved again when Noah's dad escapes from jail, but the police don't seem to care. The conflict between Jasper and Noah continues when Jasper actually hurts Noah this time. Shelly builds tension by confirming that the *Coral Queen* is still dumping waste into the ocean. Tension also builds when Abbey runs away."

Meeting Students' Needs

Reviewing homework holds all students accountable for reading the novel and completing their homework.

B. Unpacking Learning Targets (2 minutes)

- Invite students to silently follow along as you read the learning targets aloud:
  - "I can find the gist of "Florida 'A Paradise of Scandals'" Excerpt 1."
  - "I can use evidence from the text to answer text-dependent questions."
  - "I can identify evidence of Carl Hiaasen's perspective of his geographic location in *Flush*."
- Remind students of what *gist* and *perspective* mean and explain that *geographic location* means the place he lives in, for example Carl Hiaasen lives in Florida. His geographic location is Florida.
- Explain that students will begin reading a new text as they continue working on those learning targets in this lesson.

Meeting Students' Needs

- Learning targets are a research-based strategy that helps all students, especially challenged learners.
- Posting learning targets allows students to reference them throughout the lesson to check their understanding. Learning targets also provide a reminder to students and teachers about the intended learning behind a given lesson or activity.
- Discussing and clarifying the language of learning targets helps build academic vocabulary.

Work Time

A. Reading for Gist: "Florida 'A Paradise of Scandals'" Excerpt 1 (8 minutes)

- Display and distribute **"Florida 'A Paradise of Scandals'" Excerpt 1**.
- Invite students to follow along silently as you read the excerpt aloud slowly, fluently, and without interruption.
- Invite new pairs to work together to read for gist, annotate the gist in the margin of their texts, and record unfamiliar words on their **Flush Word-Catchers**.
- Distribute **dictionaries**. Remind students that if they aren't sure what a word means after looking for context clues and looking in the dictionary, they should leave the definition to be discussed with the whole group later on.
- Circulate and support students as they read. For those who need more support, ask them to practice telling you the gist of a section before they write it down. This is quite a challenging text, but allow students to grapple. They will have the opportunity to study the text more closely with a guided close reading later in the lesson.
- Invite students to get into their regular triads to compare what they wrote for their gist statements and to help each other with any unfamiliar vocabulary they haven't been able to figure out.
- Refocus the whole class and invite students to share any unfamiliar vocabulary words they found, along with the definition. If students were unable to work out the definition from the context or find it in a dictionary, encourage other students to assist them with the meaning.

- Focus students on the words *urban sprawl*. Ask students to discuss in their triads what they think *urban* means.
- Select volunteers to share their responses with the whole group. If no one knows, invite a volunteer to look it up in the dictionary. Make sure students understand that urban is related to cities.
- Ask students to discuss in triads what they think *sprawl* means. Ask:
  - "What does *sprawl* mean? When you describe something as *sprawled out*, what do you mean?"
- Cold-call students to share their responses. Listen for students to explain that sprawl means spread out.
- Invite students to put those two words together:
  - "So what is *urban sprawl*?"
- Consider using equity sticks to select students to share their responses with the whole group. Listen for students to explain that urban sprawl is a lot of buildings, for example houses and stores, spread out over a large area.
- Other words students may struggle with include: *quaint*, *strip malls*, *appealing*, *appalling*, *manufacture*, *tourism*, *therapy*, *transformed*, and *collision*. Be sure to address these words here by taking each one at a time and asking if any students know what they mean. If no one knows what they mean, either invite a student to look up the word in the dictionary to share with the whole group, or consider telling students if you are running short of time.

Meeting Students' Needs

- Hearing a complex text read slowly, fluently, and without interruption or explanation promotes fluency for students. They are hearing a strong reader read the text aloud with accuracy and expression and are simultaneously looking at and thinking about the words on the printed page. Be sure to set clear expectations that students read along silently in their heads as you read the text aloud.
- Allow students to grapple with a complex text before explicit teaching of vocabulary. After students have read for gist, they can identify challenging vocabulary for themselves.
- Asking students to identify challenging vocabulary helps them monitor their understanding of a complex text. When students annotate the text by circling these words, it can also provide a formative assessment for the teacher.

B. Guided Close Reading and Answering Text-Dependent Questions: "Florida 'A Paradise of Scandals'" Excerpt 1 (20 minutes)

- Display and distribute **Gathering Evidence of Hiaasen's Perspective: Part 2 Graphic Organizer**. Remind students that the purpose of the graphic organizer is to support them in meeting the learning targets.
- Invite students to reread the following learning target along with you:
  - "I can use evidence from the text to answer text-dependent questions."

- Follow **"Florida 'A Paradise of Scandals'" Excerpt 1: Close Reading Guide (Teacher Reference)** to guide students through closely reading the text and filling out the Questions and Answers columns on their graphic organizers.

Meeting Students' Needs

- Asking students to discuss challenging questions before recording them helps to ensure that all students have an idea about what to write and can give students confidence in their responses.
- Some students may benefit from having key sections pre-highlighted in their texts. This will help them focus on small sections rather than scanning the whole text for answers.

Closing and Assessment

A. Inferring Carl Hiaasen's Perspective of Florida (7 minutes)

- Remind students that *perspective* means "how you see something based on your background and your previous experiences."
- Ask students to discuss in triads:
  - "Based on what you have read so far, how has being born and raised in Florida affected Carl Hiaasen's perspective of the place?"
- Select volunteers to share their answers with the whole group. Listen for students to explain something like: "Carl Hiaasen is very angry with the people responsible for the development in Florida and the way it is destroying the natural beauty and, as a result, he makes bad things happen to the bad guys in his novels." Use **Gathering Evidence of Hiaasen's Perspective: Part 2 Graphic Organizer (Teacher Reference)** as a guide.
- Invite students to record their ideas in the Perspective column of their graphic organizers.
- Distribute **Structured Notes: Chapters 11 and 12** and **evidence flags** for homework.

Meeting Students' Needs

Asking students to discuss challenging questions before recording their answer helps to ensure that all students have an idea about what to write and can give students confidence in their responses.

Homework

- Read chapters 11 and 12 of *Flush*. As you read, mark the text with at least three evidence flags to help you answer this focus question in your structured notes:
  - "What happens in these chapters and how do those events contribute to the plot development?"
- Record any new vocabulary on your word-catcher.

"Florida 'A Paradise of Scandals'" Excerpt 1

Name: _____

Date: _____

Rebecca Leung

Do you need to be angry to be funny?

"Some days, yeah," he says. "Yeah."

Much of that anger is reserved for the forces of development, which have transformed Florida from a quaint tropical postcard where Hiaasen grew up, to urban sprawl, strip malls, and skyscrapers. Hiaasen sees it as a daily collision between nature and the unnatural, the appealing and the appalling, as manatees fight for space with manatee mailboxes, and developers pave over 450 acres of green space a day.

"The one word that no politician will ever speak, is 'enough.' Enough," says Hiaasen. "This is an economy that's based on growth—growth for the sake of growth. We don't manufacture anything. We don't produce anything except, you know, oranges and handguns. This is all about growth, tourism and growth."

Why did he decide to start writing novels?

"Therapy," says Hiaasen laughing. "Actually, with the novels, you have this wonderful opportunity to write your own endings—to have the bad guys get not only exactly what they deserve, but in some poetic, you know, miserable way."

Source: From a CBS *60 Minutes* interview with Carl Hiaasen from April 17, 2005. Copyright 2005 CBS. All rights reserved.

Gathering Evidence of Hiaasen's Perspective: Part 2 Graphic Organizer

Name: _____

Date: _____

Learning targets:

- "I can use evidence from the text to answer text-dependent questions."
- "I can identify evidence of Carl Hiaasen's perspective of his geographic location in *Flush*."

Questions	Answers	Perspective
	(Use evidence from the text to support your answers.)	**Based on what you have read so far, how has being born and raised in Florida affected Carl Hiaasen's perspective of the place?**
"Florida 'A Paradise of Scandals'" Excerpt 1		
1. According to the text, what does Hiaasen reserve his anger for?		
2. According to the text, how has Florida changed?		

Questions	Answers	Perspective
	(Use evidence from the text to support your answers.)	Based on what you have read so far, how has being born and raised in Florida affected Carl Hiaasen's perspective of the place?
3. According to the text, how much green space is paved over in Florida each day?		
4. What does Carl Hiaasen say is produced in Florida?		
5. According to the text, why did Carl Hiaasen start writing novels?		

"Florida 'A Paradise of Scandals'" Excerpt 1 Close Reading Guide
(Teacher Reference)

Time: 20 minutes

Directions and Questions	Teaching Notes

1. According to the text, what does Hiaasen reserve his anger for?
 	
2. According to the text, how has Florida changed?
	(5 minutes)
	• Invite students to reread the part of the text that says, "Much of that anger is reserved for the forces of development . . ."
	• Ask students to discuss in triads:
	  • "What does it mean when it says that 'Much of that anger is reserved . . .'? When you reserve anger for something, what are you doing?"
	• Cold-call students to share their responses. Listen for students to explain that it means saving the anger you have and directing it at something in particular.
	• Remind students that in the excerpt of text they read in the previous lesson, *development* meant building, for example houses and roads. Ask students to discuss in triads:
	  • "So what are the *forces of development*?"
	• Consider using equity sticks to select students to share their responses. Listen for students to explain that the *forces of development* probably means the people responsible for the development.
	• Ask students to discuss Question 1 in triads and record their answers in the Answers column of their graphic organizers.
	• Cold-call students to share their answers with the whole group. Refer to Gathering Evidence of Hiaasen's Perspective: Part 2 Graphic Organizer (Teacher Reference) to guide students.
	• Focus students' attention on the rest of the sentence, ". . . which have transformed Florida from a quaint tropical postcard where Hiaasen grew up, to urban sprawl, strip malls, and skyscrapers."
	• Students should already be familiar with the words *quaint, urban sprawl,* and *strip malls* from the vocabulary discussion after reading for the gist.
	• Ask students to discuss in triads:
	  • "What does *transformed* mean?"

Directions and Questions	Teaching Notes
	• Select volunteers to share their responses with the whole group. Listen for students to explain that it means changed. • Ask students to discuss Question 2 in triads and record their answers on their graphic organizers. • Cold-call students to share their answers with the whole group. Refer to the Gathering Evidence of Hiaasen's Perspective: Part 2 Graphic Organizer (Teacher Reference) to guide students.

3. According to the text, how much green space is paved over in Florida each day?	**(5 minutes)**
	• Focus students' attention on the part of the text that says, "Hiaasen sees it as a daily collision between nature and the unnatural, the appealing and the appalling, as manatees fight for space with manatee mailboxes, and developers pave over 450 acres of green space a day."
	• Ask students:
	  • "What is a *collision*?"
	• Consider using equity sticks to select students to share their responses. Listen for students to explain that a collision is when two things crash together.
	• Ask students to discuss in triads:
	  • "Thinking about the first part of this paragraph in which the text describes how Carl Hiaasen is angry about the development happening in Florida and the way the natural landscape has been turned into sprawling cities, what do you think a collision between the natural and the unnatural means?"
	• Select volunteers to share their responses. Listen for students to explain that it means that he sees natural beauty in Florida, but then he also sees ugly cities.
	• Ask students to discuss in triads:
	  • "Which is appealing and which is appalling? Do you think he means that the natural side of Florida is appealing? Or the development? How do you know?"
	• Select volunteers to share their responses. Listen for students to explain that it means he finds the natural side appealing and the unnatural—the development—appalling. We know because we have already read that he is angry about the development, so he obviously doesn't find it appealing.

TEACHER GUIDE AND RESOURCE BOOK • Grade 6 • Module 3B • Unit 2 • Lesson 7 Supporting Materials

Directions and Questions	Teaching Notes

	• Explain to students that manatees are animals that live in the waters of Florida. Ask students to discuss in triads:
	  • "Do manatees really fight for space with mailboxes? What kind of language is this?"
	• Consider using equity sticks to select students to share their responses. Listen for students to explain that it is figurative language.
	• Ask students to discuss in triads:
	  • "So what does it mean? Do manatees really fight for space with mailboxes?"
	• Select volunteers to share their responses. Listen for students to explain that it means that areas that manatees live in are being taken over by houses. For example, wetlands are drained for development.
	• Explain to students that in this context *pave over* means to build on. Ask students to discuss Question 3 in triads and record their answers on their graphic organizers.
	• Cold-call students to share their answers with the whole group. Refer to Gathering Evidence of Hiaasen's Perspective: Part 2 Graphic Organizer (Teacher Reference) to guide students.

4. What does Carl Hiaasen say is produced in Florida?	**(5 minutes)** • Focus students' attention on the part of the text that says, "'The one word that no politician will ever speak, is 'enough.' Enough,' says Hiaasen. 'This is an economy that's based on growth—growth for the sake of growth. We don't manufacture anything. We don't produce anything except, you know, oranges and handguns. This is all about growth, tourism and growth.'" • Explain to students that this part of the interview continues on from the discussion about development. Ask students to discuss in triads: • "So what does he mean by *enough*? Enough of what?" • Select volunteers to share their responses with the whole group. Listen for students to explain that he means enough developing. • Explain to students that the *economy* is the wealth and resources of an area, particularly in terms of how much is produced and how much is used. Remind students of what *manufacture* means, as they should have already discussed this word when discussing unfamiliar vocabulary after reading for gist.

Directions and Questions	Teaching Notes
	• It would be useful here to provide an illustration of one acre to help students to understand just how big the area discussed in the text is. For example, "one acre is the size of the playground, so can you imagine how big 450 acres is?" • Ask students to discuss Question 4 in triads and record their answers on their graphic organizers. • Cold-call students to share their answers with the whole group. Refer to Gathering Evidence of Hiaasen's Perspective: Part 2 Graphic Organizer (Teacher Reference) to guide students. • Ask triads to discuss: • "So what does this section of the text mean? What is he saying here?" • Select students to share their responses. Students may struggle with this, so listen for and guide students to understand that he is saying that there is too much development and it needs to stop. He is also saying that the development is growing, there are lots more houses and things for tourists, but they don't produce anything else.
5. According to the text, why did Carl Hiaasen start writing novels?	**(5 minutes)** • Focus students' attention on the part of the text that says "'Therapy,' says Hiaasen laughing. 'Actually, with the novels, you have this wonderful opportunity to write your own endings—to have the bad guys get not only exactly what they deserve, but in some poetic, you know, miserable way.'" • Ask students to discuss in triads: • "What does he mean by *therapy* here? And why does he laugh?" • Consider using equity sticks to select students to share their responses. Students may struggle with this, so listen for and guide students to understand that he means he uses writing to control his anger about things like development. He laughs because writing is his own form of therapy. • Ask students to discuss Question 5 in triads and record their answers on their graphic organizers. • Cold-call students to share their answers with the whole group. Refer to Gathering Evidence of Hiaasen's Perspective: Part 2 Graphic Organizer (Teacher Reference) to guide students.

TEACHER GUIDE AND RESOURCE BOOK • Grade 6 • Module 3B • Unit 2 • Lesson 7 Supporting Materials

Gathering Evidence of Hiaasen's Perspective: Part 2 Graphic Organizer

(Teacher Reference)

Questions	Answers	Perspective
	(Use evidence from the text to support your answers.)	Based on what you have read so far, how has being born and raised in Florida affected Carl Hiaasen's perspective of the place?
"Florida 'A Paradise of Scandals'" Excerpt 1		
1. According to the text, what does Hiaasen reserve his anger for?	For the people responsible for the development. It says, "Much of that anger is reserved for the forces of development."	He likes the natural side of Florida and is very angry with the people responsible for its development for taking over the green spaces and natural beauty and changing Florida from a tropical paradise into an urban sprawl.
2. According to the text, how has Florida changed?	It has changed from being naturally beautiful to having lots of buildings and cities. It says, "which have transformed Florida from a quaint tropical postcard where Hiaasen grew up, to urban sprawl, strip malls, and skyscrapers."	
3. According to the text, how much green space is paved over in Florida each day?	450 acres. It says, "developers pave over 450 acres of green space a day."	
4. What does Carl Hiaasen say is produced in Florida?	Oranges and handguns. It says, "We don't produce anything except, you know, oranges and handguns."	

Questions	Answers	Perspective
	(Use evidence from the text to support your answers.)	Based on what you have read so far, how has being born and raised in Florida affected Carl Hiaasen's perspective of the place?
5. According to the text, why did Carl Hiaasen start writing novels?	As therapy, so he could channel his anger by making the bad guys get what they deserve. It says, "'Therapy,' says Hiaasen laughing. 'Actually, with the novels, you have this wonderful opportunity to write your own endings—to have the bad guys get not only exactly what they deserve, but in some poetic, you know, miserable way.'"	

Structured Notes: Chapters 11 and 12

Name: _____

Date: _____

Chapter	Homework Focus Question	Answer to Homework Focus Question with Evidence from the Text (include page numbers)

LESSON 8

Carl Hiaasen's Perspective of Florida: Part 3

Long-Term Target Addressed (Based on ELA CCSS)

- I can explain how an author develops the point of view of the narrator or speaker in a text. (RL.6.6)

Supporting Learning Targets

- I can find the gist of "Florida 'A Paradise of Scandals'" Excerpt 2.
- I can use evidence from the text to answer text-dependent questions.
- I can infer Carl Hiaasen's perspective of Florida.

Ongoing Assessment

- Structured Notes: Chapters 11 and 12 (from homework)
- Gathering Evidence of Hiaasen's Perspective: Part 3 Graphic Organizer

Agenda

1. Opening
    A. Engaging the Reader: Chapters 11 and 12 of *Flush* (10 minutes)
    B. Unpacking Learning Targets (3 minutes)
    C. Feedback from Mid-Unit 2 Assessment (6 minutes)
2. Work Time
    A. Reading for Gist: "Florida 'A Paradise of Scandals'" Excerpt 2 (8 minutes)
    B. Text-Dependent Questions: "Florida 'A Paradise of Scandals'" Excerpt 2 (10 minutes)
3. Closing and Assessment
    A. Identifying Carl Hiaasen's Perspective of Florida (8 minutes)

4. Homework

   A. Read chapters 13 and 14 of *Flush*. As you read, mark the text with evidence flags to help you answer the focus question in your structured notes.

   B. Record any new vocabulary words on your word-catcher.

Teaching Notes

- Lesson 8 is similar in structure to previous lessons. Students read Excerpt 2 of "Florida 'A Paradise of Scandals'" and complete most of the Gathering Evidence of Hiaasen's Perspective: Part 3 Graphic Organizer.
- In preparation for the end of unit assessment, this lesson continues to gradually release students to work more independently.
- In advance:
  - Prepare to hand back the Mid-Unit 2 Assessment during this lesson.
  - Read "Florida 'A Paradise of Scandals'" Excerpt 2, focusing on gist.
  - Review Gathering Evidence of Hiaasen's Perspective: Part 3 Graphic Organizer (Teacher Reference).
- Post: learning targets; *Flush* Plot Development Anchor Chart.

Lesson Vocabulary

poling, skiff, therapeutic, agent, sane

Materials

- *Flush* (book; distributed in Lesson 1; one per student)
- Structured Notes: Chapters 11 and 12 (from homework)
- Equity sticks
- *Flush* Plot Development Anchor Chart (from Lesson 2)
- *Flush* Word-Catcher (begun in Lesson 1)
- Mid-Unit 2 Assessments (with teacher feedback)
- "Florida 'A Paradise of Scandals'" Excerpt 2 (one per student and one to display)
- Dictionaries (several, for students' reference)
- Gathering Evidence of Hiaasen's Perspective: Part 3 Graphic Organizer (one per student and one to display)
- Gathering Evidence of Hiaasen's Perspective: Part 3 Graphic Organizer (Teacher Reference)
- Structured Notes: Chapters 13 and 14 (one per student)
- Evidence flags (at least three per student)

Opening

A. Engaging the Reader: Chapters 11 and 12 of *Flush* (10 minutes)

- Invite students to refer to *Flush* and their **Structured Notes: Chapters 11 and 12** homework and ask triads to discuss the plot development of chapters 11 and 12 by prompting them with these familiar questions:
    - "What happened in chapters 11 and 12 of *Flush*?"
    - "How did those events contribute to the rising action of the plot?"
- Refocus the whole class and consider using **equity sticks** to call on a few students to summarize the plot development in chapters 11 and 12. Add to the posted *Flush* **Plot Development Anchor Chart** something like: "11 and 12—Tension increases as Noah's mom forces Noah's dad to apologize to Dusty Muleman, who is mean and sarcastic in return. Tension is relieved when Abbey is found, but builds again when Noah's dad is taken back to jail for tampering with the tag. Tension about the sewage problem grows when Noah, Abbey, and Shelly see a turtle swimming in the sewage."

Meeting Students' Needs

Reviewing homework holds all students accountable for reading the novel and completing their homework.

B. Unpacking Learning Targets (3 minutes)

- Invite students to read today's learning targets with you aloud:
    - "I can find the gist of "Florida 'A Paradise of Scandals'" Excerpt 2."
    - "I can use evidence from the text to answer text-dependent questions."
    - "I can identify evidence of Carl Hiaasen's perspective of his geographic location in *Flush*."
- Tell students that today they will look at how Hiaasen uses this kind of language in *Flush* to share his perspective.

Meeting Students' Needs

- Learning targets are a research-based strategy that helps all students, especially challenged learners.
- Posting learning targets allows students to reference them throughout the lesson to check their understanding. Learning targets also provide a reminder to students and teachers about the intended learning behind a given lesson or activity.
- Discussing and clarifying the language of learning targets helps build academic vocabulary.

C. Feedback from Mid-Unit 2 Assessment (6 minutes)

- Hand back the **Mid-Unit 2 Assessments (with teacher feedback)** and invite students to spend time reading your feedback and thinking about:
  - "How can this feedback help you to improve your work on Carl Hiaasen's perspective?"
- Invite students to write their names on the board if they have questions so that you can follow up either immediately or later on in the lesson.

Work Time

A. Reading for Gist: "Florida 'A Paradise of Scandals'" Excerpt 2 (8 minutes)

- Display and distribute **"Florida 'A Paradise of Scandals'" Excerpt 2**.
- Invite students to follow along silently as you read Excerpt 2 slowly, fluently, and without interruption.
- Invite students to independently annotate the gist in the margin of the text and record unfamiliar words on their word-catchers.
- Have several **dictionaries** available to the class. Remind students that if they aren't sure what a word means after looking for context clues and looking in the dictionary, they should leave the definition to be discussed with the whole group later on.
- Circulate and support students as they read. For those who need more support, ask them to practice telling you the gist of a section before they write it down.
- Invite students to get into triads to compare what they wrote for their gist statements and to help each other with any unfamiliar vocabulary they haven't been able to figure out.
- Refocus the whole class and invite students to share any unfamiliar vocabulary words they found, along with the definition. If students were unable to work out the definition from the context or find it in a dictionary, encourage other students to assist them with the meaning.
- Ask students to discuss in triads:
  - "Hiaasen describes being out on the water fishing as being 'like a church' for him. What do you think he means by this? What do people usually do in churches?"
- Select volunteers to share their responses. Students may struggle with this, so listen for and guide students to understand that he probably means it is peaceful and quiet like a church—somewhere he can think without being interrupted. Explain to students that he may also mean it in a religious sense, like perhaps he uses the time to pray, but this isn't clear.
- Focus students' attention on the word *therapeutic*. Ask:
  - "What root word that we already discussed in a previous lesson can you see or hear in the word *therapeutic*?"
- Cold-call students to share their responses. Listen for students to explain that *therapy* is a root in this word.

- Ask students to discuss in triads:
  - "Knowing the word *therapy* means 'to help to make yourself feel better,' what do you think *therapeutic* might mean?"
- Consider using equity sticks to select students to share their responses. Listen for and guide students to understand that *therapeutic* means "something that makes you feel better."
- These are other words students may struggle with, so be sure to address them here: *poling*, *skiff*, *agent*, and *sane* by taking each one at a time and asking if any students know what they mean. If no one knows what they mean, either invite a student to look up the word in the dictionary to share with the whole group, or consider telling students if you are running short of time.

Meeting Students' Needs

- Hearing a complex text read slowly, fluently, and without interruption or explanation promotes fluency for students. Be sure to set clear expectations that students follow along silently as you read the text aloud.
- Allow students to grapple with a complex text before explicit teaching of vocabulary. After students have read for gist, they can identify challenging vocabulary for themselves.
- Asking students to identify challenging vocabulary helps them monitor their understanding of a complex text. When students annotate the text by circling these words, it can also provide a formative assessment for the teacher.

B. Text-Dependent Questions: "Florida 'A Paradise of Scandals'" Excerpt 2 (10 minutes)

- Display and distribute **Gathering Evidence of Hiaasen's Perspective: Part 3 Graphic Organizer**. Remind students that the purpose of the organizer is to support them with the learning targets.
- Invite students to follow along as you reread the learning target they will focus on next:
  - "I can use evidence from the text to answer text-dependent questions."
- Invite students to read the questions on the graphic organizer with you as you read them aloud. Remind students that, as in the two previous lessons, they need to reread the questions in column 1, review their excerpt, and then record the answers to the questions in column 2. Today they will do the work independently. Clarify directions as needed.
- Invite students to work independently to write their responses on the graphic organizer.
- Circulate and observe students as they work. As needed, support students by asking them to use evidence from the excerpt to answer the questions. While circulating, identify a student with a strong example of responding to the questions. Ask that student if he or she will present his or her work to the class when everyone refocuses as a whole group.
- Refocus the whole class after a few minutes. Invite the preselected student to share his or her responses with the class and clarify any questions from peers. Support the student and guide class responses using **Gathering Evidence of Hiaasen's Perspective: Part 3 Graphic Organizer (Teacher Reference)**. Invite students to revise their organizers as necessary.

Meeting Students' Needs

- Some students may benefit from having access to "hint cards": small slips of paper or index cards that they turn over for hints about how/where to find the answers to text-dependent questions. For example, a hint card might say, "Look in the third paragraph."
- Some students may benefit from having key sections pre-highlighted in their texts. This will help them focus on small sections rather than scanning the whole text for answers.

Closing and Assessment

A. Identifying Carl Hiaasen's Perspective of Florida (8 minutes)

- Ask students to discuss in triads:
  - "Based on what you have read so far, what do you know about how being born and raised in Florida has affected Carl Hiaasen's perspective of the place?"
- Select volunteers to share their answers with the whole group. Listen for students to explain something like: "Carl Hiaasen loves Florida, loves the water, and thinks it is gorgeous."
- Record this in the third column of the displayed graphic organizer as a model for students. Invite students to record their ideas in the third column of their own organizers.
- Collect students' Gathering Evidence of Hiaasen's Perspective: Part 3 Graphic Organizers and explain that you are going to look over them and provide some formative feedback for students in the next lesson.
- Preview homework and distribute **Structured Notes: Chapters 13 and 14** and **evidence flags**.

Homework

- Read chapters 13 and 14 of *Flush*. As you read mark the text with at least three evidence flags to help you answer this focus question in your structured notes:
  - "What happens in these chapters and how do those events contribute to the plot development?"
- Record any new vocabulary on your word-catcher.

"Florida 'A Paradise of Scandals'" Excerpt 2

Name: _____

Date: _____

Rebecca Leung

Note: Kroft is the person who is conducting the interview.

... says Hiaasen. "My escape is to just get in a boat and disappear on the water."

Most days when he's finished writing, he's out in Florida Bay, usually alone, poling his skiff and looking for bonefish on the edge of the Everglades.

"It's like church for me anyway. It's gorgeous," says Hiaasen.

"So we're away from the weirdness now?" asks Kroft

"Yeah. We are totally away from the weirdness, except for me," says Hiaasen. "All these little fish and all the sting rays and little sharks and everything. You're right in the middle of it, which makes it so much fun. Even if you're not catching any fish, it's a blast to be out here. It's certainly therapeutic."

His agent says that Hiaasen is a fisherman who happens to write. "I would take that as a compliment any day," says Hiaasen. "I need to do it to stay sane, so I think that, you know, the official version is it's number three on my list behind the writing and behind my family."

Source: From a CBS *60 Minutes* interview with Carl Hiaasen from April 17, 2005. Copyright 2005 CBS. All rights reserved.

Gathering Evidence of Hiaasen's Perspective: Part 3 Graphic Organizer

Name: _____

Date: _____

Learning targets:

- "I can use evidence from the text to answer text-dependent questions."
- "I can infer Carl Hiaasen's perspective of Florida."

Questions	Answers	Perspective
	(Use evidence from the text to support your answers.)	Based on what you have read so far, how has being born and raised in Florida affected Carl Hiaasen's perspective of the place?
"Florida 'A Paradise of Scandals'" Excerpt 2		
1. How does Carl Hiaasen escape?		
2. How does he describe what it's like out on the water for him?		
3. What is more important than fishing to Carl Hiaasen?		
4. Why does Carl Hiaasen say he needs to fish?		

Gathering Evidence of Hiaasen's Perspective: Part 3 Graphic Organizer
(Teacher Reference)

Questions	Answers	Perspective
	(Use evidence from the text to support your answers.)	Based on what you have read so far, how has being born and raised in Florida affected Carl Hiaasen's perspective of the place?
"Florida 'A Paradise of Scandals'" Excerpt 2		
1. How does Carl Hiaasen escape?	*He gets on his boat to get away from everything. He says in the interview, "My escape is to just get in a boat and disappear on the water."*	*He thinks it is "gorgeous." He loves the water and the fish.*
2. How does he describe what it's like out on the water for him?	*He says, "It's like church for me anyway. It's gorgeous," and, "All these little fish and all the sting rays and little sharks and everything. You're right in the middle of it, which makes it so much fun. Even if you're not catching any fish, it's a blast to be out here. It's certainly therapeutic."*	
3. What is more important than fishing to Carl Hiaasen?	*Writing and his family. He says, "... it's number three on my list behind the writing and behind my family."*	
4. Why does Carl Hiaasen say he needs to fish?	*To stay sane. He says, "I need to do it to stay sane..."*	

Structured Notes: Chapters 13 and 14

Name: _____

Date: _____

Chapter	Homework Focus Question	Answer to Homework Focus Question with Evidence from the Text (include page numbers)

LESSON 9

Finding Evidence of Carl Hiaasen's Perspective in *Flush*

Long-Term Target Addressed (Based on ELA CCSS)

- I can explain how an author develops the point of view of the narrator or speaker in a text. (RL.6.6)

Supporting Learning Target

- I can identify evidence of Carl Hiaasen's perspective in *Flush*.

Ongoing Assessment

- Structured Notes: Chapters 13 and 14 (from homework)
- Finding Evidence of Carl Hiaasen's Perspective in *Flush* Graphic Organizer

Agenda

1. Opening
   A. Engaging the Reader: Chapters 13 and 14 of *Flush* (10 minutes)
   B. Unpacking Learning Targets (2 minutes)
2. Work Time
   A. Summarizing Carl Hiaasen's Perspective of Florida (10 minutes)
   B. Identifying Evidence of Hiaasen's Perspective in *Flush* (20 minutes)
3. Closing and Assessment
   A. Debrief (3 minutes)
4. Homework
   A. Read chapters 15 and 16 of *Flush*. As you read, mark the text with evidence flags to help you answer the focus question in your structured notes.
   B. Record new vocabulary on your word-catcher.

Teaching Notes

- In this lesson, students work in triads to identify evidence of Carl Hiaasen's perspective of Florida in *Flush*. In order to gather as much evidence as possible, each student in the triad will analyze a different excerpt of *Flush*. To save time, be prepared to assign excerpts to students.

- Collect students' Finding Evidence of Carl Hiaasen's Perspective in *Flush* Graphic Organizer at the end of the lesson and look them over to determine which students might need extra guidance or assistance before they are assessed against these standards in Lesson 11.

- In advance:
  - Review the Mix and Mingle protocol activity in Opening A and have music ready to use for the opening of this lesson.

- Post: learning targets; *Flush* Plot Development Anchor Chart.

Lesson Vocabulary

None

Materials

- Structured Notes: Chapters 13 and 14 (from homework)
- Equity sticks
- *Flush* Plot Development Anchor Chart (from Lesson 2)
- Finding Evidence of Carl Hiaasen's Perspective in *Flush* Graphic Organizer (one per student and one for display)
- Finding Evidence of Carl Hiaasen's Perspective in *Flush* Graphic Organizer (Teacher Reference)
- *Flush* (book; distributed in Lesson 1; one per student)
- Structured Notes: Chapters 15 and 16 (one per student)
- Evidence flags (at least three per student)

Opening

A. Engaging the Reader: Chapters 13 and 14 of *Flush* (10 minutes)

- Remind students that for homework they were to read chapters 13 and 14 and record their answers to the focus question in their **Structured Notes: Chapters 13 and 14**. Ask students to retrieve the handout and prepare for Mix and Mingle.

- Mix and Mingle:
  1. Play music. Invite students to move around the room with their structured notes.
  2. After 15 seconds, stop the music.

3. Invite students to share their answer to the following question with the person standing closest to them: "What happens in chapter 12?"
4. Repeat Steps 1 and 2.
5. Invite students to share their answer to the following question with the person standing closest to them: "What happens in chapter 13?"
6. Repeat Steps 1 and 2.
7. Invite students to share their answer to the following question with the person standing closest to them: "How do those events contribute to the rising action of the plot?"

- Refocus the whole class and consider using **equity sticks** to call on a few students to summarize the plot development in chapters 13 and 14. Add to the posted *Flush* **Plot Development Anchor Chart** something like: "13 and 14—Another conflict between Jasper and Noah is stopped by a new character, an old man. Bull comes to apologize, which relieves some of the tension in that conflict. Tension builds as Noah, Shelly, and Abbey cook up a dangerous plan to put food dye in the sewage system of the *Coral Queen*."

Meeting Students' Needs

Reviewing homework holds all students accountable for reading the novel and completing their homework.

B. Unpacking the Learning Target (2 minutes)

- Invite students to silently follow along as you read the learning target aloud:
  - "I can identify evidence of Carl Hiaasen's perspective in *Flush*."
- Remind students of what *perspective* means.

Meeting Students' Needs

- Learning targets are a research-based strategy that helps all students, especially challenged learners.
- Posting learning targets allows students to reference them throughout the lesson to check their understanding. Learning targets also provide a reminder to students and teachers about the intended learning behind a given lesson or activity.
- Discussing and clarifying the language of learning targets helps build academic vocabulary.

Work Time

A. Summarizing Carl Hiaasen's Perspective of Florida (10 minutes)

- Display and distribute **Finding Evidence of Carl Hiaasen's Perspective in *Flush* Graphic Organizer**.

- Invite students to read through the first three directions on the first page of the graphic organizer with you:
  - Read back through all the inferences you have made about Carl Hiaasen's perspective of Florida on your Gathering Evidence of Hiaasen's Perspective Graphic Organizers from Lessons 6–8.
  - Look for the common themes in each of the perspectives you have inferred and combine those to write a short summary (no more than two sentences) describing Carl Hiaasen's perspective of Florida, using the sentence starter in the top row of the Claim column.
  - Record that summary in the Claim column.
- Model the process with a volunteer student. Ask the student:
  - "What similarities do you see between all of the perspectives you have inferred? What are some common ideas and themes?"
- Listen for the student to suggest things like: "He loves Florida," "He loves the nature and the water," and "He doesn't like the development and exploitation." Record these themes on the displayed organizer and explain that identifying these common themes will help students to summarize Carl Hiaasen's perspective of Florida.
- Model combining those themes into one short paragraph. Use **Finding Evidence of Carl Hiaasen's Perspective in *Flush* Graphic Organizer (Teacher Reference)** to help you fill out the first column of the displayed graphic organizer.
- Invite students to follow the first three directions in the same way to independently summarize the perspectives of Florida that they have inferred. Explain that they may talk to other students, but this is independent work, so ultimately the ideas and writing should be their own.
- Circulate to assist. Ask:
  - "What similarities do you see between all of the perspectives you have inferred? What are some common ideas and themes?"
- "How can you combine those ideas into one summary paragraph of just a couple of sentences?"

Meeting Students' Needs

Some students may benefit from saying their summary aloud to you before recording it on their organizer. Invite those students to sit in a group close to you so that you can work with them.

B. Identifying Evidence of Hiaasen's Perspective in *Flush* (20 minutes)

- Tell students that now that they have inferred how being born and raised in Florida has affected Carl Hiaasen's perspective of the place, they need to look for evidence of that perspective in *Flush*.
- Tell students that in triads they are going to reread excerpts of ***Flush*** to look for evidence of where Carl Hiaasen may have communicated his perspective of Florida.
- Invite students to read steps 4–7 with you in the directions. Emphasize to students that each student in their triad needs to be assigned one set of page numbers to analyze.

- Tell students that you are going to model this with pages 27–29. Fill out the displayed organizer as a model for the whole group. Refer to the Finding Evidence of Carl Hiaasen's Perspective in *Flush* Graphic Organizer (Teacher Reference).
- Invite students to follow steps 4–7 to do the same thing with the page numbers listed.
- Circulate to listen to triad discussions. Ask the following question as necessary to help students stay focused on the task:
  - "How is that evidence of Carl Hiaasen's perspective of Florida?"
- Refocus the whole group. Consider using equity sticks to select students to share their responses with the whole group. Guide students using Finding Evidence of Carl Hiaasen's Perspective in *Flush* Graphic Organizer (Teacher Reference).
- Collect students' Finding Evidence of Carl Hiaasen's Perspective in *Flush* Graphic Organizers at the end of the lesson and look them over to determine which students might need extra guidance or assistance before they are assessed against these standards in Lesson 11.

Meeting Students' Needs

Asking students to discuss prompts before recording their answers helps to ensure that all students have an idea about what to write and can give students confidence in their responses.

Closing and Assessment

A. Debrief (3 minutes)

- Fist-to-Five: Ask students to share how confident they feel about their progress on the learning targets by holding up anywhere from zero (low) to five (high) fingers. Make a note of those students who hold low numbers of fingers in order to address their concerns in the next lesson before they are assessed in Lesson 11.
- Preview homework and distribute **Structured Notes: Chapters 15 and 16** and **evidence flags**.

Meeting Students' Needs

Inviting students to self-assess can help you gauge who requires additional support and guidance before the end of unit assessment.

Homework

- Read chapters 15 and 16 of *Flush*. As you read, mark the text with at least three evidence flags to help you answer this focus question in your structured notes:
  - "What happens in these chapters and how do those events contribute to the plot?"
- Record any new vocabulary on your word-catcher.

Finding Evidence of Carl Hiaasen's Perspective in *Flush* Graphic Organizer

Name: _____

Date: _____

Learning target:

- "I can identify evidence of Carl Hiaasen's perspective in *Flush*."

Directions

1. Read back through all the inferences you have made about Carl Hiaasen's perspective of Florida on your Gathering Evidence of Hiaasen's Perspective Graphic Organizers from Lessons 6–8.

2. Look for the common themes in each of the perspectives you have inferred and combine those to write a short summary (no more than two sentences) describing Carl Hiaasen's perspective of Florida, using the sentence starter in the top row of the Claim column.

3. Record that summary in the Claim column.

4. Assign each student in your triad one of the following excerpts: pages 44–46, 66–68, 102–104, and 138–141 looking for connections to Carl Hiaasen's perspective of Florida.

5. Each triad member should read his or her assigned section, marking any evidence of Carl Hiaasen's perspective of Florida with evidence flags.

6. Share and discuss the evidence you marked with your triad and determine which evidence you think clearly shows his perspective and how he channels that in his writing.

7. Record the evidence in the Evidence column and use the sentence starters in the top row to explain how this shows evidence of Carl Hiaasen's perspective.

Claim	Evidence
As a result of being born and raised in Florida, Carl Hiaasen's perspective is that . . .	In his novel *Flush*, he writes . . . This shows evidence of the claim that . . . because . . .

Finding Evidence of Carl Hiaasen's Perspective in *Flush* Graphic Organizer

(Teacher Reference)

Learning target:

- "I can identify evidence of Carl Hiaasen's perspective in *Flush*."

Claim As a result of being born and raised in Florida, Carl Hiaasen's perspective is that…	Evidence In his novel *Flush*, he writes… This shows evidence of the claim that… because…
As a result of being born in Florida, Carl Hiaasen's perspective is that he loves and cares about the state and sees it as a special place. He thinks it is "gorgeous" and loves the natural, unspoiled side of Florida, including the water and the fish, but he doesn't like the way it is being developed and exploited.	• In his novel *Flush*, he writes, "I've always liked watching the sky drop down like a foamy purple curtain when a summer storm rumbles across Florida Bay" (pages 27–28). This shows evidence of the claim that Carl Hiaasen loves Florida because Noah is showing a love for the weather in Florida. • In his novel *Flush*, he writes, "I was glad to see that the water was okay, especially when a big loggerhead turtle bobbed up to the surface. The three of us stayed real quiet because we thought the turtle might be coming ashore to lay her eggs.… We wouldn't have bothered her if she decided to crawl up and dig a nest.… The momma turtles down here don't have lots of options, so we leave them alone" (pages 28–29). This shows evidence of the claim that he cares about Florida and loves the natural, unspoiled side of it because this evidence shows how much Noah cares about the water and the wildlife.

Claim	Evidence
As a result of being born and raised in Florida, Carl Hiaasen's perspective is that . . .	In his novel *Flush*, he writes . . . This shows evidence of the claim that . . . because . . .
	• In his novel *Flush*, he writes, "... when he spotted Derek Mays stringing a gill net near Little Rabbit Key. Gill nets were outlawed years ago in Florida because they kill everything that gets tangled, not just the baitfish but sharks, reds, snook, tarpon, turtles—you name it, it dies. To make things worse, the island where Derek Mays was poaching was deep in the Everglades National Park, which is totally protected. Or supposed to be. . . . By the time the park rangers had arrived, Dad had wrapped up Derek in his own net, like a big dumb mullet" (page 45). This shows evidence of the claim that he cares about Florida and loves the natural unspoiled side of it because this evidence shows how Noah's dad cared about the ocean life enough to cause trouble with someone who was endangering it. • In his novel *Flush*, he writes, "I started thinking about all the great times we'd had—Dad, Abbey, and me—on our sunset trips. My mother wasn't keen on fishing, but she was always happy when we'd come back with a cooler full of snapper" (page 67). This shows evidence of the claim that he loves Florida and sees it as a special place to be taken care of because Noah has memories of fishing with his family that makes Florida a special place, just like Hiaasen has many emotional attachments to places in Florida.

Claim	Evidence
As a result of being born and raised in Florida, Carl Hiaasen's perspective is that . . .	In his novel *Flush*, he writes . . . This shows evidence of the claim that . . . because . . .
	• In his novel *Flush*, he writes, "I bet there hasn't been a mutton snapper on these flats in ages. Lots of reasons—fish trappers, pollution, too many boats. That's what people do when they find a special place that's wild and full of life, they trample it to death" (page 104). This shows evidence of the claim that he is angry about the development and exploitation of Florida because this evidence includes Noah's dad talking about exploitation in a negative way. • In his novel *Flush*, he writes, "Abbey turned to me. 'The fish are gone. Those little green minnows we always see here.' 'They'll be back,' I said, 'when the water clears up.' Suddenly a loggerhead stuck up its knobbly brown head . . . 'No!' my sister cried out. 'Noah, do something!'. . . So I charged back into the waves, kicking and splashing and hollering like a lunatic. It wasn't the brightest thing I've ever done, but it definitely got that loggerhead's attention. In a fright it ducked under and scooted off, leaving only a boiling swirl" (pages 140–141). This shows evidence of the claim that he cares about Florida and loves the natural unspoiled side of it because this evidence shows how Noah cared enough about the turtle to risk his own health by scaring it away.

Structured Notes: Chapters 15 and 16

Name: _____

Date: _____

Chapter	Homework Focus Question	Answer to Homework Focus Question with Evidence from the Text (include page numbers)

LESSON 10

Illustrating Carl Hiaasen's Perspective of Florida in *Flush*

Long-Term Target Addressed (Based on ELA CCSS)

- I can draw evidence from literary or informational texts to support analysis, reflection, and research. (W.6.9)

Supporting Learning Target

- I can illustrate a scene from *Flush* that shows evidence of Carl Hiaasen's perspective of Florida.

Ongoing Assessment

- Structured Notes: Chapters 15 and 16 (from homework)
- Illustrating a Scene Showing Perspective

Agenda

1. Opening
    A. Engaging the Reader: Chapters 15 and 16 of *Flush* (10 minutes)
    B. Unpacking Learning Targets (2 minutes)
2. Work Time
    A. Illustrating a Scene from *Flush* (20 minutes)
    B. Whole-Group Critique (8 minutes)
3. Closing and Assessment
    A. Revising Work (5 minutes)
4. Homework
    A. Read chapter 17 of *Flush*. As you read, mark the text with evidence flags to help you answer the focus question in your structured notes.
    B. Record any new vocabulary on your word-catcher.

Teaching Notes

- To prepare students to address W.6.9 in the End-of-Unit 2 Assessment in the next lesson, students will illustrate a scene from *Flush* that shows evidence of Carl Hiaasen's perspective of Florida. In this lesson, the word *illustrate* means students can choose to either sketch and label or write about the scene and how it shows evidence of Carl Hiaasen's perspective, depending on their preferred way of expressing their ideas.

- This lesson involves teacher modeling of sketching the scene, so if you are not confident about modeling sketching skills or you are concerned about the amount of time it may take, consider preparing artwork in advance and then model annotating it to describe how the scene you have chosen shows evidence of Carl Hiaasen's perspective of Florida. For example, you could draw a picture of a turtle surfacing in the water with people watching on the shore. You could then label it with the caption, "Carl Hiaasen loves nature and wants to protect it. In *Flush*, Noah and his friends see a turtle in the water, but Noah describes how they leave it alone in case she wants to come ashore and lay eggs, showing evidence of the perspective of loving nature and taking care of it."

- This lesson involves a whole-group critique of student work. Take care to select volunteers who are willing to have their work critiqued and ensure that the critique process is done sensitively and carefully to provide volunteers with constructive feedback.

- As students are working, consider brief meetings with students who may need additional support in inferring Carl Hiaasen's perspective of Florida or finding evidence of his perspective in *Flush* (based on the Finding Evidence of Carl Hiaasen's Perspective in *Flush* Graphic Organizer collected in the previous lesson). You may also consider working with students who showed low numbers of fingers in the Fist-to-Five in the Closing and Assessment of the previous lesson.

- As students are reading two chapters of this novel per night, consider providing catch-up reading time to ensure all students are at the same place in the text as they go into the End-of-Unit 2 Assessment in the next lesson.

- In advance:
  - Review the Concentric Circles protocol (see appendix).
- Post: learning targets; *Flush* Plot Development Anchor Chart.

Lesson Vocabulary

illustrate

Materials

- Structured Notes: Chapters 15 and 16 (from homework)
- *Flush* Plot Development Anchor Chart (from Lesson 2)
- *Flush* (book; distributed in Lesson 1; one per student)
- Finding Evidence of Carl Hiaasen's Perspective in *Flush* Graphic Organizer (collected in Lesson 9)
- Illustrating a Scene Showing Perspective (one per student and one for display)

- Structured Notes: Chapter 17 (one per student)
- Evidence flags (at least three per student)

Opening

A. Engaging the Reader: Chapters 15 and 16 of *Flush* (10 minutes)

- Invite students to refer to their **Structured Notes: Chapters 15 and 16** homework and the answer they wrote to the homework focus question:
  - "What happened in chapters 15 and 16? How did those events contribute to the plot development?"
- Remind students of the Concentric Circles protocol:
  1. Split the group in half. Invite one half to make a circle facing out and the other half to make a circle around them, facing in.
  2. Ensure that all students are facing someone opposite them.
  3. Ask: "What happened in chapter 15? How did it contribute to the plot development?"
  4. Invite students to share their answers with the person opposite them.
  5. Invite students on the inside circle to move two people to the right.
  6. Ask: "What happened in chapter 16? How did it contribute to the plot development?"
  7. Invite students to share their answers with the person opposite them.
- Refocus the whole group. Direct students' attention to the posted *Flush* **Plot Development Anchor Chart** and ask:
  - "Is the action still rising? How do you know? Where are we on the chart now?"
- Select volunteers to share their responses. Listen for students to explain that they have reached the climax of the story now. We know because Noah and Abbey did something big by going on the *Coral Queen* and flushing food dye down the toilets that will help the police to catch Dusty Muleman.
- Record a summary of the climax on the *Flush* Plot Development Anchor Chart that reads something like: "15 and 16—Noah gets on the *Coral Queen* and flushes food dye down the toilet. He and Abbey nearly get caught and get stranded at sea for a night until they are rescued by their dad."

Meeting Students' Needs

Reviewing homework holds all students accountable for reading the novel and completing their homework.

B. Unpacking Learning Targets (2 minutes)

- Invite students to follow along silently as you read the learning target aloud:
  - "I can illustrate a scene from *Flush* that shows evidence of Carl Hiaasen's perspective of Florida."

- Explain that *illustrate* means to either draw or write about the scene. Tell students that today they are going to illustrate a scene from **Flush** that shows evidence of Carl Hiaasen's perspective.

Meeting Students' Needs

- Learning targets are a research-based strategy that helps all students, especially challenged learners.
- Posting learning targets allows students to reference them throughout the lesson to check their understanding. Learning targets also provide a reminder to students and teachers about the intended learning behind a given lesson or activity.
- Discussing and clarifying the language of learning targets helps build academic vocabulary.

Work Time

A. Illustrating a Scene from *Flush* (20 minutes)

- Return **Finding Evidence of Carl Hiaasen's Perspective in *Flush* Graphic Organizer** collected at the end of Lesson 9.
- Display and distribute **Illustrating a Scene Showing Perspective**.
- Tell students that they are going to select a scene from *Flush* that clearly shows evidence of Carl Hiaasen's perspective of Florida. Remind them that in the previous lesson they found evidence of his perspective in *Flush*, so it would be a good idea to choose a scene that one of those pieces of evidence was taken from.
- Model this with the class and emphasize choosing something they think they will be able to sketch or write about. Using a completed Finding Evidence of Carl Hiaasen's Perspective in *Flush* Graphic Organizer, do a think-aloud. For example:
  - "The claim I have made states that Carl Hiaasen's perspective of Florida is "As a result of being born in Florida, Carl Hiaasen's perspective is that he loves and cares about the state and sees it as a special place. He thinks it is 'gorgeous' and loves the natural, unspoiled side of Florida, including the water and the fish, but he doesn't like the way it is being developed and exploited."
  - "All of these pieces of evidence should show evidence of that perspective. I think I want to sketch rather than write, and there are a lot of people in this scene and I'm not very good at drawing a lot of people. There is a turtle in the water in this scene. I think I can draw that."
- Model using the page numbers recorded on the organizer to go back and reread the scene in the book. Do a think-aloud of what you might draw after reading the scene. For example:
  - "In this scene on pages 28–29, the three boys are standing on the shore watching the turtle as it surfaces. So I would need to draw the water with the turtle head poking out and then the shore with three boys standing on it."

- Complete a sketch of the scene on the spot or use a sketch created prior to the lesson and model how to caption the artwork. Think aloud as you caption your artwork. For example:
  - "Just like when I was choosing evidence yesterday, my caption needs to describe how this shows evidence of Carl Hiaasen's perspective of Florida. So something like: 'In this scene, Noah and his friends are watching from the shore as a turtle surfaces on the water. Noah describes how they stay away from the turtle just in case it wants to come ashore to lay eggs. This shows evidence of Carl Hiaasen's perspective of Florida because Carl Hiaasen loves the natural, unspoiled side of Florida and wants to protect it, which is reflected in Noah's thoughts and actions.'"
- Record some sentence starters that students could use on the board:
  - In this scene . . .
  - This shows evidence of Carl Hiaasen's perspective of Florida because . . .
- Explain that students who don't like to sketch can write using the same sentence starters. Rather than sketch the scene, they will describe the scene in their own words and then explain how it shows evidence of Carl Hiaasen's perspective.
- Model how to do this with the same scene that was sketched.
- Invite students to work independently to illustrate a scene from *Flush*.
- Circulate to support students in choosing their scene, drawing their artwork, and labeling it or writing their description of the scene. Ask guiding questions:
  - "How does this scene show Carl Hiaasen's perspective of Florida?"
  - "Who is doing what in this scene? Why?"

Meeting Students' Needs

Modeling a process for students with a think-aloud can guide students in how to do something, and it can also provide them with expectations for their work.

B. Whole-Group Critique (8 minutes)

- Refocus the whole group. Seek two volunteers—one who has completed a sketch and one who has used writing—who would like to share their work with the whole group and engage in a critique.
- First ask the students to share which scene they have chosen and why. Ensure that students explain how their scene shows evidence of Carl Hiaasen's perspective of Florida.
- Invite the students to read the scenes they have chosen from *Flush* to the whole group and then share their sketch of (or description of) the scene.
- Ask the group:
  - "How can (s)he improve his/her work to make the scene clearer? Is there anything in the scene that is missing from the work?"
  - "Is there anything that could be more clear?"

- "What about the label—does it clearly explain what is happening in the scene and how it shows evidence of Carl Hiaasen's perspective?"
- Invite students to make suggestions sensitively and invite the volunteer students to either make notes about revisions to work on later or to make those revisions in real time as the class provides them with suggestions.

Meeting Students' Needs

A whole class critique can provide all students with ideas and suggestions for improving their own work.

Closing and Assessment

A. Revising Work (5 minutes)

- Invite students to revise their work based on pointers given to the volunteer students in the whole-group critique.
- Inform students that in the next lesson they are going to be completing their End-of-Unit 2 Assessment in which they will look for evidence of Carl Hiaasen's perspective in a new excerpt, and they will also illustrate a scene showing evidence of Carl Hiaasen's perspective, just as they have in this lesson.
- Preview homework and distribute **Structured Notes: Chapter 17** and **evidence flags**.

Homework

- Read chapter 17 of *Flush*. As you read, mark the text with at least three evidence flags to help you answer this focus question in your structured notes:
  - "What happens in this chapter and how do those events contribute to the plot?"
- Record any new vocabulary on your word-catcher.

Illustrating a Scene Showing Perspective

Name: _____

Date: _____

Learning target:

- I can draw evidence from literary or informational texts to support analysis, reflection, and research. (W.6.9)

Page number: _____

Structured Notes: Chapter 17

Name: _____

Date: _____

Chapter	Homework Focus Question	Answer to Homework Focus Question with Evidence from the Text (include page numbers)

LESSON 11

End-of-Unit 2 Assessment

Finding Evidence of Carl Hiaasen's Perspective in *Flush* and Illustrating Perspective

Long-Term Targets Addressed (Based on ELA CCSS)

- I can explain how the author develops the point of view of the narrator or speaker in a text. (RL.6.6)
- I can draw evidence from literary or informational texts to support analysis, reflection, and research. (W.6.9)

Supporting Learning Targets

- I can identify evidence of Carl Hiaasen's perspective in *Flush*.
- I can illustrate a scene from *Flush* that shows evidence of Carl Hiaasen's perspective of Florida.

Ongoing Assessment

- Structured Notes: Chapter 17 (from homework)
- End-of-Unit 2 Assessment

Agenda

1. Opening
    A. Engaging the Reader: Chapter 17 of *Flush* (10 minutes)
    B. Unpacking Learning Targets (2 minutes)
2. Work Time
    A. End-of-Unit 2 Assessment (30 minutes)
3. Closing and Assessment
    A. Debrief (3 minutes)

4. Homework

    A. Read to the end of *Flush*. As you read, mark the text with evidence flags to help you answer the focus question in your structured notes.

    B. Record new vocabulary on your word-catcher.

Teaching Notes

- This is the End-of-Unit 2 Assessment. Assess student responses on the end of unit assessment using the Grade 6 2-Point Rubric—Short Response, and the Illustrating Perspective Rubric (see supporting materials). Use the End-of-Unit 2 Assessment: Finding Evidence of Carl Hiaasen's Perspective in *Flush* and Illustrating Perspective (Teacher Reference) to guide you in your assessment, but be aware that this is just an example of the kinds of things students may have written.

- Students who finish early may want to continue reading *Flush*. Homework for this lesson is to finish the book. Students may need more time to do this than has been allocated, so consider making additional time for students to finish the novel before moving on to Unit 3.

- In advance:
    - Read the beginning of chapter 18 of *Flush* from "The food coloring didn't show up as brightly in the sea as it did in the store bottles" to "Dusty Muleman was officially busted" on page 219 to familiarize yourself with the events and how they might show evidence of Carl Hiaasen's perspective. This will help you prepare to grade students' assessments.
    - Review the Back-to-Back and Face-to-Face protocol (see Appendix).

- Post: learning targets.

Lesson Vocabulary

Do not preview vocabulary.

Materials

- Structured Notes: Chapter 17 (from homework)
- *Flush* Plot Development Anchor Chart (from Lesson 2)
- End-of-Unit 2 Assessment: Finding Evidence of Carl Hiaasen's Perspective in *Flush* and Illustrating Perspective (one per student)
- *Flush* (book; distributed in Lesson 1; one per student)
- Evidence flags (five per student for the assessment; three additional per student for homework)
- End-of-Unit 2 Assessment: Finding Evidence of Carl Hiaasen's Perspective in *Flush* and Illustrating Perspective (Teacher Reference)
- Grade 6 2-Point Rubric—Short Response (Teacher Reference)
- Illustrating Perspective Rubric (Teacher Reference)
- Structured Notes: End of *Flush* (one per student)

Opening

A. Engaging the Reader: Chapter 17 of *Flush* (10 minutes)

- Invite students to refer to their **Structured Notes: Chapter 17** homework and the answer they wrote to the homework focus question:
    - "What happened in chapter 17? How did it contribute to the plot development?"
- Back-to-Back and Face-to-Face:
    1. Invite students to pair up with their structured notes and to sit back-to-back.
    2. Ask: "What happened in chapter 17? How did it contribute to the plot development?"
    3. Give students time think and to refer to their structured notes.
    4. Invite students to turn face-to-face to share their answers.
- Refocus the whole group. Direct students' attention to the **Flush Plot Development Anchor Chart** and ask:
    - "Where are we on the chart now?"
- Select volunteers to share their responses. Listen for students to explain that they are now moving toward the resolution.
- Record a summary next to the resolution line on the *Flush* Plot Development Anchor Chart that reads something like: "17—Noah meets his grandfather and hears his story."

B. Unpacking Learning Targets (2 minutes)

- Invite students to read the learning targets with you:
    - "I can identify evidence of Carl Hiaasen's perspective in *Flush*."
    - "I can illustrate a scene from *Flush* that shows evidence of Carl Hiaasen's perspective of Florida."
- Remind students that these are the same learning targets they have been working with during the past several lessons. Today they will show how well they can demonstrate these targets independently in an assessment.

Meeting Students' Needs

- Learning targets are a research-based strategy that helps all students, especially challenged learners.
- Posting learning targets allows students to reference them throughout the lesson to check their understanding. Learning targets also provide a reminder to students and teachers about the intended learning behind a given lesson or activity.
- Discussing and clarifying the language of learning targets helps build academic vocabulary.

Work Time

A. End-of-Unit 2 Assessment (30 minutes)

- Distribute the **End-of-Unit 2 Assessment: Finding Evidence of Carl Hiaasen's Perspective in *Flush* and Illustrating Perspective**. Invite students to read the directions at the top with you.
- Remind students that they will need their novel *Flush*.
- Distribute **evidence flags**.
- Remind the class that because this is an assessment, it is to be completed independently. However, if students need assistance, they should raise their hand.
- Circulate and support students as they work. During an assessment, prompting should be minimal.
- At the end of the allotted time, collect the assessments. Assess them using **End-of-Unit 2 Assessment: Finding Evidence of Carl Hiaasen's Perspective in *Flush* and Illustrating Perspective (Teacher Reference)**, **Grade 6 2-Point Rubric—Short Response**, and **Illustrating Perspective Rubric**.

Meeting Students' Needs

- If students receive accommodations for assessment, communicate with the cooperating service providers regarding the practices of instruction in use during this study, as well as the goals of the assessment.
- For some students, this assessment may require more than the 30 minutes allotted. Consider providing students time over multiple days if necessary.

Closing and Assessment

A. Debrief (3 minutes)

- Fist-to-Five: Invite students to reread each of the learning targets with you and to show on their fingers how well they achieved each target with 0 being "not at all" and 5 being "achieved it successfully."
- Summarize to the whole group what you see with the Fist-to-Five.
- Preview homework and distribute **Structured Notes: End of *Flush*** and **evidence flags**.

Meeting Students' Needs

Developing self-assessment and reflection supports all learners.

Homework

- Read to the end of *Flush*. As you read, mark the text with at least three evidence flags to help you answer this focus question in your structured notes:
  - "What is the resolution?"
- Record any new vocabulary on your word-catcher.

End-of-Unit 2 Assessment

Finding Evidence of Carl Hiaasen's Perspective in *Flush* and Illustrating Perspective

Name: _____

Date: _____

Learning targets:

- "I can identify evidence of Carl Hiaasen's perspective in *Flush*."
- "I can illustrate a scene from *Flush* that shows evidence of Carl Hiaasen's perspective of Florida."

Directions

1. Revisit the summarized claim you made about Carl Hiaasen's perspective of Florida in Lesson 9 on your Finding Evidence of Carl Hiaasen's Perspective Graphic Organizer and record it in the first column of the organizer on the following page.

2. Read a new excerpt of *Flush* from the beginning of chapter 18, "The food coloring didn't show up as brightly in the sea as it did in the store bottles," to "Dusty Muleman was officially busted" on page 219.

3. Reread that excerpt of *Flush*, using evidence flags to mark where you find evidence of Carl Hiaasen's perspective of Florida.

4. Record the evidence you find in the second column of the organizer.

1. Finding Evidence of Carl Hiaasen's Perspective

Claim As a result of being born and raised in Florida, Carl Hiaasen's perspective is that . . .	Evidence

2. Use your graphic organizer to write a response to the following prompt:

   How has being born and raised in Florida affected Carl Hiaasen's perspective of the place? Where is the evidence of this perspective in the excerpt you have read today of the novel *Flush*? How does the evidence you have selected illustrate his perspective?

   _____
   _____
   _____
   _____
   _____
   _____
   _____
   _____
   _____
   _____

3. Illustrate a scene from the excerpt you've read from chapter 18 of *Flush* that shows how Carl Hiaasen's perspective of Florida is evident in this excerpt. Explain how Carl Hiaasen's perspective is evident in this scene.

   Page numbers: _____

   - In this scene . . .

   - This shows evidence of Carl Hiaasen's perspective of Florida because . . .

End-of-Unit 2 Assessment

Finding Evidence of Carl Hiaasen's Perspective in *Flush* and Illustrating Perspective

(Teacher Reference)

1. Finding Evidence of Carl Hiaasen's Perspective

Claim As a result of being born and raised in Florida, Carl Hiaasen's perspective is that . . .	**Evidence** In his novel *Flush*, he writes . . . This shows evidence of the claim that . . . because . . .
He loves and cares about the state and sees it as a special place. He thinks it is "gorgeous" and loves the natural, unspoiled side of Florida, including the water and the fish, but he doesn't like the way it is being developed and exploited.	• In his novel Flush he writes, "At first I thought she was mad at Abbey and me, but it turned out that she wasn't. She was mad at Dusty Muleman. 'Unbelievable!' she exploded finally. 'How can a person do something like that! A father, for heaven's sake! All the kids on the island go swimming here—and he's poisoning the place with all this . . . this . . .'" (page 217). This shows evidence of the claim that he doesn't like the way the place is being exploited because in this scene Noah's mom is angry that Dusty Muleman has been polluting the water. • In his novel Flush he writes, "'Sure? Anyways, it was helluva catch,' said Grandpa Bobby. 'That was back before they dropped fish traps all over the reefs. Back before certain creeps started dumping their crapola in the sea.' There was a rumbly edge to his voice, like he was struggling to keep his temper under control" (pages 217–218). This also show evidence of his perspective that he doesn't like the way the place is being developed and exploited because Grandpa Bobby is angry that people are exploiting the ocean with particular fishing techniques. Grandpa Bobby is also angry with people like Dusty Muleman for dumping sewage into the ocean.

2. Use your graphic organizer to write a response to the following prompt:

   How has being born and raised in Florida affected Carl Hiaasen's perspective of the place? Where is the evidence of this perspective in the excerpt you have read today of the novel *Flush*? How does the evidence you have selected illustrate his perspective?

As a result of being born and raised in Florida, Carl Hiaasen loves and cares about the place and sees it as very special. He thinks it is "gorgeous" and loves the natural, unspoiled side of Florida, including the water and the fish, but he doesn't like the way it is being developed and exploited.

In his novel Flush *he writes, "At first I thought she was mad at Abbey and me, but it turned out that she wasn't. She was mad at Dusty Muleman. 'Unbelievable!' she exploded finally. 'How can a person do something like that! A father, for heaven's sake! All the kids on the island go swimming here—and he's poisoning the place with all this . . . this . . .'" (page 217). This shows evidence of Carl Hiaasen's perspective that he doesn't like the way the place is being exploited because in this scene Noah's mom is angry that Dusty Muleman has been exploiting the water.*

In his novel Flush, *Hiaasen also writes, "'Sure? Anyways, it was helluva catch,' said Grandpa Bobby. 'That was back before they dropped fish traps all over the reefs. Back before certain creeps started dumping their crapola in the sea.' There was a rumbly edge to his voice, like he was struggling to keep his temper under control" (pages 217–218). This also show evidence of his perspective that he doesn't like the way the place is being developed and exploited because Grandpa Bobby is angry that people are exploiting the ocean with particular fishing techniques. Grandpa Bobby is also angry with people like Dusty Muleman for dumping sewage into the ocean.*

Grade 6 2-Point Rubric—Short Response
(Teacher Reference)

Use the rubric below for determining scores on short answers in this assessment.

The features of a **2-point response** are:

- Valid inferences and/or claims from the text where required by the prompt
- Evidence of analysis of the text where required by the prompt
- Relevant facts, definitions, concrete details, and/or other information from the text to develop response according to the requirements of the prompt
- Sufficient number of facts, definitions, concrete details, and/or other information from the text as required by the prompt
- Complete sentences where errors do not impact readability

The features of a **1-point response** are:

- A mostly literal recounting of events or details from the text as required by the prompt
- Some relevant facts, definitions, concrete details, and/or other information from the text to develop response according to the requirements of the prompt
- Incomplete sentences or bullets

The features of a **0-point response** are:

- A response that does not address any of the requirements of the prompt or is totally inaccurate
- No response (blank answer)
- A response that is not written in English
- A response that is unintelligible or indecipherable

If the prompt requires two texts and the student references only one text, the response can be scored no higher than a 1.

Illustrating Perspective Rubric
(Teacher Reference)

	4	3	2	1
I can draw evidence from literary or informational texts to support analysis, reflection, and research. (W.6.9)	Student has clearly created a piece of artwork or text illustrating a scene from the excerpt of *Flush*.	Student has created a piece of artwork or text illustrating a scene from the excerpt of *Flush*.	Student has created a piece of artwork or text related to the excerpt of *Flush*.	Student work is not really relevant to the excerpt of *Flush*.
I can draw evidence from literary or informational texts to support analysis, reflection, and research. (W.6.9)	Student has clearly described in detail how his/her scene shows evidence of Carl Hiaasen's perspective of Florida.	Student has described in detail how his/her scene shows evidence of Carl Hiaasen's perspective of Florida.	Student has described how his/her scene shows evidence of Carl Hiaasen's perspective of Florida.	Student work does not really show evidence of Carl Hiaasen's perspective of Florida.

Structured Notes: End of *Flush*

Name: _____

Date: _____

Chapter	Homework Focus Question	Answer to Homework Focus Question with Evidence from the Text (include page numbers)

LESSON 12

Analyzing Plot Development across *Flush*

Long-Term Target Addressed (Based on ELA CCSS)

- I can analyze how a particular sentence, stanza, scene, or chapter fits in and contributes to the development of a literary text. (RL.6.5)

Supporting Learning Targets

- I can explain how chapters 18–21 contribute to plot development.
- I can explain how Carl Hiaasen develops the plot across the novel.
- I can write a Reader's Review of the novel *Flush*.

Ongoing Assessment

- Structured Notes: End of *Flush* (from homework)
- Reader's Review of *Flush*
- Optional Supplementary Assessment Items

Agenda

1. Opening
   A. Unpacking Learning Targets (3 minutes)
2. Work Time
   A. Plot Development throughout the Novel (10 minutes)
   B. Reader's Review (17 minutes)
3. Closing and Assessment
   A. Independent Reading Launch (15 minutes)
4. Homework
   A. Read your independent reading book.

Teaching Notes

- This is the final lesson of this unit. It has been included after the End-of-Unit 2 Assessment to ensure students have time to synthesize their learning about plot development in the novel *Flush* and to capture their thinking about the novel.
- Independent reading is launched at the end of this lesson. See Launching Independent Reading in Grades 6–8: Sample Plan—which provides practical guidance for a robust independent reading program. Having launched independent reading in Module 2, you may find students don't need as much time for the launch in this module; however, allocate time according to the needs of your particular students.
- Students may require more time to finish reading the novel before this lesson.
- Post: learning targets.
- Review: Launching Independent Reading in Grades 6–8: Sample Plan.

Lesson Vocabulary

None

Materials

- Structured Notes: End of *Flush* (from homework)
- *Flush* (book; distributed in Lesson 1; one per student)
- *Flush* Plot Development Anchor Chart (from Lesson 2)
- Reader's Review: *Flush* (one per student and one for display)
- Launching Independent Reading in Grades 6–8: Sample Plan (Teacher Reference) (see Teaching Notes)

Opening

A. Unpacking Learning Targets (3 minutes)

- Invite students to read aloud the learning targets with you:
    - "I can explain how chapters 18–21 contribute to plot development."
    - "I can explain how Carl Hiaasen develops the plot across the novel."
    - "I can write a Reader's Review of the novel *Flush*."
- Congratulate students on finishing the novel and on their good thinking on point of view, perspective, and plot development. Explain that in this lesson, they are going to finish up their work on the novel.

Meeting Students' Needs

- Learning targets are a research-based strategy that helps all students, especially challenged learners.
- Posting learning targets allows students to reference them throughout the lesson to check their understanding. Learning targets also provide a reminder to students and teachers about the intended learning behind a given lesson or activity.

Work Time

A. Plot Development throughout the Novel (10 minutes)

- Invite students to refer to their **Structured Notes: End of *Flush*** and their novel, *Flush*, to share the answers they wrote to the homework focus question with their triads:
  - "What happened in the remaining chapters of *Flush*? How did that contribute to plot development?"
- Point out the ideas recorded on the Rising Action section of the ***Flush* Plot Development Anchor Chart** and ask students to discuss in triads:
  - "What issues/problems were introduced throughout the story? How did each of them contribute to the plot?"
- Select volunteers to share their responses. Listen for students to list the things from the Rising Action part of the anchor chart.
- Ask students to discuss in triads:
  - "How were those issues/problems resolved in the final chapters?"
- Cold-call students to share their responses. Listen for them to explain that the problem of the *Coral Queen* polluting the ocean was resolved when the food coloring made a purple river in the water from the *Coral Queen* out to sea, and the conflict between Noah and Jasper Jr. ended when Noah stood up to him and forced him to apologize.
- Record student responses in the Resolutions box on the *Flush* Plot Development Anchor Chart.
- Ask students to synthesize their learning about plot development in triads:
  - "So how did Carl Hiaasen develop the plot of *Flush*? What did he do?"
- Cold-call students to share their responses. Listen for them to explain that he introduced a big problem early on that needed to be resolved, and he added tensions associated with that problem along the way as characters tried to resolve the problem, including conflicts and tensions between characters.

B. Reader's Review (17 minutes)

- Explain that now that students have finished the novel, they are going to write a Reader's Review of it to synthesize their thinking about it.

- Display and distribute the **Reader's Review: *Flush***. Invite students to read through the questions silently in their heads as you read them aloud.
- Invite students to ask any clarifying questions.
- Explain that because a Reader's Review contains opinions about a book, you would like them to complete this independently without talking to anyone else. Explain that you would like them to be honest about the book and to think carefully about their responses. Remind students that they need to justify their responses.
- Circulate to support students as they work. Ask guiding questions:
  - "What happened?"
  - "What did you notice?"
  - "What did this book make you think about? Did you make any connections to other texts?"
  - "Why would you give it that star rating?"
- Refocus the whole group. Invite students to share parts of their Reader's Reviews with the whole group.

Meeting Students' Needs

- Reading the instructions with students will ensure that all of them understand what is expected of them.
- Consider inviting students who may struggle with putting their thoughts into writing to say them aloud to you before writing.

Closing and Assessment

A. Independent Reading Launch (15 minutes)

- Follow the **Launching Independent Reading in Grades 6–8: Sample Plan** for practical guidance in launching the independent reading program.

Homework

Read your independent reading book.

Reader's Review: *Flush*

Name: _____

Date: _____

1. What happened?

   In this text, _____

   _____

   _____

   _____

   _____

2. What did you notice? (structure, author's language and word choice, writing style, etc.)

   I noticed, _____

   _____

   _____

   _____

   _____

3. What did this book make you wonder/think about/connect to?

   Reading this book made me think about/wonder/connect to _____

   _____

   _____

   _____

   _____

4. How would you rate this book?

   I would give this book 1/2/3/4/5 stars because _____

   _____

   _____

   _____

Supplementary Assessment Items

Flush

Name: _____

Date: _____

Directions: Read the following passage. Answer the questions that follow.

I grabbed my bike and headed full speed down the old road. I'd had a bad feeling about Lice Peeking from the beginning, and now it looked like I might be right. If he was Dad's best hope for a witness against Dusty Muleman, we might be in deep trouble.

Halfway to the trailer park it started pouring, and I was drenched by the time I got there. I knocked so hard that the door swung open.

Dripping like a dog, I stepped inside. The TV was blaring—some station that shows country-music videos all day long. I turned it off and called out, "Helloooo?"

Nothing.

"Anybody home? Mr. Peeking?"

From the rear of the trailer came a muffled *thump-thump* of footsteps, and I tensed up. I was ready to run if Lice came out bombed or acting crazy.

But it was Shelly who walked up the hall, all alone. She looked red in the cheeks and not very happy. She was wearing the top half of a blue bathing suit and a Hawaiian-style wraparound skirt. Her brassy blond hair was pinned in a bun, and she was limping. I noticed that her right foot was wrapped in tape, and I wondered if it had something to do with the baseball bat she was carrying.

"Sorry for barging in," I said, taking a backward step toward the door. "I knocked for a long time but nobody heard me."

"I was busy redecorating. What do you want?"

"Mr. Peeking was supposed to stop over today and look at my dad's bonefish boat."

"And he didn't show up? My darlin' Lice? What a surprise." Shelly laughed in a cold way that made me shudder.

"Is he here?" I asked.

"Nope."

For several moments we stood there not saying anything, the rain drumming on the aluminum roof.

"What happened to your foot?" I heard myself ask.

Source: Flush by Carl Hiaasen (pp. 68–71).

"I believe I busted it," Shelly replied.

"How?"

"Kicking the toilet to death."

"Oh," I said.

"I was pretending it was Lice's butt. He's gone, by the way, in case you hadn't figured that out."

"Gone where?"

"Wherever it is that gutless, lazy, lowlife boyfriends go," she said. "Bolted last night while I was in the shower. Took my Jeep, too. The cops found it abandoned this morning up near the toll plaza at Cutler Ridge."

I didn't know what to say, but I had to be careful. Shelly looked like she was aching to use that baseball bat.

"But Mr. Peeking told me he doesn't have a driver's license," I said.

"A minor technicality," said Shelly, "for a weasel like him. Have a seat, Noah."

"I really should be going."

"I said *have a seat*."

So I did.

"Some man came by to see Lice last night," she said, "just before he ran off. A big bald-headed guy with a weird foreign accent—French or Russian or something."

"He was bald?" I thought of the stranger who'd grabbed Abbey at the marina.

"Like a bowling ball," Shelly said. "Plus, he looked like somebody gave him a nose job with a socket wrench. Lice went outside to talk, and he came back white as a ghost. Wouldn't tell me anything, either. Waited until I was in the shower, then he took off. Did I mention he grabbed all the cash?"

"No, ma'am."

"A hundred and eighty-six bucks. Everything I had."

"That stinks." I felt queasy, like somehow it was all my fault.

"Funny," Shelly said, "but Lice didn't say nothin' about buyin' your daddy's boat."

"I've really got to go now."

"Remember what I told you about lying, Noah?"

"Yes, ma'am."

"Besides, you can't be out in this rain. You'll catch strep."

I was more than ready to risk it. "Please," I said. "My mom's gonna be worried."

Shelly nodded toward the telephone. "Then give her a jingle."

Of course, I didn't move.

Shelly smiled. "Tell me about Lice and your daddy's boat," she said. "Tell me everything, okay? I'm sure it won't take long."

I couldn't take my eyes off the wooden bat, which she was slapping from one palm to the other.

"Relax, kid, this isn't for you," she said.

I wasn't taking any chances. Without hesitating, I told her all about the secret deal between my father and Lice Peeking. I figured she'd just laugh and tell me I was stupid for trusting her no-good boyfriend, but I was wrong.

What she said was: "Noah, I think I can help you."

Which was the last thing I expected.

This question has two parts. First answer Part A. Then answer Part B.

Part A: How does Noah's attitude toward Shelly change in this passage?

- A. From sorry to helpful
- B. From scared to comforted
- C. From confused to confident
- D. From worried to understanding

Part B: Which **two** details from the passage **best** support the change described in the correct answer to Part A?

- A. "If he was Dad's best hope for a witness . . . we might be in deep trouble."
- B. "I was ready to run if Lice came out bombed or acting crazy."
- C. "I wondered if it had something to do with the baseball bat she was carrying."
- D. "'What happened to your foot?' I heard myself ask."
- E. "I didn't know what to say, but I had to be careful."
- F. "I wasn't taking any chances. Without hesitating, I told her all about the secret."
- G. "'Noah, I think I can help you.' Which was the last thing I expected."

The following question has two parts. First answer Part A. Then, answer Part B.

Part A: How does Lice's disappearance move the plot forward?

- A. It creates a setback for Noah.
- B. It makes Shelly feel sorry for herself.
- C. It causes Noah to be suspicious of Lice.
- D. It means Lice's plan to buy Noah's dad's boat is not a secret.

Part B: Which detail from the passage supports the correct answer to Part A?

A. "If he was Dad's best hope for a witness against Dusty Muleman, we might be in deep trouble."

B. "'Took my Jeep, too. The cops found it abandoned this morning up near the toll plaza at Cutler Ridge.'"

C. "'Waited until I was in the shower, then he took off. Did I mention he grabbed all the cash?'"

D. "'Tell me about Lice and your daddy's boat,' she said. 'Tell me everything, okay?'"

Read the following sentences from the passage.

"Wherever it is that gutless, lazy, lowlife boyfriends go," she said. "Bolted last night while I was in the shower. Took my Jeep, too. The cops found it abandoned this morning up near the toll plaza at Cutler Ridge."

What is the connotative meaning of the word *bolted* in this context?

A. securely fastened
B. hastily departed
C. fiercely struck
D. tightened fast

Supplementary Assessment Items Answer Key

Flush

Standards Assessed: RL.6.3, RL.6.4, RL.6.6

Note: Supplementary Assessment Items are located in the Teacher Guide and Resource Book only. Distribute a copy of the student version of this assessment to each student.

Directions: Read the following passage. Answer the questions that follow.

I grabbed my bike and headed full speed down the old road. I'd had a bad feeling about Lice Peeking from the beginning, and now it looked like I might be right. If he was Dad's best hope for a witness against Dusty Muleman, we might be in deep trouble.

Halfway to the trailer park it started pouring, and I was drenched by the time I got there. I knocked so hard that the door swung open.

Dripping like a dog, I stepped inside. The TV was blaring—some station that shows country-music videos all day long. I turned it off and called out, "Helloooo?"

Nothing.

"Anybody home? Mr. Peeking?"

From the rear of the trailer came a muffled *thump-thump* of footsteps, and I tensed up. I was ready to run if Lice came out bombed or acting crazy.

But it was Shelly who walked up the hall, all alone. She looked red in the cheeks and not very happy. She was wearing the top half of a blue bathing suit and a Hawaiian-style wraparound skirt. Her brassy blond hair was pinned in a bun, and she was limping. I noticed that her right foot was wrapped in tape, and I wondered if it had something to do with the baseball bat she was carrying.

"Sorry for barging in," I said, taking a backward step toward the door. "I knocked for a long time but nobody heard me."

"I was busy redecorating. What do you want?"

"Mr. Peeking was supposed to stop over today and look at my dad's bonefish boat."

"And he didn't show up? My darlin' Lice? What a surprise." Shelly laughed in a cold way that made me shudder.

"Is he here?" I asked.

"Nope."

For several moments we stood there not saying anything, the rain drumming on the aluminum roof.

"What happened to your foot?" I heard myself ask.

"I believe I busted it," Shelly replied.

"How?"

"Kicking the toilet to death."

Source: Flush by Carl Hiaasen (pp. 68–71).

"Oh," I said.

"I was pretending it was Lice's butt. He's gone, by the way, in case you hadn't figured that out."

"Gone where?"

"Wherever it is that gutless, lazy, lowlife boyfriends go," she said. "Bolted last night while I was in the shower. Took my Jeep, too. The cops found it abandoned this morning up near the toll plaza at Cutler Ridge."

I didn't know what to say, but I had to be careful. Shelly looked like she was aching to use that baseball bat.

"But Mr. Peeking told me he doesn't have a driver's license," I said.

"A minor technicality," said Shelly, "for a weasel like him. Have a seat, Noah."

"I really should be going."

"I said *have a seat*."

So I did.

"Some man came by to see Lice last night," she said, "just before he ran off. A big bald-headed guy with a weird foreign accent—French or Russian or something."

"He was bald?" I thought of the stranger who'd grabbed Abbey at the marina.

"Like a bowling ball," Shelly said. "Plus, he looked like somebody gave him a nose job with a socket wrench. Lice went outside to talk, and he came back white as a ghost. Wouldn't tell me anything, either. Waited until I was in the shower, then he took off. Did I mention he grabbed all the cash?"

"No, ma'am."

"A hundred and eighty-six bucks. Everything I had."

"That stinks." I felt queasy, like somehow it was all my fault.

"Funny," Shelly said, "but Lice didn't say nothin' about buyin' your daddy's boat."

"I've really got to go now."

"Remember what I told you about lying, Noah?"

"Yes, ma'am."

"Besides, you can't be out in this rain. You'll catch strep."

I was more than ready to risk it. "Please," I said. "My mom's gonna be worried."

Shelly nodded toward the telephone. "Then give her a jingle."

Of course, I didn't move.

Shelly smiled. "Tell me about Lice and your daddy's boat," she said. "Tell me everything, okay? I'm sure it won't take long."

I couldn't take my eyes off the wooden bat, which she was slapping from one palm to the other.

"Relax, kid, this isn't for you," she said.

I wasn't taking any chances. Without hesitating, I told her all about the secret deal between my father and Lice Peeking. I figured she'd just laugh and tell me I was stupid for trusting her no-good boyfriend, but I was wrong.

What she said was: "Noah, I think I can help you."

Which was the last thing I expected.

This question has two parts. First answer Part A. Then answer Part B.

Part A: How does Noah's attitude toward Shelly change in this passage?

- A. From sorry to helpful
- B. From scared to comforted
- C. From confused to confident
- D. From worried to understanding

Part A: Choice B is correct. Although Noah is worried that he has lost the best chance for helping his father, his initial encounter with Shelly is based on fear. He does not know if she will use the baseball bat on him because he entered the trailer uninvited. Choice A is not fully supported by the text because although he shows concern for Shelly's foot or for the loss of her Jeep and money, he does not offer to help her. Choice C is not supported because the text doesn't suggest that Noah has gained confidence in this interaction. Even when he shares his story, he does not expect the response Shelly gives him. Choice D is not supported because although Noah is worried at the beginning there is no evidence he is more understanding by the end of the passage.

Part B: Which **two** details from the passage **best** support the change described in the correct answer to Part A?

- A. "If he was Dad's best hope for a witness . . . we might be in deep trouble."
- B. "I was ready to run if Lice came out bombed or acting crazy."
- C. "I wondered if it had something to do with the baseball bat she was carrying."
- D. "'What happened to your foot?' I heard myself ask."
- E. "I didn't know what to say, but I had to be careful."
- F. "I wasn't taking any chances. Without hesitating, I told her all about the secret."
- G. "'Noah, I think I can help you.' Which was the last thing I expected."

Part B: Choices E and G are correct. Choice E indicates the fear Noah feels because Shelly is holding a baseball bat and he has entered the trailer uninvited. Choice G indicates that Noah was relieved when Shelly offers to help him, not hurt him. Choice D indicates Noah's concern for Shelly's foot, but this does not support the major change in his attitude. Choice B does not involve his interaction with Shelly. Choice F shows his compliance was based on fear. Choice C adds to the tension, but the bat is in Shelly's hand as intimidation more than as a threat.

The following question has two parts. First answer Part A. Then, answer Part B.

Part A: How does Lice's disappearance move the plot forward?

    A. It creates a setback for Noah.

    B. It makes Shelly feel sorry for herself.

    C. It causes Noah to be suspicious of Lice.

    D. It means Lice's plan to buy Noah's dad's boat is not a secret.

Part A: Choice A is correct. The scene opens with Noah acknowledging that he had a bad feeling about Lice all along. Lice's disappearance means that Noah's father lost a key witness. This creates a setback for Noah as he tries to clear his father's name. Choice B could be inferred because Lice takes Shelly's Jeep and the last of her cash in an attempt to flee, but she does not react in a way that suggests she feels sorry for herself. Choice C is not supported by the text. There is no indication in this passage that Noah is suspicious of Lice. Choice D is not supported by the text. Lice is not planning to purchase the boat.

Part B: Which detail from the passage supports the correct answer to Part A?

    A. "If he was Dad's best hope for a witness against Dusty Muleman, we might be in deep trouble."

    B. "'Took my Jeep, too. The cops found it abandoned this morning up near the toll plaza at Cutler Ridge.'"

    C. "'Waited until I was in the shower, then he took off. Did I mention he grabbed all the cash?'"

    D. "'Tell me about Lice and your daddy's boat,' she said. 'Tell me everything, okay?'"

Part B: Choice A is correct. Lice's disappearance gives Noah a terrible feeling that his father may have lost a key witness who could have helped clear his name. This is a setback for Noah. Choices B and C show setbacks for Shelly more than for Noah's father. Choice D shows Shelly's need to know why Lice has left so quickly and shows she is starting to relax around Noah, but it does not directly support that Lice's disappearance is a setback for Noah's father.

Read the following sentences from the passage.

"Wherever it is that gutless, lazy, lowlife boyfriends go," she said. "Bolted last night while I was in the shower. Took my Jeep, too. The cops found it abandoned this morning up near the toll plaza at Cutler Ridge."

What is the connotative meaning of the word *bolted* in this context?

A. securely fastened

B. hastily departed

C. fiercely struck

D. tightened fast

Choice B is correct. This usage indicates a swift and hasty departure. The context clues "he ran off" and "he took off" support this answer. Choices A and D indicate that bolted means fastened. Choice C implies a forceful blow, like lightning.

GRADE 6   Module 3B: Unit 3

UNIT OVERVIEW

Reading Closely and Writing to Learn: Point of View and Perspective

Researching and Interpreting Information: What You Need to Know When Buying Fish

In this unit, students delve more deeply into learning about overfishing methods and case studies of specific fish depletion to answer the question: What do you need to know when buying fish? Students begin by researching factual information about overfishing methods, sustainable fishing methods, case studies, and ways to buy fish caught using sustainable methods, and record what they find on graphic organizers. In the second half of the unit, students analyze consumer guides to learn about the features. Students then evaluate the information they have collected through research to determine what is most compelling to include in their guides. They organize their information to create an eye-catching consumer guide to answer the research question.

Guiding Questions and Big Ideas

- How do human activities affect the balance of our ecosystem?
- How can we make a difference?
- What does a consumer need to know when buying fish?
- *Organisms and their environment have an interconnected relationship. Human choices affect this relationship.*
- *Information needs to be presented in an eye-catching and emotionally appealing way to encourage people to follow the advice presented.*

Mid-Unit 3 Assessment

Part 1: Researching Information about How to Buy Fish Caught Using Sustainable Methods

This assessment addresses ELA CCSS W.6.7. There are two parts to this assessment. In Part 1, students interpret the information presented in diverse media and formats to answer the question: How can we buy fish caught using sustainable methods? They record the information they find on a graphic organizer.

Part 2: Explaining How New Information Connects to the Topic

This assessment addresses ELA CCSS SL.6.2. In Part 2, students explain orally how the resources they have looked at contribute to the topic of overfishing and fish depletion.

End-of-Unit 3 Assessment

Draft of Written Content of Informative Consumer Guide: What You Need to Know When Buying Fish

This assessment addresses ELA CCSS RI.6.7, W.6.2.a–f, W.6.4, and W.6.9. Students write a first draft of their informative consumer guide to answer the question: What does a consumer need to know when buying fish? They select factual information from research that is most compelling and include all of the features of an informative guide that they have identified from authentic consumer guides.

Performance Task

Informative Consumer Guide: What You Need to Know When Buying Fish

This task addresses ELA CCSS W.6.2, W.6.4, W.6.6 (optional), W.6.7, L.6.2, L.6.2.a, L.6.2.b, L.6.3, L.6.3.a, and L.6.3.b. In this performance task, students have an opportunity to apply what they have learned about fish depletion and the issue of overfishing to create an informative consumer guide to be handed out in grocery stores about buying sustainably caught fish. They research overfishing, sustainable fishing methods, specific case studies of fish having their numbers depleted, and suggestions for ways to buy fish caught using sustainable fishing methods. They then compile all this information in an eye-catching guide that consumers will want to pick up when they are at the fish counter in a grocery store.

Supplementary Assessment Items

This unit also includes a small set of optional selected-response items. These are supplementary items that provide additional information about student mastery of a subset of the standards for this unit.

- Supplementary assessment items and teacher-facing answer keys are available at the end of each unit.
- To provide teachers with flexibility around how and when to use these materials, supplementary assessment items are located in this Teacher Guide And Resource Book only.

Content Connections

This module is designed to address English Language Arts standards as students read a literary non-fiction text about the causes of and solutions to the issue of fish depletion in the oceans. However,

the module intentionally incorporates social studies themes and practices to support potential interdisciplinary connections to this compelling content. Descriptions of these intentional connections follow.

Social Studies Themes

- Time, Continuity, and Change
  - Analyzing causes and consequences of events and developments
- Geography, Humans, and the Environment
  - Relationship between human populations and the physical world (people, places, and environment)
  - Impact of human activities on the environment
- Creation, Expansion, and Interaction of Economic Systems
  - Scarcity of resources and the challenges of meeting wants and needs
  - Supply/demand and the coordination of individual choices
- Science, Technology, and Innovation
  - Relationship between human populations and the physical world
  - Interactions between regions, locations, places, people, and environments

Social Studies Practices

- Gathering, Interpreting, and Using Evidence
  - Identify, effectively select, and analyze different forms of evidence used to make meaning in social studies
- Identify evidence and explain content, authorship, point of view, purpose, and format; identify bias; explain the role of bias and potential audience.

Central Texts

1. Mark Kurlansky, *World Without Fish* (New York: Workman Publishing, 2011), ISBN: 978-0-7611-8500-0. (1160L)
2. Marine Conservation Institute, "Destructive Fishing," October 23, 2015. (1280L)
3. National Resources Defense Council, "Protecting Ocean Habitat from Bottom Trawling," October 23, 2013. (1420L)
4. "Threat 1: Overfishing." Overfishing. Save Our Seas, Feb. 19, 2014. (1350L)
5. PBS Newshour Extra, "A Rapidly Disappearing Fish." (1160L)
6. "Case Study: Atlantic Bluefin Tuna," Overfishing, Feb. 19, 2014. (1280L)
7. Sunset. "Sustainable Fishing Methods." (1160L)

8. National Geographic, "Sustainable Fishing." (1130L)

9. Vancouver Aquarium. "Sustainable Seafood," available at https://seafood.ocean.org/sustainable-seafood/. (1310L)

Unit-at-a-Glance Calendar

This unit is approximately 2.5 weeks or 13 sessions of instruction.

Lesson	Lesson Title	Long-Term Learning Targets	Supporting Learning Targets	Ongoing Assessment	Anchor Charts and Protocols
1	Analyzing a Model Informative Consumer Guide	• I can write informative/explanatory texts that convey ideas and concepts using relevant information that is carefully selected and organized. (W.6.2) • I can use evidence from a variety of grade-appropriate texts to support analysis, reflection, and research. (W.6.9)	• I can find the gist of the model informative consumer guide. • I can determine the main ideas of a model informative consumer guide. • I can explain the purpose of an informative consumer guide.	• Annotations on model informative consumer guide	• Informative Consumer Guide Anchor Chart

Lesson	Lesson Title	Long-Term Learning Targets	Supporting Learning Targets	Ongoing Assessment	Anchor Charts and Protocols
2	Researching Information about Overfishing	• I can write informative/explanatory texts that convey ideas and concepts using relevant information that is carefully selected and organized. (W.6.2) • I can conduct short research projects to answer a question. (W.6.7) • I can interpret information presented in different media and formats. (SL.6.2)	• I can research overfishing to find relevant and compelling factual information and quotes.	• Structured Notes: Chapter 7, Pages 87–97 of *World Without Fish* (from homework) • Researching Graphic Organizer: Lesson 2	

Lesson	Lesson Title	Long-Term Learning Targets	Supporting Learning Targets	Ongoing Assessment	Anchor Charts and Protocols
3	Researching Case Studies of a Depleted Fish Species	• I can write informative/explanatory texts that convey ideas and concepts using relevant information that is carefully selected and organized. (W.6.2) • I can conduct short research projects to answer a question. (W.6.7)	• I can research to find relevant and compelling factual information and quotes about depleted fish species to use as a case study in my informative consumer brochure.	• Structured Notes: Chapter 7, Pages 98–106 of *World Without Fish* (from homework) • Researching Graphic Organizer: Lesson 3	
4	Researching Information about Sustainable Fishing	• I can write informative/explanatory texts that convey ideas and concepts using relevant information that is carefully selected and organized. (W.6.2)	• I can research to find relevant and compelling factual information and quotes about sustainable fishing methods to use in my informative consumer brochure.	• Structured Notes: Chapter 8 of *World Without Fish* (from homework) • Researching Graphic Organizer: Lesson 4	

Lesson	Lesson Title	Long-Term Learning Targets	Supporting Learning Targets	Ongoing Assessment	Anchor Charts and Protocols
		• I can conduct short research projects to answer a question. (W.6.7)			
5	Mid-Unit 3 Assessment Part 1: Researching Information about Buying Fish Caught Using Sustainable Methods	• I can conduct short research projects to answer a question. (W.6.7) • I can use several sources in my research. (W.6.7) • I can refocus or refine my question when appropriate. (W.6.7) • I can interpret information presented in different media and formats. (SL.6.2)	• I can interpret information from different resources as part of my research about what consumers need to know about overfishing and fish depletion when buying fish. • I can refine the research question to focus my research.	• Mid-Unit 3 Assessment, Part 1: Researching Information about Buying Fish Caught Using Sustainable Fishing Methods	

Lesson	Lesson Title	Long-Term Learning Targets	Supporting Learning Targets	Ongoing Assessment	Anchor Charts and Protocols
6	Mid-Unit 3 Assessment Part 2: Explaining How New Information Connects to the Topic	• I can interpret information presented in different media and formats. (SL.6.2) • I can explain how new information connects to a topic, text, or issue I am studying. (SL.6.2)	• I can explain how the new information I found through research deepens my understanding of what consumers need to know about overfishing and fish depletion when buying fish.	• Structured Notes: Chapter 9 through Page 127 of *World Without Fish* (from homework) • Mid-Unit 3 Assessment, Part 2: Explaining How New Information Connects to the Topic (oral)	
7	Evaluating Research	• I can write informative/ explanatory texts that convey ideas and concepts using relevant information that is carefully selected and organized. (W.6.2)	• I can evaluate research to choose the most relevant and compelling factual information and quotes for my consumer guide.	• Structured Notes: Chapter 9, Pages 128–134 of *World Without Fish* (from homework) • Circled information and quotes on Researching Graphic Organizer from Lesson 2	• Back-to-Back and Face-to-Face protocol

Lesson	Lesson Title	Long-Term Learning Targets	Supporting Learning Targets	Ongoing Assessment	Anchor Charts and Protocols
		• I can use evidence from a variety of grade-appropriate texts to support analysis, reflection, and research. (W.6.9)			
8	Planning Content of Informative Consumer Guide: The Issue of Overfishing and Fish Depletion	• I can write informative/explanatory texts that convey ideas and concepts using relevant information that is carefully selected and organized. (W.6.2) • I can produce clear and coherent writing that is appropriate to task, purpose, and audience. (W.6.4) • I can use evidence from a variety of grade-appropriate texts to	• I can organize the information and quotes I have chosen about overfishing and the issue of fish depletion into a Quote Sandwich Graphic Organizer. • I can evaluate research to choose the most relevant and compelling factual information and quotes for my informative consumer guide.	• Structured Notes: Chapter 10 of *World Without Fish* (from homework) • Quote Sandwich Graphic Organizer for the issue of overfishing and fish depletion • Circled information and quotes on Researching Graphic Organizer from Lessons 2 and 3	

Lesson	Lesson Title	Long-Term Learning Targets	Supporting Learning Targets	Ongoing Assessment	Anchor Charts and Protocols
		support analysis, reflection, and research. (W.6.9)			
9	Planning Content of Informative Consumer Guide: Sustainable Fishing Methods	• I can write informative/explanatory texts that convey ideas and concepts using relevant information that is carefully selected and organized. (W.6.2) • I can produce clear and coherent writing that is appropriate to task, purpose, and audience. (W.6.4) • I can use evidence from a variety of grade-appropriate texts to support analysis, reflection, and research. (W.6.9)	• I can evaluate research to choose the most relevant and compelling factual information and quotes for my informative consumer guide. • I can organize the information and quotes I have chosen about sustainable fishing methods into a Quote Sandwich Graphic Organizer.	• Circled information and quotes on Researching Graphic Organizer from Lesson 4 • Quote Sandwich for sustainable fishing methods • Circled information and quotes on the graphic organizer from the Mid-Unit 3 Assessment (from Lesson 5)	

Lesson	Lesson Title	Long-Term Learning Targets	Supporting Learning Targets	Ongoing Assessment	Anchor Charts and Protocols
10	End-of-Unit 3 Assessment: Drafting the Informative Consumer Guide	• I can write informative/explanatory texts that convey ideas and concepts using relevant information that is carefully selected and organized. (W.6.2) • I can introduce the topic of my text. (W.6.2.a) • I can organize my information using various strategies (e.g., definition/classification, comparison/contrast, cause/effect). (W.6.2.a) • I can include headings, graphics, and multimedia to help readers understand my ideas. (W.6.2.a)	• I can use domain-specific vocabulary in my informative consumer guide. • I can draft the written content of a relevant and compelling informative consumer guide to inform people who are buying fish about how and why to buy fish caught using sustainable methods. • I can maintain a formal style in my writing.	• End-of-Unit 3 Assessment: Draft of Written Content of Informative Consumer Guide	• Formal Style Anchor Chart

Lesson	Lesson Title	Long-Term Learning Targets	Supporting Learning Targets	Ongoing Assessment	Anchor Charts and Protocols
		• I can develop the topic with relevant facts, definitions, concrete details, and quotations. (W.6.2.b) • I can use transitions to clarify relationships among my ideas. (W.6.2.c) • I can use contextually specific language/vocabulary to inform or explain about a topic. (W.6.2.d) • I can establish and maintain a formal style in my writing. (W.6.2.e) • I can construct a concluding statement or section of an informative/explanatory text. (W6.2.f)			

Lesson	Lesson Title	Long-Term Learning Targets	Supporting Learning Targets	Ongoing Assessment	Anchor Charts and Protocols
		• I can use evidence from a variety of grade-appropriate texts to support analysis, reflection, and research. (W.6.9)			
11	Analyzing the Features of an Informative Consumer Guide	• I can write informative/explanatory texts that convey ideas and concepts using relevant information that is carefully selected and organized. (W.6.2) • I can integrate information presented in different media or formats (e.g., visually, quantitatively) as well as in words to develop a coherent understanding of a topic or issue. (RI.6.7)	• I can identify the features of an informative consumer guide. • I can select visuals like images, charts, and graphs to make my informative consumer guide eye-catching and to help consumers better understand the issue of overfishing and fish depletion.	• Annotated informative consumer guides	• Informative Consumer Guide Anchor Chart

Lesson	Lesson Title	Long-Term Learning Targets	Supporting Learning Targets	Ongoing Assessment	Anchor Charts and Protocols
12	Revising the Informative Consumer Guide: Sentence Structure, Transitions, and Works Cited	• I can use a variety of sentence structures to make my writing and speaking more interesting. (L.6.3.a) • I can maintain consistency in style and tone when writing and speaking. (L.6.3.b)	• I can use a variety of sentence structures to make my informative consumer guide more interesting. • I can use appropriate transitions to make the informative consumer guide flow smoothly.	• Revised Draft of Written Content of Informative Consumer Guide • Self-assessment on row 3 of the Grades 6–8 Expository Writing Evaluation Rubric	
13	Performance Task: Final Informative Consumer Guide	• I can write informative/explanatory texts that convey ideas and concepts using relevant information that is carefully selected and organized. (W.6.2) • I can introduce the topic of my text. (W.6.2.a) • I can organize my information using various strategies (e.g., definition/classification, comparison/contrast, cause/effect). (W.6.2.a)	• I can use formative feedback from the teacher to revise my informative consumer guide. • I can use peer feedback to revise my writing to further meet the expectations of the rubric. • I can write a final draft of an interesting, accurate, and objective informative consumer guide.	• Performance Task: Final draft of informative consumer guide	

Lesson	Lesson Title	Long-Term Learning Targets	Supporting Learning Targets	Ongoing Assessment	Anchor Charts and Protocols
		• I can include headings, graphics, and multimedia to help readers understand my ideas. (W.6.2.a) • I can develop the topic with relevant facts, definitions, concrete details, and quotations. (W.6.2.b) • I can use transitions to clarify relationships among my ideas. (W.6.2.c) • I can use contextually specific language/vocabulary to inform or explain about a topic. (W.6.2.d) • I can establish and maintain a formal style in my writing. (W.6.2.e)			

Lesson	Lesson Title	Long-Term Learning Targets	Supporting Learning Targets	Ongoing Assessment	Anchor Charts and Protocols
		• I can construct a concluding statement or section of an informative/explanatory text. (W.6.2.f) • I can produce clear and coherent writing that is appropriate to task, purpose, and audience. (W.6.4) • I can use evidence from a variety of grade-appropriate texts to support analysis, reflection, and research. (W.6.9) • I can apply sixth-grade reading standards to literary nonfiction (e.g., "Trace and evaluate the argument and specific claims in a text,			

Lesson	Lesson Title	Long-Term Learning Targets	Supporting Learning Targets	Ongoing Assessment	Anchor Charts and Protocols
		distinguishing claims that are supported by reasons and evidence from claims that are not"). (W.6.9.a) • I can use a variety of sentence structures to make my writing and speaking more interesting. (L.6.3.a) • I can maintain consistency in style and tone when writing and speaking. (L.6.3.b) • I can integrate information presented in different media or formats (e.g., visually, quantitatively) as well as in words to develop a coherent understanding of a topic or issue. (RI.6.7)			

Optional: Experts, Fieldwork, and Service

Experts

- Invite fishermen to speak to the students about the methods they use for catching fish and the rules and regulations they have to follow.
- Invite a scientist to speak to the students about biodiversity and fish depletion.

Fieldwork

- Arrange for a visit to a local aquarium so students can learn more about biodiversity in the oceans.
- Arrange for a visit to a museum or exhibit about the Industrial Revolution.
- Arrange for a visit to a grocery store so students can see the fish available to buy.

Optional: Extensions

- An in-depth case study of depleted fish species and the impact of the depletion on humans and other species
- A study of extinct species
- A study of the depletion of a particular extinct species and the circumstances that led to their extinction; for example, the baiji white dolphin or the Javan tiger

Preparation and Materials

This unit includes a number of routines that involve stand-alone documents.

Reading Calendar

- Students read excerpts of *World Without Fish* for homework each night for Lessons 1–7 and answer a focus question. In Unit 1, students read excerpts of the text in the lesson before rereading them at home. In this unit, students read the text excerpts for the first time at home because they should be familiar now with Mark Kurlansky's writing style, the subject matter, and domain-specific vocabulary, and should have built reading stamina over the course of the module. The purpose of this independent reading of *World Without Fish* in the first half of the unit is to prepare them for the research they will carry out in lessons on the ideas and topics discussed in the book. The purpose of the reading in the second half is for students to complete the unit with a solid understanding of all of Mark Kurlansky's ideas about fish depletion.
- Consider providing a reading calendar to help students, teachers, and families understand what is due and when. See stand-alone document.

Structured Notes

- Structured notes record students' thinking about a focus question specific to what they have been asked to read. They are organized by chapter and require students to read the excerpt, answer the focus question for the excerpt, and record evidence from the excerpt to support their answers to the questions.

Research

- The research materials provided in the research folders in this unit are purposely of a range of Lexile measures to challenge students of all abilities. Guide students to choose research materials from the folders that are at an appropriate level for them. Glossaries have been provided for each of the articles, so have students use the glossaries with the articles to gain a greater understanding of the text. Be prepared to provide support to students who will struggle with all of the texts in a group—choose one text for all of them to work with and read it for the gist as a group.

Reading Calendar *World Without Fish*

The calendar below shows what is due on each day.

You may modify this document to include dates instead of lessons.

Due at Lesson	Reading	Focus Question
2	Chapter 7: pages 87–97	• Read to the end of page 97 of chapter 7 of *World Without Fish*. Remember to record new words on your word-catcher. Answer the focus questions on your structured notes: • According to Mark Kurlansky, what are some solutions to the issue of fish depletion? According to Kurlansky, why won't they work? • **Key vocabulary:** domestic, indiscriminately, domestication, ferocious, ancestors, resembles, offspring, spawning, enzyme, menace, penalties, regulating, quotas, incentive, by-catch
3	Chapter 7: page 98 to the end of the chapter	• Read the rest of chapter 7 of *World Without Fish*. Remember to record new words on your word-catcher. Answer the focus question on your structured notes: • According to Mark Kurlansky, what are some other solutions to the issue of fish depletion? According to Kurlansky, why won't they work? • **Key vocabulary:** gear, concentrated, discontinued, underutilized, self-regulation, monitored, noncommercial, bureaucracy
4	Chapter 8	• Read chapter 8 of *World Without Fish*. Remember to record new words on your word-catcher. Answer the focus question on your structured notes: • What are the sustainable fishing methods Mark Kurlansky suggests? What makes them sustainable? • **Key vocabulary:** efficient, banned, outrage, auctions, overwhelmed, harpooning

Due at Lesson	Reading	Focus Question
5	Chapter 11 pages 144–153	• Read chapter 11 of *World Without Fish* through page 153. Remember to record new words on your word-catcher. Answer the focus question on your structured notes: • According to Mark Kurlansky, what are some things that we can do to help solve the problem of fish depletion? • **Key vocabulary:** modifications, recognition, environmentalists, decline, appreciate, deprive, boycott
6	Chapter 9 pages 117–127	• Read chapter 9 of *World Without Fish* to the end of page 127. Remember to record new words on your word-catcher. Answer the focus question on your structured notes: • According to Mark Kurlansky, what is pollution doing to fish? How? • **Key vocabulary:** tremendous, hazardous, components, pristine, legislation, catastrophe, restitution, vehemently, renewable, consequently
7	Chapter 9 pages 128–134	• Read to the end of chapter 9 of *World Without Fish*. Remember to record new words on your word-catcher. Continue to answer the focus question on your structured notes: • According to Mark Kurlansky, what is pollution doing to fish? How? • **Key vocabulary:** ingesting, beneficial, corrosion, opaqueness, receptacle, deficiency, genetic, subtle
8	Chapter 10	• Read chapter 10 of *World Without Fish*. Remember to record new words on your word-catcher. Continue to answer the focus question on your structured notes: • According to Mark Kurlansky, what is global warming doing to fish? How? • **Key vocabulary:** emitted, observable, salinity, excessive, correlates

LESSON 1

Analyzing a Model Informative Consumer Guide

Long-Term Targets Addressed (Based on ELA CCSS)

- I can write informative/explanatory texts that convey ideas and concepts using relevant information that is carefully selected and organized. (W.6.2)
- I can use evidence from a variety of grade-appropriate texts to support analysis, reflection, and research. (W.6.9)

Supporting Learning Targets

- I can find the gist of the model informative consumer guide.
- I can determine the main ideas of a model informative consumer guide.
- I can explain the purpose of an informative consumer guide.

Ongoing Assessment

- Annotations on Model Informative Consumer Guide

Agenda

1. Opening
   A. Unpacking Learning Targets (2 minutes)
   B. Partner Discussion: The Purpose of an Informative Consumer Guide (6 minutes)
2. Work Time
   A. Unpacking the Prompt and Introducing the Rubric (12 minutes)
   B. Reading the Model Informative Consumer Guide (15 minutes)
3. Closing and Assessment
   A. Analyzing Content of the Model Informative Consumer Guide (10 minutes)

4. Homework

    A. Read up to page 97 of chapter 7 of *World Without Fish*. Remember to record new words on your word-catcher. Use evidence flags to gather evidence as you read to answer the focus question on your structured notes:

        • According to Mark Kurlansky, what are some solutions to the issue of fish depletion? According to Kurlansky, why won't they work?

    B. Continue reading your independent reading book.

Teaching Notes

- This lesson launches the performance task in which students will create an informative consumer guide to answer the question: What do consumers need to know about overfishing and fish depletion when buying fish? The task requires students to research about overfishing methods, sustainable fishing methods, case studies of depletion of particular fish species, and suggestions for how to buy fish that have been caught using sustainable methods. They then compile this research into an informative consumer guide using evidence from research sources to support their claims.

- The Grades 6–8 Expository Writing Evaluation Rubric will be used to assess student informative consumer guides. Students will review the rubric briefly in this lesson, but will use it to evaluate their own writing in later lessons.

- In later lessons, students will need their annotated Model Informative Consumer Guide. Use routines of your classroom to help students keep track of these resources.

- Students continue the homework routine of taking structured notes and using evidence flags. Consider giving each student one baggie with evidence flags, rather than distributing new flags each day.

- For Lesson 2, prepare the research materials for each triad (see supporting materials).

- In advance:

    • Review the Model Informative Consumer Guide (see supporting materials).

    • Consider preparing the research materials each triad will need in Lesson 2 (see supporting materials for Lesson 2). Each triad needs to be allocated one research article and you need enough of each article for one per student. The articles provided range in difficulty—determine how to allocate them by considering the reading level of students in each triad. Each triad needs to be given a glossary for its article, too.

- Post: learning targets.

Lesson Vocabulary

gist, main idea

Materials

- Informative Consumer Guide Anchor Chart (new; co-created with students during Opening B)
- Performance Task Prompt: Informative Consumer Guide (one per student and one for display)
- Equity sticks
- Grades 6–8 Expository Writing Evaluation Rubric (one per student and one to display)
- Model Informative Consumer Guide (one per student and one to display)
- Evidence flags (three per student for homework)
- Structured Notes: Chapter 7, Pages 87–97 (one per student)
- *World Without Fish* Word-Catcher (one per student)

Opening

A. Unpacking Learning Targets (2 minutes)

- Direct students' attention to the posted learning targets and read them aloud:
  - "I can find the gist of the model informative consumer guide."
  - "I can determine the main ideas of a model informative consumer guide."
  - "I can explain the purpose of an informative consumer guide."
- Remind students of what finding the *gist* means. Tell students that their performance task will be to create an informative consumer guide for people about buying fish that have been caught using sustainable fishing methods.

Meeting Students' Needs

- Learning targets are a research-based strategy that helps all students, especially challenged learners.
- Posting learning targets allows students to reference them throughout the lesson to check their understanding. Learning targets also provide a reminder to students and teachers about the intended learning behind a given lesson or activity.

B. Partner Discussion: The Purpose of an Informative Consumer Guide (6 minutes)

- Pair students up and ask them to discuss:
  - "What is an informative consumer guide?"
- Cold-call pairs to share their ideas. Listen for and guide students to the understanding that an informative consumer guide is a brochure to guide people in making choices when they are buying something.
- Post the following questions. Then ask students to discuss in pairs:
  - "What is the purpose of an informative consumer guide?"
  - "What do consumers need/expect from an informative guide? Why?"

- Cold-call pairs to share their ideas. This is only an initial discussion as students have not yet looked at any guides and some students may never have seen one before.
- Record student ideas on the **Informative Consumer Guide Anchor Chart**. Ensure the list includes:
  - Describes the problem: describes the problem and the link to the products they are looking to buy
  - Provides a solution: explains how the problem can be solved
  - Provides an example/case study: evidence and elaboration
  - Provide consumers with advice and suggestions: how and what to buy to help with this issue

Meeting Students' Needs

Capturing whole-class thinking on an anchor chart can ensure quick reference later on.

Work Time

A. Unpacking the Prompt and Introducing the Rubric (12 minutes)

- Display and distribute **Performance Task Prompt: Informative Consumer Guide**.
- Invite students to follow along with you as you read the prompt aloud.
- Ask students to circle any unfamiliar words. Clarify words as needed.
- Ask students to think back to the work they did in Unit 1. Remind them that they read the first five chapters of Mark Kurlansky's *World Without Fish*, in which the problem of fish depletion due to overfishing was presented.
- Ask students to discuss in pairs:
  - "What can you remember about the issue of fish depletion and overfishing?"
- Consider using **equity sticks** to select students to share out their responses.
- Ask students to discuss in pairs:
  - "What is a consumer? What is an informative consumer guide?"
- Select students to share out their ideas. Listen for students to explain that a consumer is someone who buys something and an informative consumer guide is a guide that provides information about what to buy.
- Ask students to discuss in pairs:
  - "What is the Performance Task Prompt asking you to do?"
  - "What will your writing have to include to address the question?"
- Circulate and listen for students to list each of the bullet points on the prompt when describing what their writing should include.
- Display and distribute the **Grades 6–8 Expository Writing Evaluation Rubric**.

- Remind students that they should be familiar with this rubric from previous modules and that they will be assessed according to this rubric.
- Ask students to review the criteria of the rubric with you. Select volunteers to read aloud each criterion.
- Invite students to turn and talk with their partner:
  - "Which criterion do you think is a strength for you? Why?"
  - "Which criterion do you think is a challenge for you? Why? How can you work on this?"
- Cold-call students to share out their responses.

Meeting Students' Needs

Consider providing select students with a pre-highlighted version of the Performance Task Prompt that highlights the explicit actions students must take to complete the task.

B. Reading the Model Informative Consumer Guide (15 minutes)

- Congratulate students for unwrapping the Performance Task Prompt.
- Display and distribute the **Model Informative Consumer Guide**.
- Tell them they will now begin reading like a writer by studying a model informative consumer guide.
- Give students the focus question for the model:
  - "What do consumers need to know about chemical pesticides and fertilizers when buying fresh fruit and vegetables?"
- Guide students to see the difference between the focus question in the prompt versus the model by asking students to discuss in pairs:
  - "What is the difference between the focus question in your prompt and the focus question in this model?"
- Select students to share their responses with the whole group. Listen for students to explain that the focus questions are very similar, but instead of discussing the issue of fish depletion and overfishing in relation to buying fish, the model discusses the issue of pesticides and buying fruit and vegetables.
- Invite students to follow along while you read the Model Informative Consumer Guide aloud.
- Ask students to discuss in pairs:
  - "What is this model mostly about?"
- Consider using equity sticks to select students to share their responses. Listen for students to explain that the model is mostly about how chemical pesticides and fertilizers are used in the process of growing fruits and vegetables and that they can cause health issues, so where possible, we should buy organic fruits and vegetables because they are grown without chemical pesticides and fertilizers.

- Explain that now students will work in pairs to reread and annotate each paragraph of the model for the gist or to get an idea of what each of the paragraphs is mostly about.
- Remind students to discuss the gist of each paragraph in their pairs before recording anything.
- Ask students to begin.
- Circulate and observe student annotations and invite students who are struggling to say the gist aloud to you before recording it.

Meeting Students' Needs

- Hearing a complex text read slowly, fluently, and without interruption or explanation promotes fluency for students; they are hearing a strong reader read the text aloud with accuracy and expression, and are simultaneously looking at and thinking about the words on the printed page. Be sure to set clear expectations that students read along silently in their heads as you read the text aloud.
- Consider allowing students to grapple with a complex text prior to explicit teaching of vocabulary. After students have read for the gist, they can identify challenging vocabulary for themselves. Teachers can address student-selected vocabulary as well as predetermined vocabulary upon subsequent encounters with the text. However, in some cases and with some students, pre-teaching selected vocabulary may be necessary.

Closing and Assessment

A. Analyzing Content of the Model Informative Consumer Guide (10 minutes)

- Explain to students that now they will synthesize their thinking about the Model Informative Consumer Guide.
- Give students 1 minute to review their annotations.
- Then, have them turn to a new partner and discuss their annotations.
- Invite students to share their annotations with the whole group. Ask:
  - "What is the main idea of the first paragraph in the model informative consumer guide?"
  - "What is the main idea of the second paragraph?"
- Select volunteers to share their responses. Listen for students to explain:
  - Some fruits and vegetables are grown using chemical pesticides and fertilizers that may cause health problems.
  - Research shows that some pesticides may be linked to ADHD and the development and growth of children.
  - Eating organic food is a way to prevent consuming pesticides because it is grown without chemical pesticides and fertilizers.

- - Research shows that eating organic fruits and vegetables can lower the levels of certain pesticides in urine.
  - Suggestions for consuming fewer chemicals from non-organic fertilizers and pesticides.
- Preview homework and distribute the **Structured Notes: Chapter 7, Pages 87–97** and **evidence flags**.

Homework

- Read to the end of page 97 of chapter 7 of *World Without Fish*. Remember to record new words on your **word-catcher**. Use evidence flags to gather evidence as you read to answer the focus question on your structured notes:
  - According to Mark Kurlansky, what are some solutions to the issue of fish depletion? According to Kurlansky, why won't they work?
- Continue reading your independent reading book.

Performance Task Prompt

Informative Consumer Guide

Name: _____

Date: _____

Learning targets:

- I can write informative/explanatory texts that convey ideas and concepts using relevant information that is carefully selected and organized. (W.6.2)
- I can produce clear and coherent writing that is appropriate to task, purpose, and audience. (W.6.4)

Focus question: What do consumers need to know about overfishing and fish depletion when buying fish?

For this performance task, you are going to create an informative consumer guide to be placed in a grocery store, near the fish counter, to inform people about the issue of fish depletion due to overfishing and to guide them in how to buy fish caught using sustainable fishing methods.

Your guide should fit onto one piece of paper so consumers don't have to carry a lot of paper around in the store with them. It should explain the problem, provide a case study to highlight the impact of the problem, and provide suggestions for how to buy fish caught using sustainable fishing methods. It should be eye-catching to encourage consumers to pick it up when they stand at the fish counter deciding which fish to buy, and compelling to encourage them to read to the end.

Your informative consumer guide needs to include relevant and compelling factual information and quotes about:

- The issue: overfishing and how it causes fish depletion.
- A case study of a fish species that has been severely depleted and the impact that it has had.
- A solution: sustainable methods for catching fish.
- Suggestions: ways to buy fish that have been caught using sustainable methods.

Your informative consumer guide also needs to:

- Fit onto one piece of letter-sized paper.
- Include the features of a consumer guide: headline and subheadings.
- Include visuals like pictures and charts or graphs to make it eye-catching and to improve consumer understanding of the issue.
- Include a Works Cited list.

Grades 6–8 Expository Writing Evaluation Rubric

Criteria	CCSS	4	3	2	1	0
CONTENT AND ANALYSIS: The extent to which the newspaper article objectively conveys complex ideas and information clearly and accurately in order to logically support the author's analysis of different points of view	W.2 R.1.9	• Clearly conveys the topic in a manner that is objective, compelling, and follows logically from the task and purpose • Demonstrates insightful analysis of the text(s) by referencing different points of view of the event	• Clearly conveys the topic in a manner that is objective and follows from the task and purpose • Demonstrates grade-appropriate analysis of the text(s) by referencing different points of view of the event	• Conveys the topic in a manner that follows generally from the task and purpose • Demonstrates a literal comprehension of the text(s) by referencing different points of view of the event	• Conveys the topic in a manner that does not logically follow from the task and purpose • Demonstrates little understanding of the text(s) by attempting to reference different points of view of the event	• Claim and reasons demonstrate a lack of comprehension of the text(s) or task

Criteria	CCSS	4	3	2	1	0
COMMAND OF EVIDENCE: The extent to which the newspaper article presents evidence from the various media to support analysis and reflection through the use of newspaper article features* *headline, byline, subheading, graphic image with caption, and quotations	W.9 R.1.9	• Develops the topic with relevant, well-chosen facts, concrete details, quotations, other information and examples from the text(s), and features of a newspaper article* • Sustains the use of varied, relevant evidence • Skillfully and logically selects evidence to support the angle of the newspaper article	• Develops the topic with relevant facts, concrete details, quotations, other information and examples from the text(s), and features of a newspaper article* • Sustains the use of relevant evidence, with some lack of variety • Logically selects evidence to support the angle of the newspaper article	• Partially develops the topic with the use of some textual evidence and features of a newspaper article,* some of which may be irrelevant • Uses relevant evidence inconsistently • Sometimes logically selects evidence to support the angle of the newspaper article	• Demonstrates an attempt to use evidence and features of a newspaper article,* but develops ideas with only minimal, occasional evidence that is generally invalid or irrelevant • Attempts to select evidence to support the angle of the newspaper article	• Provides no evidence or provides evidence that is completely irrelevant • Does not explain how evidence supports the angle of the newspaper article

Criteria	CCSS	4	3	2	1	0
COHERENCE, ORGANIZATION, AND STYLE: The extent to which the newspaper article logically organizes complex ideas, concepts, and information using the inverted pyramid structure* and formal and precise language *newspaper article uses the inverted pyramid structure, organizing details in order from major to minor	W.2 L.3 L.6	• Exhibits clear newspaper article organization,* with the skillful use of appropriate and varied transitions to create a unified whole and enhance meaning • Establishes and maintains a formal style, using grade-appropriate, stylistically sophisticated descriptive language and domain-specific vocabulary with a notable sense of voice • Uses a variety of sentence structures to make writing more compelling and interesting	• Exhibits clear newspaper article organization,* with the use of appropriate transitions to create a unified whole • Establishes and maintains a formal style using precise descriptive language and domain-specific vocabulary • Uses a variety of sentence structures to make writing more interesting	• Exhibits some attempt at newspaper article organization,* with inconsistent use of transitions • Establishes but fails to maintain a formal style, with inconsistent use of descriptive language and domain-specific vocabulary • Inconsistent use of a variety of sentence structures to make writing more interesting	• Exhibits little attempt at newspaper article organization,* or attempts to organize are irrelevant to the task • Lacks a formal style, using language that is not descriptive or is inappropriate for the text(s) and task • Rarely uses a variety of sentence structures to make writing more interesting	• Exhibits no evidence of newspaper article organization* • Uses language that is predominantly incoherent or copied directly from the text(s) • Does not use a variety of sentence structures to make writing more interesting

TEACHER GUIDE AND RESOURCE BOOK • Grade 6 • Module 3B • Unit 3 • Lesson 1 Supporting Materials

Criteria	CCSS	4	3	2	1	0
CONTROL OF CONVENTIONS: The extent to which the essay demonstrates command of the conventions of standard English grammar, usage, capitalization, punctuation, and spelling	W.2 L.1 L.2	• Demonstrates grade-appropriate command of conventions, with few errors	• Demonstrates grade-appropriate command of conventions, with occasional errors that do not hinder comprehension	• Demonstrates emerging command of conventions, with some errors that may hinder comprehension	• Demonstrates a lack of command of conventions, with frequent errors that hinder comprehension	• Demonstrates minimal command of conventions, making assessment of conventions unreliable

Model Informative Consumer Guide

Are You Buying Fruit and Vegetables Today?

What you need to know...

Some fruits and vegetables are grown using chemical pesticides and fertilizers to prevent, destroy and reduce the possibility of pests, rodents, weeds, fungi, bacteria and viruses; however, research suggests that consuming fruit and vegetables sprayed with chemical pesticides and fertilizers can have a negative impact on our health. The US Environmental Protection Agency website explains that "By their nature, most pesticides create some risk of harm – Pesticides can cause harm to humans, animals, or the environment because they are designed to kill or otherwise adversely affect living organisms." When buying fruit and vegetables consumers should know that there are options that haven't been sprayed with pesticides and fertilizers during the growing process.

Negative Impact of Pesticides

One of the suggested negative impacts on our health is outlined in the journal *Pediatrics* describing research linking ADHD and a certain type of pesticide called an organophosphate. "Exposure to organophosphates has been associated with adverse effects on neurodevelopment, such as behavioral problems and lower cognitive function." (*Pediatrics*, Page e1270). The research goes on to describe how children who were found to have higher concentrations of the chemicals found in this pesticide in their urine were more likely to be diagnosed with ADHD. Kathryn Topei, M.S. also explains a possible negative impact of exposure to organophosphate pesticides for children, "The effect of low-level, long-term exposure to pesticides from food is not well understood but the concern is that organophosphate (OP) pesticides, a commonly used group of insecticides, could affect the development and growth of young children." (Reducing pesticide exposure in children and pregnant women. Page 9).

Pesticide Residue in Produce
Percent of Samples Testing Positive Under Different Production Systems
www.Traditional-Foods.com

	Fruit	Vegetables
Conventional	82	61
Int Pest Mng	49	44
Organic	23	9

Source: Baker et al. 2002
Food Additives and contaminants 19 (5)427-446
Excludes residues of banned pesticides

A solution

Studies suggest that eating organic fruit and vegetables, which have been grown without the use of chemical pesticides can lower health risks when eating fresh fruit and vegetables. A study in 2003 comparing pesticide levels in urine between children who ate organic foods and those who ate non-organic produce showed that children eating non-organic produce had pesticide levels up to six times higher (Reducing pesticide exposure in children and pregnant women).

A recent study...

Another study at the University of Washington found that when children were put on organic food diets including organic fresh fruits and vegetables for five days, lower levels of organophosphates were found in their urine (Northwest Bulletin).

What can I do?

1. When buying fruit and vegetables, buy organic where you can. They will have been grown without chemical pesticides and fertilizers.
2. There are twelve fruits and vegetables that have been found by the Environmental Working Group to contain more pesticides than others. Try to buy organic when buying any of these: apples, celery, sweet bell peppers, peaches, strawberries, nectarines, grapes, spinach, lettuce, cucumbers, blueberries, and potatoes.
3. Look for the USDA Organic Seal on fruits and vegetables in the grocery store. This means the food has been grown without chemical pesticides and fertilizers.
4. If you can't buy organic fruit and vegetables, make sure you wash and scrub the produce well before eating it. Peel the fruit and vegetables to reduce pesticides.

Works Cited

Bouchard, M.F., Bellinger, D.C., Wright, R.O., & Weisskopf, M.G. "Attention-deficit/hyperactivity disorder and urinary metabolites of organophosphate pesticides." *Pediatrics*, 2010. 125:e1270–1277.

Environmental Working Group. Methodology. Available at: http://www.ewg.org/foodnews/methodology.php. Accessed on October 23, 2013.

Green Planet Ethics. "Pesticide Residue in Produce." Available at: http://greenplanetethics.com/wordpress/pesticides-in-food-the-dirty-dozen-foods-list-plus-safest-food-to-buy-2012/. Accessed on November 6, 2013.

U.S. Environmental Protection Agency. "About Pesticides." Available at: http://www.epa.gov/pesticides/about/index.htm. Accessed on October 23, 2013.

Washington State Department of Family and Child Health. "Reducing pesticide exposure in children and pregnant women." Fall/Winter 2006. Available at: http://depts.washington.edu/nwbfch/PDFs/NWBv21n1.pdf. Accessed on: October 23, 2013.

Structured Notes: Chapter 7, Pages 87–97

Name: _____

Date: _____

Chapter	Homework Focus Question	Answer with Evidence from the Text (include page number)
_____	According to Mark Kurlansky, what are some solutions to the issue of fish depletion? According to Kurlansky, why won't they work?	

World Without Fish Word-Catcher

Name: _____

Date: _____

Mark literary words with an * (for example: *text feature).

A	B	C	D	E
F	G	H	I	J
K	L	M	N	O
P	Q	R	S	T
U	V	W	X	Y
Z	Use this space for notes.			

LESSON 2

Researching Information about Overfishing

Long-Term Targets Addressed (Based on ELA CCSS)

- I can write informative/explanatory texts that convey ideas and concepts using relevant information that is carefully selected and organized. (W.6.2)
- I can conduct short research projects to answer a question. (W.6.7)
- I can interpret information presented in different media and formats. (SL.6.2)

Supporting Learning Target

- I can research overfishing to find relevant and compelling factual information and quotes.

Ongoing Assessment

- Structured Notes: Chapter 7, Pages 87–97 of *World Without Fish* (from homework)
- Researching Graphic Organizer: Lesson 2

Agenda

1. Opening
   A. Engaging the Reader: Chapter 7 of *World Without Fish* (5 minutes)
   B. Unpacking Learning Targets (3 minutes)
2. Work Time
   A. Modeling How to Fill In the Researching Graphic Organizer for a Video (15 minutes)
   B. Researching Facts: Part 1 of the Jigsaw (15 minutes)
3. Closing and Assessment
   A. Triad Share: Part 2 of the Jigsaw (7 minutes)

4. Homework

   A. Read the rest of chapter 7 of *World Without Fish*. Remember to record new words on your word-catcher. Use evidence flags to gather evidence as you read to answer the focus question on your structured notes:

   - According to Mark Kurlansky, what are some other solutions to the issue of fish depletion? According to Kurlansky, why won't they work?

   B. Continue reading your independent reading book.

Teaching Notes

- In this lesson, students work in triads to research information about overfishing. This is done in a Jigsaw, so each triad is given a different research resource, and they partner up with another triad in the Closing and Assessment to share their findings.

- To practice SL.6.2, students are given Researching Graphic Organizers and also watch an excerpt of a video called "Ending Overfishing" (accessed here: www.youtube.com/watch?v=F6nwZUkBeas) as part of their research. How you choose to manage this depends on the technology you have available. You may choose to show it to the whole group, or have it set up on devices for students to access independently. As with other research resources, it needs to be reviewed multiple times to be used effectively. Please note and explain to students that this video was made by and for Europeans, so many of the measurements they use, like meters and kilos, may not be familiar to them. There is a transcription of the video included in the supporting materials that you can read to your class if you do not have access to audiovisual equipment.

- As in Unit 1, continue to emphasize to students that the ideas presented are just one point of view and that there are other points of view out there on overfishing and fish depletion.

- In advance:

  - Prepare the research articles for each triad (see supporting materials). Each triad needs to be allocated one research article, and you need enough of each article for one per student. The articles provided range in difficulty—determine how to allocate articles by considering the reading level of students in each triad. Each triad needs to be given a glossary for its vocabulary article, too. An excerpt of *World Without Fish* is also used as a research resource, so consider allocating this to triads with students who require more support with reading, as they should already be familiar with the text.

  - Review: Concentric Circles protocol (see Appendix).

- Post: learning target.

Lesson Vocabulary

factual information, relevant, compelling; see glossaries for vocabulary words pertaining to specific research resources

Materials

- Structured Notes: Chapter 7, Pages 87–97 (from homework)
- Performance Task Prompt: Informative Consumer Guide (from Lesson 1)
- Researching Graphic Organizer: Lesson 2 (one per student and one for display)
- Colored pencils or markers (one for each student)
- "Ending Overfishing" video (up to 2:40)
- "Ending Overfishing" Video Transcript (teacher reference)
- Research articles and glossaries (one per student in assigned triad; see Teaching Notes):
  - *World Without Fish*: pages 36 and 37 (book; distributed in Unit 1; one per student)
  - "Threat 1: Overfishing"
  - "Destructive Fishing"
  - "Protecting Ocean Habitat from Bottom Trawling"
- Evidence flags (three per student for homework)
- Structured Notes: Chapter 7, Pages 98–106 (one per student)

Opening

A. Engaging the Reader: Chapter 7 of *World Without Fish* (5 minutes)

- Remind students of the homework: Read to the end of page 97 in chapter 7 of *World Without Fish* and answer the focus question.
- Ask students to take out their **Structured Notes: Chapter 7, Pages 87–97** and review them.
- Invite students to follow the Concentric Circles protocol to share their structured notes:
  - Divide the group in half and invite both halves to get into two circles, one inside the other with their structured notes. The circle on the inside should be facing out and the circle on the outside should be facing in.
  - Remind students of the of the homework focus question: According to Mark Kurlansky, what are some solutions to the issue of fish depletion? According to Kurlansky, why won't they work?
  - Invite students to refer to their structured notes from their homework.
  - Invite students in the inside circle to share their responses with the person opposite them in the outside circle.
  - Invite students in the outside circle to do the same.
  - Invite students in the inside circle to move two people to the left.
  - Repeat three to five times until each student has spoken to three people.
- Ask students to return to their seats.

- Invite students to make revisions to their structured notes where necessary based on their discussions during the Concentric Circles protocol.
- Select volunteers to share their answers to the focus question with the whole group. Listen for students to explain that fish farming is one solution, but it won't work because farmed fish are fed wild fish that have been caught at sea. Another solution is limiting the number of fish that fishermen can catch, but this is hard to manage and encourages fishermen, when they have caught more fish than they are allowed, to just throw back the dead fish into the water. The fish have been caught and killed either way.

Meeting Students' Needs

- Opening the lesson by asking students to share their homework makes them accountable for completing it. It also gives you the opportunity to monitor which students are not doing their homework.
- Consider pairing ELL students who speak the same first language to deepen their discussion and understanding.

B. Unpacking Learning Targets (3 minutes)

- Announce triads. Ask students to quietly move to sit with their triads.
- Direct students' attention to the posted learning target and ask for a volunteer to read it aloud:
    - "I can research overfishing to find relevant and compelling factual information and quotes."
- Ask students to discuss in triads:
    - "What is *factual information*? Why are you looking for factual information?"
    - "What does *relevant* mean?"
    - "What does *compelling* mean?"
- Cold-call students to share out their ideas with the whole group. Listen for students to explain that factual information is information that is undeniably true and that they are researching factual information because this brochure is informative—they are aiming to inform the consumer with factual information rather than to try to persuade them with opinions. Listen for students to explain that *relevant* means that it is appropriate to the topic, and *compelling* means it sparks the interest of the reader and makes them want to continue reading to the end. We want readers to read to the end of the consumer guides to be fully informed of the issue.
- Ask students to discuss in triads:
    - "Where have you already read some information about overfishing?"
- Select volunteers to share their ideas. Listen for students to explain that *World Without Fish* contains information about overfishing.
- Explain to students that today some of them will be revisiting an excerpt of this text in their research.

- Remind students that as in Unit 1 with Mark Kurlansky's *World Without Fish*, there are different points of view about overfishing and fish depletion, so they should not accept everything they read as fact. Make it clear that good readers question everything—they don't believe everything that they read, but instead they consider ideas they read and use them as a jumping point to find out more.

Meeting Students' Needs

- Learning targets are a research-based strategy that helps all students, especially challenged learners.
- Posting learning targets allows students to reference them throughout the lesson to check their understanding. Learning targets also provide a reminder to students and teachers about the intended learning behind a given lesson or activity.

Work Time

A. Modeling How to Fill In the Researching Graphic Organizer for a Video (15 minutes)

- Display the **Performance Task Prompt: Informative Consumer Guide** and invite students to refer to their own copies.
- Direct students' attention to the list of requirements for the informative consumer guide, focusing on the first bullet: "The issue: overfishing and how it causes fish depletion."
- Ask students to discuss with their triads:
  - "How are you going to find out more about the issue of overfishing and fish depletion? What does this lesson's learning target say?"
  - "We read about overfishing and fish depletion in *World Without Fish*, so why are we not just going to the information from that book?"
- Select students to share their responses. Listen for them to explain that they are going to find out more by researching, as the learning target suggests, and they are not just going to use the information in *World Without Fish*. To ensure they are including the most accurate information, they should read other resources to check that the information in *World Without Fish* is accurate.
- Display and distribute the **Researching Graphic Organizer: Lesson 2**. Focus students on the line for a "Refined research question" at the top of the page.
- Tell students to discuss in triads:
  - "You will be researching to find more information about overfishing and fish depletion in this lesson. What do you think a refined research question might be for this lesson? Why?"
- Select volunteers to share their ideas with the class. Listen for students to suggest a question like: "What is overfishing and how does it contribute to the issue of fish depletion?"
- Invite students to record a refined research question on the lines of their graphic organizer.

- Invite students to read through the directions and the column headings on the Researching Graphic Organizer with you.
- Tell students that they are going to be researching informative facts about the issue of overfishing that they could use in their informative consumer guides.
- Explain that they will begin by watching a video about overfishing. Tell students you are going to play the video and you would like them to just watch it through the first time without recording anything on their graphic organizer to see all of the content. You will give them time at the end of the video to make notes on their organizers and you will also replay the video. Emphasize that this video was made by Europeans for Europeans, so many of the measurements they hear, like kilos and meters, may not be familiar to them, but they should still be able to understand the main points the video is making.
- Play the **"Ending Overfishing" video** (https://www.youtube.com/watch?v=F6nwZUkBeas) up to 2:40 for the class without stopping it.
- Invite students to talk with an elbow partner about the compelling and relevant factual information and quotes they saw on the video.
- Select students to share their ideas with the whole group.
- Model filling in the displayed Researching Graphic Organizer with the title and source ("Ending Overfishing" Ocean 2012) and student ideas.
- Tell students that you are going to replay the video, and this time they can make notes on their Researching Graphic Organizers as they watch.
- Replay the video.
- Invite students to talk with an elbow partner about the compelling and relevant factual information and quotes they saw on the video and recorded on their graphic organizer.
- Select students to share their ideas with the whole group.
- Continue to model filling in the displayed Researching Graphic Organizer with students' ideas.

Meeting Students' Needs

- Consider pairing up ELL students who speak the same first language to encourage deeper discussion about the video.
- Modeling how to fill in the Researching Graphic Organizer will ensure all students know what is expected of them when they begin working independently; it will also provide them with the confidence necessary to begin working on their own.

B. Researching Facts: Part 1 of the Jigsaw (15 minutes)

- Tell students they are going to do a Jigsaw so each triad will have a different article to use for research. Then, they will come together at the end to share what they have found; this way, they can share the workload of researching facts.
- Distribute the **research articles and glossaries**.

- Choose a team to model following the directions and filling in the displayed Researching Graphic Organizer with just the first couple of paragraphs of their article.
- Remind students to discuss their ideas before writing anything on their individual graphic organizers.
- Invite triads to begin.
- Circulate to support students in reading the texts and underlining factual information. Ask probing questions as necessary:
    - "Does this information answer your refined focus question?"
    - "Is this relevant factual information? Is it something that is undeniably true?"
    - "What makes this information/quote compelling?"

Meeting Students' Needs

If students have been grouped homogeneously, focus your attention on those triads that need additional support reading the research materials.

Closing and Assessment

A. Triad Share: Part 2 of the Jigsaw (7 minutes)

- Invite triads to pair up with another triad to share the factual information they collected on the issue of overfishing.
- Invite triads to add any new pieces of factual information to their graphic organizer.
- Invite triads to repeat this process with other groups until they have shared information from each article.
- Preview homework and distribute **Structured Notes: Chapter 7, Pages 98–106** and **evidence flags**.

Meeting Students' Needs

Inviting triads to share their work can function as a self-check and enables triads to push each other's thinking further.

Homework

- Read the rest of chapter 7 of *World Without Fish*. Remember to record new words on your **word-catcher**. Use evidence flags to gather evidence as you read to answer the focus question on your structured notes:
    - According to Mark Kurlansky, what are some other solutions to the issue of fish depletion? According to Kurlansky, why won't they work?
- Continue reading your independent reading book.

Researching Graphic Organizer: Lesson 2

Name: _____

Date: _____

Refined research question:

_____

_____

Directions

1. Read through the text carefully. Use the glossary to help you with words that are unfamiliar.
2. Reread the text and discuss in your triads the relevant factual information that will help you describe the issue to consumers.
3. If you are reading a paper text, underline any relevant factual information that will help you describe the issue to consumers.
4. Reread the text and discuss in your triads any relevant and compelling quotes that will help you describe the problem to consumers.
5. In a different color, underline any relevant and compelling quotes that will help you describe the issue in a compelling way to consumers.
6. Record the source in the first column (title and author).
7. Record the information/quotes in the second column. Record quotes in quotation marks.
8. In the third column, describe how this information/quote answers your refined question.

Source (title and author)	Information/Quotes (copy quotes word for word in quotation marks)	How does it answer the question?

Source (title and author)	Information/Quotes (copy quotes word for word in quotation marks)	How does it answer the question?

"Ending Overfishing" Video Transcript
(Teacher Reference)

The earth. There are currently 7 billion people living on 30 percent of its surface and all of them are dependent on the remaining 70 percent: the ocean. The ocean is the largest source of food in the world. Fish is the main daily source of protein for 1.2 billion people. But fishers are more and more frequently returning home with empty nets.

Let's turn the clock back a little. Some scientists say that in the last 60 years, stocks of large fish have fallen by 90 percent. They are warning that we are facing the collapse of all types of fish species in less than 50 years. The reason for this: overfishing.

Long-line fishing vessels deploy 1.4 billion hooks a year. 1.4 billion hooks, each with a slice of fish hanging from them as bait. There are trawling vessels that cast nets with an opening of up to 23,000 meters squared. The size of four football (soccer) pitches and big enough to hold 13 jumbo jets, or more commonly, 500 tons of fish. Amongst these 500 tons of fish there is a lot of by-catch. By-catch is marine creatures incidentally caught, often at large quantity. Typically shrimp trawlers throw 80-90 percent of the marine creatures caught back overboard. This means that for 1 kilo of shrimp, up to 9 kilos of other marine wildlife is caught and wasted.

To relieve the strain on wild fish, 47 percent of our seafood demand is farmed fish. But marine aquaculture is more of a nail in a coffin than a lifeline. Many of the farmed fish are carnivorous; that is, they eat other smaller fish. Five kilos of captured wild fish are needed to produce one kilo of farm-reared salmon. Aquaculture just converts low-value small fish into higher-value bigger ones. It does not create more fish.

Source: www.youtube.com/watch?v=F6nwZUkBeas

Threat 1: Overfishing

Overview

Overfishing occurs when fish and other marine species are caught faster than they can reproduce. It is the result of growing demand for seafood around the world, combined with poor management of fisheries and the development of new, more effective fishing techniques. If left unchecked, it will destroy the marine ecosystem and jeopardise the food security of more than a billion people for whom fish are a primary source of protein.

Sustainable fishing

The statistics are grim: 3/4 of the world's fish stocks are being harvested faster than they can reproduce. Eighty percent are already fully exploited or in decline. Ninety percent of all large predatory fish—including tuna, sharks, swordfish, cod and halibut—are gone. Scientists predict that if current trends continue, world food fisheries could collapse entirely by 2050.[1]

The most prized species are already disappearing. The 1990s saw the widely-publicised collapse of several major cod fisheries, which have failed to recover even after fishing was stopped. WWF predicts that the breeding population of Atlantic bluefin tuna—one of the ocean's largest and fastest predators, and sought-after as a delicacy used for sushi—will disappear within three years unless catches are drastically reduced.

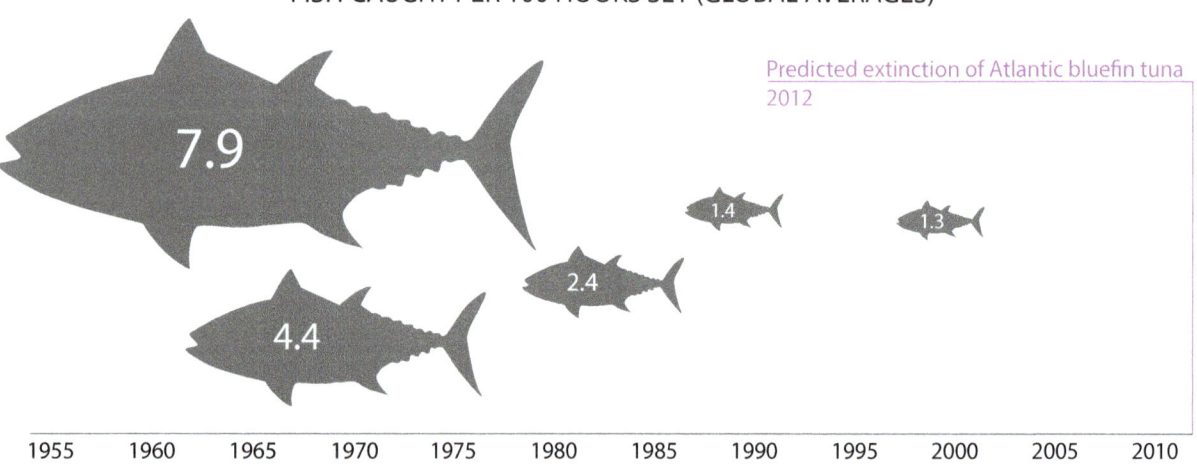

As fish populations closer to shore dwindle, commercial fishing operations have shifted their focus to largely unregulated deep-sea fisheries—as much as 40 percent of the world's trawling grounds are now in waters deeper than 200 meters. In doing so, they target species which are particularly vulnerable to

Source: "Threat 1: Overfishing." Overfishing. Save Our Seas, Web. 19 Feb. 2014. http://saveourseas.com/threats/overfishing

overexploitation, like the orange roughy. Like many other deep-sea fish, this species matures late and lives very long—over 150 years. Its low fecundity means populations become depleted more quickly than inshore species when they are overfished, and take much longer to recover. Indeed, many orange roughy stocks have already collapsed, and recently discovered substitute stocks are also rapidly dwindling.

The good news is that areas with competent fisheries management and coast guard policing, mainly in the developed world, have experienced some dramatic recoveries of fish populations. The bad news is that most overfishing takes place in the waters of poor countries where there is no adequate regulation or policing; areas where rogue fleets—some of which hail from developed countries—equipped with high-tech ships can poach without consequences. Using methods like bottom trawling and long-lining, these fleets are capable of wiping out entire fisheries in a single season. And they don't just catch the fish they target.

Bycatch

Modern fishing vessels catch staggering amounts of unwanted fish and other marine life. It's estimated that anywhere from 8 to 25 percent of the total global catch is discarded, cast overboard either dead or dying.[2] That's up to 27 million tonnes of fish thrown out each year — the equivalent of 600 fully-laden Titanics. And the victims aren't just fish. Every year, an estimated 300,000 whales, dolphins and porpoises die entangled in fishing nets, along with thousands of critically-endangered sea turtles.

ANATOMY OF A BOTTOM TRAWL

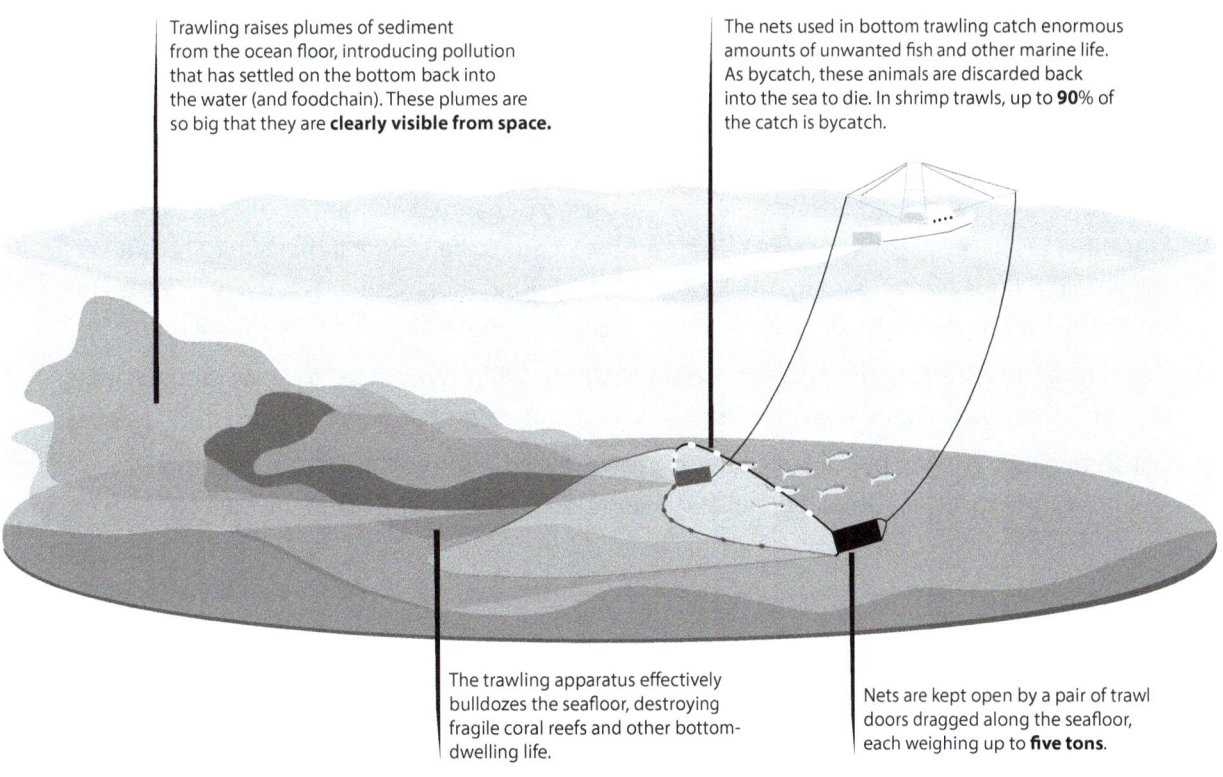

Trawling raises plumes of sediment from the ocean floor, introducing pollution that has settled on the bottom back into the water (and foodchain). These plumes are so big that they are **clearly visible from space.**

The nets used in bottom trawling catch enormous amounts of unwanted fish and other marine life. As bycatch, these animals are discarded back into the sea to die. In shrimp trawls, up to **90%** of the catch is bycatch.

The trawling apparatus effectively bulldozes the seafloor, destroying fragile coral reefs and other bottom-dwelling life.

Nets are kept open by a pair of trawl doors dragged along the seafloor, each weighing up to **five tons**.

Long-line fisheries also kill huge numbers of seabirds. Over 100,000 Albatrosses die this way every year, and many species are endangered as a result of bycatch.

All modern forms of commercial fishing produce bycatch, but shrimp trawling is by far the most destructive: it is responsible for a third of the world's bycatch, while producing only 2% of all seafood.

Shrimp (and many deep-sea fish) are caught using a fishing method called bottom trawling, which usually involves dragging a net between two trawl doors weighing several tons each across the ocean bed. This has a destructive impact on seabed communities, particularly on fragile deep water coral—a vital part of the marine ecosystem that scientists are just beginning to understand.[3] The effect of bottom trawling on the seafloor has been compared to forest clear-cutting, and the damage it causes can be seen from space. The UN Secretary General reported in 2006 that 95 percent of damage to seamount ecosystems worldwide is caused by deep sea bottom trawling.

Remedies

What can be done? The next few years will be pivotal for the oceans. If strong measures are implemented now, much of the damage can still be reversed. In terms of what needs to happen, preventing overfishing is fairly straightforward: first and foremost, scientifically-determined limits on the number of fish caught must be established for individual fisheries, and these limits must be enforced. Second, fishing methods responsible for most bycatch must either be modified to make them less harmful, or made illegal. And third, key parts of the ecosystem, such as vulnerable spawning grounds and coral reefs, must be fully protected.

In practical terms, this means:

- Putting pressure on governments to limit fishing subsidies, estimated at tens of billions of dollars per year. Eliminating subsidies of this scale lowers the financial incentives to continuously expand fishing fleets far beyond sustainability.
- Establishing and expanding Marine Protected Areas (MPAs), areas of the ocean where natural resources are protected and fishing is either restricted or banned altogether (no-take areas). Presently, 1% of the oceans are MPAs. This number needs to be bigger if they are to help reverse the damage done by overfishing. The Save Our Seas Foundation has been actively involved in supporting MPAs through our projects in the Cocos (Keeling) Islands and the Maldives.
- Better monitoring and policing of the fish trade. Pirate fishing continues to grow in scope, and though illegal, fish caught in such operations often end up on our plates.
- Consumers choosing to buy sustainably-sourced seafood and avoiding threatened species. Overfishing is driven by global demand—lowering the demand will lower the damage.

Glossary: "Threat 1: Overfishing"

Threat 1: Overfishing	
reproduce	Have babies
ecosystem	The relationships between living things in an area
jeopardize	Put at risk of losing
exploited	Made full use of
dwindle	Shrink down
fecundity	Ability to reproduce
competent	Having the skills to do something successfully
discarded	Thrown away

Destructive Fishing

Overfishing—catching more fish than the ocean can produce—has been an ongoing challenge for fisheries managers for decades. Today over a fourth of U.S. fish stocks are overfished, which has led to the collapse of some very important fisheries and fishing communities.

Related to overfishing is the question of how we catch the fish. Certain types of fishing methods destroy or damage the very seafloor habitats where fishes and many other seafloor animals reside. Certain fishing methods are notorious for catching large amounts of by-catch—fish, sea turtles, seabirds, and marine mammals—that are unintentionally caught and often incidentally killed in fishing operations.

Among all the fishing methods, bottom trawling, a fishing method that drags a large net across the seafloor is the most destructive to our oceans. To protect the ocean ecosystems from the impacts of bottom trawling, Marine Conservation Institute has been a world leader in providing solutions to policy makers in the U.S. and abroad.

What is bottom trawling? Bottom trawling is an industrial fishing method where a large net with heavy weights is dragged across the seafloor, scooping up everything in its path—from the targeted fish to the incidentally caught centuries-old corals. Bottom trawls are used in catching marine life that live on the seafloor, like shrimp, cod, sole, and flounder. In the U.S., bottom trawling occurs on the Pacific, Atlantic, and Gulf coasts, capturing more than 800,000,000 pounds of marine life in 2007. Bottom trawls are also commonly used by other fishing nations and on the high seas.

Why is it a problem? Bottom trawling is unselective and severely damaging to benthic ecosystems. The net indiscriminately catches every life and object it encounters. Thus, many creatures end up mistakenly caught and thrown overboard dead or dying, including endangered fish and even vulnerable deep-sea corals, which can live for several hundred years. This collateral damage, called by-catch, can amount to 90 percent of a trawl's total catch. In addition, the weight and width of a bottom trawl can destroy large areas of seafloor habitats that give marine species food and shelter. Such habitat destructions can leave the marine ecosystem permanently damaged.

What do we do? Marine Conservation Institute has successfully pushed trawling impacts to the forefront of the marine conservation debate. We have produced peer-reviewed science that examined the ecological impacts of bottom trawling. We advocate keeping bottom trawls out of vulnerable marine habitats and our National Marine Sanctuaries and switching from high-impact fishing methods, like the bottom trawling, to less destructive fishing methods.

Source: Marine Conservation Institute. "Destructive Fishing." Available at: http://www.marine-conservation.org/what-we-do/program-areas/how-we-fish/destructive-fishing/. Accessed on October 23, 2013.

Glossary: "Destructive Fishing"

Destructive Fishing	
notorious	Famous
ecosystems	The relationships among living things in an area
incidentally	By chance
benthic	At the bottom of a body of water
indiscriminately	Not selective; at random
collateral	Additional; secondary

Protecting Ocean Habitat from Bottom Trawling

If bottom trawling happened on land instead of at sea, someplace where we could see it and where cameras could film it, perhaps it would provoke the same sort of public outcry that strip-mining does. But unlike the raw, torn earth laid bare by strip-mining, the similar devastation of the ocean floor caused by bottom trawling is hidden beneath thousands of feet of water. In some cases, the damage could be irreparable.

Bottom trawlers drag giant weighted nets along the ocean floor, ripping up or scooping out whatever they encounter, including ancient coral forests, gardens of anemones, and entire fields of sea sponges. Unwanted and undersized fish hauled up by bottom trawlers are thrown back dead or dying—in some areas, as many as four pounds of fish are discarded for every one pound brought to market.

Today's technology is bringing bottom trawlers into areas ships couldn't reach before. Trawling nets, huge weighted bags, can be 200 feet wide and 40 feet high, weigh as much as 1,000 pounds, and can be sunk to depths of 5,000 feet or more beneath the water's surface. Heavier, stronger gear allows trawl nets to plow over rocky bottoms, destroying the underwater corals, sponges, and rock structures that provide important habitat for fish. Advanced navigation technology brings trawl nets deeper and farther from shore, into areas populated with slow-growing deep-sea fish and corals, which are especially slow to recover from repeated trawling.

Bottom Trawling in International Waters

On the high seas, unregulated bottom trawlers operating in waters well off the coast are laying waste to huge swaths of the ocean floor. Seamounts—volcanic mountains and hills that rise from the ocean floor but do not break the surface—are being damaged by these industrial fishing practices, and the wealth of flora and fauna clustered around seamounts is being wiped out in the process. Many rare, ancient, and even unknown species—some of which hold promise for biomedical research or are critical to undersea biodiversity—are at risk, including:

- Cold-water corals, which are as exotic and colorful as their warm-water counterparts. Red tree corals form ancient forests, stretching up to 7 feet tall and 25 feet wide, providing shelter for fish, shellfish, and sea stars. Corals on seamounts can live up to 8,000 years and tend to take branching, tree-like forms, making them particularly susceptible to trawl damage.
- Sponges, which form giant fields in the deep, creating stretches of habitat up to a mile long and 50 feet high.
- Fish, including orange roughy, which take decades to mature and can live for 125 years.
- New species of flora and fauna tucked away on seamounts and other deep-sea habitats. Just like the creatures of the Galapagos Islands, many seamount species have evolved in isolation, resulting in unique species. Scientists studying a cluster of seamounts near New Caledonia have determined that nearly one-third of the species there have never been seen anywhere else.
- Novel chemical compounds that hold promise for the treatment of cancer and other diseases after their discovery by scientists investigating the biomedical properties of deep-sea organisms.

Source: Natural Resources Defense Council. "Protecting Ocean Habitat from Bottom Trawling." Available at: http://www.nrdc.org/water/oceans/ftrawling.asp. Accessed on October 23, 2013.

Bottom Trawling in U.S. Waters

Closer to U.S. shores, bottom trawling can be just as destructive. Bottom trawlers have taken a huge toll on sport and commercial fish such as Pacific rockfish, a family of more than 60 species of colorful fish uniquely adapted to the rocky reefs, rugged canyons, pinnacles, and kelp forests of the Pacific coast. Marketed as Pacific red snapper or as rock cod, they are popular with fishermen and diners. Once greatly abundant, several populations are now so depleted that scientists consider them at risk of extinction.

Rockfish have several characteristics that make them susceptible to overfishing, and particularly to bottom trawling. Some rockfish species live as long as 100 years, are slow to mature and may reproduce successfully only once a decade. Because different species school together, powerful trawl gear catches the vulnerable types along with the more productive, and these deep-dwelling fish cannot survive the trauma of being brought to the surface and then tossed overboard.

Glossary: "Protecting Ocean Habitat from Bottom Trawling"

Protecting Ocean Habitat from Bottom Trawling	
irreparable	Can't be repaired
unregulated	Not controlled by regulations or laws
swaths	Areas

Structured Notes: Chapter 7, Pages 98–106

Name: _____

Date: _____

Chapter	Homework Focus Question	Answer with Evidence from the Text (include page number)
_____	According to Mark Kurlansky, what are some other solutions to the issue of fish depletion? According to Kurlansky, why won't they work?	

LESSON 3

Researching Case Studies of Depleted Fish Species

Long-Term Targets Addressed (Based on ELA CCSS)

- I can write informative/explanatory texts that convey ideas and concepts using relevant information that is carefully selected and organized. (W.6.2)
- I can conduct short research projects to answer a question. (W.6.7)

Supporting Learning Target

- I can research to find relevant and compelling factual information and quotes about depleted fish species to use as a case study in my informative consumer brochure.

Ongoing Assessment

- Structured Notes: Chapter 7, Pages 98–106 of *World Without Fish* (from homework)
- Researching Graphic Organizer: Lesson 3

Agenda

1. Opening
    A. Engaging the Reader: The Rest of Chapter 7 of *World Without Fish* (5 minutes)
    B. Unpacking Learning Targets (3 minutes)
2. Work Time
    A. Researching Facts: Part 1 of the Jigsaw (27 minutes)
3. Closing and Assessment
    A. Triad Share: Part 2 of the Jigsaw (10 minutes)

4. Homework

   A. Read chapter 8 of *World Without Fish*. Remember to record new words on your word-catcher. As you read, mark the text with evidence flags to help you answer the focus question on your structured notes:

   - What are the sustainable fishing methods Mark Kurlansky suggests? What makes them sustainable?

   B. Continue reading your independent reading book.

Teaching Notes

- In this lesson, students work in triads to research a case study of a depleted fish species. As in Lesson 2, this is done in a Jigsaw, so each triad is given a different research resource, and they partner with another triad in the Closing and Assessment to share what they have found.
- Continue to emphasize to students that the ideas presented are just one point of view and that there are other points of view out there about the idea of overfishing and fish depletion.
- In advance:
  - Prepare the research articles for each triad (see supporting materials). Each triad needs to be allocated one research article, and you need enough of each article for one per student. The articles provided range in difficulty—determine how to allocate articles by considering the reading level of students in each triad. Each triad needs to be given a glossary for its vocabulary article, too. An excerpt of *World Without Fish* is also used as a research resource, so consider allocating this to triads with students who require more support with reading, as they should already be familiar with the text.
- Post: learning target.

Lesson Vocabulary

factual information, relevant, compelling, case study; see glossaries for vocabulary words

Materials

- Structured Notes: Chapter 7, Pages 98–106 (from homework)
- Performance Task Prompt: Informative Consumer Guide (from Lesson 1)
- Researching Graphic Organizer: Lesson 3 (one per student)
- Colored pencils or markers (one for each student)
- Research articles and glossaries (one per student in assigned triad; see Teaching Notes):
  - *World Without Fish*: Pages 46–49 (book; distributed in Unit 1; one per student)
  - "A Rapidly Disappearing Fish" (one per student)
  - "Case Study: Atlantic Bluefin Tuna" (one per student)

- Evidence flags (three per student for homework)
- Structured Notes: Chapter 8 (one per student)

Opening

A. Engaging the Reader: The Rest of Chapter 7 of *World Without Fish* (5 minutes)

- Remind students of the homework: to read the rest of chapter 7 of *World Without Fish* and to answer the focus question on their structured notes: According to Mark Kurlansky, what are some other solutions to the issue of fish depletion? According to Kurlansky, why won't they work?
- Ask students to take out their **Structured Notes: Chapter 7, Pages 98–106.**
- Invite students to turn to an elbow partner and share what they wrote for homework on their structured notes.
- Remind them to make revisions where necessary.
- Select volunteers to share their answers with the whole group. Listen for students to explain that limiting the amount of time fishermen spend fishing is one solution, but it won't work because fishermen will lose money. Another solution is to temporarily close off some fishing areas, but that won't work because fishermen then move on to destroy somewhere else.

Meeting Students' Needs

Opening the lesson by asking students to share their homework makes them accountable for completing it. It also gives you the opportunity to monitor which students are not doing their homework.

B. Unpacking Learning Targets (3 minutes)

- Direct students' attention to the posted learning target and read it aloud:
  - "I can research to find relevant and compelling factual information and quotes about depleted fish species to use as a case study in my informative consumer brochure."
- Remind students that *factual information* is information that is undeniably true, *relevant* information is that which is on the topic being researched, and *compelling* quotes are those that will encourage the reader to keep reading. Although informative, we want readers to read all the way to the end to be fully informed of the issue.
- Ask students to take their **Performance Task Prompt: Informative Consumer Guide** and quietly move to sit with their triads.
- Ask students to discuss in triads:
  - "What is a case study?"
  - "Why do you think it is useful to include a case study in your informative consumer brochure? How does reading a case study help the consumer understand the problem better?"

- Cold-call students to share their responses. Listen for students to explain that a case study is a particular example that highlights the problem. It is useful because it emotionally involves consumers and helps them understand the issue with an example.

Meeting Students' Needs

Learning targets are a research-based strategy that helps all students, especially challenged learners.

Work Time

A. Researching Facts: Part 1 of the Jigsaw (27 minutes)

- Distribute **Researching Graphic Organizer: Lesson 3**.
- Display the Performance Task Prompt: Informative Consumer Guide and invite students to refer to their own copies.
- Direct students' attention to the list of requirements for the informative consumer guide, focusing on the second bullet of the Performance Task Prompt: "A case study of a fish species that has been severely depleted and the impact it has had."
- Turn students' attention to their Researching Graphic Organizer, asking them to focus on the line for a "Refined research question" at the top of the page. Tell students to discuss in triads:
  - "You are going to research more about a specific species of fish that has been depleted due to overfishing by reading a case study. What do you think a refined research question might be for this lesson? Why?"
- Select volunteers to share their ideas with the class. Listen for students to suggest a question like: "What happened to a particular species of fish that became depleted?"
- Invite students to record a refined research question on the lines of their Researching Graphic Organizer.
- Invite students to read through the directions and the column headings with you.
- Tell students that they will research a case study to include in their informative consumer guides. Explain that similar to the previous lesson, they will do a Jigsaw, where different triads read different articles about the depletion of different fish species to research. Then, they will come together during the Closing and Assessment to share what they found out; this way, they can share the workload of researching.
- Distribute the **research articles and glossaries**.
- Remind students to discuss their ideas before writing anything on their individual graphic organizers.
- Invite triads to begin researching.

- Circulate to support students in reading the texts and underlining factual information. Ask probing questions as necessary:
    - "Does this information answer your refined focus question?"
    - "Is this factual information? Is it something that is undeniably true?"
    - "Why is this quote compelling?"

Meeting Students' Needs

If students have been grouped homogeneously, focus your attention on those triads that need additional support reading the research materials.

Closing and Assessment

A. Triad Share: Part 2 of the Jigsaw (10 minutes)

- Invite triads to pair up with another triad to share the factual information they collected about case studies of fish depletion.
- Invite triads to add any new pieces of factual information to their graphic organizer.
- Invite triads to repeat this process with other groups until they have shared information from each article.
- Preview homework and distribute **Structured Notes: Chapter 8** and **evidence flags**.

Meeting Students' Needs

Inviting triads to share their work can function as a self-check and can enable triads to push each other's thinking further.

Homework

- Read chapter 8 of *World Without Fish*. Remember to record new words on your word-catcher. As you read, mark the text with evidence flags to help you answer the focus question on your structured notes:
    - What are the sustainable fishing methods Mark Kurlansky suggests? What makes them sustainable?
- Continue reading your independent reading book.

Researching Graphic Organizer: Lesson 3

Name: _____

Date: _____

Refined research question:

_____

_____

Directions

1. Read through the text carefully. Use the glossary to help you with words that are unfamiliar.
2. Reread the text and discuss in your triads the relevant factual information that will help you describe the issue to consumers.
3. If you are reading a paper text, underline any relevant factual information that will help you describe the issue to consumers.
4. Reread the text and discuss in your triads any relevant and compelling quotes that will help you describe the problem to consumers.
5. In a different color, underline any relevant and compelling quotes that will help you describe the issue in a compelling way to consumers.
6. Record the source in the first column (title and author).
7. Record the information/quotes in the second column. Record quotes in quotation marks.
8. In the third column, describe how this information/quote answers your refined question.

Source (title and author)	Information/Quotes (copy quotes word for word in quotation marks)	How does it answer the question?

Source (title and author)	Information/Quotes (copy quotes word for word in quotation marks)	How does it answer the question?

A Rapidly Disappearing Fish

Chilean sea bass is one of the most popular fishes sold in restaurants and grocery stores in the United States.

The fish, which is really called the "Patagonian toothfish" by fishermen, was virtually unknown 15 years ago. In the mid-1990s, its popularity rose both here and in Asia, causing massive increases in catches.

The toothfish is a very slow-growing species found in the cold waters of the southern hemisphere. Typically, the fish can live as long as 50 years, but most fish are caught before they have the chance to reproduce.

Legal and illegal fishermen are overfishing this rapidly disappearing species now to the point of extinction. It is difficult to properly regulate the amount of fish many "pirate" fishermen bring in and many areas are in danger of being depleted completely.

Fishermen continue in search of illegal groups of the Chilean sea bass because of their high worth at market (about $10 per pound in the U.S.). Environmental groups like Greenpeace and others are lobbying major food stores to convince them to stop carrying the fish. It's impossible to know whether public demand or the fish supply will end first.

Source: PBS Newshour Extra.

Case Study: Atlantic Bluefin Tuna

They can weigh over half a ton, grow to over four meters in length, and dive to depths of 1,000 meters. They accelerate as fast as a sports car and reach speeds of 70 km/h, propelled by a rapidly vibrating, whip-thin tail. They even raise their body temperature far above that of the surrounding water in order to traverse frigid arctic waters.

Bluefin tuna are unique, perfectly adapted products of evolution. They are also dangerously close to becoming extinct.

Coveted for their dense, dark red meat used in sushi (where it is known as "toro"), bluefin support an unsustainable $7.2 billion industry that has driven tuna stocks to the brink of collapse. In 2009, WWF predicted that without drastic measures, Atlantic bluefin will disappear by 2012. Unfortunately, attempts to implement such measures—most recently at the 2010 Convention on International Trade in Endangered Species of Wild Fauna and Flora (CITES)—have failed.

Source: "Case Study: Atlantic Bluefin Tuna" Overfishing. Save Our Seas, Web. 19 Feb. 2014. http://saveourseas.com/threats/overfishing

Glossary: "Case Study: Atlantic Bluefin Tuna"

Case Study: Atlantic Bluefin Tuna	
propelled	Moved along
traverse	Cross
frigid	Very cold
coveted	Wanted

Structured Notes: Chapter 8

Name: _____

Date: _____

Chapter	Homework Focus Question	Answer with Evidence from the Text (include page number)
_____	What are the sustainable fishing methods Mark Kurlansky suggests? What makes them sustainable?	

LESSON 4

Researching Information about Sustainable Fishing

Long-Term Targets Addressed (Based on ELA CCSS)

- I can write informative/explanatory texts that convey ideas and concepts using relevant information that is carefully selected and organized. (W.6.2)
- I can conduct short research projects to answer a question. (W.6.7)

Supporting Learning Target

- I can research to find relevant and compelling factual information and quotes about sustainable fishing methods to use in my informative consumer brochure.

Ongoing Assessment

- Structured Notes: Chapter 8 of *World Without Fish* (from homework)
- Researching Graphic Organizer: Lesson 4

Agenda

1. Opening
   A. Engaging the Reader: Chapter 8 of *World Without Fish* (5 minutes)
   B. Unpacking Learning Targets (3 minutes)
2. Work Time
   A. Researching Facts: Part 1 of the Jigsaw (27 minutes)
3. Closing and Assessment
   A. Triad Share: Part 2 of the Jigsaw (10 minutes)

4. Homework

   A. Read chapter 11 of *World Without Fish* through page 153. Remember to record new words on your word-catcher. As you read, mark the text with evidence flags to help you answer the focus question on your structured notes:

   - According to Mark Kurlansky, what are some things that we can do to help solve the problem of fish depletion?

   B. Continue reading your independent reading book.

Teaching Notes

- In this lesson, students work in triads to research information about sustainable fishing methods. As in Lessons 2 and 3, this is done in a Jigsaw. Each triad is given a different research resource and they partner up with another triad in the Closing and Assessment to share what they found.
- Continue to emphasize to students that the ideas presented are just one point of view and that there are other points of view out there about the idea of overfishing and fish depletion.
- For homework, students jump ahead to read chapter 11. Make it clear to students that the reason for this is to ensure they have read the parts of the book that will most help them by providing useful information for the performance task.
- In advance:
  - Prepare the research materials for each triad (see supporting materials). Each triad needs to be allocated one research article, and you need enough of each article for one per student. The articles range in difficulty—determine how to allocate articles by considering the reading level of students in each triad. Each triad needs a glossary for its article, too. An excerpt of *World Without Fish* is also used as a research resource, so consider allocating this to triads of students who require more support with reading, as they should already be familiar with the text.
  - Review the Mix and Mingle protocol activity in Opening A and have music ready to use for the opening of this lesson.
- Post: learning targets.

Lesson Vocabulary

factual information, relevant, compelling; see glossaries for vocabulary words

Materials

- Structured Notes: Chapter 8 (from homework)
- Performance Task Prompt: Informative Consumer Guide (from Lesson 1)
- Researching Graphic Organizer: Lesson 4 (one per student)
- Colored pencils or markers (one for each student)

- Research articles and glossaries (one per student in assigned triad; see Teaching Notes):
  - *World Without Fish*: Pages 112–115 (book; distributed in Unit 1; one per student)
  - "Sustainable Fishing Methods" (one per student)
  - "Sustainable Fishing" (one per student)
  - "Sustainable Seafood" (one per student)
- Evidence flags (three per student for homework)
- **Structured Notes: Chapter 11 through Page 153** (one per student)

Opening

A. Engaging the Reader: Chapter 8 of *World Without Fish* (5 minutes)

- Remind students of the homework: to read chapter 8 of *World Without Fish* and to answer the focus questions on their structured notes: What are the sustainable fishing methods Mark Kurlansky suggests? What makes them sustainable?
- Ask students to take out their **Structured Notes: Chapter 8**.
- Invite students to Mix and Mingle to review their answers on their structured notes.
- Review the protocol as necessary.
- Mix and Mingle:
  1. Play music.
  2. Invite students to move around the room with their structured notes.
  3. After 15 seconds, stop the music and invite students to share the answers to the homework focus questions with the person closest to them.
  4. Repeat until students have shared their answer with three other students.
- Invite students to revise the answers on their structured notes based on the discussions they had with other students in the Mix and Mingle.
- Select volunteers to share their answers with the whole group. Listen for students to explain that Mark Kurlansky suggests old practices like hook-and-line fishing and harpooning.

Meeting Students' Needs

- Opening the lesson by asking students to share their homework makes them accountable for completing it. It also gives you the opportunity to monitor which students are not doing their homework.
- Consider pairing ELL students who speak the same first language to deepen their discussion and understanding.

B. Unpacking Learning Targets (3 minutes)

- Direct students' attention to the posted learning target and read it aloud:
  - "I can research to find relevant and compelling factual information and quotes about sustainable fishing methods to use in my informative consumer brochure."
- Remind students that *factual information* is information that is undeniably true, *relevant* information is that which is on the topic being researched, and *compelling* quotes are those that will encourage the reader to keep reading. Although informative, we want readers to read all the way to the end to be fully informed of the results of overfishing.

Meeting Students' Needs

- Learning targets are a research-based strategy that helps all students, especially challenged learners.
- Posting learning targets allows students to reference them throughout the lesson to check their understanding. Learning targets also provide a reminder to students and teachers about the intended learning behind a given lesson or activity.

Work Time

A. Researching Facts: Part 1 of the Jigsaw (27 minutes)

- Ask students to take their **Performance Task Prompt: Informative Consumer Guide** and move to sit with their triads.
- Distribute **Researching Graphic Organizer: Lesson 4**.
- Display the Performance Task Prompt: Informative Consumer Guide and invite students to refer to their own copies.
- Direct students' attention to the list of requirements for the informative consumer guide, focusing students on the third bullet: "A solution: sustainable methods for catching fish." Ask students to discuss in triads:
  - "How are you going to find out more about sustainable methods for catching fish? What does the learning target say?"
- Select students to share their responses. Listen for students to explain that they are going to find out more by researching, as the learning target suggests.
- Turn students' attention to their Researching Graphic Organizer, asking them to focus on the line for a "Refined research question" at the top of the page.

- Ask students to discuss in triads:
  - "You are going to be researching to find out more information about sustainable fishing methods in this lesson. What do you think a refined research question might be for this lesson? Why?"
- Select volunteers to share their ideas with the class. Listen for students to suggest a question like: "What do consumers need to know about sustainable fishing methods?"
- Invite students to record a refined research question on the lines of their Researching Graphic Organizer.
- Invite them to read through the directions and the column headings with you.
- Tell them that they will be researching informative facts about sustainable fishing methods to use in their informative consumer guides. Explain that they are going to be doing a Jigsaw, so different triads will have different articles to research. Then they will come together to share what they found; this way, they can share the research workload.
- Distribute the **research articles and glossaries**.
- Remind students to discuss their ideas before writing anything on their individual graphic organizers.
- Invite triads to begin researching.
- Circulate to support students in reading the texts and underlining factual information. Ask probing questions as necessary:
  - "Does this information answer your refined focus question?"
  - "Is this relevant factual information? Is it something that is undeniably true?"
  - "Why is this information/quote compelling?"

Meeting Students' Needs

If students have been grouped homogeneously, focus your attention on those triads that need additional support reading the research materials.

Closing and Assessment

A. Triad Share: Part 2 of the Jigsaw (10 minutes)

- Invite triads to pair up with another triad to share the factual information they collected.
- Invite them to add any new pieces of factual information to their graphic organizer.
- Invite triads to repeat this process with other groups until they have shared information from each article.
- Preview homework and distribute **Structured Notes: Chapter 11 through Page 153** and **evidence flags**.

Meeting Students' Needs

Inviting triads to share their work can function as a self-check and can enable triads to push each other's thinking further.

Homework

- Read chapter 11 of *World Without Fish* through page 153. Remember to record new words on your word-catcher. As you read, mark the text with evidence flags to help you answer the focus question on your structured notes:
  - According to Mark Kurlansky, what are some things that we can do to help solve the problem of fish depletion?
- Continue reading your independent reading book.

Researching Graphic Organizer: Lesson 4

Name: _____

Date: _____

Refined research question:

_____

_____

Directions

1. Read through the text carefully. Use the glossary to help you with words that are unfamiliar.
2. Reread the text and discuss in your triads the relevant factual information that will help you describe the issue to consumers.
3. If you are reading a paper text, underline any relevant factual information that will help you describe the issue to consumers.
4. Reread the text and discuss in your triads any relevant and compelling quotes that will help you describe the problem to consumers.
5. In a different color, underline any relevant and compelling quotes that will help you describe the issue in a compelling way to consumers.
6. Record the source in the first column (title and author).
7. Record the information/quotes in the second column. Record quotes in quotation marks.
8. In the third column, describe how this information/quote answers your refined question.

Source (title and author)	Information/Quotes (copy quotes word for word in quotation marks)	How does it answer the question?

TEACHER GUIDE AND RESOURCE BOOK • Grade 6 • Module 3B • Unit 3 • Lesson 4 Supporting Materials

Source (title and author)	Information/Quotes (copy quotes word for word in quotation marks)	How does it answer the question?

Sustainable Fishing Methods

Some fishing methods are decidedly unsustainable, but others aren't so bad, depending on the fishery in which they're used. Harmful and sometimes-harmful methods (for superb illustrations of these, see the Monterey Bay Aquarium's Seafood Watch site):

Dredging

Dragging a metal mesh bag along the bottom of the seafloor to catch bottom-dwelling shellfish (such as clams, scallops, and oysters).

Dredging causes significant habitat damage. The mesh bags also scoop up other types of marine life—everything from fish to sponges—which tend not to survive the experience.

Gillnetting

Using a curtain of netting that hangs in the water at various depths; the openings are big enough for a fish's head but not its body, trapping the fish as it attempts to swim through (the openings are sized according to the fish being caught).

In some areas, gillnetting is not a responsible form of fishing because it can accidentally entangle and kill sea turtles and other marine animals. However, in Alaska, salmon are sustainably caught using gillnets because of the low levels of by-catch in those waters.

Long-lining

Fishing with one very long fishing line that can extend either near the ocean surface (pelagic long-lining) or just off the ocean floor (bottom long-lining) for up to 50 miles. Individual lines with hooks dangle from the central line.

Pelagic long-lining can attract lots of unintended species, including birds, resulting in large by-catches. In addition, when fishermen let their lines sit in the water for long periods of time before hauling them in, the by-catch numbers rise.

When the lines are sunk deeper, or when special hooks are used that can release by-catch, the environmental impact eases.

Purse seining

Like a giant drawstring purse, the seine encircles a school of fish; then the fishermen pull the "drawstring" at the net's bottom beneath the fish, trapping them.

This method works well for catching small fish like herring. However, when it's used for tuna, all kinds of other species are caught and die—most notoriously dolphins, since they often swim with tuna.

Source: Sunset. "Sustainable Fishing Methods." Available at: http://www.sunset.com/food-wine/flavors-of-the-west/sustainable-fishing-methods-00400000053176/. Accessed on October 28, 2013.

Even though many nets are now equipped with devices to release the dolphins, the stress of capture alone may cause injury.

Trawling

Responsible for the largest percentage of commercially available fish. This involves towing a funnel-shaped net through the water, at varying depths.

When they're used on or near the ocean floor, trawlnets can be really destructive to the habitat; by-catch is a concern, too. When used higher up (usually to scoop up whole schools of fish), their impact is nowhere near as severe.

Sustainable Methods

In general, the following methods do no harm to the oceans, but if used improperly, some can.

Hook and lining (also called pole catching)

Use of a rod (fishing pole) with one line and several hooks.

It's a responsible fishing method because fisherman can quickly release unwanted catch from their hooks soon after it was caught.

Harpooning

Catching larger fish such as swordfish with hand-thrown harpoons (just like in the whaling days) or with barbs fired from a gun. By-catch is almost nonexistent, since the fishermen are aiming at individual targets.

Traps

In general, this is a good method. Floating traps and weirs, which guide the fish into ever-smaller boxes, harm neither fish nor the environment.

Reef nets, used for salmon in the Northwest, are shallow, near-the-surface nets that the salmon swim right into, then are tipped into holding tanks.

Wire-mesh traps that lie on the bottom can damage the ocean floor if they're dragged, which has led to their being banned in some parts of the world. Used properly, they're usually not harmful.

Trolling

Another method of hooking fish individually, but rather than each line being handheld as it is in hook-and-line fishing, trolling involves towing individual anchored lines from a moving boat. It's still sustainable because by-catch is minimal and can be quickly released.

Glossary: "Sustainable Fishing Methods"

Sustainable Fishing Methods	
habitat	An area of land or sea that species of plants, animals, or living things live on or in
by-catch	Fish and other sea animals caught by mistake
seine	A special kind of fishing net
notoriously	Famously (in a bad way)
nonexistent	Doesn't exist
weirs	A fence across the water to catch fish

Sustainable Fishing

There are ways to fish sustainably, allowing us to enjoy seafood while ensuring that populations remain for the future. In many indigenous cultures, people have fished sustainably for thousands of years. Today's sustainable fishing practices reflect some lessons learned from these cultures.

In the Philippines, the Tagbanua people have traditionally employed fishing practices that simultaneously harvest and maintain fish populations. They continue to follow these practices today. Tagbanuas fish for specific species only during certain times of the year, determined by tides and the moon, allowing fish stocks to replenish themselves. They set aside certain areas, such as coral reefs, as protected spots in which fishing is prohibited. When they do fish, these traditional fishers primarily use hook-and-line methods, catching only what they need to feed themselves and their communities. A 2007 study lauded traditional Tagbanua practices as a way to prevent injury and death to local Irrawaddy dolphins, which become entangled in more modern fishing gear like nets and traps.

Traditional Polynesian cultures of the South Pacific have also always relied on the ocean's resources. Their most common historical fishing practices were hook and line, spearfishing, and cast nets. Hooks constructed of bone, shell, or stone were designed to catch specific species. Fishers would also craft 2-meter (6-foot) spears. They would dive underwater or spear fish from above, again targeting specific animals. Cast nets were used by fishers working individually or in groups. The nets could be cast from shore or canoes, catching groups of fish. All of these methods targeted fish needed for fishers' families and local communities.

Some of these sustainable fishing practices are still used today. Native Hawaiians practice cast-net fishing and spearfishing. Modern spearfishing is practiced all over the world, including in South America, Africa, Australia, and Asia. In many cases, spearguns are now used to propel the spear underwater. Spearfishing is a popular recreational activity in some areas of the United States, including Florida and Hawaii. This fishing method is considered sustainable because it targets one fish at a time and results in very little by-catch.

If you have ever gone fishing, chances are you used a rod and reel. Rod-and-reel fishing is a modern version of traditional hook-and-line. Rods and reels come in different shapes and sizes, allowing recreational and commercial fishers to target a wide variety of fish species in both freshwater and saltwater. The different types of rods and reels, coupled with different locations and bait, mean fishers can catch pelagic fish like sailfish, bottom-dwellers like flounder, and freshwater species such as catfish and trout. Rod-and-reel fishing results in less by-catch because non-targeted species can be released immediately. Additionally, only one fish is caught at a time, preventing overfishing. For commercial fishers, rod-and reel-fishing is a more sustainable alternative to long-lining.

Source: Copyright © National Geographic. Used by permission and not subject to Creative Commons license.

Glossary: "Sustainable Fishing"

Sustainable Fishing	
indigenous	Originating in a place
replenish	Fill up again
prohibited	Not allowed
lauded	Praised
recreational	Done for enjoyment
pelagic	Close to the bottom

Sustainable Seafood

Fishing Techniques

All fishing techniques have to address a certain level of by-catch; however, the type of harvesting technique determines the typical amount of by-catch associated. Certain fishing techniques are commonly associated with *high* by-catch such as trawling, dredging, and pelagic long-lining. Examples of seafood that typically involve high by-catch issues include shrimp, orange roughy, groundfish, scallops, and other wild-caught shellfish, large pelagic species such as mahi mahi, tuna, and swordfish. However, many of these species can be harvested with limited by-catch if the fishing method is sustainable. Sustainable fishing techniques associated with low by-catch include trolling, hook and line, pot and traps.

Certain fishing techniques can be associated with habitat damage and negative environmental impacts. Fishing methods that have detrimental effects on marine ecosystems include bottom trawling and dredging. In some cases, trawlers may sweep the same piece of seafloor many times a year, leaving no time for re-growth or recovery. Species that are typically caught by bottom trawl include: orange roughy, cod, shrimp, and groundfish such as flounder and sole. Dredges rake the ocean's bottom habitat, creating a disturbance in the seabed in order to sift out the targeted species, typically shellfish. Alternative sustainable fishing methods that limit habitat damage include trolling, hook and line, and bottom long-lining.

Source: Vancouver Aquarium. "Sustainable Seafood." Available at: http://www.oceanwise.ca/about/sustainable-seafood. Accessed on October 29, 2013.

Glossary: "Sustainable Seafood"

Sustainable Seafood	
typical	Usual
pelagic	Close to the bottom
trolling	A method of fishing in which one or more fishing lines with bait attached are dragged through the water
detrimental	Harmful

Structured Notes: Chapter 11 through Page 153

Name: _____

Date: _____

Chapter	Homework Focus Question	Answer with Evidence from the Text (include page number)
_____	According to Mark Kurlansky, what are some things that we can do to help solve the problem of fish depletion?	

LESSON 5

Mid-Unit 3 Assessment, Part 1

Researching Information about Buying Fish Caught Using Sustainable Methods

Long-Term Targets Addressed (Based on ELA CCSS)

- I can conduct short research projects to answer a question. (W.6.7)
- I can use several sources in my research. (W.6.7)
- I can refocus or refine my question when appropriate. (W.6.7)
- I can interpret information presented in different media and formats. (SL.6.2)
- I can explain how new information connects to a topic, text, or issue I am studying. (SL.6.2)

Supporting Learning Targets

- I can interpret information from different resources as part of my research about what consumers need to know about overfishing and fish depletion when buying fish.
- I can refine the research question to focus my research.

Ongoing Assessment

- Mid-Unit 3 Assessment, Part 1: Researching Information about Buying Fish Caught Using Sustainable Fishing Methods

Agenda

1. Opening
   A. Unpacking Learning Targets (4 minutes)
2. Work Time
   A. Mid-Unit 3 Assessment, Part 1: Interpreting Resources (38 minutes)

3. Closing and Assessment

    A. Debrief (3 minutes)

4. Homework

    A. Read chapter 9 of *World Without Fish* to the end of page 127. Remember to record new words on your word-catcher. As you read, mark the text with evidence flags to help you answer the focus question on your structured notes:

    - According to Mark Kurlansky, what is pollution doing to fish? How?

    B. Continue reading your independent reading book.

Teaching Notes

- This lesson is the Mid-Unit 3 Assessment. There are two parts to this assessment. Students complete Part 1, in which they analyze and interpret the information presented in different kinds of media including photographs, charts, and maps to find answers to the question: What do consumers need to know about overfishing and fish depletion when buying fish? They fill in the graphic organizer included with the Mid-Unit 3 Assessment, which is very similar to the Researching Graphic Organizers they used in Lessons 2–4. This is to assess W.6.7 and to prepare for SL.6.2.

- To address SL.6.2, students watch a video titled "How to Buy Fresh, Sustainable Seafood" (accessed here: www.youtube.com/watch?v=C7mMzL9Snqc) as part of their research. How you choose to manage this depends on the technology you have available. You may choose to show it to the whole group, or have it set up on devices for students to access independently.

- Please bear in mind that YouTube, social media video sites, and other website links may incorporate inappropriate content via comment banks and ads. While some lessons include these links as the most efficient means to view content in preparation for the lesson, be sure to preview links, and/or use a filter service, such as www.safeshare.tv, for actually viewing these links in the classroom.

- In the next lesson, students will complete Part 2 of the Mid-Unit 3 Assessment, in which they orally explain in a triad discussion with the teacher how the resources they analyzed in Part 1 deepen their understanding of what consumers need to know about sustainable fishing when buying fish. This is to complete the assessment of SL.6.2.

- Consider using the Grade 6 2-Point Rubric—Short Response (see supporting materials) and the Mid-Unit 3 Assessment (Teacher Reference) to assess W.6.7. Please note that students may have responses that differ from those on the suggested answer key—use your judgment as you assess.

- Students will need Part 1 of the Mid-Unit 3 Assessment in order to complete Part 2 in the following lesson, so be aware of this as you collect students' work at the end of Work Time A.

- Continue to emphasize to students that the ideas presented are just one point of view and that there are other points of view out there about the idea of overfishing and fish depletion.

- In advance:
  - Prepare the assessment research folders. Note where these materials can be accessed. These guides are updated regularly, and it is important that students are given the most up-to-date information to research from:
    - Monterey Bay Aquarium Seafood Watch Pocket Guide: https://www.seafoodwatch.org/seafood-recommendations/consumer-guides, select your state
    - Marine Conservation Society's "Good Fish Guide": https://www.mcsuk.org/goodfishguide/search
- Post: learning targets.

Lesson Vocabulary

None

Materials

- Performance Task Prompt: Informative Consumer Guide (from Lesson 1)
- Mid-Unit 3 Assessment, Part 1: Researching Information about Buying Fish Caught Using Sustainable Methods (one per student; one for display)
- Colored pencils or markers (one for each student)
- Assessment research folder (one of each article per student; distributed by teacher during Work Time A)
  - "Choosing Sustainable"
  - "What We Eat Makes a Difference"
  - Monterey Bay Aquarium Seafood Watch Pocket Guide (see Teaching Notes regarding downloading best version)
  - Marine Conservation Society "Good Fish Guide" (see Teaching Notes regarding downloading best version)
- *World Without Fish*: Pages 150–153 and 160–164 up to "We need more information" on page 164 (book; distributed in Unit 1; one per student)
- "How to Buy Fresh, Sustainable Seafood" video (see link in Teaching Notes)
- Evidence flags (three per student for homework)
- Structured Notes: Chapter 9 through Page 127 (one per student)
- Grade 6 2-Point Rubric—Short Response (Teacher Reference)

Opening

A. Unpacking Learning Targets (4 minutes)

- Direct students' attention to the posted learning targets and ask a volunteer to read them aloud:
  - "I can interpret information from different resources as part of my research about what consumers need to know about overfishing and fish depletion when buying fish."
  - "I can refine the research question to focus my research."
- Explain to students that in this lesson they will complete Part 1 of their Mid-Unit 3 Assessment, which is researching to find out more information to answer the question that will be the focus of their informative consumer guide: What do consumers need to know about sustainable fishing when buying fish?

Meeting Students' Needs

- Learning targets are a research-based strategy that helps all students, especially challenged learners.
- Posting learning targets allows students to reference them throughout the lesson to check their understanding. Learning targets also provide a reminder to students and teachers about the intended learning behind a given lesson or activity.

Work Time

A. Mid-Unit 3 Assessment, Part 1: Interpreting Resources (38 minutes)

- Ask students to take out their **Performance Task Prompt: Informative Consumer Guide**; display a copy and invite students to refer to their own copies.
- Direct students' attention to the list of requirements for the informative consumer guide, focusing students on the fourth bullet: "Suggestions: ways to buy fish that have been caught using sustainable methods."
- Display and distribute the **Mid-Unit 3 Assessment, Part 1: Researching Information about Buying Fish Caught Using Sustainable Methods**.
- Invite students to read through the directions with you and the columns of the graphic organizer.
- Point out that the graphic organizer on the Mid-Unit 3 Assessment should look familiar to them, as it is identical to the Researching Graphic Organizer they used in Lessons 2–4.
- Invite students to ask any questions they may have about the assessment. Ensure you do not answer any of the assessment questions students are expected to answer.
- Distribute **assessment research folders**.

- Also direct students to the relevant pages in **World Without Fish** by posting those page numbers:
  - Pages 150–153
  - Page 160–164 up to "We need more information" on page 164
- Explain that students should analyze each resource in the folder and the posted pages of *World Without Fish* using their Mid-Unit 3 Assessment graphic organizer.
- If you are going to play the **"How to Buy Fresh, Sustainable Seafood"** video to the whole group at once, you may choose to play it here a couple of times before they begin working with the assessment research folders; however, if you have set it up for students to watch the video on devices independently, explain to students how this will work.
- Remind them that since this is an assessment, they will be doing it individually. They are not to discuss their ideas with other students. Ask students to begin.
- Circulate to answer students' questions. Some students may require additional support in reading some of the texts.
- Collect students' Mid-Unit 3 Assessments and assessment research folders.

Meeting Students' Needs

- For some students, this assessment may require more than the 38 minutes allotted. Consider providing students time over multiple days if necessary.
- If students receive accommodations for assessments, communicate with the cooperating service providers regarding the practices of instruction in use during this study as well as the goals of the assessment.

Closing and Assessment

A. Debrief (3 minutes)

- Ask students to turn and talk with an elbow partner:
  - "What did you learn about buying fish caught using sustainable methods from the resources you analyzed and interpreted in this lesson?"
  - "Could any of this information be useful to use in your informative consumer guide?"
- Preview homework and distribute **Structured Notes: Chapter 9 through Page 127 and evidence flags**.

Meeting Students' Needs

The debrief after the assessment can help build a culture of achievement in your classroom.

Homework

- Read chapter 9 of *World Without Fish* to the end of page 127. Remember to record new words on your word-catcher. As you read, mark the text with evidence flags to help you answer the focus question on your structured notes:
    - According to Mark Kurlansky, what is pollution doing to fish? How?
- Continue to read your independent reading book.

Mid-Unit 3 Assessment, Part 1

Researching Information about Buying Fish Caught Using Sustainable Methods

Long-Term Learning Targets Assessed

- I can conduct short research projects to answer a question. (W.6.7)
- I can use several sources in my research. (W.6.7)
- I can refocus or refine my question when appropriate. (W.6.7)
- I can interpret information presented in different media and formats. (SL.6.2)
- I can explain how new information connects to a topic, text, or issue I am studying. (SL.6.2)

Focus question: What do consumers need to know about overfishing and fish depletion when buying fish?

Refined research question:

_____

_____

Directions

1. Choose a resource.
2. Read through it carefully using the glossary to help you understand what it means.
3. Reread the text and consider how it answers your questions.
    a. What factual information is included to answer the main question: What do consumers need to know about sustainable fishing when buying fish?
    b. Which quotes are the most compelling to make the consumer want to read on?
4. Underline factual information in one color.
5. Underline compelling quotes in another color.
6. Record the source in the first column (title and author).
7. Record the factual information and quotes that you have underlined in the second column. Make sure you copy quotes word for word in quotation marks.
8. In the third column, describe how this fact answers the question: What do consumers need to know about sustainable fishing when buying fish?
9. Repeat with another resource.

Source (title and author)	Information/Quotes (copy quotes word for word in quotation marks)	How does it answer the question?

Choosing Sustainable

Sustainable seafood is a hot topic these days. "Sustainability" is based on a simple principle—meeting today's needs without compromising the ability of future generations to meet their needs. In terms of seafood, this means catching or farming seafood responsibly, with consideration for the long-term health of the environment and the livelihoods of the people that depend upon the environment.

How do you know the seafood at the market or on your menu came from sustainable sources? Here are some tips that can guide you and your purchases to support sustainable practices:

- If it's harvested in the United States, it is inherently sustainable as a result of the rigorous U.S. management process that ensures fisheries are continuously monitored, improved, and sustainable.
- Stay informed and make sure you're using the most up-to-date, credible resources. FishWatch is one of those resources.
- Buy seafood from knowledgeable, reputable dealers. Many retailers and chefs are implementing seafood purchasing policies, making sustainable sourcing a priority.
- Ask questions about seafood to learn how to identify high-quality, sustainable seafood. Where is it from? Does that country manage its fisheries sustainably?
- Imported seafood can also be safe and sustainable, but comes from a variety of sources and may not be produced to the same standards as U.S. seafood. In the United States, our standard is sustainability.

Be sure to follow the tips above to make sure you know the facts about your seafood.

Guides, Eco-Labels, and Fishwatch

Over the years, many organizations have developed seafood guides, ecolabels, and certification programs to guide seafood purchasing. The majority of these products are based on the scientific data and standards that NOAA Fisheries uses to manage and enforce U.S. fisheries.

Seafood guides: A number of nonprofit organizations have created seafood guides that rate seafood, typically based on environmental and biological criteria for species, fisheries, or aquaculture practices. The ratings found in these guides generally reflect an organization's policy stance regarding these issues, and as a result, the guides sometimes contradict each other.

Eco-labels: An eco-label is a "seal of approval" awarded to fisheries and aquaculture operations deemed sustainable and responsible by third-party certification bodies. The certification process typically involves an assessment of the operation of the fishery or farm, how it's regulated, and its impact on the environment. If the fishery or farm meets the eco-label's standards, it is certified. Eco-labels also often include chain of custody requirements: the measures that guarantee the product bearing the eco-label really came from the certified fishery or farm. It's important to note, however, that the certification process can require a large investment of time and money—resources that some fisheries and aquaculture operations cannot afford.

Source: Courtesy NOAA Fisheries.

FishWatch: FishWatch does not rank or rate one species or fishery over another because the species profiled are being legally harvested under the responsible fisheries management process of the United States. With FishWatch, you have access to the most up-to-date information on the status, science, and enforcement sustaining our nation's fisheries and the seafood they provide. Remember that you have a choice when purchasing seafood—make it a smart one. FishWatch can help you support U.S. fisheries and seafood jobs and make sustainable choices.

Glossary: "Choosing Sustainable"

Choosing Sustainable	
livelihoods	Income
inherently	Exists permanently
credible	Trustworthy
implementing	Putting in place
imported	Brought in from other places
aquaculture	The farming of things that live in water
deemed	Considered to be
third-party	People from outside who do not work for the company being certified
chain of custody requirements	Collecting all of the evidence to prove that something is what it claims to be

What We Eat Makes a Difference

What We Eat Makes a Difference

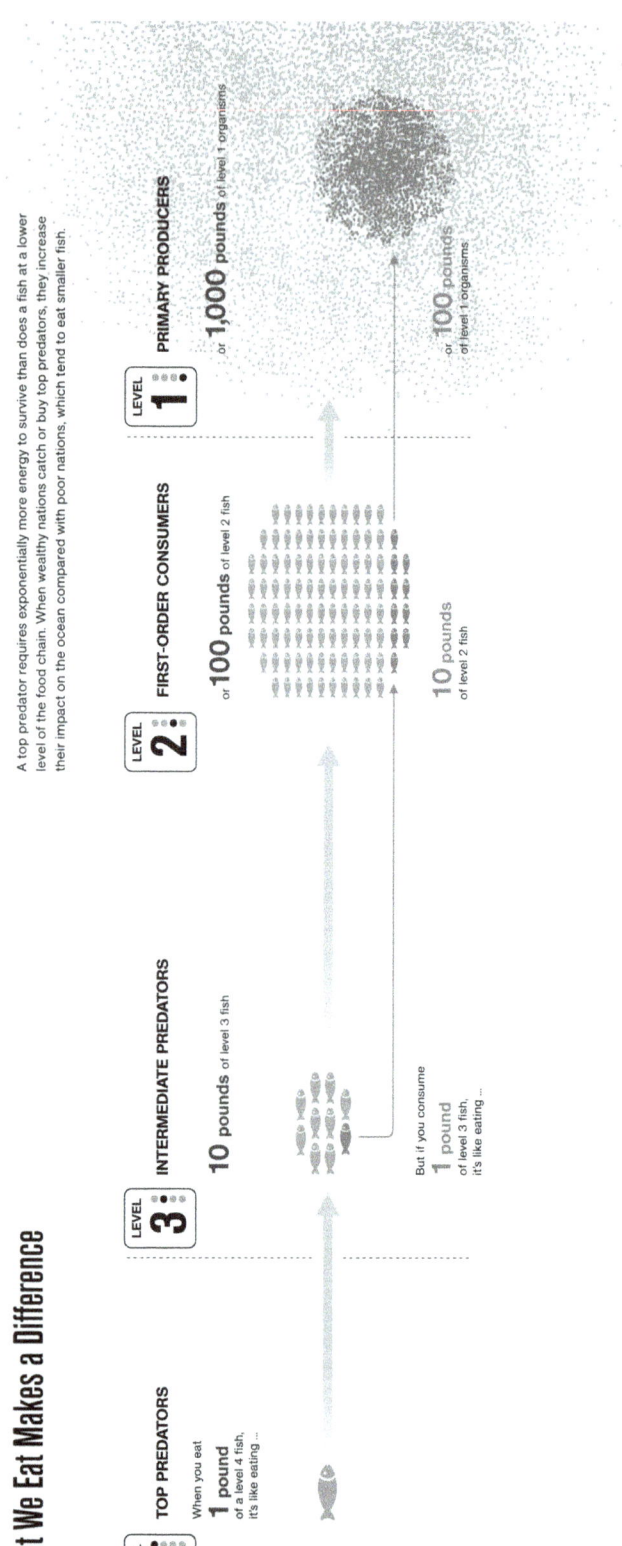

Copyright © National Geographic. Used by permission and not subject to Creative Commons license.

Structured Notes: Chapter 9 through Page 127

Name: _____

Date: _____

Chapter	Homework Focus Question	Answer with Evidence from the Text (include page number)
_____	According to Mark Kurlansky, what is pollution doing to fish? How?	

TEACHER GUIDE AND RESOURCE BOOK • Grade 6 • Module 3B • Unit 3 • Lesson 5 Supporting Materials   453

Grade 6 2-Point Rubric—Short Response
(Teacher Reference)

Use the following rubric for determining scores on short answers in this assessment.

The features of a **2-point response** are:

- Valid inferences and/or claims from the text where required by the prompt
- Evidence of analysis of the text where required by the prompt
- Relevant facts, definitions, concrete details, and/or other information from the text to develop response according to the requirements of the prompt
- Sufficient number of facts, definitions, concrete details, and/or other information from the text as required by the prompt
- Complete sentences where errors do not impact readability

The features of a **1-point response** are:

- A mostly literal recounting of events or details from the text as required by the prompt
- Some relevant facts, definitions, concrete details, and/or other information from the text to develop response according to the requirements of the prompt
- Incomplete sentences or bullets

The features of a **0-point response** are:

- A response that does not address any of the requirements of the prompt or is totally inaccurate
- No response (blank answer)
- A response that is not written in English
- A response that is unintelligible or indecipherable

If the prompt requires two texts and the student references only one text, the response can be scored no higher than a 1.

LESSON 6

Mid-Unit 3 Assessment, Part 2
Explaining How New Information Connects to the Topic

Long-Term Targets Addressed (Based on ELA CCSS)

- I can interpret information presented in different media and formats. (SL.6.2)
- I can explain how new information connects to a topic, text, or issue I am studying. (SL.6.2)

Supporting Learning Target

- I can explain how the new information I found through research deepens my understanding of what consumers need to know about overfishing and fish depletion when buying fish.

Ongoing Assessment

- Structured Notes: Chapter 9, Pages 128–134
- Mid-Unit 3 Assessment, Part 2: Explaining How New Information Connects to the Topic (oral)

Agenda

1. Opening
   A. Unpacking Learning Targets (2 minutes)
2. Work Time
   A. Mid-Unit 3 Assessment, Part 2: Explaining How New Information Connects to a Topic (40 minutes)
3. Closing and Assessment
   A. Debrief (3 minutes)

4. Homework

   A. Read to the end of chapter 9 of *World Without Fish*. Remember to record new words on your word-catcher. As you read, mark the text with evidence flags to help you continue to answer the focus question on your structured notes:

   - According to Mark Kurlansky, what is pollution doing to fish? How?

   B. Continue to read your independent reading book.

Teaching Notes

- In this lesson, students complete Part 2 of the Mid-Unit 3 Assessment. For this part of the assessment, students explain orally in a triad discussion how the resources they analyzed in Part 1 of the assessment deepen their understanding of what consumers need to know about sustainable fishing when buying fish. You will observe, in order to assess SL.6.2.
- Depending on the size of your class, you may need to spend more than the allocated time on this assessment.
- Work Time A includes discussion questions that enable you to score students' achievement of SL.6.2. Assess students' responses using the Mid-Unit 3 Assessment, Part 2: Explaining How New Information Connects to the Topic, Rubric provided in the supporting materials. Note that you will need to return the assessment with feedback in Lesson 9.
- In advance:
  - Prepare and post a discussion schedule so students can see when they will take part in the discussion with you. When they are not participating in their discussion, they should focus on independent reading or an independent reading assessment that you prepare.
  - This may be a good time to assess the independent reading standards RL.6.11.a and RL.6.11.b. See Launching Independent Reading in Grades 6–8: Sample Plan
- Post: learning target.

Lesson Vocabulary

None

Materials

- Discussion schedule (new; teacher-created, see Teaching Notes; one to display)
- Mid-Unit 3 Assessment, Part 1 (from Lesson 5; students' completed copies)
- Assessment research folders (from Lesson 5)
- Mid-Unit 3 Assessment, Part 2: Explaining How New Information Connects to the Topic Rubric (one per student)
- Evidence flags (three per student for homework)
- Structured Notes: Chapter 9, Pages 128–134 (one per student)

Opening

A. Unpacking Learning Target (2 minutes)

- Direct students' attention to the posted learning target and ask for a volunteer to read it aloud:
  - "I can explain how the new information I found through research deepens my understanding of what consumers need to know about overfishing and fish depletion when buying fish."
- Explain to students that in this lesson they are going to be finishing their Mid-Unit 3 Assessment by having a discussion with you.
- Point to the posted **discussion schedule**.

Meeting Students' Needs

- Learning targets are a research-based strategy that helps all students, especially challenged learners.
- Posting learning targets allows students to reference them throughout the lesson to check their understanding. Learning targets also provide a reminder to students and teachers about the intended learning behind a given lesson or activity.

Work Time

A. Mid-Unit 3 Assessment, Part 2: Explaining How New Information Connects to the Topic (40 minutes)

- Set students on independent reading and/or an independent reading assessment (see Teaching Notes).
- Invite students to get into triads.
- Hand back students' **Mid-Unit 3 Assessment, Part 1** and **assessment research folders**.
- Invite the first triad to take their Mid-Unit 3 Assessment, Part 1 and assessment research folders and move to meet with you.
- Ask this triad to discuss:
  - "What do you now know about sustainable fishing when buying fish that you didn't know before you saw those resources?"
  - "What factual information did you find out? Which resource did it come from? How did it answer the question?"
  - "What compelling quotes did you find? Which resource did it come from? How did they deepen your understanding?"
- Ensure all students contribute. If students do not contribute, cold-call on them to do so.

- Assess each student using the **Mid-Unit 3 Assessment, Part 2: Explaining How New Information Connects to the Topic Rubric**.
- Collect the **Mid-Unit 3 Assessment: Part 1** and the assessment research folder to review and provide feedback in time for Lesson 9.

Meeting Students' Needs

If students receive accommodations for assessments, communicate with the cooperating service providers regarding the practices of instruction in use during this study as well as the goals of the assessment.

Closing and Assessment

A. Debrief (3 minutes)

- Refocus the whole group.
- Ask students to discuss in triads:
  - "Now that you have done all of your research, what do you think your next steps should be in creating your informative consumer guide?"
- Select volunteers to share their responses.
- Guide students to understand that now they need to evaluate their factual information and quotes to determine which ones they will use in their informative consumer guides.
- Preview homework and distribute **Structured Notes: Chapter 9, Pages 128–134** and **evidence flags**.

Meeting Students' Needs

The debrief after the assessment can help build a culture of achievement in your classroom.

Homework

- Read to the end of chapter 9 of *World Without Fish*. Remember to record new words on your word-catcher. As you read, mark the text with evidence flags to help you continue to answer the focus question on your structured notes:
  - According to Mark Kurlansky, what is pollution doing to fish? How?
- Continue to read your independent reading book.

Mid-Unit 3 Assessment, Part 2

Explaining How New Information Connects to the Topic Rubric

Name: _____

Date: _____

	4	3	2	1
Student interprets information presented in diverse media and formats (e.g., visually, quantitatively, orally) and explains how it contributes to a topic, text, or issue under study.	Student clearly explains the content of the resource and how it deepens his/her understanding of what consumers need to know about sustainable fishing when buying fish.	Student explains the content of the resource and how it deepens his/her understanding of what consumers need to know about sustainable fishing when buying fish.	Student has a basic understanding of the content of the resource and how it deepens his/her understanding of what consumers need to know about sustainable fishing when buying fish.	Student struggles to explain the content of the resource and how it deepens his/her understanding of what consumers need to know about sustainable fishing when buying fish.

Structured Notes: Chapter 9, Pages 128–134

Name: _____

Date: _____

Chapter	Homework Focus Question	Answer with Evidence from the Text (include page number)
_____	According to Mark Kurlansky, what is pollution doing to fish? How?	

LESSON 7

Evaluating Research

Long-Term Targets Addressed (Based on ELA CCSS)

- I can write informative/explanatory texts that convey ideas and concepts using relevant information that is carefully selected and organized. (W.6.2)
- I can use evidence from a variety of grade-appropriate texts to support analysis, reflection, and research. (W.6.9)

Supporting Learning Target

- I can evaluate research to choose the most relevant and compelling factual information and quotes for my consumer guide.

Ongoing Assessment

- Structured Notes: Chapter 9 of *World Without Fish* (from homework)
- Circled information and quotes on Researching Graphic Organizer from Lesson 2

Agenda

1. Opening
   A. Engaging the Reader: Chapter 9 of *World Without Fish* (10 minutes)
   B. Unpacking Learning Targets (3 minutes)
2. Work Time
   A. Identifying Relevant and Compelling Factual Information and Quotes (22 minutes)
3. Closing and Assessment
   A. Pair Share (10 minutes)

4. Homework

   A. Read chapter 10 of *World Without Fish*. Remember to record new words on your word-catcher. As you read, mark the text with evidence flags to help you answer the focus question on your structured notes:

   • According to Mark Kurlansky, what is global warming doing to fish? How?

   B. Continue to read your independent reading book.

Teaching Notes

- In this lesson, students evaluate the information and quotes they recorded on their Researching Graphic Organizers in Lesson 2 about the issue of overfishing and fish depletion to identify relevant and compelling information to use in their informative consumer guides. Students may find this challenging and may require more modeling than the lesson suggests.

- In the next lesson, students will use the information and quotes they select to begin writing their informative consumer guide.

- Emphasize to students that they are continuing to read *World Without Fish* for homework because while they are not discussing other issues that he discusses, like pollution, on their informative consumer guides, it is important for them to understand all of the ideas Mark Kurlansky suggests in his book so they have an idea of the bigger picture of fish depletion outside overfishing. Explain that it is also important for them to recognize the connections between the texts they have been reading across the module.

- In advance:
  - Review: Back-to-Back and Face-to-Face protocol (see Appendix).
- Post: learning target.

Lesson Vocabulary

evaluate

Materials

- Structured Notes: Chapter 9, Pages 128–134 (from homework)
- Performance Task Prompt: Informative Consumer Guide (from Lesson 1)
- Researching Graphic Organizer (from Lesson 2)
- Evidence flags (three per student for homework)
- Structured Notes: Chapter 10 (one copy per student)

Opening

A. Engaging the Reader: Chapter 9 of *World Without Fish* (10 minutes)

- Remind students of the homework: read the rest of chapter 9 of *World Without Fish* and answer the focus question.
- Invite students to take out their **Structured Notes: Chapter 9, Pages 128–134**.
- Tell students they will now use the Back-to-Back and Face-to-Face protocol to review what they wrote in their structured notes.
- Review the protocol as necessary.
- Back-to-Back, Face-to-Face:
    1. Pair students up and ask them to sit back-to-back.
    2. Ask them the homework focus questions: "According to Mark Kurlansky, what is pollution doing to fish? How?"
    3. Ask students to review the answers to the questions on their structured notes.
    4. Invite students to turn face-to-face to share their answers.
    5. Ask students to return to their seats.
- Invite students to make revisions as necessary based on the discussions they just had.
- Select volunteers to share their answers with the whole group. Listen for students to explain that pollution, like oil and poisonous metals, are consumed and poison sea life. Other sea life then eats the poisoned sea life and becomes poisoned and so on and so forth.
- Ask students to turn and talk:
    - "How does this issue link to *Flush* and the work you did in Unit 2?"
- Select volunteers to share their responses. Listen for students to explain that a big idea in *Flush* is the way dumping bad things in the water can kill marine life, which is exactly what chapter 9 in *World Without Fish* is all about.
- Emphasize to students here that while they are not discussing pollution on their informative consumer guides, it is important to understand all of the ideas that Mark Kurlansky suggests in his book to have an idea of the bigger picture of fish depletion outside overfishing. Explain that it is also important for them to recognize the connections between the texts they have been reading across the module.

Meeting Students' Needs

- Opening the lesson by asking students to share their homework makes them accountable for completing it. It also gives you the opportunity to monitor which students are not doing their homework.
- Consider pairing ELL students who speak the same first language to deepen their discussion and understanding.

B. Unpacking Learning Targets (3 minutes)

- Direct students' attention to the posted learning target and read it aloud:
  - "I can evaluate research to choose the most relevant and compelling factual information and quotes for my consumer guide."
- Ask students to turn and talk:
  - "What does *evaluate* mean?"
  - "Why do you need to do evaluate your information? Why not just use all of the information and quotes you have collected?"
- Cold-call students to share their ideas with the whole group. Listen for students to explain that *evaluate* means to compare the research recorded to determine which is the most relevant and compelling to use in their informative consumer guide. Listen also for students to explain that they can't use all of the information and quotes they have collected in research because the informative consumer guide needs to fit on one piece of letter paper.

Work Time

A. Identifying Relevant and Compelling Factual Information and Quotes (22 minutes)

- Explain to students that now that they have collected all of the factual information and quotes they need for their informative consumer guide, they now need to think about the content of their guides. They have collected a lot of information and now they need to determine what is most relevant and compelling.
- Ask students to take out their copy of the **Performance Task Prompt: Informative Consumer Guide** and reread it, focusing particularly on the text: "Your informative consumer guide needs to include relevant and compelling factual information and quotes about: The issue: overfishing and how it causes fish depletion."
- Remind students that their informative consumer guide needs to be no longer than one piece of letter-sized paper. Therefore, they need to select the information that is most relevant and compelling while providing all of the essential information consumers will need to buy fish caught using sustainable fishing methods.
- Explain that in this lesson, students are going to evaluate their information and quotes from Lesson 2 about how overfishing causes fish depletion to choose what to use in their informative consumer guide.
- Invite students to take out their **Researching Graphic Organizer** from Lesson 2.
- Ask one student to borrow their Researching Graphic Organizer and display it for the class.
- Model how to evaluate the information on the graphic organizer and choose the most relevant and compelling information about how overfishing can cause fish depletion.

- Go through each piece of information and ask students:
  - "Is this something that consumers must know to understand the issue of overfishing and how it causes fish depletion?"
  - "Is it relevant?"
  - "Is it compelling?"
- Ask for a show of hands for those who think the information should be used. Select a student to explain why it should be used.
- Tell students that until they start looking at their own information and quotes, it is okay if they aren't sure yet. If they think there is a chance they might like to use it, encourage them to put a star next to the information or quote.
- Repeat with the next few pieces of information and quotes recorded on the graphic organizer.
- Once you have at least two pieces of information and/or quotes starred, invite students to compare those pieces of information and also to consider whether any of the quotes that have been starred support the recorded information.
- Ask students:
  - "Are both of these starred pieces of information/quotes necessary for consumers to know?"
  - "Is there one that is more relevant and compelling?"
  - "Does the quote support any of the pieces of information you have recorded? Or does it provide relevant information in a compelling way itself?"
- The information/quotes that students want to use should be circled; use your judgment and student input to determine whether or not to circle any starred information on the students' graphic organizers.
- Invite students to work together in pairs to evaluate all of the factual information and quotes in their Researching Graphic Organizers to identify the most relevant and compelling of those on the issue of overfishing and fish depletion.
- Circulate to assist students. Ask guiding questions:
  - "Why have you put a star next to this?"
  - "Why do people need to know this information?"
  - "Which of these pieces of information/quotes about overfishing is most relevant and compelling? Or do you need to use them both?"
  - "Does the quote support a particular piece of information? Or does it provide relevant information in a compelling way itself?"

Meeting Students' Needs

Modeling the activity for students can provide them with the expectations you have of their independent work. It can also provide students with the confidence to work independently, giving you time to support students who require additional support.

Closing and Assessment

A. Pair Share (10 minutes)

- Invite students to get into new pairs to share their circled information and quotes and to justify why they have chosen them.
- Encourage students to help each other to ensure they have selected only the most relevant and compelling information and quotes.
- Remind students that they will only have one piece of letter-sized paper and they need to include the other information, like the case study, sustainable fishing methods, and suggestions for buying fish caught using sustainable methods, as well.
- Preview homework and distribute **Structured Notes: Chapter 10** and **evidence flags**.

Homework

- Read chapter 10 of *World Without Fish*. Remember to record new words on your word-catcher. As you read, mark the text with evidence flags to help you answer the focus question on your structured notes:
    - According to Mark Kurlansky, what is global warming doing to fish? How?
- Continue to read your independent reading book.

Structured Notes: Chapter 10

Name: _____

Date: _____

Chapter	Homework Focus Question	Answer with Evidence from the Text (include page number)
_____	According to Mark Kurlansky, what is global warming doing to fish? How?	

LESSON 8

Planning Content of Informative Consumer Guide

The Issue of Overfishing and Fish Depletion

Long-Term Targets Addressed (Based on ELA CCSS)

- I can write informative/explanatory texts that convey ideas and concepts using relevant information that is carefully selected and organized. (W.6.2)
- I can produce clear and coherent writing that is appropriate to task, purpose, and audience. (W.6.4)
- I can use evidence from a variety of grade-appropriate texts to support analysis, reflection, and research. (W.6.9)

Supporting Learning Targets

- I can organize the information and quotes I have chosen about overfishing and the issue of fish depletion into a Quote Sandwich Graphic Organizer.
- I can evaluate research to choose the most relevant and compelling factual information and quotes for my informative consumer guide.

Ongoing Assessment

- Structured Notes: Chapter 10 of *World Without Fish* (from homework)
- Quote Sandwich Graphic Organizer for the issue of overfishing and fish depletion
- Circled information and quotes on Researching Graphic Organizer from Lessons 2 and 3

Agenda

1. Opening
   A. Engaging the Reader: Chapter 10 of *World Without Fish* (5 minutes)
   B. Unpacking Learning Targets (3 minutes)

2. Work Time
   A. Modeling the Quote Sandwich (8 minutes)
   B. Working on a Quote Sandwich (12 minutes)
   C. Identifying Relevant and Compelling Factual Information and Quotes (10 minutes)
3. Closing and Assessment
   A. Pair Share (7 minutes)
4. Homework
   A. Using the information and quotes you have circled about a depleted fish species on your Researching Graphic Organizer from Lesson 3, complete the Quote Sandwich Graphic Organizer to plan the paragraph for your informative consumer guide. Remember that you may not be able to use all of the information and quotes you have circled, in which case you may need to reevaluate which ones you use.
   B. Continue reading your independent reading book.

Teaching Notes

- This lesson begins with students revisiting what they read in chapter 10 for homework. As global warming can be a controversial issue, make it clear to students that this is Mark Kurlansky's opinion, but that other people may have different opinions about global warming.

- Emphasize to students that they are continuing to read *World Without Fish* for homework because while they are not discussing other issues that he discusses, like global warming, in their informative consumer guides, it is important to understand all of the ideas that Mark Kurlansky suggests in his book to have an idea of the bigger picture of fish depletion outside overfishing.

- In this lesson, students use the Quote Sandwich Graphic Organizer to arrange their chosen information and quotes about overfishing and fish depletion into a paragraph that could be used in their informative consumer guide. The process of filling in a Quote Sandwich Graphic Organizer is modeled in this lesson with a paragraph from the model informative consumer guide. Students are then released to practice independently.

- Students then evaluate the information and quotes gathered on their Researching Graphic Organizers from Lesson 3 about the depleted fish species (case study) in the same way they evaluated the information and quotes about overfishing in the previous lesson.

- For homework, students organize their information and quotes about the depleted fish species (case study) onto a new Quote Sandwich Graphic Organizer. This will further prepare them to complete their informative consumer guide.

- In advance:
  - Plan to return students' Mid-Unit 3 Assessments in Lesson 9, with your feedback.
- Post: learning targets.

Lesson Vocabulary

evaluate

Materials

- Structured Notes: Chapter 10 (from homework)
- Model Informative Consumer Guide (from Lesson 1)
- Model Quote Sandwich Graphic Organizer: Are You Buying Fruits and Vegetables Today? (one to display)
- Quote Sandwich Graphic Organizers (two per student)
- Researching Graphic Organizer: Lesson 2 (students' completed organizers)
- Performance Task Prompt: Informative Consumer Guide (from Lesson 1)
- Researching Graphic Organizers: Lesson 3 (students' completed organizers)

Opening

A. Engaging the Reader: Chapter 10 of *World Without Fish* (5 minutes)

- Remind students of the homework: read chapter 10 of *World Without Fish* and answer the focus questions: According to Mark Kurlansky, what is global warming doing to fish? How?
- Invite students to take out their **Structured Notes: Chapter 10.**
- Ask students to pair up to share their answers on their structured notes and to make revisions where they think necessary.
- Select volunteers to share their answers with the whole group. Listen for students to explain that Kurlansky thinks global warming could kill fish because some species of fish need cold ocean temperatures. Listen for students to also explain that he thinks global warming is melting the polar ice caps, which over time will cause the water to be less salty and could kill some species of fish.
- Emphasize to students that they are continuing to read *World Without Fish* for homework because while they are not discussing other issues that he discusses, like global warming, on their informative consumer guides, it is important for them to understand all of the ideas that Mark Kurlansky suggests in his book to have an idea of the bigger picture of fish depletion outside overfishing. Remind students that if they only read about overfishing, they only understand one of the three problems that he highlights.

Meeting Students' Needs

- Opening the lesson by asking students to share their homework makes them accountable for completing it. It also gives you the opportunity to monitor which students are not doing their homework.
- Consider pairing ELL students who speak the same first language to deepen their discussion and understanding.

B. Unpacking Learning Targets (3 minutes)

- Direct students' attention to the posted learning targets and read them aloud:
  - "I can organize the information and quotes I have chosen about overfishing and the issue of fish depletion into a Quote Sandwich Graphic Organizer."
  - "I can evaluate research to choose the most relevant and compelling factual information and quotes for my informative consumer guide."
- Remind students that they have used the Quote Sandwich Graphic Organizers in Module 2 to organize their evidence.
- Remind students also of what *evaluate* means.

Meeting Students' Needs

- Reviewing key academic vocabulary in learning targets can prepare students for vocabulary they may encounter in the lesson.
- Posting learning targets allows students to reference them throughout the lesson to check their understanding. Learning targets also provide a reminder to students and teachers about the intended learning behind a given lesson or activity.

Work Time

A. Modeling the Quote Sandwich (8 minutes)

- Have students retrieve their copy of the **Model Informative Consumer Guide** from Lesson 1.
- Invite them to reread the first paragraph of the model aloud.
- Display **Model Quote Sandwich Graphic Organizer: Are You Buying Fruits and Vegetables Today?**
- Point out the three parts of the Quote Sandwich.
- Invite students to discuss with an elbow partner:
  - "How has the author used the Quote Sandwich to plan this paragraph?"
- Select volunteers to share their responses. Listen for them to explain that each part of the Quote Sandwich is a part of the paragraph. In organizing the information and quotes on the Quote Sandwich, the author has planned the content of the paragraph.
- Make sure students understand that while the quote is in the middle, there is also researched information to introduce the issue. Students should combine their researched information and quotes using the Quote Sandwich Graphic Organizer.

Meeting Students' Needs

Showing a model of a completed organizer that is connected to the model essay guides students in the expectations you have of them.

B. Working on a Quote Sandwich (12 minutes)

- Distribute the **Quote Sandwich Graphic Organizer**.
- Explain that students will do the same thing that you have modeled, independently using the evidence they have circled on their **Researching Graphic Organizer: Lesson 2**.
- Explain to students that they may not be able to use all of the information and quotes they have circled, in which case they may need to reevaluate and choose new ones.
- They may discuss ideas with an elbow partner, but this work is to be their own. Invite students to begin working.
- Circulate to support students in filling in their organizers. Ask guiding questions:
  - "How can you introduce the issue? What information do you have from research that would introduce the issue well?"
  - "How can you include the quotes you have selected?"
  - "How can you explain the quotes you have selected? Do you have any other information that you can use to explain the quotes you have selected?"

Meeting Students' Needs

Consider seating students who may need additional support in one area to work with them as a group.

C. Identifying Relevant and Compelling Factual Information and Quotes (10 minutes)

- Ask students to take out their copy of the **Performance Task Prompt: Informative Consumer Guide** and reread it, focusing particularly on the text: "Your informative consumer guide needs to include relevant and compelling factual information and quotes about: A case study of a fish species that has been severely depleted and the impact that it has had."
- Remind students that their informative consumer guide needs to be no longer than one piece of letter-sized paper containing all of the information listed in the bullet points, so they need to select the information that is most relevant and compelling while providing all of the information the consumers will need to buy fish caught using more sustainable fishing methods.
- Explain that for the rest of this lesson, students will evaluate their information and quotes about a depleted fish species from Lesson 3 to choose what to use in their informative consumer guide.
- Remind students they did this in the previous lesson for the information and quotes they had researched about overfishing and fish depletion.
- Invite students to take out their **Researching Graphic Organizer: Lesson 3**.
- Invite students to work together in pairs to evaluate all of the factual information and quotes in their Researching Graphic Organizers to identify the most relevant and compelling of those on the issue of overfishing and fish depletion.

- Circulate to assist students. Ask guiding questions:
  - "Why have you put a star next to this?"
  - "Why do people need to know this information?"
  - "Which of these pieces of information/quotes about the depleted fish species is most relevant and compelling? Or do you need to use them both?"
  - "Does the quote support a particular piece of information? Or does it provide relevant information in a compelling way itself?"

Meeting Students' Needs

Modeling the activity for students can provide them with the expectations you have of their independent work. It can also provide students with the confidence to work independently, giving you time to support students who require additional support.

Closing and Assessment

A. Pair Share (7 minutes)

- Invite students to get into new pairs to share the information and quotes they have circled and to justify why they have circled them.
- Encourage students to help each other to ensure they have only selected the most relevant and compelling information and quotes. Remind students that they will only have one piece of letter-sized paper, and they need to include other information, like the case study, sustainable fishing methods, and suggestions for buying fish caught using sustainable methods, as well.
- Distribute a new Quote Sandwich Graphic Organizer to each student.

Homework

- Using the information and quotes you have circled about a depleted fish species on your Researching Graphic Organizer from Lesson 3, complete the Quote Sandwich Graphic Organizer to plan the paragraph for your informative consumer guide. Remember that you may not be able to use all of the information and quotes you have circled, in which case you may need to reevaluate which ones you use.
- Continue reading your independent reading book.

Model Quote Sandwich Graphic Organizer

Are You Buying Fruits and Vegetables Today?

A sandwich is made up of three parts—the bread on top, the filling in the middle, and the bread on the bottom. A "Quote Sandwich" is similar; it is how you use evidence in your writing. First, you introduce evidence. Then, you include the evidence. Last, you explain the evidence.

Introduce the Evidence

Some fruits and vegetables are grown using chemical pesticides and fertilizers to prevent, destroy, and reduce the possibility of pests, rodents, weeds, fungi, bacteria, and viruses; however, research suggests that consuming fruits and vegetables sprayed with chemical pesticides and fertilizers can have a negative impact on our health.

Include the Evidence (in quotation marks)

The U.S. Environmental Protection Agency website explains that "By their nature, most pesticides create some risk of harm—pesticides can cause harm to humans, animals, or the environment because they are designed to kill or otherwise adversely affect living organisms."

Explain the Evidence

When buying fruits and vegetables, consumers should know that there are options that haven't been sprayed with pesticides and fertilizers during the growing process.

Some fruits and vegetables are grown using chemical pesticides and fertilizers to prevent, destroy, and reduce the possibility of pests, rodents, weeds, fungi, bacteria, and viruses; however, research suggests that consuming fruits and vegetables sprayed with chemical pesticides and fertilizers can have a negative impact on our health. The U.S. Environmental Protection Agency website explains that "By their nature, most pesticides create some risk of harm—pesticides can cause harm to humans, animals, or the environment because they are designed to kill or otherwise adversely affect living organisms." When buying fruits and vegetables, consumers should know that there are options that haven't been sprayed with pesticides and fertilizers during the growing process.

Quote Sandwich Graphic Organizer

Name: _____

Date: _____

A sandwich is made up of three parts—the bread on top, the filling in the middle, and the bread on the bottom. A "Quote Sandwich" is similar; it is how you use evidence in your writing. First, you introduce evidence. Then, you include the evidence. Last, you explain the evidence.

Subheading:

Introduce the Evidence

Include the Evidence (in quotation marks)

Explain the Evidence

LESSON 9

Planning Content of Informative Consumer Guide
Sustainable Fishing Methods

Long-Term Targets Addressed (Based on ELA CCSS)

- I can write informative/explanatory texts that convey ideas and concepts using relevant information that is carefully selected and organized. (W.6.2)
- I can produce clear and coherent writing that is appropriate to task, purpose, and audience. (W.6.4)
- I can use evidence from a variety of grade-appropriate texts to support analysis, reflection, and research. (W.6.9)

Supporting Learning Targets

- I can evaluate research to choose the most relevant and compelling factual information and quotes for my informative consumer guide.
- I can organize the information and quotes I have chosen about sustainable fishing methods into a Quote Sandwich Graphic Organizer.

Ongoing Assessment

- Circled information and quotes on Researching Graphic Organizer from Lesson 4
- Quote Sandwich for sustainable fishing methods
- Circled information and quotes on the graphic organizer from the Mid-Unit 3 Assessment (from Lesson 5)

Agenda

1. Opening
   A. Receiving Feedback from the Mid-Unit 3 Assessment (5 minutes)
   B. Unpacking Learning Targets (3 minutes)

2. Work Time
   A. Identifying Relevant and Compelling Factual Information and Quotes (10 minutes)
   B. Working on the Quote Sandwich (10 minutes)
   C. Identifying More Relevant and Compelling Factual Information and Quotes (10 minutes)
3. Closing and Assessment
   A. Whole-Group Share (7 minutes)
4. Homework
   A. Review and revise (where necessary, if at all) all of your completed Quote Sandwich Graphic Organizers. Look at the subheadings on the Model Informative Consumer Guide and notice how they are very short and guide the consumer to understand what will follow. Think of a short subheading for each of your Quote Sandwiches that accurately represents the information you are presenting.
   B. Continue reading your independent reading book.

Teaching Notes

- Be prepared to return students' Mid-Unit 3 Assessments from Lessons 5 and 6 with feedback at the beginning of this lesson.
- This lesson is very similar to Lesson 8; however, students begin by evaluating the information and quotes gathered in Lesson 4 about sustainable fishing methods and then use the Quote Sandwich Graphic Organizer to arrange their chosen information and quotes into a paragraph that could be used on their informative consumer guide.
- Students also evaluate the information and quotes gathered in Lesson 5 as part of the Mid-Unit 3 Assessment about suggestions for buying fish caught using sustainable fishing methods to choose the most relevant and compelling factual information and quotes; however, students will not complete a Quote Sandwich Graphic Organizer for buying fish caught using sustainable methods because this section should be a bulleted list on their informative consumer guide (see Model Informative Consumer Guide).
- Post: learning targets.

Lesson Vocabulary

evaluate

Materials

- Mid-Unit 3 Assessment, Parts 1 and 2 (from Lessons 5 and 6, with teacher feedback)
- Performance Task Prompt: Informative Consumer Guide (from Lesson 1)
- Researching Graphic Organizer: Lesson 4 (students' completed copies)
- Quote Sandwich Graphic Organizer (one per student)
- Model Informative Consumer Guide (from Lesson 1)

Opening

A. Receiving Feedback from the Mid-Unit 3 Assessment (5 minutes)

- Hand back students' **Mid-Unit 3 Assessments, Parts 1 and 2**.
- Invite students to spend time reading your feedback.
- Ask students to write their name on the board if they have questions so you can follow up either immediately or later on in the lesson.

B. Unpacking Learning Targets (3 minutes)

- Direct students' attention to the posted learning targets and ask for volunteers to read them aloud:
  - "I can evaluate research to choose the most relevant and compelling factual information and quotes for my informative consumer guide."
  - "I can organize the information and quotes I have chosen about sustainable fishing methods into a Quote Sandwich Graphic Organizer."
- Remind students that they practiced using Quote Sandwiches in the previous lesson and they have experience with them from Module 2 as well.
- Remind students also of what *evaluate* means.

Meeting Students' Needs

- Learning targets are a research-based strategy that helps all students, especially challenged learners.
- Reviewing the key academic vocabulary in learning targets can prepare students for vocabulary they may encounter in the lesson.
- Posting learning targets allows students to reference them throughout the lesson to check their understanding. Learning targets also provide a reminder to students and teachers about the intended learning behind a given lesson or activity.

Work Time

A. Identifying Relevant and Compelling Factual Information and Quotes (10 minutes)

- Ask students to take out their copy of the **Performance Task Prompt: Informative Consumer Guide** and reread it, focusing particularly on the text: "Your informative consumer guide needs to include relevant and compelling factual information and quotes about: A solution: sustainable methods for catching fish."
- Remind students that their informative consumer guide needs to be no longer than one piece of letter-sized paper containing all of the information listed in the bullet points, so they need to select the information that is most relevant and compelling while providing all of the information consumers will need to buy fish caught using more sustainable methods.

- Explain that they will evaluate their information and quotes about a depleted fish species from Lesson 4 to choose what to use in their informative consumer guide.
- Invite students to take out their **Researching Graphic Organizer: Lesson 4**.
- Ask students to work together in pairs to evaluate all of the factual information and quotes on their Researching Graphic Organizers to identify what is most relevant and compelling about sustainable fishing methods.
- Circulate to assist students. Ask guiding questions:
  - "Why have you put a star next to this?"
  - "Why do people need to know this information?"
  - "Which of these pieces of information/quotes about sustainable fishing methods is most relevant and compelling? Or do you need to use them both?"
  - "Does the quote support a particular piece of information? Or does it provide relevant information in a compelling way itself?"

B. Working on the Quote Sandwich (10 minutes)

- Distribute a new **Quote Sandwich Graphic Organizer**.
- Tell students that they are now going to organize the information and quotes about sustainable fishing methods they have circled on their Researching Graphic Organizer from Lesson 4.
- Remind students that they completed Quote Sandwich Graphic Organizers in the previous lesson for the issue of overfishing and for homework for a depleted fish species.
- Explain to them that they may not be able to use all of the information and quotes they have circled, in which case they may need to reevaluate and choose new ones.
- They may discuss ideas with an elbow partner, but this work is to be their own. Invite students to begin working.
- Circulate to support students in filling in their organizers. Ask guiding questions:
  - "How can you introduce sustainable fishing methods? What information do you have from research that would introduce them well?"
  - "How can you include the quotes you have selected?"
  - "How can you explain the quotes you have selected? Do you have any other information that you can use to explain the quote you have selected?"

Meeting Students' Needs

Consider seating students who may need additional support in one area to work with them as a group.

C. Identifying More Relevant and Compelling Factual Information and Quotes (10 minutes)

- Redirect students' attention to their Performance Task Prompt: Informative Consumer Guide.

- Invite them to reread the prompt, focusing particularly on the text: "Your informative consumer guide needs to include relevant and compelling factual information and quotes about: Suggestions: ways to buy fish that have been caught using sustainable methods."
- Display the **Model Informative Consumer Guide**.
- Invite students to reread the "What Can I Do?" section.
- Tell students that they need to include as many suggestions in their informative consumer guides as they can to give consumers as much help as possible in choosing fish that have been caught using sustainable methods.
- Invite students to refer to their Mid-Unit 3 Assessment, Part 1: Researching Information about Buying Fish Caught Using Sustainable Methods.
- Explain that this time, when evaluating, they still must choose relevant and compelling suggestions, but at the end they should have as many suggestions as possible.
- Invite students to work together in pairs to evaluate all of the factual information and quotes they have collected on their Researching Graphic Organizers to identify those that are most relevant and compelling about suggestions for buying fish caught using sustainable methods.
- Ask students to begin working.
- Circulate to assist students. Ask guiding questions:
  - "Why have you put a star next to this?"
  - "Why do people need to know this information?"
  - "How does it guide consumers toward what to buy?"

Closing and Assessment

A. Whole-Group Share (7 minutes)

- Tell students that they aren't going to complete a Quote Sandwich Graphic Organizer for the suggestions because, as seen on the model, these should be in a bulleted or numbered list rather than recorded in a paragraph to make them clear for consumers.
- Invite a volunteer to share his/her Quote Sandwich, completed for sustainable fishing methods, with the class.
- Invite the volunteer to read what he/she has recorded to the class and to justify the information and quotes chosen.
- Take the Quote Sandwich section by section and invite students to suggest ways each section could be improved. Ask them:
  - "This already looks good, but how can he or she make it better? Why?"
- Invite the volunteer to make any notes for revisions on his/her Quote Sandwiches.
- Tell students to remember the discussion and revisions suggested by the class when they review and revise their own Quote Sandwiches for homework.

Homework

- Review and revise (where necessary, if at all) all of your completed Quote Sandwich Graphic Organizers. Look at the subheadings on the Model Informative Consumer Guide and notice how they are very short and guide the consumer to understand what will follow. Think of a short subheading for each of your Quote Sandwiches that accurately represents the information you are presenting.

- Continue reading your independent reading book.

Quote Sandwich Graphic Organizer

Name: _____

Date: _____

A sandwich is made up of three parts—the bread on top, the filling in the middle, and the bread on the bottom. A "Quote Sandwich" is similar; it is how you use evidence in your writing. First, you introduce evidence. Then, you include the evidence. Last, you explain the evidence.

Subheading:

Introduce the Evidence

Include the Evidence (in quotation marks)

Explain the Evidence

LESSON 10

End-of-Unit 3 Assessment

Drafting the Informative Consumer Guide

Long-Term Targets Addressed (Based on ELA CCSS)

- I can write informative/explanatory texts that convey ideas and concepts using relevant information that is carefully selected and organized. (W.6.2)
- I can introduce the topic of my text. (W.6.2.a)
- I can organize my information using various strategies (e.g., definition/classification, comparison/contrast, cause/effect). (W.6.2.a)
- I can include headings, graphics, and multimedia to help readers understand my ideas. (W.6.2.a)
- I can develop the topic with relevant facts, definitions, concrete details, and quotations. (W.6.2.b)
- I can use transitions to clarify relationships among my ideas. (W.6.2.c)
- I can use contextually specific language/vocabulary to inform or explain about a topic. (W.6.2.d)
- I can establish and maintain a formal style in my writing. (W.6.2.e)
- I can construct a concluding statement or section of an informative/explanatory text. (W6.2.f)
- I can use evidence from a variety of grade-appropriate texts to support analysis, reflection, and research. (W.6.9)

Supporting Learning Targets

- I can use domain-specific vocabulary in my informative consumer guide.
- I can draft the written content of a relevant and compelling informative consumer guide to inform people who are buying fish about how and why to buy fish caught using sustainable methods.
- I can maintain a formal style in my writing.

Ongoing Assessment

- End-of-Unit 3 Assessment: Draft of Written Content of Informative Consumer Guide

Agenda

1. Opening
    A. Partner Feedback: Subheadings (3 minutes)
    B. Unpacking Learning Targets (4 minutes)
2. Work Time
    A. Language Mini Lesson: Formal Style (10 minutes)
    B. Drafting the Informative Consumer Guide (25 minutes)
3. Closing and Assessment
    A. Debrief (3 minutes)
4. Homework
    A. If you haven't already done so, finish writing the content of your informative consumer guide.
    B. Continue reading your independent reading book.

Teaching Notes

- In this lesson, students begin the End-of-Unit 3 Assessment. To do so, they draft the written content of their informative consumer guide using their Quote Sandwich Graphic Organizers. Make it clear to students that they do not have to plan the layout of their consumer guide or think about visual images or charts in this lesson. This is assessing only written content. The performance task will assess the completed guide.
- This is the first lesson in which students will draft their bulleted list of suggestions for ways to buy fish caught using sustainable fishing methods.
- Assess informative consumer guides against rows 1 and 3 of the Grades 6–8 Expository Writing Evaluation Rubric. Provide students with a star (something they have done well) and a step (something they could improve on) for each of rows 1 and 3 of the rubric. Students will need their drafts in Lesson 12 for a peer critique, but they will not need teacher feedback from the End-of-Unit 3 Assessment until Lesson 13.
- Students will need the draft for revision in Lesson 12; however, they don't need to receive teacher feedback until Lesson 13. You many chose to collect drafts from those students who finish during class time to have adequate time to have feedback ready for students in Lesson 13.
- Some students may need additional time to finish their drafts. Allow these students to take their work home to finish it, but emphasize that it must be returned in the next lesson so you can assess it.
- Post: learning targets.

Lesson Vocabulary

domain-specific vocabulary

Materials

- Quote Sandwich Graphic Organizers (from Lessons 8 and 9)
- Word-Catchers (completed across the module)
- Mid-Unit 3 Assessment, Part 1: Researching Information about Buying Fish Caught Using Sustainable Methods (completed in Lesson 5)
- End-of-Unit 3 Assessment: Draft of Written Content of Informative Consumer Guide (one per student)
- Performance Task Prompt: Informative Consumer Guide (from Lesson 1)
- Model Informative Consumer Guide (from Lesson 1)
- Model Quote Sandwich Graphic Organizer: Are You Buying Fruits and Vegetables Today? (from Lesson 8)
- Formal Style Examples (one to display)
- Formal Style Anchor Chart (new; co-created during Work Time A)
- Grades 6–8 Expository Writing Evaluation Rubric (from Lesson 1)

Opening

A. Partner Feedback: Subheadings (3 minutes)

- Invite students to take out their **Quote Sandwich Graphic Organizers**.
- Tell students they will be sharing the subheadings drafted for homework with a partner.
- Ask students to find an elbow partner to share with.
- Record the following sentence starters on the board:
    1. "Your subheadings lead me to expect . . . will follow"
    2. "The words that draw me in are . . ."
- Invite students to review the subheadings of their elbow partners' Quote Sandwiches and to use the two sentence starters provided to give feedback.
- Invite students to revise their headline and subheading based on the feedback they received if needed.

Meeting Students' Needs

Reviewing homework can hold students accountable for completing homework. It can also give you an opportunity to see who is completing homework and who isn't.

B. Unpacking Learning Targets (4 minutes)

- Direct students' attention to the posted learning targets and read them aloud:
    - "I can use domain-specific vocabulary in my informative consumer guide."
    - "I can draft the written content of a relevant and compelling informative consumer guide to inform people who are buying fish about how and why to buy fish caught using sustainable methods."
    - "I can maintain a formal style in my writing."
- Tell students that *domain-specific vocabulary* is words specific to a topic or study.
- Tell students to take out their **word-catchers** for the whole module.
- Ask students to consider:
    - "What words are good examples of domain-specific vocabulary that you want to use in your informative consumer guides?"
- Ask for volunteers and listen for examples such as: *trawling, depleted, extinct, hook-and-line, ecosystem, environment, by-catch*, etc.
- Consider making a Word Wall list from student examples that can be referenced while students are writing.
- Invite students to turn and talk:
    - "Now that you have seen the learning targets for this lesson, what do you think you will be doing today?"
- Listen for: "We are going to use our Quote Sandwich Graphic Organizers to draft the written content of our informative consumer guides, making sure we use domain-specific words."
- Remind students to use their Quote Sandwich Graphic Organizers for all of the sections they need to include apart from the suggestions for buying fish caught using sustainable methods. That section should be a bulleted or numbered list rather than a paragraph like the other sections. Remind students that they have circled the suggestions they would like to use on their **Mid-Unit 3 Assessment, Part 1: Researching Information about Buying Fish Caught Using Sustainable Methods**.
- Distribute **End-of-Unit 3 Assessment: Draft of Written Content of Informative Consumer Guide**.
- Invite students to read the directions.

Meeting Students' Needs

- Learning targets are a research-based strategy that helps all students, especially challenged learners.
- Posting learning targets allows students to reference them throughout the lesson to check their understanding. Learning targets also provide a reminder to students and teachers about the intended learning behind a given lesson or activity.

Work Time

A. Language Mini Lesson: Formal Style (10 minutes)

- Display the **Performance Task Prompt: Informative Consumer Guide** and invite students to reread it to ground themselves in what is expected of them on the End-of-Unit 3 Assessment.
- Ask students to take out their **Model Informative Consumer Guide** and **Model Quote Sandwich Graphic Organizer: Are You Buying Fruits and Vegetables Today?**
- Invite them to reread both of these documents.
- Ask students to turn and talk with an elbow partner:
  - "How did the author of the Model Informative Consumer Guide use the Quote Sandwich to write that paragraph of the model essay?"
- Select volunteers to share their responses. Listen for them to explain that the author joined the pieces of the Quote Sandwich together to write the paragraph.
- Explain that students are going to do exactly that as they draft the paragraphs for their informative consumer guide.
- Remind them that the learning target requests that they maintain a formal style.
- Display the **Formal Style Examples**.
- Explain that the first example is the paragraph from the Model Informative Consumer Guide, and the second example is a less formal version. Invite them to read both of the examples with you aloud.
- Ask students to turn and talk:
  - "In what ways does the first example sound more formal?"
- Cold-call students to share their responses. Listen for them to explain that the first example is more formal because it sounds like something you would read in a textbook—it sounds like the person writing is an expert who really knows what he or she is talking about, whereas the second example sounds like someone speaking to a friend. The vocabulary in the first example is more precise and complex, and the vocabulary in the second is simple and includes slang.
- Record students' responses on the **Formal Style Anchor Chart**. Ensure that the following are included:
  - Avoid using contractions (e.g., instead of *don't*, use *do not*).
  - Avoid using slang (e.g., instead of *awesome*, use *very good*).
  - Use more varied and mature vocabulary (e.g., *negative* instead of *bad*).

Meeting Students' Needs

Providing good and bad examples for students to compare can highlight the differences between good and bad work and provide them with guidelines and expectations.

B. Drafting the Informative Consumer Guide (25 minutes)

- Reassure students that they don't have to have the final informative consumer guide finished by the end of this lesson—just a draft of the written content. Make it clear that they will add images, charts, and graphs in the next lesson.
- Display the **Grades 6–8 Expository Writing Evaluation Rubric**. Invite students to read the level 3 column to remind themselves of what their writing should include.
- Direct student's attention to the Content and Analysis row, where it says: "Clearly introduce a topic in a manner that follows from the task and purpose."
- Ask students:
  - "What information are you going to include first to introduce the topic and to prepare the reader for what comes next?"
- Ask volunteers to share their responses. Listen for students to explain that they need to introduce their information about the issue of overfishing and fish depletion before anything else, so the reader understands the issue and understands why the rest of the information is important.
- Direct students' attention to Coherence, Organization, and Style row, third bullet, where it says: "Provide a concluding statement or section that follows from the topic and information presented."
- Ask students:
  - "What information are you going to use to conclude the informative consumer guide? What are you going to leave the consumer with to think about? Why?"
- Select volunteers to share their responses. Listen for students to explain that they need to finish with the suggestions for how to buy fish caught using sustainable methods, so the consumers remember and apply what they have learned when making their fish purchases.
- Tell students that now they are going to draft the written content of their informative consumer guides. Make it clear that students do not need to be concerned about the layout or the look of it—this assessment is only assessing the written content.
- Remind students to use all the resources they have collected as a class over the past weeks to write their paragraphs. List the resources on the board:
  - Performance Task Prompt: Informative Consumer Guide
  - Model Informative Consumer Guide
  - Grades 6–8 Expository Writing Evaluation Rubric
  - Their completed Quote Sandwich Graphic Organizers
  - Their completed Mid-Unit 3 Assessment, Part 1: Researching Information about Buying Fish Caught Using Sustainable Methods
  - Formal Style Anchor Chart
- Ask students to begin independently drafting the written content of their informative consumer guide.
- Circulate to support students by reviewing the model with them as an example as needed.

Meeting Students' Needs

Some students may benefit from speaking ideas aloud before writing them down. Organize these students into a group to work with you away from other students who need to work quietly.

Closing and Assessment

A. Debrief (3 minutes)

- Refocus the whole group.
- Ask students to look over their drafts and to discuss in triads:
  - "How do you think you have done? What went well in your drafting? Why?"
  - "What didn't go so well? Why not?"
  - "What do you think you could improve upon? Why?"
- Collect the End-of-Unit 3 Assessment from students who have completed their drafts.

Meeting Students' Needs

The debrief after the assessment can help build a culture of achievement in your classroom.

Homework

- If you haven't already done so, finish writing the content of your informative consumer guide.
- Continue reading your independent reading book.

End-of-Unit 3 Assessment

Draft of Written Content of Informative Consumer Guide

Name: _____

Date: _____

Long-Term Learning Targets Assessed

- I can write informative/explanatory texts that convey ideas and concepts using relevant information that is carefully selected and organized. (W.6.2)
- I can introduce the topic of my text. (W.6.2.a)
- I can organize my information using various strategies (e.g., definition/classification, comparison/contrast, cause/effect). (W.6.2.a)
- I can include headings, graphics, and multimedia to help readers understand my ideas. (W.6.2.a)
- I can develop the topic with relevant facts, definitions, concrete details, and quotations. (W.6.2.b)
- I can use transitions to clarify relationships among my ideas. (W.6.2.c)
- I can use contextually specific language/vocabulary to inform or explain about a topic. (W.6.2.d)
- I can establish and maintain a formal style in my writing. (W.6.2.e)
- I can construct a concluding statement or section of an informative/explanatory text. (W6.2.f)
- I can use evidence from a variety of grade-appropriate texts to support analysis, reflection, and research. (W.6.9)

Directions: Use your Quote Sandwich Graphic Organizers and your Mid-Unit 3 Assessment, Part 1: Researching Information about Buying Fish Caught Using Sustainable Methods to draft the written content of your informative consumer guide. Write your information in the order it will appear in your final informative consumer guide, but don't worry about the layout or the visual images or charts. You will put all of the pieces together in later lessons to create your final informative consumer guide for the performance task at the very end of the unit.

Formal Style Examples

Example 1

Some fruits and vegetables are grown using chemical pesticides and fertilizers to prevent, destroy, and reduce the possibility of pests, rodents, weeds, fungi, bacteria, and viruses; however, research suggests that consuming fruits and vegetables grown using chemical pesticides and fertilizers can have a negative impact on our health. The U.S. Environmental Protection Agency website explains that "By their nature, most pesticides create some risk of harm—pesticides can cause harm to humans, animals, or the environment because they are designed to kill or otherwise adversely affect living organisms." When buying fruits and vegetables, there are options that do not involve food grown using pesticides and fertilizers.

Example 2

These chemicals called pesticides and fertilizers are put on vegetables and fruit that are growing to stop stuff like pests and diseases from killing the plants, but some research says this is bad for us and can make us pretty sick. It says on this website, "By their nature, most pesticides create some risk of harm—pesticides can cause harm to humans, animals, or the environment because they are designed to kill or otherwise adversely affect living organisms." So basically, don't buy stuff that has been sprayed with pesticides and fertilizers.

LESSON 11

Analyzing the Features of an Informative Consumer Guide

Long-Term Targets Addressed (Based on ELA CCSS)

- I can write informative/explanatory texts that convey ideas and concepts using relevant information that is carefully selected and organized. (W.6.2)
- I can integrate information presented in different media or formats (e.g., visually, quantitatively) as well as in words to develop a coherent understanding of a topic or issue. (RI.6.7)

Supporting Learning Targets

- I can identify the features of an informative consumer guide.
- I can select visuals like images, charts, and graphs to make my informative consumer guide eye-catching and to help consumers better understand the issue of overfishing and fish depletion.

Ongoing Assessment

- Annotated informative consumer guides

Agenda

1. Opening
    A. Unpacking Learning Targets (3 minutes)
2. Work Time
    A. Identifying the Features of an Informative Consumer Guide (15 minutes)
    B. Selecting Visuals for the Informative Consumer Guide (20 minutes)
3. Closing and Assessment
    A. Pair Share (7 minutes)

4. Homework

   A. Look at the layout of the model and consider the layout of the informative consumer guides you have studied today. Sketch out on your blank paper where you are going to record each of your paragraphs of information, subheadings, and visuals. You don't need to actually write the paragraphs or draw the images; just draw boxes relative in size to the writing or feature to mark how everything will fit on the page.

   B. Continue reading your independent reading book.

Teaching Notes

- In this lesson, students analyze authentic informative consumer guides to determine the features they need to include on their own guides.

- Students also select images they would like to use in their guides in this lesson. Depending on the technology you have available for students, this could be done in different ways. If students are creating their guides on the computer, they could insert clip art or images/charts from the Web found through internet searches; for example, "Overfishing charts." If students are handwriting their guides, they could either cut out printed images, charts, and graphs or hand-copy from *World Without Fish* and the research materials used in Lessons 2–5. Give students who enjoy creative art the opportunity to draw their own images and designs, but emphasize that somewhere there should be an informative visual, like a graph or chart.

- For those students who needed additional time to complete the End-of-Unit 3 Draft, collect those during today's lesson. Remember that students will need the drafts to complete revisions in Lesson 12 and will need to receive teacher feedback by Lesson 13.

- In advance:
  - Prepare age-appropriate informative consumer guides. Where possible, try to give each triad a different guide. The Model Informative Consumer Guide from Lesson 1 could be used as a teacher model. Ensure there are as many of the features listed in Work Time B in each one as possible. Students may want to refer to these models once they begin drafting their own guides in Lesson 12.
  - Prepare resources for students to access images and charts to use on their guides and determine how they are going to record their choices. For example, if you are providing them with print-outs of images to cut out and use, they will need to store those somewhere until they are ready to use them. If they are using visuals on the computer, they will need to be able to store their selected visuals in an easily accessible folder.

- Post: learning targets.

Lesson Vocabulary

None

Materials

- Examples of informative consumer guides (one per triad and one to display, see Teaching Notes)
- Marker (one per team and one for teacher)
- Informative Consumer Guide Anchor Chart (begun in Lesson 1)
- Performance Task Prompt: Informative Consumer Guide (from Lesson 1)
- Images and charts (see Teaching Notes)
- Blank paper (two pieces per student)

Opening

A. Unpacking Learning Targets (3 minutes)

- Direct students' attention to the posted learning targets and read them aloud:
  - "I can identify the features of an informative consumer guide."
  - "I can select visuals like images, charts, and graphs to make my informative consumer guide eye-catching and to help consumers better understand the issue of overfishing and fish depletion."
- Ask students to discuss with an elbow partner:
  - "Why are we identifying the features of an informative consumer guide? How will that help us to create an informative consumer guide about buying fish caught using sustainable methods?"
- Listen for students to explain that identifying the features of an informative consumer guide will help them ensure that they include all of those features in their informative consumer guides, which will make consumers more likely to pick up their guide to use when buying fish.

Meeting Students' Needs

- Learning targets are a research-based strategy that helps all students, especially challenged learners.
- Posting learning targets allows students to reference them throughout the lesson to check their understanding. Learning targets also provide a reminder to students and teachers about the intended learning behind a given lesson or activity.

Work Time

A. Identifying the Features of an Informative Consumer Guide (15 minutes)

- Ask students to arrange themselves into triads. Explain that today students are going to be looking at real informative consumer guides to determine the features. Ask students:
  - "What do I mean by features?"

- Cold-call students for their responses. Listen for and guide students to understand that the features are the things outside of the content. For example, a title is a feature.
- Explain that not only are they going to identify features but they are going to identify the purpose of each feature, too.
- Display an informative consumer guide. Circle the title with a marker. Ask students to discuss in triads:
  - "What is the purpose of the title?"
- Select students to share their responses. Listen for them to explain that the purpose is to catch the readers' attention and give them an idea of what the informative consumer guide is about.
- Annotate the title of the consumer guide with the purpose. Distribute **examples of informative consumer guides** and **markers**, one to each team, and invite triads to do the same.
- Circulate to assist triads. Ask guiding questions:
  - "Why have you circled that feature?"
  - "What is the purpose of that feature?"
- Refocus the whole group. Cold-call triads to share what they found with the whole group.
- Record student suggestions on the **Informative Consumer Guide Anchor Chart**. Ensure the following is included:
  - Title—to grab the readers' attention and give them an idea of what the content of the guide is about
  - Large and colorful font—to grab the readers' attention
  - Images—to make the guide look appealing so that people want to pick it up and support the content of the text
  - Charts and graphs—to provide consumers with more information and to help them understand the information presented
  - Subheadings—to organize the information and to make the content appear more manageable to read
  - Bite-sized pieces of information—to make the information easy to read

Meeting Students' Needs

Inviting students to analyze authentic models can give them a clearer idea of what their final product should look like.

B. Selecting Visuals for the Informative Consumer Guide (20 minutes)

- Ask students to take out their **Performance Task Prompt: Informative Consumer Guide** and to reread it.
- Invite students to focus on the text that reads: "Include visuals such as pictures and charts or graphs to make it eye-catching and to improve consumer understanding of the issue."

- Remind students of visuals on the informative consumer guides they just analyzed with their triad. Emphasize that there are just enough visuals for the guides to be eye-catching, but not so many that they are cluttered. Explain to students that if there are too many images, it can make it less eye-catching, and it can distract the consumer from the important information captured in the writing.
- Direct students' attention to the **images and charts** available (dependent on your resources).
- Explain that in the same way they evaluated the information and quotes they collected in research to choose the content of their writing for their guides, they are going to evaluate the images and charts to choose which ones will go into their guides.
- Explain that students may also be creative and draw their own images and designs to make their guides eye-catching, but they also need to include informative visuals like charts and/or graphs to inform consumers.
- Emphasize that students should consider the information and quotes recorded on their Quote Sandwich Graphic Organizers when evaluating, selecting, and designing visuals because the visuals they select should support the content of their writing.
- Invite students to evaluate and select the visuals to use on their guides.
- Students who are designing their own visuals or copying from other resources will need **blank paper** to practice their designs on.

Closing and Assessment

A. Pair Share (7 minutes)

- Invite students to get into new pairs to share the visuals they have chosen and to justify why they have chosen them.
- Encourage students to help each other ensure that they have only selected the most relevant visuals for their content. Remind students that they will only have one piece of letter-sized paper and they need to make sure the information is clear, so they don't want too many visuals.
- Distribute a second sheet of blank paper for homework.

Meeting Students' Needs

- Asking students to justify their choices to another student can help them realize whether the choices they have made are appropriate or not.
- Consider pairing ELL students to deepen the discussion they have about the choices they have made.

Homework

- Look at the layout of the model and consider the layout of the informative consumer guides you have studied today. Sketch out on your blank paper where you are going to record each of your paragraphs of information, subheadings, and visuals. You don't need to actually write the paragraphs or draw the images; just draw boxes relative in size to the writing or feature to mark how everything will fit on the page.
- Continue reading your independent reading book.

There are no new supporting materials in this lesson.

LESSON 12

Revising the Informative Consumer Guide
Sentence Structure, Transitions, and Works Cited

Long-Term Targets Addressed (Based on ELA CCSS)

- I can use a variety of sentence structures to make my writing and speaking more interesting. (L.6.3.a)
- I can maintain consistency in style and tone when writing and speaking. (L.6.3.b)

Supporting Learning Targets

- I can use a variety of sentence structures to make my informative consumer guide more interesting.
- I can use appropriate transitions to make the informative consumer guide flow smoothly.

Ongoing Assessment

- Revised Draft of Written Content of Informative Consumer Guide
- Row 3 of the Grades 6–8 Expository Writing Evaluation Rubric: Self-Assessment

Agenda

1. Opening
   A. Unpacking Learning Targets (2 minutes)
2. Work Time
   A. Mini Lesson: Sentence Structure (16 minutes)
   B. Mini Lesson: Transitions (7 minutes)
   C. Writing a Works Cited List (12 minutes)
3. Closing and Assessment
   A. Self-Assessment Against the Rubric (8 minutes)
4. Homework
   A. Continue reading your independent reading book.

Teaching Notes

- Students need the End-of-Unit 3 Assessment: Draft of Written Content of Informative Consumer Guides from Lesson 10 returned in this lesson for revision; however, they don't need to receive teacher feedback until the next lesson.
- To address Language Standards L.6.3.a and L.6.3.b, students have mini lessons on sentence structure and appropriate transitions to improve the flow of their informative consumer guides. Students then revise their guide drafts with this new knowledge in mind.
- In the next lesson, students will create their final informative consumer guides for the performance task. If you require more time to provide feedback on the End-of-Unit 3 Assessment, consider adding lessons in which students read independently and/or complete the independent reading assessment. See Launching Independent Reading in Grades 6–8: Sample Plan.
- Post: learning targets.

Lesson Vocabulary

appropriate transitions

Materials

- Sentence Structure and Transitions (one per student and one to display)
- End-of-Unit 3 Assessment: Draft of Written Content of Informative Consumer Guide (from Lesson 10, see Teaching Notes)
- Grades 6–8 Expository Writing Evaluation Rubric (from Lesson 1)
- Model Informative Consumer Guide (from Lesson 1)
- Researching Graphic Organizers (from Lessons 2–4)
- Mid-Unit 3 Assessment, Part 1: Researching Information about Buying Fish Caught Using Sustainable Methods (from Lesson 5)
- Row 3 of the Grades 6–8 Expository Writing Evaluation Rubric: Self-Assessment (one per student)

Opening

A. Unpacking Learning Targets (2 minutes)

- Invite students to sit in their triads.
- Direct students' attention to the posted learning targets and read them aloud:
  - "I can use a variety of sentence structures to make my informative consumer guide more interesting."
  - "I can use appropriate transitions to make the informative consumer guide flow smoothly."

- Invite students to Think-Pair-Share:
  - "What are *appropriate transitions*? Why are they important?"
- Select volunteers to share their ideas. Listen for students to explain that appropriate transitions are the words and phrases used to connect sentences and paragraphs, and they are important because they help writing flow well.

Meeting Students' Needs

- Learning targets are a research-based strategy that helps all students, especially challenged learners.
- Posting learning targets allows students to reference them throughout the lesson to check their understanding. Learning targets also provide a reminder to students and teachers about the intended learning behind a given lesson or activity.

Work Time

A. Mini Lesson: Sentence Structure (16 minutes)

- Display **Sentence Structure and Transitions** with only the top of the handout showing to students—the boxes with the A and B examples of sentences.
- Direct students to determine which one is more interesting: A or B, and why.
- Read each box aloud.
- Ask for a volunteer to share which one was more interesting and why. Listen for the student to explain something like: "B flowed more easily, was not as choppy, and had some variety to the sentence structure."
- Distribute the Sentence Structure and Transitions handout to each student.
- Read the bulleted notes under the A and B boxes. Direct students to answer question 2 on the handout.
- Ask them to read their sentence aloud to their triad and make any changes if it didn't flow well when they read it aloud.
- Circulate and support students as needed. You might have a student say a new sentence aloud first if he or she is stuck writing one down.
- Refocus the whole class. Cold-call on one or two triads to whom you were not able to circulate to extend your check for understanding.
- Write down their sentences on the displayed Sentence Structure and Transitions handout.
- Think aloud about how the students combined the sentences while keeping the language and style. An example of a new sentence might be: "Bottom dragging destroys a lot of life on the seabed and it also results in a lot of by-catch."

- Hand back students' **End-of-Unit 3 Assessment: Draft of Written Content of Informative Consumer Guide**. Give directions:
  - Choose one paragraph to revise for more interesting sentence structure.
  - Review the sentences in that paragraph and combine them if needed, writing the new sentences in the margins of your draft.
  - Read your whole paragraph through in your head and determine if the sentences flow together well. If not, revise the sentences that seemed choppy.
- Circulate and support students with their sentence combining and revision.

Meeting Students' Needs

Consider supporting some students by helping them make a next-steps list at the top of their draft. This helps students chunk the task for revision into smaller steps.

B. Mini Lesson: Transitions (7 minutes)

- Display the **Grades 6–8 Expository Writing Evaluation Rubric**.
- Circle row 3 and read aloud to students: "Exhibits clear organization with the use of appropriate and varied transitions to create a unified whole."
- Ask them to discuss in triads:
  - "What does 'transitions to create a unified whole' mean?"
- Cold-call on a student and listen for: "Transition words help connect one paragraph to the next."
- Emphasize that because informative consumer guides present information in relatively small chunks, they use transitions a little differently than a literary analysis or a narrative. While there are still sometimes transitional words and phrases at the beginning of paragraphs, where there is a subheading dividing paragraphs, we know that the subheading provides the transition by signaling the start of a new topic or idea.
- Ask students to take out their copies of the **Model Informative Consumer Guide** and reread it, paying particular attention to the transitions.
- Invite students to discuss in triads.
  - "What do you notice about transitions?"
- Select volunteers to share their responses. Listen for them to notice that there are a few transitions like "One of the suggested negative impacts on our health . . ." and "Another study . . ." but mostly the paragraphs are connected by content with subheadings to divide different topics.
- Invite students to review and revise the transitions in their informative consumer guide drafts.

C. Writing a Works Cited List (12 minutes)

- Remind students of the final bullet on the Performance Task Prompt: "Include a Works Cited List."
- Invite students to refer to the Works Cited list at the bottom of the model informative consumer guide.

- Ask students to look at the format of the Works Cited list:
  - Author's last name, author's first name and middle initial. "Name of text." Where the text was found and when it was published. When the text was found.
- Invite students to revisit their **Researching Graphic Organizers** as well as their **Mid-Unit 3 Assessment, Part 1** to write a Works Cited list for the evidence they have used in their informative consumer guide drafts.
- Circulate to support students in writing their Works Cited list.

Closing and Assessment

A. Self-Assessment Against the Rubric (8 minutes)

- Distribute **Row 3 of the Grades 6–8 Expository Writing Evaluation Rubric: Self-Assessment**.
- Invite students to read the Criteria column and level 3 aloud with you.
- Tell students they are going to score their informative consumer guide drafts against the rubric. Ask them to underline on the rubric where their writing fits best. Then, they should justify how they have scored themselves using evidence from their draft writing on the lines following the rubric.
- Remind students to be honest when self-assessing because identifying where there are problems with their work will help them improve their work in the next draft. Remind students that writing is a set of skills that have to be learned over time. Encourage them to give their best assessment.
- Invite students to begin.
- Circulate and encourage students to think carefully about their scoring choices. Consider prompting students with this question as needed:
  - "You have underlined this part of your rubric. Why? Where is the evidence in your draft to support this?"
- Students who finish quickly can begin to revise their informative consumer guide draft based on their scoring against the rubric.
- Congratulate students on their focus and effort at revision.
- Collect the revised drafts and the self-assessments from students to continue providing feedback for the End-of-Unit 3 Assessment.

Meeting Students' Needs

Self-assessment can enable students to recognize the issues in their own work, so giving them a sense of ownership and responsibility for correcting their mistakes.

Homework

- Continue reading your independent reading book.

Sentence Structure and Transitions

1. Which set of sentences is more interesting and why?

A	B
Some fruits and vegetables are grown using chemical pesticides and fertilizers. They prevent, destroy, and reduce the possibility of pests, rodents, weeds, fungi, bacteria, and viruses. Research suggests that consuming fruits and vegetables sprayed with chemical pesticides and fertilizers can have a negative impact on our health.	Some fruits and vegetables are grown using chemical pesticides and fertilizers to prevent, destroy, and reduce the possibility of pests, rodents, weeds, fungi, bacteria, and viruses; however, research suggests that consuming fruits and vegetables sprayed with chemical pesticides and fertilizers can have a negative impact on our health.

- All the sentences in A are simple sentences.
- Having a variety of simple and complex (shorter and longer) sentences makes your writing more interesting to read.
- To create more interesting sentences, spend time combining some sentences. Read your sentences aloud to hear how they flow.
- When we combine sentences, we want to make sure we keep the descriptive words and formal style of language.

2. Practice combining these two sentences into one interesting sentence: "Bottom dragging destroys a lot of life on the seabed. There is a lot of by-catch from bottom dragging."

_____

_____

_____

Row 3 of the Grades 6–8 Expository Writing Evaluation Rubric: Self-Assessment

Name: _____

Date: _____

Criteria	CCSS	4	3	2	1	0
COHERENCE, ORGANIZATION, AND STYLE: The extent to which the newspaper article logically organizes complex ideas, concepts, and information using the inverted pyramid structure* and formal and precise language	W.2 L.3 L.6	• Exhibits clear newspaper article organization,* with the skillful use of appropriate and varied transitions to create a unified whole and enhance meaning • Establishes and maintains a formal style, using grade-appropriate, stylistically sophisticated descriptive language and domain-specific vocabulary with a notable sense of voice	• Exhibits clear newspaper article organization,* with the use of appropriate transitions to create a unified whole • Establishes and maintains a formal style using precise descriptive language and domain-specific vocabulary • Uses a variety of sentence structures to make writing more interesting	• Exhibits some attempt at newspaper article organization,* with inconsistent use of transitions • Establishes but fails to maintain a formal style, with inconsistent use of descriptive language and domain-specific vocabulary	• Exhibits little attempt at newspaper article organization,* or attempts to organize are irrelevant to the task • Lacks a formal style, using language that is not descriptive or is inappropriate for the text(s) and task	• Exhibits no evidence of newspaper article organization* • Uses language that is predominantly incoherent or copied directly from the text(s) • Does not use a variety of sentence structures to make writing more interesting

Criteria	CCSS	4	3	2	1	0
*newspaper article uses the inverted pyramid structure, organizing details in order from major to minor		• Uses a variety of sentence structures to make writing more compelling and interesting		• Inconsistent use of a variety of sentence structures to make writing more interesting	• Rarely uses a variety of sentence structures to make writing more interesting	

What score are you giving yourself for Row 3 today? Why? Provide specific evidence from your writing.

LESSON 13

Performance Task

Final Informative Consumer Guide

Long-Term Targets Addressed (Based on ELA CCSS)

- I can write informative/explanatory texts that convey ideas and concepts using relevant information that is carefully selected and organized. (W.6.2)
    a. I can introduce the topic of my text.
    a. I can organize my information using various strategies (e.g., definition/classification, comparison/contrast, cause/effect).
    a. I can include headings, graphics, and multimedia to help readers understand my ideas.
    b. I can develop the topic with relevant facts, definitions, concrete details, and quotations.
    c. I can use transitions to clarify relationships among my ideas.
    d. I can use contextually specific language/vocabulary to inform or explain about a topic.
    e. I can establish and maintain a formal style in my writing.
    f. I can construct a concluding statement or section of an informative/explanatory text.
- I can produce clear and coherent writing that is appropriate to task, purpose, and audience. (W.6.4.a)
- I can use evidence from a variety of grade-appropriate texts to support analysis, reflection, and research. (W.6.9)
- I can apply sixth-grade reading standards to literary nonfiction (e.g., "Trace and evaluate the argument and specific claims in a text, distinguishing claims that are supported by reasons and evidence from claims that are not."). (W.6.9.a)
- I can use a variety of sentence structures to make my writing and speaking more interesting. (L.6.3.a)
- I can maintain consistency in style and tone when writing and speaking. (L.6.3.b)
- I can integrate information presented in different media or formats (e.g., visually, quantitatively) as well as in words to develop a coherent understanding of a topic or issue. (RI.6.7)

Supporting Learning Targets

- I can use formative feedback from the teacher to revise my informative consumer guide.
- I can use peer feedback to revise my writing to further meet the expectations of the rubric.
- I can write a final draft of an interesting, accurate, and objective informative consumer guide.

Ongoing Assessment

- Performance Task: Final copy of informative consumer guide
- Optional Supplementary Assessment Items

Agenda

1. Opening
    A. Unpacking Learning Targets (2 minutes)
2. Work Time
    A. Reviewing Formative Feedback (5 minutes)
    B. Peer Critique: Stars and Steps (10 minutes)
    C. Creating the Final Copy (25 minutes)
3. Closing and Assessment
    A. Debrief (3 minutes)
4. Homework
    A. Continue reading your independent reading book.

Teaching Notes

- Be prepared to give students feedback on their End-of-Unit 3 Assessments in this lesson. If you need more time to provide feedback, consider adding more lessons in which students read independently or are assessed on the independent reading standards RL.1.1.a and RL.1.1.b. See Launching Independent Reading in Grades 6–8: Sample Plan.
- In previous lessons, students drafted and revised the written content of their informative consumer guide. In this lesson, students write/create their final, best version of their guide including the visual images, charts, and graphs. Depending on the technology students are using, this may require more time and instruction. If students are using computers, consider working with a media technology educator to help students learn the skills of constructing columns, text-wrapping and sizing graphics, and using different colors and sizes of fonts.
- Before creating their final copy, students participate in peer critiquing. Set up peer critiquing carefully to ensure students feel safe giving and receiving feedback. Students must be given a set of clear guidelines for behavior (see supporting materials), and they need to see the teacher model how to do it successfully. Asking students to provide feedback to their peers based on explicit

criteria in the rubric benefits both parties in clarifying what a strong piece of writing should look like. Students can learn from both the strengths and weaknesses that they notice in the work of peers.

- In advance:
  - Prepare the visual components for the final informative consumer guides. Students will need to be able to insert the visual components they have chosen into their guides.
  - Review: Peer Critique Guidelines.
- Post: learning targets.

Lesson Vocabulary

formative feedback, peer critique

Materials

- End-of-Unit 3 Assessment (from Lesson 10, returned in this lesson with teacher feedback)
- Peer Critique Guidelines (one to display)
- Grades 6–8 Expository Writing Evaluation Rubric (from Lesson 1)
- Stars and Steps Recording Form (one per student)
- Performance Task Prompt: Informative Consumer Guide (from Lesson 1)
- Row 3 of the Grades 6–8 Expository Writing Evaluation Rubric: Self-Assessment (from Lesson 12)
- Visual Component(s) (from Lesson 11; various per student)
- Draft layout (from Lesson 11 homework)

Opening

A. Unpacking Learning Targets (2 minutes)

- Direct students' attention to the posted learning targets and read them aloud:
  - "I can use formative feedback from the teacher to revise my informative consumer guide."
  - "I can use peer feedback to revise my writing to further meet the expectations of the rubric."
  - "I can write a final draft of an interesting, accurate, and objective informative consumer guide."
- Invite students to Think-Pair-Share:
  - "What does *formative feedback* mean?"
- Listen for and guide students to explain that formative feedback is where you get suggestions for how to improve your writing.
- Invite students to Think-Pair-Share:
  - "What does *peer critique* mean?"
  - "Why is peer critiquing useful?"

- Listen for: "Peer critique means to look at someone else's work and give them feedback that will help them improve their writing."
- Clarify as needed, then ask:
  - "Now that you have seen the learning targets for this lesson, what do you think you will be doing today? Why?"
- Ask for volunteers to share. Listen for: "Creating a final, best version of the informative consumer guide using the feedback from you and from the peer critique."

Meeting Students' Needs

- Learning targets are a research-based strategy that helps all students, especially challenged learners.
- Posting learning targets allows students to reference them throughout the lesson to check their understanding. Learning targets also provide a reminder to students and teachers about the intended learning behind a given lesson or activity.

Work Time

A. Reviewing Formative Feedback (5 minutes)

- Hand back students' **End-of-Unit 3 Assessment** with feedback.
- Ask students to look over your comments quietly and independently and make sure they understand them.
- Invite students to raise their hands to ask questions if they have them. Alternatively, create a "Help List" on the board and invite students to add their names to it if they need questions answered.
- Remind students that this feedback helps them develop as a writer and that it takes practice. No one is born knowing how to write. Tell them to use the feedback to determine how they can improve the whole guide, not just where the teacher comments are.

Meeting Students' Needs

- Consider supporting some students by helping them make a next-steps list at the top of their draft. This helps students chunk the task for revision into smaller steps.
- The use of leading questions in feedback helps struggling students understand what areas they should improve.

B. Peer Critique: Stars and Steps (10 minutes)

- Remind students that a peer critique is when we look over someone else's work and provide that person with feedback. Explain that peer critiquing must be done carefully because we want to be helpful to our peers so they can use our suggestions to improve their work. We don't want to make them feel bad.
- Post the **Peer Critique Guidelines** and invite students to read them with you.
- Display the **Grades 6–8 Expository Writing Evaluation Rubric**.
- Ask students to take out their own copy of the rubric.
- Focus students on row 3: "Coherence, Organization, and Style." In level 3, highlight/underline this section: "establish and maintain a formal style using precise language and domain-specific vocabulary."
- Emphasize to students that their job is to make sure that their peers' writing maintains a formal style and uses domain-specific vocabulary as discussed in Lesson 10. Distinguish peer critiquing from proofreading; it is fine if they catch small errors in each other's work, but the goal is to make the thinking in the writing as strong as possible.
- Tell students they will present feedback in the form of stars and steps. Remind them that they have done this in the first module. Today they will give one "star" and one "step" based on the criteria.
- Briefly model how to give "kind, specific, helpful" stars. Be sure to connect your comments directly to the Grades 6–8 Expository Writing Evaluation Rubric. For example: "You have maintained a formal style all of the way through."
- Repeat, briefly modeling how to give "kind, specific, helpful" steps. For example: "Could you use more domain-specific vocabulary in this section; for example, rather than excess fish, could you use the term *by-catch*?"
- Emphasize that it is especially important to be kind when giving steps. Asking a question of the writer is often a good way to do this: "I wonder if . . .?" "Have you thought about . . .?" "I'm not sure what you meant by . . ."
- Distribute the **Stars and Steps Recording Form**.
- Explain that today, students will record the star and step for their partner on this sheet so their partners can remember the feedback they receive. They are to write the name of their partners at the top of their paper.
- Pair up students. Invite pairs to swap their informative consumer guide drafts and to spend 3 minutes reading them in silence.
- Ask students to record a star and step for their partner on the recording form.
- Circulate to assist students who may struggle with articulating or recording their feedback.
- Ask students to return the draft and the Stars and Steps Recording Form to their partners and explain the star and step they recorded for their partners.
- Invite students to question their partners where they don't understand the star or step given.

C. Creating the Final Copy (25 minutes)

- Display the **Performance Task Prompt: Informative Consumer Guide**.
- Ask students to reread it to ground themselves again in what is expected of their work.
- Invite students to use the feedback from the following to create the final copy of their informative consumer guides:
  - End-of-Unit 3 Assessment (today)
  - Step from the peer critique (today)
  - **Row 3 of the Grades 6–8 Expository Writing Evaluation Rubric: Self-Assessment** (Lesson 12)
  - **Visual Component(s)** (Lesson 11)
  - **Draft layout** (Lesson 11 homework)
- Ask students to begin working.
- Circulate to assist as necessary.
- Collect students' final informative consumer guides.

Closing and Assessment

A. Debrief (3 minutes)

- Redirect students' attention to the posted learning targets.
- Read each one aloud, pausing after each to ask students to show a Fist-to-Five to demonstrate how well they feel they have achieved the target.

Homework

- Continue reading your independent reading book.

Peer Critique Guidelines

1. **Be kind:** Always treat others with dignity and respect. This means we never use words that are hurtful, including sarcasm.

2. **Be specific:** Focus on particular strengths and weaknesses rather than making general comments like, "It's good," or "I like it." Provide insight into why it is good or what, specifically, you like about it. For example: "I like the word choice here," or "I am confused by this sentence. Can you rewrite it to be clearer?"

3. **Be helpful:** The goal is to positively contribute to the individual or the group, not to simply be heard. Echoing the thoughts of others or cleverly pointing out details that are irrelevant wastes time. Really be the audience and help your peer.

4. **Participate:** Peer critique is a process to support each other, and your feedback is valued!

Stars and Steps Recording Form

Partner's Name: _____

Date: _____

Learning target:

- "Establish and maintain a formal style using precise language and domain-specific vocabulary."

Star:

_____

_____

Step:

_____

_____

Supplementary Assessment Items

Writing to Inform

Name: _____

Date: _____

A student is doing research to write a pamphlet about overfishing and the danger to fish populations. She found these three possible sources for her pamphlet. Read the sources and answer the questions that follow.

Source 1: From *World Without Fish* by Mark Kurlansky (pp. 112–113).

[1]The biggest hope for banning bottom dragging is the marketplace where fish is sold. If offered the choice between buying a fish caught in a net and one caught on a hook and line, most people would prefer the line-caught fish if they could see them. Net-caught fish can spend hours together, thousands of them—slithering, squirming, slapping one another—crushed against the net so that they arrive at the market scratched and bruised.

[2]Until recently, the fish-selling business operated with very little inspection. Now, however, there's a growing trend toward selling fish in what are called "display auctions." At these auctions, all of the fish are sorted by species and fishery. So cod from a bottom dragger would be in a different bin than cod caught on a hook and line.

[3]What people are finding in display auctions around the world is that fish that are caught on a hook and line are fetching higher prices than net-caught fish. What that means is that there is a real financial incentive for fishermen to abandon bottom dragging for the old-fashioned method of hook-and-line fishing. Because fishermen are being asked to catch fewer fish, their only hope for survival is to be paid more for the fewer fish they catch.

Source 2: "Threat 1: Overfishing." Overfishing. Save Our Seas, Web. 19 Feb. 2014. http://saveourseas.com/threats/overfishing.

Bycatch

[1]Modern fishing vessels catch staggering amounts of unwanted fish and other marine life. It's estimated that anywhere from 8 to 25 percent of the total global catch is discarded, cast overboard either dead or dying. That's up to 27 million tonnes of fish thrown out each year—the equivalent of 600 fully-laden Titanics. And the victims aren't just fish. Every year, an estimated 300,000 whales, dolphins and porpoises die entangled in fishing nets, along with thousands of critically-endangered sea turtles. Long-line fisheries also kill huge numbers of seabirds. Over 100,000 Albatrosses die this way every year, and many species are endangered as a result of bycatch.

[2]All modern forms of commercial fishing produce bycatch, but shrimp trawling is by far the most destructive: it is responsible for a third of the world's bycatch, while producing only 2% of all seafood.

[3]Shrimp (and many deep-sea fish) are caught using a fishing method called bottom trawling, which usually involves dragging a net between two trawl doors weighing several tons each across the ocean bed. This has a destructive impact on seabed communities, particularly on fragile deep water coral—a vital part of the marine ecosystem that scientists are just beginning to understand. The effect of bottom trawling on the seafloor has been compared to forest clear-cutting, and the damage it causes can be seen from space. The UN Secretary General reported in 2006 that 95 percent of damage to seamount ecosystems worldwide is caused by deep sea bottom trawling.

Source 3: From "Threat 1: Overfishing" infographic.

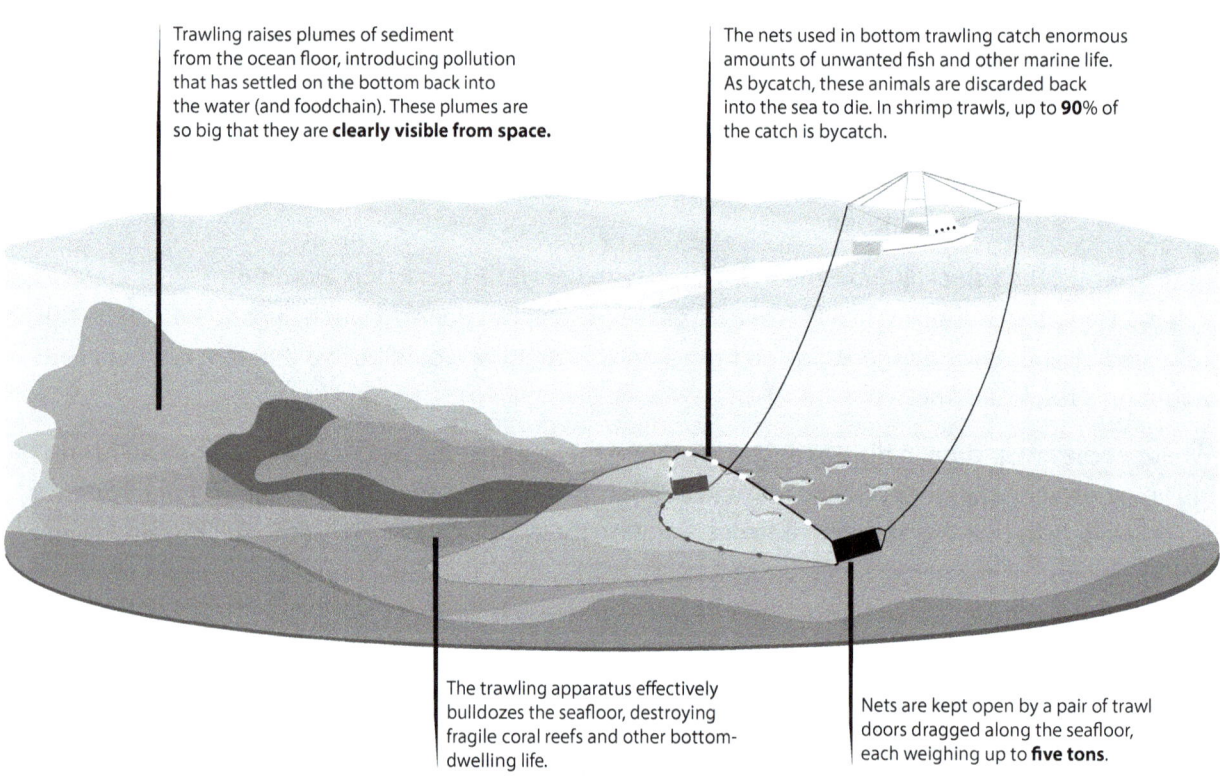

Source: http://saveourseas.com/threats/overfishing.

The student made three categories for her pamphlet. Look at the categories in the table. Decide which source or sources, if any, support each category and put a checkmark in the appropriate box.

	Source 1: *World Without Fish*	Source 2: "Bycatch" from "Threat 1: Overfishing"	Source 3: Infographic from "Threat 1: Overfishing"	Neither texts nor infographic support category
Category 1. What you need to know about overfishing				
Category 2. Solutions that may help control overfishing				
Category 3. Steps you can take				

This question has two parts. First answer Part A. Then answer Part B.

Part A: What is the main purpose of the infographic in "Threat 1: Overfishing"?

   A. to show the damage the use of fishing nets creates

   B. to describe the risk to the seafloor if coral reefs are lost

   C. to illustrate the visibility of the sediment plumes created when the seafloor is stirred up

   D. to show how shrimp trawlers create a massive amount of waste and damage the seafloor

Part B: Which detail from Source 2 supports the correct answer to Part A?

   A. "Long-line fisheries also kill huge numbers of seabirds. Over 100,000 Albatrosses die this way every year."

   B. "Shrimp trawling is by far the most destructive: it is responsible for a third of the world's bycatch, while producing only 2% of all seafood."

   C. "This has a destructive impact on seabed communities, particularly on fragile deep water coral."

   D. "The effect of bottom trawling on the seafloor has been compared to forest clear-cutting, and the damage it causes can be seen from space."

Supplementary Assessment Items Answer Key

Writing to Inform

Standards Assessed: W.6.2, W.6.2.a-f, RI.6.7

Note: Supplementary Assessment Items are located in the Teacher Guide and Resource Book only. Distribute a copy of the student version of this assessment to each student.

A student is doing research to write a pamphlet about overfishing and the danger to fish populations. She found these three possible sources for her pamphlet. Read the sources and answer the questions that follow.

Source 1: From *World Without Fish* by Mark Kurlansky (pp. 112–113).

The biggest hope for banning bottom dragging is the marketplace where fish is sold. If offered the choice between buying a fish caught in a net and one caught on a hook and line, most people would prefer the line-caught fish if they could see them. Net-caught fish can spend hours together, thousands of them—slithering, squirming, slapping one another—crushed against the net so that they arrive at the market scratched and bruised.

Until recently, the fish-selling business operated with very little inspection. Now, however, there's a growing trend toward selling fish in what are called "display auctions." At these auctions, all of the fish are sorted by species and fishery. So cod from a bottom dragger would be in a different bin than cod caught on a hook and line.

What people are finding in display auctions around the world is that fish that are caught on a hook and line are fetching higher prices than net-caught fish. What that means is that there is a real financial incentive for fishermen to abandon bottom dragging for the old-fashioned method of hook-and-line fishing. Because fishermen are being asked to catch fewer fish, their only hope for survival is to be paid more for the fewer fish they catch.

Source 2: "Threat 1: Overfishing." Overfishing. Save Our Seas, Web. 19 Feb. 2014. http://saveourseas.com/threats/overfishing

Bycatch

Modern fishing vessels catch staggering amounts of unwanted fish and other marine life. It's estimated that anywhere from 8 to 25 percent of the total global catch is discarded, cast overboard either dead or dying. That's up to 27 million tonnes of fish thrown out each year—the equivalent of 600 fully-laden Titanics. And the victims aren't just fish. Every year, an estimated 300,000 whales, dolphins and porpoises die entangled in fishing nets, along with thousands of critically-endangered sea turtles. Long-line fisheries also kill huge numbers of seabirds. Over 100,000 Albatrosses die this way every year, and many species are endangered as a result of bycatch.

All modern forms of commercial fishing produce bycatch, but shrimp trawling is by far the most destructive: it is responsible for a third of the world's bycatch, while producing only 2% of all seafood.

Shrimp (and many deep-sea fish) are caught using a fishing method called bottom trawling, which usually involves dragging a net between two trawl doors weighing several tons each across the ocean bed. This has a destructive impact on seabed communities, particularly on fragile deep water coral—a vital part of the marine ecosystem that scientists are just beginning to understand. The effect of bottom trawling on the seafloor has been compared to forest clear-cutting, and the damage it causes can be seen from space. The UN Secretary General reported in 2006 that 95 percent of damage to seamount ecosystems worldwide is caused by deep sea bottom trawling.

Source 3: From "Threat 1: Overfishing" infographic.

ANATOMY OF A BOTTOM TRAWL

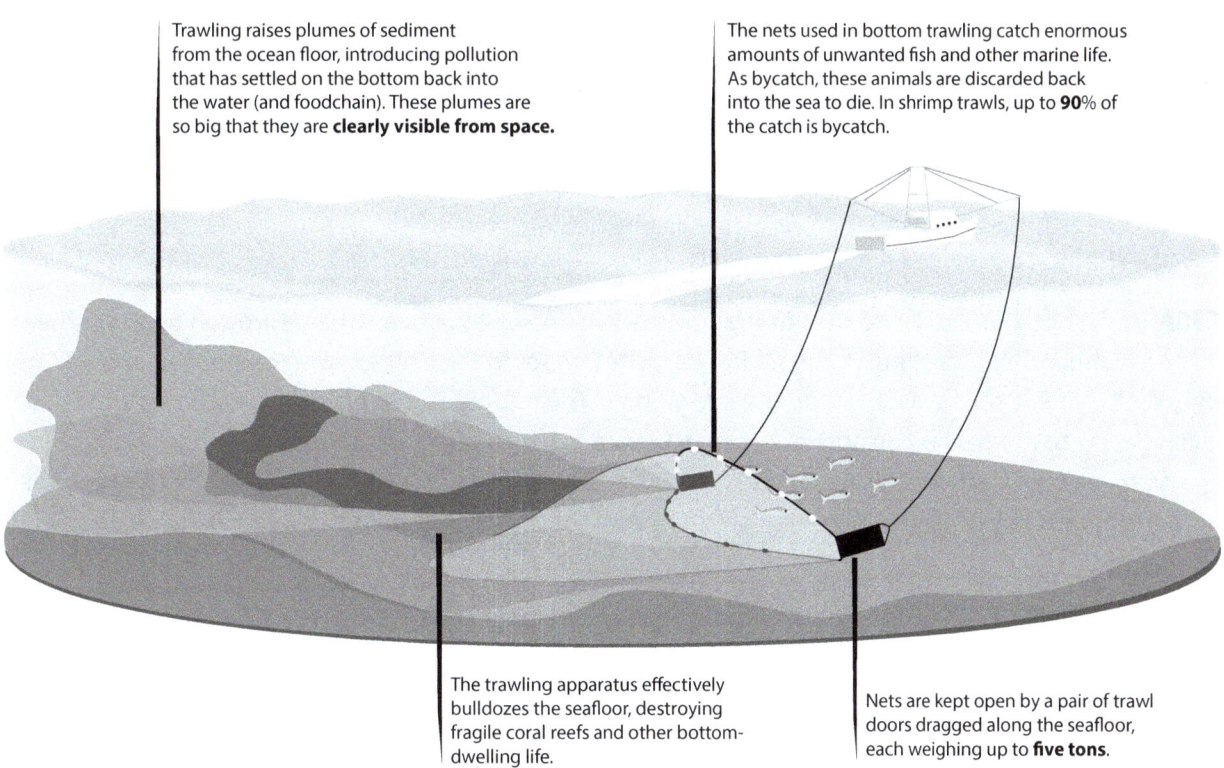

Trawling raises plumes of sediment from the ocean floor, introducing pollution that has settled on the bottom back into the water (and foodchain). These plumes are so big that they are **clearly visible from space.**

The nets used in bottom trawling catch enormous amounts of unwanted fish and other marine life. As bycatch, these animals are discarded back into the sea to die. In shrimp trawls, up to **90**% of the catch is bycatch.

The trawling apparatus effectively bulldozes the seafloor, destroying fragile coral reefs and other bottom-dwelling life.

Nets are kept open by a pair of trawl doors dragged along the seafloor, each weighing up to **five tons**.

Source: http://saveourseas.com/threats/overfishing.

The student made three categories for her pamphlet. Look at the categories in the table. Decide which source or sources, if any, support each category and put a checkmark in the appropriate box.

	Source 1: *World Without Fish*	Source 2: "Bycatch" from "Threat 1: Overfishing"	Source 3: Infographic from "Threat 1: Overfishing"	Neither texts nor infographic support category
Category 1. What you need to know about overfishing		√	√	
Category 2. Solutions that may help control overfishing	√			
Category 3. Steps you can take				√

Explanation

Category 1: Both Source 2 and the infographic explain one facet of overfishing through bycatch. The destructive nature of trawling on the seafloor and its impact to the ecosystems are detailed in both the article "Threat 1: Overfishing" and the infographic. The infographic explains that up to 90% of what is caught in shrimp nets is considered bycatch. Source 1, which offers an alternative to net fishing, mentions banning bottom fishing, but this is not the passage's focus. Instead, Kurlansky focuses on the differences between the inferior quality of fish caught through nets versus the more valuable hook-and-line caught.

Category 2: Only Source 1 focuses on possible solutions that may slow the negative effects of overfishing by focusing on the profitability of using old-fashioned methods to catch fish. Sources 2 and 3 only focus on the problem, not the solution.

Category 3: Neither the texts nor the infographic offer solutions for the consumer who buys fish for personal consumption. Neither article offers suggestions concerning what to look for or what questions to ask when purchasing fish, nor do they offer alternatives or solutions for the average consumer. This would have to come from an outside source.

This question has two parts. First answer Part A. Then answer Part B.

Part A: What is the main purpose of the infographic in "Threat 1: Overfishing"?

A. to show the damage the use of fishing nets creates

B. to describe the risk to the seafloor if coral reefs are lost

C. to illustrate the visibility of the sediment plumes created when the seafloor is stirred up

D. to show how shrimp trawlers create a massive amount of waste and damage the seafloor

Part A: Choice D is correct. The central idea of the two paragraphs is the mass destruction to sea life as a by-product of the shrimping industry. All three paragraphs focus on the destruction to the seafloor and all the ecosystems it supports, along with the devastation to birds and fish caught in the net's wide path. Choices A, B, and C may be inferred, but each are small details in the infographic, not its main purpose.

Part B: Which detail from Source 2 supports the correct answer to Part A?

A. "Long-line fisheries also kill huge numbers of seabirds. Over 100,000 Albatrosses die this way every year."

B. "Shrimp trawling is by far the most destructive: it is responsible for a third of the world's bycatch, while producing only 2% of all seafood."

C. "This has a destructive impact on seabed communities, particularly on fragile deep water coral."

D. "The effect of bottom trawling on the seafloor has been compared to forest clear-cutting, and the damage it causes can be seen from space."

Part B: Choice B is correct. This detail supports a similar claim made in the article: "Shrimp trawling is by far the most destructive: it is responsible for a third of the world's bycatch, while producing only 2% of all seafood." This statistic is startling and forces the reader to question if the cost of all that bycatch is worth the long-term impact to ocean ecosystems. This is then supported in the infographic with the caption: "In shrimp trawls, up to 90% of the catch is bycatch." This statistic supports what is stated in the article and speaks to the devastation and destruction to marine life supported by the article. Choice C is about part of the sea life impacted by this practice, but the impact of the coral reef destruction is not the focus of the article. Choice A focuses on birds, while the infographic focuses on the seafloor. Choice D introduces the idea that seafloor trawling can be seen from space. However, the purpose of the infographic is not to demonstrate how the plume is able to be seen from space.

Vocabulary Included in This Module

- abundant
- accustomed
- adapt
- advantages
- agent
- anatomy
- appalling
- appealing
- appropriate transitions
- aquatic species
- avocations
- bail
- beam trawler
- biodiversity
- biologically
- boon
- bounty
- case study
- cataclysm
- class
- coined
- collision
- colony
- commissions
- compelling
- compensates
- conflict
- connotative language
- contempt
- convey
- cooperation
- cormorants
- culprit

- Darwinism
- debate
- decline
- deposit
- development
- diminution
- domain-specific vocabulary
- dominate
- economy
- ecosystem
- efficient
- elaborate
- eliminated
- emotional attachment
- evaluate
- Everglades
- evidence
- evolution
- evolve
- exhaustion
- exploitation
- exposition
- extinct
- factual information
- figurative language
- first person
- fish depletion
- fishing territories
- flush
- foreigners
- formative feedback
- gambling
- generation
- genetic
- geographic location

- gist
- glaciers
- grave
- hunkered
- idly
- illustrate
- indestructible
- Industrial Revolution
- industry
- infer
- influential
- inhabit
- innovations
- intensified
- interconnected
- interfering
- invertebrates
- krill
- lava-encrusted
- literal language
- lucrative
- main idea
- mangroves
- manufacture
- marina
- metaphor
- minuscule
- misconception
- myth
- neglected
- objecting
- omniscient
- organism
- origin
- peer critique

- perspective
- pitiful
- plot
- point of view
- poling
- politics
- polyp
- posthumously
- preservation
- productive
- promoting
- quaint
- rational
- refuted
- relevant
- reproduce
- reservation
- revolting
- rising action
- sail power
- sane
- satire
- scarce
- simile
- skiff
- smuggling
- snuffed
- squall
- staunch
- strip malls
- synopsis
- technique
- technological
- teeming
- tendency

- therapeutic
- therapy
- third person
- thus
- tone
- tourism
- transformed
- trawler
- unforeseen
- unobservant
- unprecedented
- unravel
- urban sprawl
- variations
- various
- vertebrates
- Viking
- voraciously
- well boats

www.ingramcontent.com/pod-product-compliance
Lightning Source LLC
LaVergne TN
LVHW080134260326
834688LV00042B/1168